POLICY ANALYSIS IN BRAZIL

International Library of Policy Analysis

*Series editors: Iris Geva-May and Michael Howlett,
Simon Fraser University, Canada*

This major new series brings together for the first time a
detailed examination of the theory and practice of policy
analysis systems at different levels of government and by non-
governmental actors in a specific country. It therefore provides
a key addition to research and teaching in comparative policy
analysis and policy studies more generally.

Each volume includes a history of the country's policy analysis
which offers a broad comparative overview with other
countries as well as the country in question. In doing so, the
books in the series provide the data and empirical case studies
essential for instruction and for further research in the area.
They also include expert analysis of different approaches to
policy analysis and an assessment of their evolution
and operation.

Early volumes in the series will cover the following countries:

Brazil • China • France • Germany • India • Israel •
Netherlands • New Zealand • Norway • Russia •
South Africa • Taiwan • UK • USA

and will build into an essential library of key reference works.
The series will be of interest to academics and students
in public policy, public administration and management,
comparative politics and government, public organisations and
individual policy areas. It will also interest people working in the
countries in question and internationally.

In association with the ICPA-Forum and *Journal of Comparative Policy Analysis*.
See more at http://goo.gl/raJUX

INTERNATIONAL COMPARATIVE POLICY ANALYSIS FORUM
affiliated with JOURNAL OF COMPARATIVE POLICY ANALYSIS

POLICY PRESS
at the University of Bristol

POLICY ANALYSIS IN BRAZIL

Edited by
Jeni Vaitsman, José Mendes Ribeiro
and Lenaura Lobato

First published in Great Britain in 2013 by

Policy Press
University of Bristol
6th Floor
Howard House
Queen's Avenue
Bristol BS8 1SD
UK
t: +44 (0)117 331 5020
f: +44 (0)117 331 5367
tpp-info@bristol.ac.uk
www.policypress.co.uk

North America office:
Policy Press
c/o The University of Chicago Press
1427 East 60th Street
Chicago, IL 60637, USA
+1 773 702 7700
+1 773 702 9756
sales@press.uchicago.edu
www.press.uchicago.edu

© Policy Press 2013

British Library Cataloguing in Publication Data
A catalogue record for this book is available from the British Library.

Library of Congress Cataloging-in-Publication Data
A catalog record for this book has been requested.

ISBN 978 1 4473 0684 9 hardcover

The right of Jeni Vaitsman, José Mendes Ribeiro and Lenaura Lobato to be identified as editors of this work has been asserted by them in accordance with the Copyright, Designs and Patents Act 1988.

Cover design by Qube Design Associates, Bristol
Front cover: image kindly supplied by www.istock.com
Printed and bound in Great Britain by TJ International, Padstow.
Policy Press uses environmentally responsible print partners.

Contents

PART FOUR: ACADEMIC AND RESEARCH INSTITUTE-BASED POLICY ANALYSIS

List of tables and figures

Tables

Figures

Notes on contributors

Aline Gazola Hellmann

Sociologist and researcher at the Centro de Estudos Internacionais Sobre Governo and the Núcleo de Estudos em Tecnologia, Indústria e Economia Internacional at Universidade Federal do Rio Grande do Sul, Brazil, where she is a PhD candidate in development economics, working in the field of policy monitoring and evaluation. Aline has had articles published on social inequality and South–South cooperation in social development.

Aline Inglez-Dias

MPH (Master in public health), PhD candidate at the Escola Nacional de Saúde Pública Sérgio Arouca, Fundação Oswaldo Cruz, Brazil, and specialist in public policies and governmental management at Rio de Janeiro city government's Secretaria Estadual de Assistência Social e Direitos Humanos, Aline has participated in health policy research projects, especially regarding HIV prevention, mental health and drug use, on which subjects she has published various articles and book chapters.

Armando Castelar Pinheiro

Coordinator of applied economic research at IBRE/FGV (Instituto Brasileiro de Economia/Fundação Getulio Vargas (Brazilian Institute of Economy/Getulio Vargas Foundation) and professor of economics at the Universidade Federal do Rio de Janeiro, Armando previously worked at Gavea Investimentos, the Instituto de Pesquisa Econômica Aplicada and Brazil's Banco Nacional de Desenvolvimento Econômico e Social. He holds a PhD in economics from the University of California, Berkeley, USA, Master's degrees in statistics and business administration and a Bachelor's degree in electronic engineering. He is a member of the Conselho Superior Temático de Economia of the Federação das Indústrias do Estado de São Paulo and writes monthly columns in the *Valor Econômico* and *Correio Braziliense* newspapers.

Carlos Alberto Vasconcelos Rocha

Professor and researcher at the Pontifícia Universidade Católica de Minas Gerais, Brazil, Carlos holds a PhD in social sciences from Universidade Estadual de Campinas and a post-doctorate from Universidad Autónoma de Barcelona (2009). He studies public policies, citizen participation and local governance, metropolis and inequality, reform of the state, participatory democracy, and federalism. He has co-edited books and published numerous papers and book chapters.

Celina Souza

Research fellow at the Instituto de Estudos Sociais e Políticos, Universidade Estadual do Rio de Janeiro and author of *Constitutional engineering in Brazil: the politics of federalism and decentralization* (Macmillan and St. Martin's Press, 1997), Celina has written journal articles and contributed to books published in both English and Portuguese. Her most recent publications in English are 'Brazil: the prospects of a center-constraining federation in a fragmented polity', published in *Publius: The Journal of Federalism* (Spring, 2002) and 'Participatory budgeting in Brazilian cities:

limits and possibilities in building democratic institutions', published in *Environment & Urbanization* (April, 2001).

Christina W. Andrews

Senior lecturer at Universidade Federal de São Paulo, Brazil, where she teaches political theory and public policy, Christina is currently on the editorial board of the *International Review of Administrative Sciences* journal She has published articles in Brazilian and international journals, and contributed to *Improving local government: outcomes of comparative research*, edited by Michiel S. de Vries, P.S. Reddy and Shamsul Haque (Palgrave/MacMillan, 2008) and to *Value and virtue in public administration: a comparative perspective*, edited by Michiel S. de Vries and Pan Suk Kim (Palgrave/MacMillan, 2011). With Edison Bariani she co-edited *Administração Pública no Brasil: Breve História Política* (Editora Unifesp, 2010).

Cristiane Batista

Associate professor at Universidade Federal do Estado do Rio de Janeiro, Brazil, Cristiane holds a PhD in political science from Instituto Universitário de Pesquisas do Rio de Janeiro. Her research interests include ideology, political parties and public policies. She has published articles in, among others, *Dados* and the *Latin American Research Review*.

Cristina Almeida Cunha Filgueiras

PhD in sociology (École des Hautes Études en Sciences Sociales, France), Cristina is a lecturer and researcher within the postgraduate programme in social science at Pontifícia Universidade Católica de Minas Gerais, Brazil. She studies public policies, social management, social programme evaluation, poverty and inequality, and international development cooperation, and has published articles and book chapters and co-edited books in these fields.

Eliane Hollanda

Professor and researcher at the Social Science Department, Escola Nacional de Saúde Pública Sérgio Arouca, Brazil, Eliane holds a PhD in public policies from FIOCRUZ - Fundação Oswaldo Cruz. Her fields of interest include public policies, policy analysis, social indicators and health.

Elize Massard da Fonseca

Postdoctoral research fellow in political science at the Centro de Estudos da Metrópole, funded by the Fundação de Amparo à Pesquisa do Estado de São Paulo, Elize has also acted as a consultant on social protection projects for United Nations agencies, including PAHO (Panamerican Health Organization), UNODC (United Nations Office on Drugs and Crime) and UNFPA (United Nations Population Fund). Her research interests are policy change and stability and the political economy of pharmaceutical regulation. Her peer-reviewed papers have appeared in high-impact journals such as *Health Affairs*, *Public Library of Science Medicine* and *European Union Politics*, receiving significant press coverage from Reuters, the BBC and other media outlets.

Fabiano Santos

PhD in political science from Instituto Universitário de Pesquisas do Rio de Janeiro, Brazil, and now professor and researcher at Instituto de Estudos Sociais e Políticos, Universidade do Estado do Rio de Janeiro, Fabiano has published in scientific journals including *Legislative Studies Quarterly, Journal of Politics in Latin America, Regional and Federal Studies, Party Politics* and *Latin America Research Review*. He is author of *O Poder Legislativo no Presidencialismo de Coalizão* (Belo Horizonte: Editora da UFMG, 2003), *Governabilidade e Representação na América do Sul*, with Fátima Anastasia and Carlos Ranulfo Melo (Rio de Janeiro and São Paulo: Fundação Konrad Adenauer and Editora da UNESP, 2004), and *Fundamentos Informacionais do Presidencialismo de Coalizão*, with Acir Almeida (Curitiba: Editora Appris, 2011), and organised the volume *O Poder Legislativo nos Estados: Diversidade e Convergências* (Rio de Janeiro: Editora da FGV, 2001).

Fernando Lattman-Weltman

PhD in political science from the Instituto Universitário de Pesquisas do Rio de Janeiro, Fernando is professor and researcher at the Escola de Ciências Sociais e História, Centro de Pesquisa e Documentação de História Contemporânea do Brasil, Fundação Getulio Vargas, where he specialises, researches and teaches in media and politics, political theory, Brazilian political institutions, Brazilian social policy thinking, and political elites and social mobility. He has authored and co-authored books and scientific articles, including *A política domesticada: Afonso Arinos e o colapso da democracia em 1964* (Editora FGV, Rio de Janeiro, 2005), *Sistema de informação de custos na administração pública federal: uma política de Estado* (Editora FGV, Rio de Janeiro, 2010), *Mídia e política: jornalismo e ficção* (Editora FGV, Rio de Janeiro, 2003), *A imprensa faz e desfaz um presidente* (Nova Fronteira, Rio de Janeiro, 1994), and was one of the coordinators of the second edition of the *Dicionário Histórico-Biográfico Brasileiro – Pós-30* (Editora FGV. Rio de Janeiro, 2001).

Francisco I. Bastos

Senior researcher at the Fundação Oswaldo Cruz and principal investigator on large, multi-city studies of HIV and other blood-borne infections and sexually transmitted infections, including the ongoing national survey on crack cocaine and associated harms. He has published over 300 papers and book chapters on HIV and substance misuse.

Gabriela Andrade

PhD in public health from the Escola Nacional de Saúde Pública Sérgio Arouca and visiting researcher at the ENSP Social Sciences Department, Gabriela's research interests include social participation, user satisfaction and public and health policy evaluation. She has published various articles and book chapters in these fields.

Jeni Vaitsman

Sociologist, senior researcher and lecturer in the Social Sciences Department of the Escola Nacional de Saúde Pública Sérgio Arouca, Fundação Oswaldo Cruz, Brazil, Jeni has been director of evaluation and monitoring at the Brazilian Ministry of Social Development and to Combat Hunger. She has conducted evaluation studies and research projects in the fields of gender, family, values, and health and social protection policies. She has published or edited books, journal articles and book chapters in Portuguese, English and Spanish.

João Bôsco Hora Góis

Associate professor at Universidade Federal Fluminense, João holds a PhD in social service work from Pontifícia Universidade Católica de São Paulo/Boston College. He has had various articles published in Brazilian and international specialist journals on race and gender relations, social policy, corporate social responsibility and AIDS.

José Mendes Ribeiro

MD, Master's in public health, PhD in sciences, senior researcher at Fundação Oswaldo Cruz. He has published more than 60 articles and chapters in books, mainly on policy studies, policy analysis, health policies, governance and reform of the state.

Lenaura Lobato

Sociologist, professor with the Escola de Serviço Social and the Programa de Estudos Pós-graduados em Política Social at the Universidade Federal Fluminense, Rio de Janeiro, Brazil. Researcher in social policy, health and social assistance policies and systems, health reform in Brazil, and social policy analysis and evaluation. She has recently authored and co-edited the books: *Políticas e sistema de saúde no Brasil* (Rio de Janeiro: Fiocruz/Cebes, 2008), *Participação, democracia e saúde* (Rio de Janeiro: Centro Brasileiro de Estudos de Saúde [Cebes], 2009) and *Seguridade social, cidadania e saúde* (Rio de Janeiro: Cebes, 2009).

Licinio Velasco

PhD (political sciences), director of Banco Nacional de Desenvolvimento Economico e Social Participações and superintendent for privatizations at Banco Nacional de Desenvolvimento Econômico e Social, Licinio has published studies on decision-making processes and privatisation, and several articles on privatisation and reform of the state.

Marta Ferreira Santos Farah

Associate dean for MSc and PhD programmes on public administration and government at Fundação Getulio Vargas, São Paulo (FGV-SP) and professor at the Public Management Department, FGV-SP. She is the author of numerous articles on local government policies in Brazil and co-author of *Innovations in government: research, recognition, and replication* (Brookings Institution Press, 2008).

Nilson do Rosário Costa

Senior researcher, Escola Nacional de Saúde Pública Sérgio Arouca/Fundação Oswaldo Cruz, Ministry of Health, Brazil, Nilson's background is in social sciences, urban planning and economics. His main research interests today are public policy, innovation and development of social protection and of national health systems, and he has had various books and articles published in those fields.

Paulo Fábio Dantas Neto

PhD in human science/political science (Instituto Universitário de Pesquisas do Rio de Janeiro), MS in management (Universidade Federal da Bahia (UFBA)), BS in economics (UFBA,1978); professor of FFFCH/UFBA, serving in the Department of Political Science at the PostGraduate Program in Social Sciences and the Center for Human Resources. Councilman of the city of Salvador (1983–88), Bahia Deputy State (1989) and Municipal Secretary of Education of Salvador (1994). Author of *Tradição, autocracia e carisma: a política de Antonio Carlos Magalhães na modernização da Bahia (1954-1974)*[*Tradition, autocracy and charisma: the politics of Antonio Carlos Magalhães in Bahia modernization (1954-1974)*], published in 2006 by EdUFMG.

Renato Raul Boschi

PhD in political science (The University of Michigan), Renato is full professor of political science in the Institute for Social and Political Studies at University of the State of Rio de Janeiro (formerly IUPERJ). He is also retired full professor at Federal University of Minas Gerais. He was Senior Fulbright/CAPES visiting professor at City University of New York (2006), visiting professor at the Institut d'Études Politiques de Toulouse (2006,2007, 2008 and 2009) and Directeur de Recherche Associé at the Maison des Sciences de l'Homme, Paris (2009), in addition to Stanford, Duke and Michigan in previous years. He is the author of several books on entrepreneurs, interest representation, the state and capitalist development in Brazil. He is 1A top researcher and has a research grant from the Brazilian National Research Council, and coordinates the research network INCT/PPED dedicated to studying varieties of capitalism and development perspectives in Brazil. Some of his latest books include *Variedades de Capitalismo, Política e Desenvolvimento na América Latina* (UFMG Editora, 2011) and *Development and semi-periphery: post-neoliberal trajectories in South America and Central Eastern Europe* (Anthem Press, 2012).

Rômulo Paes–Sousa

Senior international associate at the Institute of Social Development Studies, University of Sussex, UK, Rômulo was Brazil's deputy minister for social development and to Combat Hunger (2009–12). His interests are social protection policies, social inequality indicators and health inequality. He has co-edited books on social protection and numerous scientific papers on social protection policies and epidemiology.

Sandra Aparecida Venâncio de Siqueira

Researcher in the Social Sciences Department at Escola Nacional de Saúde Pública Sérgio Arouca, Brazil, Sandra holds a PhD in public policies from Escola Nacional de Saúde Pública Sérgio Arouca, Fundação Oswaldo Cruz. He lectures and researches in the fields of social protection and inequality, public policies, and social indicators and health.

Soraya Vargas Côrtes

PhD in social policy (London School of Economics and Political Science), Soraya is a professor in the Department of Sociology of the Federal University of Rio Grande do Sul, Brazil, and vice-president of the Brazilian Sociological Association. Her teaching and research focus on political sociology, participative processes, public policies, political inequalities, councils and assemblies of public policies, mostly in the health field.

Tatiana Teixeira

Tatiana is a PhD candidate in political science at the Institute of Political and Social Studies of the State University of Rio de Janeiro (formerly IUPERJ). In 2012, she was a visiting scholar on the International Relations Program at University of Pennsylvania, US. Tatiana is journalist and holds an MA in international relations (Fluminense Federal University, Brazil). In 2007 she won the US Embassy's Franklin Delano Roosevelt Prize for best Master's thesis, and she has been a researcher for the US Political Observatory (OPEU, Brazil).

Acknowledgements

First, we would like to thank Iris Geva-May and Michael Howlett, general editors of the series International Library of Policy Analysis, for their invitation to coordinate the volume on Brazil and for the confidence thus placed in us. That confidence extends to the researchers from the various institutions involved, whose active engagement (on a subject still little explored in Brazil) was decisive to bringing the project satisfactorily to term.

The studies would not have been possible without institutional and financial support from: the Programa de Apoio à Pesquisa, Desenvolvimento e Inovação (INOVA) of the Escola Nacional de Saúde Pública/Fundação Oswaldo Cruz; the Fundação para o Desenvolvimento Científico e Tecnológico em Saúde (Fiotec); the Programa PRIORIDADE RIO, which supports study on what are priority issues for Rio de Janeiro State Government; the Fundação de Apoio a Pesquisa do Estado do Rio de Janeiro (Faperj); and the Conselho Nacional de Desenvolvimento Cientifico e Tecnológico (CNPq).

We are especially grateful to: Antonio Ivo de Carvalho, director of the Escola Nacional de Saúde Pública; Marcelo Rasga Moreira, vice-director of the Escola de Governo, Escola Nacional de Saúde Pública; and Maria Cristina Guilam, vice-president for teaching, Fundação Oswaldo Cruz, whose support made various stages of the project possible.

Lastly, we are also particularly grateful to Ingrid D'Ávilla for leading the various activities involved in managing the project, and to Peter Lenny, Diane Grosklaus Whitty and Christopher Peterson for their competent translation and revision of the texts.

ONE

Policy analysis in Brazil: the state of the art

Jeni Vaitsman, José Mendes Ribeiro and Lenaura Lobato

This volume, the Brazilian case in the series The International Library of Policy Analysis, constitutes a first effort to understand how the activity of policy analysis has developed in Brazil and how it stands at present. The purpose of the series is to publish studies that throw light on how policy analysis has evolved and how it is structured in different countries. When we accepted the invitation from the general editors – Professors Michael Howlett and Iris Geva-May – to coordinate the Brazilian study, we realised the challenge, but also the opportunity, of what is an innovative project in the Brazilian context, where policy analysis has never been the object of study from the perspective proposed here. The activity of policy analysis, as defined by the international project – a type of knowledge produced by different actors in public and private organisations and designed to inform public policy decision-making – has never been named, mapped and much less systematised in Brazil.

Nonetheless, it was also evident that a great variety of studies, evaluations, diagnoses, reports and research is produced in Brazil not just *about* public policies, but also *for* public policymaking. Unlike well-established academic production in the fields of the human sciences – in economics, history, sociology, political science and administration – the difficulty of the undertaking resided exactly in the lack of an academic tradition of thinking about policy analysis *for* the policy process. In that respect, to survey the state of the art in how policy analysis is taught and operated in Brazil would entail *naming* this kind of activity and endeavouring to trace its contours as an object, which was done as the research progressed. This meant that the editors, who are also chapter authors, discovered and defined the specific features of this phenomenon only to the extent that the research and discussion with the other authors advanced.

There are substantive differences to policy analysis in Brazil as compared with (particularly) its counterpart in the US, regarded as the country that pioneered policy analysis as an activity with certain specific characteristics. In the first place, there is a *lack of conceptual differentiation* as regards the very term 'policy analysis': there is no definition of *policy analysis*, as established in the North American literature, designating a specific modality of analysis oriented to public policy problem-solving. No conceptual difference has been drawn here between analysis *about* and analysis *for* the policy process (Lasswell, 1951), which gave rise in other national contexts to the separation between one area of academic study and another, and which although drawing on expertise acquired in academic institutions, is applied in view of decision-makers' needs or to influence the course of policymaking. The various types of knowledge production about public policies – studies, academic research, diagnoses and policy analysis (including those performed as consultancy and advisory services to governments) – are not the object of specific definitions, as would be the case in the US and Canadian contexts (Patton and Sawicki, 1993; Bardach, 1996; Weimer and Vining, 2005; Dobuzinskis et al, 2007).

Second, this lack of conceptual differentiation entails a *lack of methodological differentiation*. In Brazil, no use is made of what is called the *basic policy analysis method or policy analysis methodology*. That approach, spread via the US literature in the field (Weimer and Vining, 1989; Patton and Sawicki, 1993; Bardach, 1996; Geva-May, 2002), consists in an operational methodology that goes through the stages of problem definition, identification of policy options, argumentation, policy selection and implementation design. Geva-May (2002) considers this methodology as the common core of the field and it is taught on public policy courses in the US. Although some of its components are found in planning methodologies or even applied empirically by different types of policy analyst, it is not explicitly differentiated from the methodologies and research techniques used in political science, social science or economics. This type of approach is neither studied nor taught as a practical kind of activity for policy problem-solving. In Brazil – far more than identified by Wildawsky (1979) in the US context – policy analysis is 'art and craft', but exercised in practice, even though not taught separately as a discipline at universities or on public policy courses.

Third, as a result, there is no specific training in policy analysis. Training in public policy in Brazil is achieved through postgraduate courses in a variety of subject areas. Public policies appear as an object of study in disciplines such as Political Science, Economics, Public Health, Administration and Social Service and not as a specific field constituted in universities and recognised by the agencies that regulate postgraduate education. This means that policy analysis as practised in Brazil reflects the features of theoretical and methodological training in these fields. Here, too, some of these policy analysts avail themselves of already-existing theoretical and methodological resources in making their analyses. On the other hand, some postgraduate courses are beginning to use the literature specific to the policy field, although what predominates in policy analysis is what the mainstream North American policy analysis literature calls *policy research* or *policy studies*, informed by the theories used in these various different disciplinary fields.

Accordingly, two broad modalities of policy analysis have developed with conceptually indistinct, and in some situations overlapping, boundaries. The first, consisting in production *about* policies, expresses currents of political theory in the social sciences and political science. The other is policy analysis as a practical activity – production *for* policy – which was initially only undertaken from within the executive structure of government, but later was also pursued by a variety of non-governmental organisations (NGOs) and actors seeking to influence policy decision-making from outside government. This latter approach in Brazil can also be seen to involve the phenomenon that Mintrom (2007) called a *policy analysis movement*: changes that produced few immediate or obvious ruptures in administrative processes and structures associated with public governance, but which did challenge the practice of informal counselling and prompted a professionalisation of government advisory systems.

The studies in this volume that deal with the cycles of Brazilian politics focus mainly on the period since 1930, thus framing the process that laid the institutional and organisational bases of the modern Brazilian state, including the formation of a modern bureaucracy, regarded as one of the conditions for policy analysis to professionalise. Although during the imperial period and the República Velha, the state had taken a hand in sanitation, public health, transport, ports, railways and electricity and the first civil actors had begun to emerge (such as trade unions and employer associations in the early 20th century), there was still nothing like policy analysis in the sense given to the term here.

Between 1930 and 1980, as the apparatus of state modernised, policy analysis was not distinguished functionally from the activity of the senior officials of the bureaucracy. In line with formal, rational approaches, economic analysis and planning were the subject of numerous commissions, projects and institutions set up within the state to implement vertical, national policies and programmes as part of the national developmentalist debate over the nation-building project. After 1988, with the promulgation of the Federal Constitution that underpinned Brazil's re-democratisation after a military regime had held power from 1964 to 1985, policymaking became more deliberative, horizontal and bottom-up, eroding the tradition of centralisation in decision-making. The inclusion of mechanisms for public participation and deliberation – largely in response to demands from social actors during the democratisation process – required that social stakeholders become more knowledgeable about policy so as to offer more authoritative solutions in argumentative dispute in decision-making bodies. This was yet another variable that promoted policy analysis as a force in support of democracy (Ingram and Schneider, 2006). Policy analysis spread beyond the boundaries of the organisations of state to become a regular activity in various sectors and policymaking bodies in a society where policy analysis consumers, producers and intermediaries – the three groups identified by Lindquist (Dobuzinskis et al, 2007) as a precondition for policy analysis – now existed.

As policy analysis expanded, so the influence of democratisation was reflected in the new styles and activities that were introduced, especially the participatory and argumentative styles. New styles of policy analysis were adopted more as a result of increasing social complexity and the new design demarcated for public policy than from any depletion of the rational approaches, which continued to be used as well. Contestation in the form of critical policy analysis seeking alternatives to dominant arguments (Dryzek, 2006) is another characteristic of the policy analysis conducted by various NGOs and social movements (especially in the social policy field) and was accepted – and to some extent incorporated – by sectors of the public bureaucracy given that the NGOs and movements not only met up in participatory policymaking settings, but also came to form part of government bodies in some social policy areas. While the critical approach informs the origins of policy analysis as 'science for democracy' (Lasswell, 1951) and needs to be reinstated, in the Brazilian case, critique and contestation came to employ rationality and knowledge as means to gain recognition and a place in policymaking.

These issues emerge in a number of studies in this volume exploring, from different perspectives, how policy analysis is being practised by different organisations in Brazil's various policy arenas. The book is divided into four parts, which are summarised as follows.

The studies in Part One address the context in which policy analysis has emerged and professionalised as its specific contours have been shaped by the process of state modernisation, which presupposes the formation of both a modern bureaucracy and the technical elites that will form its technical staffs. Jeni Vaitsman, Lenaura Lobato and Gabriela Andrade examine the professionalisation of policy analysis as a process spanning different political regimes and built initially within structures internal to the state that were both vertical and insulated as part of the development of the state bureaucracy and the technical and intellectual elites. From the 1930s to the 1980s, these were predominantly groups or commissions convened by governments and comprising economists, administrators and sectoral academic specialists. From the mid-1980s onwards, re-democratisation and the entry of new actors into policy sectors functionally external to the state became part of the regular dynamics of government activity and of policymaking processes and arenas through horizontalised structures, which included larger numbers of policy analysis actors, styles and activities as part of policymaking.

The styles and methods employed by the new actors incorporated by the participatory design of policymaking after 1988 express the political, social and academic trajectory traced by policy analysis, as Christina W. Andrews shows. In order to analyse the methodological diversity of the analyses that predominate in Brazil, she constructs a typology by style (economic and socio-political) and scope (macro- or micro-analytical). The economic dimension, prioritised by the state and peopled by economists, developed more in the rational style and devoted itself to forming and developing its technical elite. Social concerns, meanwhile, have come to policy analysis more recently in a process directed more from society to the state. The more participatory and deliberative policymaking of the post-1988 period includes styles suited to contemporary forms of governance in democratic states.

Particularist relations are increasingly giving way to technical competences and universal procedures as the basis for forming the public bureaucracy. Celina Souza examines the role of the bureaucratic system as one of the factors that played a decisive part in modernising the Brazilian state by professionalising on the basis of technical and scientific expertise, formalising rules, and standardising procedures. Focusing on methods of recruiting for the bureaucracy, she shows that, particularly from the 2000s onwards, greater professionalisation, oversight of the bureaucracy and recruitment by competitive examination indicate that Brazil's democracy is being strengthened. She argues that in spite of the multiple mechanisms used by different governments and political regimes to recruit for the bureaucracy, the federal executive was always able to construct bureaucratic capabilities to meet its priorities.

In Part Two, the focus is on policy analysis by governments and the legislature. The chapters address government at the three federative levels in Brazil (union, state and municipal), the legislature and the main government investment bank. The studies also vary in their goals and types of approach.

The production of analyses, circulation of ideas and levels of influence of authors and institutions that gravitate around federal public organisations are discussed by José Mendes Ribeiro and Aline Inglez-Dias by reference to the case of the planning, organisation and management ministry (Ministério do Planejamento, Organização e Gestão; MPOG). Public institutions produce the greater part of the studies and analyses. The sectors closest to the government decision-making core tend to deal with the reforms with least political cost and to propose policies of an incremental nature. Issues such as the reform of the state span across governments with different political orientations, with marginal adaptations as regards the proposals' content. The participatory forums organised to debate policy proposals were an important source for government initiatives relating to administrative reform and privatisations.

Focusing on the federal executive, Rômulo Paes-Sousa and Aline Gazola Hellmann discuss the institutional mechanisms developed by the federal government to promote systematic, ongoing policy evaluation. They emphasise the historical dimension, here as regards monitoring and evaluation programmes, particularly since the 2000s. They attribute the growth of a technical culture of monitoring and evaluation to increasing government emphasis on social policy after re-democratisation, the expansion of public policy programmes at universities, the development of new information technology capabilities and the influence of international agencies on the government policy and programme evaluation agenda.

Still in the executive sphere, but focusing on the public development bank, Licinio Velasco and Armando Castelar Pinheiro offer a historical analysis of the privatisation of state enterprises in Brazil through the – initially circumstantial – activities of the Brazilian Development Bank (BNDES) in developing the models for the transfer of ownership deployed particularly by the administrations of Fernando Henrique Cardoso in line with macroeconomic adjustment in the 1990s. The long period of divestment of major assets converged with the steadily growing authority and capacity of the BNDES and its technical staff to nurture each cycle of government with information and solutions for decision-making. Despite the complexity of the factors that impelled and restrained cycles of privatisation under different governments, the authors highlight the capacity of the BNDES to influence the process, motivated both by interest as a quota-holder and by its policy agenda. The diagnoses, analyses and recommendations produced by its more strategic technical staff were crucial in reducing vetoes and taking circumstantial opportunities.

Cristina Almeida Cunha Filgueiras and Carlos Alberto Vasconcelos Rocha examine the state government agencies tasked with producing analysis, planning and providing data and economic indicators. These agencies' development is examined in historical perspective and associated with political and economic cycles, as a response to federal government inducement, as an endogenous strategy by state governments to strengthen local development or as a result of support from international institutions leveraged especially by public universities in Brazil. With re-democratisation, these agencies' expectations of power gains were frustrated by the leading role that experts came to play in policymaking and also by state governments' federative conflicts with the federal government, formerly the base from which these agencies drew local legitimacy.

Unlike in most federative countries, municipalities in Brazil are fully fledged federative entities endowed with constitutional prerogatives, fiscal attributes and objective policy responsibilities in education, health and sanitation. This means that the large municipalities are of major importance on the domestic political stage. In the chapter on policy analysis in the municipal sphere, Marta Ferreira Santos Farah shows, from a historical standpoint and in the light of the importance of the problems at different conjunctures, how knowledge was mobilised for local government programmes. The initial, 19th-century emphasis on urban and housing problems shifted to the interface between urbanism and developmentalism in the first half of the 20th century, in keeping with the state's role as the agent of development, especially from the 1930s onwards.

The patterns of policy analysis produced by municipal institutions varied according to the political regime in place in Brazil: under the military regime, centralisation and planning; with the democratic regime after 1988, decentralisation and civil society participation, together with a strengthening of municipal agendas addressing social problems. A number of policies embodied an endeavour to articulate among management, social participation and the collegiate bodies set up between government and civil society organisations, which were to become sources in the production of policy options and solutions.

As regards the federal legislature, Fabiano Santos analyses the case of Brazil's Congress in the light of the informational approach, according to which, activity on parliamentary commissions centred on building up information and intervention capacity rather than on patrimonialist benefits. On this approach, he examines the activities of the advisory offices of the lower house (the Câmara dos Deputados), their administrative structure and the distribution of professions within them. Production of analyses by legislative advisory units combines juridical, administrative and policy-orientation components through complex interaction between in-house experts and parliamentarians interested in information and influence. He shows that this expertise in the legislature produces information able to match the greater informational capacity of the executive.

The chapters of Part Three bring out more explicitly the relations between policies and politics. When considered in the light of politics, policy solutions are preceded by positionings with strong value connotations in relation to the socio-political context; they are 'unabashedly value-laden' in the terms of Goodin et al (2006).

Soraya Vargas Côrtes examines the activities of sector policy communities in Brazil, particularly the National Council for Social Assistance (Conselho Nacional de Assistência Social; CNAS). The policy community connected with social assistance was among those responsible for the transition from a model of assistance based on religious charity to one of social rights. In the neo-corporatist tradition considered by the author, the CNAS operates under government influence. In addition, throughout the 2000s, a dynamic of coalitions can be seen on the council, with government and professional and trade union associations congregated at one extreme, and religious and service provider organisations at the other. In the course of the process, she observes a transition from a situation where religious and philanthropic organisations had the initiative to one where the central bureaucracy was in control and the social rights agenda took precedence over one based on charity.

Civil society action in national policies in response to the AIDS epidemic since the 1980s, one of the prime examples of successful policy combining government capability and societal activism in Brazil, is examined by Elize Massard da Fonseca and Francisco I. Bastos. As the basis for analysing the overall policy, they focus on government policies to guarantee access to anti-retroviral drugs, looking at the role of advocacy groups in the debate over ownership of drug patents and harm-reduction policies for drug users. The World Bank's strong support for AIDS control favoured the agenda of groups and experts concerned to produce policy analyses and solutions, such as needle exchange programmes as a harm-reduction policy. Activism connected with the epidemic and AIDS control played an important role in information production for, and influence on, government decision-making, particularly in promoting universal access to drugs, in discussion forums on intellectual property and in the clash with laboratories over prices and local production rights.

The chapter by Fernando Lattman-Weltman identifies the key factors affecting how policies are received and analysed by the media. When the media are considered as a polyarchic institution, the balance of forces in the policy debate can be seen to raise or lower competitors' transactional costs. The media act fundamentally by agenda-setting, by framing issues by selecting the news and how it will be broadcast, and by the panoptic effects of exposing people's vulnerabilities. He notes how the rise of the workers' party (Partido dos Trabalhadores; PT) to government in 2002 kindled debate over review of existing communications sector regulations and the introduction of a regulatory agency, both fiercely rejected by the major media, culminating in the government's abandoning of its regulatory initiatives.

Paulo Fábio Dantas Neto analyses the activities of Brazil's main political parties since the early 1990s in a study of constitutional amendments submitted during the period. He draws attention to the fact that, in the day-to-day activities of Brazil's Congress, policy is not produced exclusively by the parties between which national contests for the executive are polarised (the PT and the Brazilian Social Democracy Party; PSDB). Unlike other routine ballots and activities, constitutional amendments reflect the political agenda of the major parties and the actions of their key leaders. The study corroborates the argument that the parties function more as processors of ideas produced outside their institutional environment than as original producers. By analysing each proposed constitutional amendment in the context of the corresponding cycle of government, he reveals that the PT administration coincided with a reduction in ideological polarisation on matters such as tax and political and social security reform.

Production of systematic policy analyses and the monitoring of strategic indicators for the industrial sector and public policy sector form the subject matter considered by Renato Raul Boschi in terms of the dynamics of business and industrial associations (particularly in the Rio de Janeiro–São Paulo area) and of semi-public corporative associations in the main sectors of the economy. He shows that accompanying Brazil's re-democratisation, the focus of interest mediation has migrated, in significant measure at least, from the executive to the legislature in a movement associated with increasingly professional lobbying activities. The study reveals a high degree of complexity in policy tracking and analysis, with internal specialisation tailored to monitoring policies of interest to specific industrial sectors. In a context of re-democratisation, the conjunctural conditions affording access to the apparatus of the state and the increasing availability of information from public agencies, as well as globalisation, have been important factors in strengthening these organisations' capacity for analysis. This has affected the pattern of industrial organisations' activities and their political agenda and has altered the traditional corporative arrangement inherited from the 1930s.

João Bôsco Hora Góis offers a conceptual discussion of policy analysis in Brazil in the light of increasing activity by social movements since re-democratisation. Advocacy practices have come to the fore especially among diversity groups representing women, black people and gay people. These movements, while voicing the demands of vulnerable groups, have appropriated studies and analyses, some with a high degree of expertise, in order to argue their ideas in the political process and have come to be acknowledged as strategic actors. Their instrumental use of analyses was directed initially to organising arguments in support of their efforts to gain recognition and then to producing change: to having their issues recognised as belonging on the state agenda and deserving of access to redistributive government funding and coverage by rights protection legislation.

Part Four comprises chapters addressing different aspects of policy analysis production in universities, research institutes and think tanks. From the second half of the 1980s onwards, the movement to re-democratise Brazil and the political and social changes that followed brought public policy gradually into the universities and research and teaching institutes. In the 2000s, policy-related teaching and research expanded, producing at the same time greater professionalisation and expertise at training centres that built on the existing tradition of research in Brazil, reinforcing the pattern of policy experts and analysts being trained on the basis of pathways through the various existing academic fields.

The *political analysis* that resulted in the adoption of the universal right to health in the 1988 Federal Constitution and the intellectual foundations of the health sector reform are examined by Nilson do Rosário Costa. In connection with the democratic transition of the 1980s, he highlights the role of political argumentation by the epistemic community of experts in the health field as central to the universalist health sector reform. The basis for argumentation in favour of the health sector reform was produced by researchers at public universities and research institutes, who challenged the idea of subordinating the reform to the social security conception in favour of the proposal for universalisation supported by general taxation. This community's analytical output concentrated on deconstructing the government's medical care policy at a time when the constitutional drafting assembly was calling for institutional arguments to justify the health sector reform project, and thus ensured the reform's approval.

In her analysis of think tanks, Tatiana Teixeira shows that, in Brazil, organisations that in other contexts may perhaps be characterised as think tanks – in that they deal with policy analysis – are not always recognised, nor recognise themselves, as having the role of influencing public policy. Aside from the fact that they are few and recent in Brazil, these institutes were founded by high-ranking technical elites in their fields, which may explain why they set themselves apart from the field of politics, an arena associated with politicians, parties and movements, where interests and ideologies prevail more explicitly than technical solutions based on high expertise.

As regards academic production of technical solutions for public policies, Cristiane Batista demonstrates how academic studies of applied policy, whether undertaken on researchers' own initiative or commissioned by government, have increased since the early 1990s. Academia has become a recognised actor in the discussion and production of policy-related knowledge, a role that the media have reinforced by circulating and discussing the results of academic studies in their communication outlets. This has contributed to increasing the visibility of – and consequently expanding the demand for – academic production *for* policymaking. Today, academia plays a fundamental role in policy evaluation, formulation and implementation in Brazil in that it proposes new concepts, new points of view and new options. It is not the only, nor the most important, source of information, but beyond a doubt, it is one of them. At the limit, it influences people's beliefs and opinions, including those of opinion leaders, pressure groups and public decision-makers, and in that way has an impact on policy.

Lastly, given that no specific training in policy analysis has developed in Brazil, Eliane Hollanda and Sandra Aparecida Venâncio de Siqueira look at instruction in the public policy field and the contribution of postgraduate education to preparing policy analysts. Political and policy analyses first related to subjects dear to Brazil's intelligentsia in the 20th century, when intellectuals and academics from various fields applied themselves basically to studying the state and the patterns of its development. Drawing a distinction between 'instruction' and 'training', the authors show that instruction forms part of the policy analyst's training, although that training is not restricted to academic instruction, but also incorporates professional practice.

What the studies collected here show quite clearly is that while policy analysis in Brazil can be differentiated from its counterparts in the countries where it originated by its lack of a clearly defined professional activity, specific training or distinctive methods and techniques, this has not stopped it developing. With its unique make-up, Brazil's vast tradition in the social and human sciences stands as a foundation for the production of analysis oriented towards increasingly multidisciplinary government decision-making. This volume and the studies it presents are a sample of the types of policy analysis being produced in Brazil by different actors and organisations in the various arenas of the policy process.

References

Bardach, E. (1996) *Policy analysis: a handbook for practice.* Berkeley, CA: Berkeley Academic Press.

Dobuzinskis, C., Howlett, M. and Laycock, P. (2007) *Policy analysis in Canada*, Toronto and London: University of Toronto Press.

Dryzek, J.S. (2006) 'Policy analysis as critique', in M. Moran, M. Rein and R.E. Goodin (eds) *The Oxford handbook of public policy*, Oxford: Oxford University Press.

Geva-May, I. (2002) 'Cultural theory: the neglected variable in the craft of policy analysis', *Journal of Comparative Policy Analysis: Research and Practice*, vol 4, pp 243–65.

Goodin, E., Rein, M. and Moran, M. (2006) 'The public and its policies', in R.E. Goodin, M. Rein and M. Moran (eds) *The Oxford handbook of public policy*, Oxford: Oxford University Press.

Ingram, H. and Schneider, A. (2006) 'Policy analysis for democracy', in M. Moran, M. Rein and R.E. Goodin (eds) *The Oxford handbook of public policy*, Oxford: Oxford University Press.

Lasswell, H. (1951) 'The policy orientation', in D. Lerner and H. Laswell (eds) *The policy sciences*, Stanford, CA: Stanford University Press.

Mintrom, M. (2007) 'The policy analysis movement', in C. Dobuzinskis, M. Howlett and P. Laycock (eds) *Policy analysis in Canada*, Toronto and London: University of Toronto Press.

Patton, C. and Sawicki, D. (1993) *Basic methods of policy analysis and planning*, New Jersey, NJ: Prentice-Hall.

Weimer, D. and Vining, A.R. (2005) *Policy analysis: concepts and practice*, New Jersey, NJ: Pearson Prentice Hall.

Wildawsky, A. (1979) *Speaking truth to power – the art and craft of policy analysis*, London: Macmillan.

PART ONE

STYLES AND METHODS OF POLICY ANALYSIS IN BRAZIL

TWO

Professionalisation of policy analysis in Brazil

Jeni Vaitsman, Lenaura Lobato and Gabriela Andrade

Introduction

The international literature identifies two main paradigms of policy analysis, which although associated with certain historical and national contexts, are not necessarily mutually exclusive (Lynn, 1999; Radin, 2000; Brooks, 2007). First is the positivist paradigm that spread from the North American context in the 1960s, characteristically making ample use of formal, rational, cost–benefit, linear planning and programming, efficiency, and effectiveness methodologies. These approaches were associated with hierarchical structures of government and with a time when policy analysis came to mean 'speaking truth to power' (Wildavsky, 1979; Patton and Sawicki, 1993; Bardach, 1996; Weimer, 1998).

The second, post-positivist, paradigm emerged in the latter decades of the 20th century, accompanying changes in the scientific and cultural discourses of contemporary democratic states and the emergence of new actors and horizontal, decentralised structures of governance (Fischer, 1980; Kenis and Schneider, 1991; Hoppe, 1999; Lynn, 1999; Radin, 2000; Howlett and Rayner, 2006; Adam and Kriesi, 2007; Howlett and Lindquist, 2007). In different policy subsystems, these actors were to produce new 'policy analysis activities and styles', such as argumentation, participation and interaction (Mayer et al, 2004), more appropriate to the needs of contemporary public policy and democracy (Dryzek, 2006; Goodin et al, 2006; Ingram and Schneider, 2006).

The professionalisation of policy analysis, as shown by Brooks (2007), entails various dimensions, including: the technical, connected with the formation of a modern bureaucracy and the rise of rational authority; the political, connected with the role of intellectuals in society and their relations with power; and the cultural, connected with the symbolic significance of experts and expertise in society, independently of the ideas and information that are associated with them.

As regards the social conditions surrounding its emergence, policy analysis as a professional activity is connected with the formation of the segment that Gouldner (1978), in the second half of the 20th century, called a 'new class' formed by the technical intelligentsia and the intellectuals. Crucially, this segment must be constituted in order to permit the social construction of professional expertise and the formation of policy communities. It is generally from this segment that the members of the technical elites, intellectuals and the professionals in government and non-government enterprises and organisations are largely drawn.

Although 'policy analysis' does not designate a 'profession' in the sense that the sociology of professions gives to the term (of exclusive command of specialised knowledge recognised and regulated by the state), but rather an unregulated activity that cuts across several different disciplines, we may state that in Brazil, policy analysis has professionalised. Even though policy analysis has not institutionalised as a field with schools, professional associations, specific publications and so on, a wide range of professionals from different background disciplines are producing knowledge for policymaking.

The technical, political, cultural and social dimensions that made it possible for policy analysis to professionalise in Brazil developed at the same time as two other movements. The first began in the 1930s and was both driven by and internal to the state. The first successful measures were taken to construct a modern bureaucracy and to form technical and intellectual elites, on a vertical and rational logic, as part of the modernising – and, at times, authoritarian – process of state-building. Although with little functional differentiation among the positions and structures tasked with performing the activities of analysis, formulation and decision-making, the first structures were put in place for producing rational policy analysis activities and styles. The second movement was set in motion in the 1990s when, well into the post-positivist period, the participatory democratic design of policymaking that emerged from the 1988 Constitution expanded the arenas and the range of stakeholders active in a variety of policy sectors. In that new context of governance, rational activities and styles came to coexist with other policy analysis activities and styles.

Two characteristics of society and state in Brazil framed the process in which the production of policy analysis professionalised. First, although the Republic was proclaimed in 1899, the regimes that followed were not always democratic. It was the democracy in place between 1945 and 1964 that presided over the expansion of insulated state structures from which public policies would be formulated and implemented, and that pattern was maintained and reinforced throughout the authoritarian regime that took power in 1964. It was not until the civil regime in 1985 and the 1988 Constitution that democracy consolidated into a decentralized federative design that yielded the necessary political conditions for arenas and actors to diversify and to influence the policy process.

Second, it was only from 1930 onwards that the Brazilian nation-state consolidated. As a centralised political and administrative structure was built up, it provided the base from which to begin slowly to meet the two requisites indicated by Geddes (1990) for a competent bureaucracy to exist: a supply of trained personnel in society and selection by merit. However, despite all the reforms and progress in professionalising public administration since then, government management by a bureaucracy organised on exclusively rational criteria did not become fully established in Brazil, but continued largely captive to a process in which the ability to bring about change depended on maintaining particularist commitments. The construction of niches in the state protected from political pressures was to give the initial impetus in building up analytical expertise for policy decision-making.

This chapter argues that the development of professionalism in policy analysis started in the vertical structures internal to the state and horizontalised when new stakeholders, in policy areas functionally external to the state, became part of the regular dynamics of government activity, policy processes and arenas. The thread running through the chapter is the development of the bureaucracy of state and the technical and intellectual elites and the proliferation of civil communities involved with policy analysis in different historical periods, political regimes and forms of governance.

Modernisation of the state after 1930

Although there was a prior history of state intervention to address public problems, the 1930s marked a milestone in terms of the conditions necessary for professional policy analysis to emerge. The Vargas government, which lasted 15 years (1930–45), eight of them (1937–45) under a dictatorial regime, took a series of political and administrative measures that brought major change to the organisation of both state and society. Centralisation in all sectors and at all territorial levels was made a key organisational principle for the state, so as to bring the power of local oligarchies under federal control. In that way, the Vargas government constructed a vertical, corporative institutional framework to organise social and economic relations.

In an intellectual climate coloured by disputes between partisans of political liberalism and state authoritarianism, construction of the nation-state figured as one of the main problems for precursors of Brazilian political thought such as Oliveira Vianna and Azevedo Amaral (Lamounier, 1982; Melo, 1999). Their historical and sociological essays were to provide an ideological underpinning for the modernisation project conducted by the state, which culminated in 1937 in the Estado Novo dictatorship.

The 1934 Constitution had introduced the principle of merit for entry into public service, and the Public Service Administrative Department (Departamento Administrativo do Serviço Público; DASP), set up in 1938, provided the first insulated structure necessary to operationalise the process. The DASP was the first organisation to produce studies for the purpose of professionalising public administration and introducing universal principles of administration, so as to separate it from politics. Although this bureaucratic insulation and universalism would continue to coexist with Brazil's other two 'political grammars' – clientelism and corporatism – noted by Nunes (1977), this point marked the origin of the technical staffs that would give rise to Brazil's modern state bureaucracy (Wahrlich, 1983; Bariani, 2010).

A public primary education system began to be constructed, as well as the first universities, which were to expand continuously. From then on, state-building, going hand in hand with policies designed to form technical elites, spread gradually to various sectors of state intervention as new public agencies were set up. These included: the Ministry of Education and Public Health (Ministério da Educação e Saúde Pública); the National Education Studies Institute (Instituto Nacional de Estudos Pedagógicos; INEP), which would produce guidelines based on modern education thinking for the education system in the states and municipalities; and the official statistics and census agency (Instituto Brasileiro de Geografia e Estatística; IBGE).

The corporative Vargas regime set up institutes, councils and associations to contemplate the interests of a range of groups and sectors. In the economic field, many of these agencies were to be leading producers of studies and proposals for industrial and infrastructure projects. In the social dimension, a strong social protection structure based on Retirement and Pensions Institutes (Institutos de Aposentadorias e Pensões) was set up for the emerging urban working class. These institutes were a key component in direct state influence on relations between capital and labour and in the trade of political support for privileges with political groups or leaders, and some of them were the source of a technical elite that produced analyses of the social security system.

It was in this period that the first strategies were established for consolidating knowledge-based modernisation. Technical input into decision-making was generated predominantly by the vertical structures internal to the state or the corporative structures set up by the Vargas regime.

The democratic period: 1945–64

The end of the Second World War brought important domestic and international changes, among them, the creation of the Bretton Woods system, the restoration of democracy and the alignment with the US, all of which produced a new political and institutional context in which policy analysis was to professionalise and expand into new areas. Insulated technical elites formed within the state, initially to conduct economic analysis and planning in the areas of finance, economy, foreign policy and national security, in a process induced from the 1950s onwards, when the Coordination for Higher Education Personnel Improvement (Coordenação de Aperfeiçoamento de Pessoal de Nível Superior; CAPES) and the National Council for Scientific and Technological Development (Conselho Nacional de Desenvolvimento Científico e Tecnológico; CNPq) were set up. These organisations paved the way for the spread of postgraduate studies, scientific research and meritocracy in Brazil.

North American diagnostic and advisory missions, including the Cooke and Abbink missions, then began to assist the formulation of economic development projects. The Joint Brazil–United States Commission's work on infrastructure projects financed from a fund of Brazilian and US capital gave rise to Brazil's National Development Bank (Banco Nacional de Desenvolvimento Econômico; BNDE), which from then on was to play a central role in the analysis, formulation and implementation of economic and industrial development policies.

In addition to technical advisory missions and commissions, not only were highly specialised agencies set up, such as the Currency and Credit Superintendency (Superintendência da Moeda e do Crédito; SUMOC), responsible for the institutional design and management of Brazil's financial system (Gouvêa, 1994), but also the first state planning agencies. Newly founded state oil, iron, steel, electricity and foreign trade enterprises fostered sectoral technical expertise. As economic department staffs were made up largely of engineers, lawyers, accountants and administrators, in order to meet that demand, investment was directed to the building up of economics courses. In addition, cooperation agreements with international organisations supported international exchanges, scholarships, funding and technical resources for capacity-building in this field (Loureiro, 1992, 1997).

With the founding of the Getúlio Vargas Foundation (Fundação Getúlio Vargas; FGV), set up in 1944 by senior members of the DASP, the professionalisation of policy analysis based on rational styles was raised to a new plateau, and the FGV went on to develop economic policy guidelines. Set up as a private law organisation with financial support from government, business and politicians, it became an important centre for postgraduate programmes and studies in public and private administration, as well as for applied economic research and macroeconomic statistics. It introduced the price index calculation and national accounts system methods into Brazil (Schwartzman et al, 2008). Diplomacy was professionalised through the Rio Branco Institute (Instituto Rio Branco), founded in 1946, which introduced a competitive examination for entry to the diplomatic corps, was exclusively responsible for training technical diplomatic personnel and would play an important part in formulating Brazilian foreign policy (Cheibub, 1985; Amorim Neto, 2011; Lopes et al, 2012). In national security, the War College (Escola Superior de Guerra; ESG) was founded in 1948 as a research and discussion centre in the area of security and development. Strategies and policies formulated there in keeping with the doctrine of national security were to justify the 1964 military takeover and subsequent economic and political project.

The insulated structures that were set up to produce and consume policy analysis were unable to eliminate traditional relations in the public administration, but did assure that economic and industrial policies were operated. In order to escape the political and bureaucratic constraints on policy management, the Kubitscheck government set up a 'parallel administration' of councils and executive groups drawn from the staffs of various insulated organisations as its core mechanism for coordinated action in development project planning, decision-making and implementation.

In the democratic period between the end of the Second World War and the 1964 military takeover, a number of institutes, associations and scientific societies – polarised between national developmentalists and advocates of openness to foreign capital – formed from civil society or in a variety of connections with the state. Left-wing parties and movements sought to influence policy directions and many intellectuals asserted their role as thinkers and formulators behind a left-wing national developmentalist project. The Brazilian Economics, Sociology and Politics Institute (Instituto Brasileiro de Economia, Sociologia e Política; IBESP) and the Higher Brazilian Studies Institute (Instituto Superior de Estudos Brasileiros; ISEB), as well as the publication Cadernos de Nosso Tempo that it gave rise to, stood as bastions of nationalism and defenders of the role of intellectuals as formulators of a political project for the country (Schwartzman, 1981).

In the foreign policy field, the Brazilian International Relations Institute (Instituto Brasileiro de Relações Internacionais; IBRI), a civil association for policy analysis and proposals, which was to publish the Brazilian international policy journal Revista Brasileira de Política Internacional, was set up with the participation of senior civil servants, diplomats, businessmen and personalities. Together with the economics journals Revista Brasileira de Economia and Conjuntura Econômica, both published by the FGV, these publications were pioneers in Brazil as vehicles for discussing the developmentalist theories of the Economic Commission for Latin America and the Caribbean (ECLAC) on the role of the state and of domestic and foreign enterprises in the development process (Almeida, 1998).

The climate of the period was one of intense political and theoretical conflict among monetarists, structuralists and national developmentalists as to the directions Brazil's economy and state should take. Right-wing organisations grew increasingly active in constructing arguments and were an influence on political change in 1964. Policy analysis was confused with political analysis based on approaches to national development.

The production of knowledge intended specifically for input into policymaking was still restricted to meeting the demands of state or corporative organisations, and focused mainly on economic and development problems, the use of planning methodologies and macroeconomic analysis, in addition to economic policy studies. Social problems were to be addressed through studies, essays and documents based on arguments, secondary data and historical comparisons. In these sectors, there was intense debate over proposals for social insurance legislation, education guidelines and land ownership issues.

The military period: 1964–85

The military dictatorship extended the modernisation project, carrying through a wide-ranging programme of reforms in several sectors. Within the state, policy analysis began to be functionally differentiated and the Applied Economic Research Institute (Instituto de Pesquisas Econômicas Aplicadas; IPEA) was set up as a government think tank for the explicit purpose of producing policy-oriented analyses (Velloso, in D'Araújo et al, 2005). Focusing on macroeconomic and industrial policies, and later on other sectors, the technical staff of the IPEA participated in preparing the large-scale infrastructure and scientific development projects outlined in the First and Second National Development Plans. Under the developmentalist influence of ECLAC, planning was directed basically to economic and industrial growth. Planning and cost–benefit analyses were extended to other areas, as in the case of the health resource planning proposed by the Pan American Health Organisation (PAHO). In parallel, in the economics research institutes and postgraduate programmes set up since the 1960s, schools of thought developed that were to have diverse influences on the economic policies adopted in the decades to follow (Loureiro, 1997).

In the second half of the 1970s, in a context of economic crisis and the military regime, Brazil had already become more modern and complex. A new working class and a new trade unionism emerged to challenge the Vargas-era corporative model, and a growing urban middle class adopted more cosmopolitan lifestyles. Against a backdrop of increasing inequalities and political repression, social grievances and demands for democracy were brought to the centre of the national debate. The resurgence of trade union activities and the struggles of social movements were to give intellectuals, political parties, professional and trade union organisations, and civil and community associations a more influential role in the political arena, strengthening the production of policy analysis outside the structures of the state. Private research centres formed by academics and intellectuals in opposition to the military regime, such as the Brazilian Centre for Analysis and Planning (Centro Brasileiro de Análise e Planejamento; CEBRAP) and the Contemporary Culture Studies Centre (Centro de Estudos de Cultura Contemporânea; CEDEC), initially funded by international financial organisations and agencies, became important players in the formulation of policy proposals.

In the 1980s, the public policy field entered the academic context with the introduction of political science postgraduate and research programmes and the founding of the Brazilian Political Science Association (Associação Brasileira de Ciência Política; ABPC) and the public policy working group of the National Association of Social Science Research and Graduate Studies (Associação Nacional de Pós-Graduação e Pesquisa em Ciências Sociais; ANPOCS) (Melo, 1999). Particularly in political science departments, a wide range of academic studies of different dimensions of the policy process, working from social science and political science approaches, related public policies to the state and to the regime (Melo, 1999; Souza, 2007).

At this time, economists entered into analysis of problems in various policy sectors, including social sectors, using the methods and tools of microeconomics recently introduced into Brazil (Paes and Barros, in D'Araújo et al, 2005); at the same time, public policy as an object of study spread into other fields, such as administration, public health, law and economics. Among social areas, the health field stands out as one of the precursors of the production of policy analysis outside the state. Its analysis was normative in nature, in opposition to the military dictatorship, but nonetheless went beyond any strictly political and ideological bias. Using arguments based on data and historical and economic analyses, it developed a critique of existing health policies and proposed alternatives. The style of analysis applied by the health care field, of policy studies with recommendations, was to influence subsequent policy analysis in other social areas.

Democracy after 1988

It was after 1988 that policy analysis in Brazil became more clearly diverse and horizontal. New forms of governance, including the adoption of horizontal and participatory management practices and the proliferation of policy analysis in civil society, deprived the state of its near monopoly over the production of systematic knowledge for decision-making processes. New problems entered the public agenda, creating new areas of demand for policy analysis and requiring further professionalisation of the bureaucracy. As a result, new policy analysis activities and styles spread.

These characteristics are connected with the changes that took place in the course of democratic consolidation. Democratisation was accompanied by: 1) a proliferation of new social actors operating through civil associations, social movements and non-governmental organisations (NGOs) that directly or indirectly came to make use of or even to produce policy analysis in order to influence policymaking; 2) the introduction of a federative design of state that brought with it new responsibilities for decentralised public policy, with new government actors and more complex policymaking; 3) the introduction of innovations in policy formulation and design (policy councils, conferences and public hearings) that not only incorporated a wide range of actors into the process, but called for supporting studies and reports; 4) the 1988 Constitution, which introduced a wide spectrum of social rights, led in turn to comprehensive, decentralised, national public policies that were subject to social oversight and called for ongoing and increasingly better-informed learning; and 5) further professionalisation of civil servants and public management, which demanded greater technical qualification in bureaucracies at the three levels of government.

The growth of policy analysis in civil society is related to the proliferation of new social actors, such as social movements, NGOs, think tanks, study centres and policy networks, which began to coordinate and voice demands and interests in all kinds of areas. The 1988 Constitution instituted a number of social rights, such as to health, housing and social assistance, rights of the elderly and disabled (Brasil, 2012), and so on, leading to growth in civil associations and NGOs addressing social needs. In addition, rights relating to race, gender and sexual orientation were widened considerably, largely as a result of the preceding period of intense mobilisation.

As the problems became more specialised, so civil associations (particularly NGOs) and social movements came to be confronted by highly diversified agendas (Gohn, 2007). New competences were required of activists and their organisations as a condition for gaining legitimacy in the political and public policy fields. This new professional field came to absorb qualified personnel to lead non-governmental associations and social movements in formulating projects and seeking funding from government bodies, international cooperation agencies, multilateral financial organisations, foundations and private enterprise.

Civil society organisations with a wide variety of goals and interests multiplied in number and went on to form policy networks that acted on political decision-making processes and produced or circulated policy analyses. These included community groups engaged in promoting local development, advisory and research intermediary organisations, think tanks, advocacy groups, foundations pursuing social interest programmes or funding third-party social projects, and social welfare and philanthropic organisations (Oliveira and Haddad, 2001).

From the 1990s on, growing numbers of economic consultancy firms provided services to the financial and industrial sectors, and the economy ceased to be the preserve of the state and its advisers, but expanded to include input from civil society. New think tanks emerged and spurred renewed debate and publication on development-related issues. The economy, even though more restricted to elite technical circles, became a focus for social movements (for example, the PlataformaBNDES[1]), particularly on issues such as infrastructure (for example, the Instituto AcendeBrasil[2] or the Trata Brasil[3]). Although these movements were engaged primarily in advocacy or social oversight, they increasingly brought specialised knowledge to bear in the endeavour to influence policymaking.

Civil associations and NGOs also grew significantly in the environment field, where there is substantial stakeholder participation and policy analysis is widespread. Until recently, much of the policy analysis in this field was performed by numerous NGOs and traditional networks in defence of the environment, comprising environmentalists and advocates for indigenous peoples' rights. Institutionalisation of the environment as a public agenda item led to the appearance of new business and academic study centres and think tanks, which either addressed environmental issues directly or incorporated the environment into their field of activity. Many of these were highly proactive in producing policy analyses.

Legislation and environmental preservation policies adopted in recent decades triggered a reaction from coalitions of landowning and agricultural interests in opposition to the environmental movement. The novelty is that in this arena too, debate has come to be framed largely by contending policy-oriented studies and reports, as seen in the activities of the national farmers' association, the Brazilian Agriculture Confederation (Confederação da Agricultura e Pecuária do Brasil; CNA).[4]

Two other areas that have become objects of policy analysis in recent years are public administration and the political system. While the state had been endeavouring for decades to improve public management and had pursued a succession of public administration reforms and reform plans, with democratisation came the need for greater oversight, accountability and transparency in its actions. Not only did the democratised state make new inroads in professionalising the administration, but civil associations were set up to monitor and propose solutions for this field. As many of the problems of public administration are connected with deadlocks in the political system, analyses and advocacy became widespread, as did proposals for political reforms and means to foster ethics in politics, for example, the initiatives of the Socioeconomic Studies Institute (Instituto de Estudos Socioeconômicos; INESC).[5]

The diversification of problems and social actors also encouraged greater participation by academics in everyday political issues. Since democratisation, numerous centres have been set up at universities to address cross-cutting themes, and particularly for policy studies. This has been catalysed by growth in studies and research commissioned by government, very often via public tender or through government teaching and research agencies, which have increased their investments, thus broadening the policy analysis market.

As regards the federative structure, the 1988 Constitution instituted three levels of government: union, states (26 plus the Federal District) and, for the first time, municipalities (5,565) as the constitutive entities of the federation. The three levels are autonomous and have their own legislations, budgets and government structures. The Constitution introduced shared responsibilities and decentralisation for a series of public policies, creating an unprecedented transformation in the structure of the Brazilian state. The municipalities became responsible for providing a series of (particularly social) services, and had to build or reform public organisations, hire trained personnel, introduce legislation and decide, format and monitor contracts. Democratisation meant that demands formerly addressed primarily to the federal government were now directed also to the states and municipalities, requiring that they professionalise further and that civil organisations become more qualified to deliberate on public problems.

Most of Brazil's municipalities are very small and, together with several states, highly dependent on federal funds. Accordingly, the process of professionalisation is not homogeneous and occurs mainly in the larger and financially more autonomous bodies, which are able and need to maintain structures for financing and contracting policy analysis. The majority, however, reproduce at the local level the administrative structure in place at the federal or state level, making it easier for them to meet state or federal guidelines for receiving funding. This calls for an intense process of negotiation involving consultations, working groups, commissions, symposia and so on, which yields institutional learning among levels of government. On the other hand, application for funding generally entails submitting projects, thus fuelling demand for NGOs, universities, research centres and the private sector to support city governments in preparing them. In the opposite direction too, growing local power stimulates the policy analysis market for civil associations and academic institutions.

Brazil's democratisation also involved wide-ranging reform of the state, both in its structure and organisation and in its relationship with civil society (Avritzer, 2011). New mechanisms were introduced for greater accountability and participation, such as public consultations, popular initiatives and public hearings. On issues where there is substantial conflict, public hearings are used increasingly by the coalitions in dispute, and studies, research and reports are the resources most used to influence the outcomes.[6]

In 2003, the Economic and Social Development Council (Conselho the Desenvolvimento Econômico e Social) was set up to advise the President on public policy. It includes representatives of workers, entrepreneurs, social movements, government and prominent leaders from a wide range of other sectors.

The 1988 Constitution also instituted a participatory design for the formulation and implementation of decentralised national policies, and made it compulsory for conferences to be held and policy councils set up with civil society participation. The conferences – regular encounters called to discuss and decide policy guidelines for a given area and period – involve parity participation by government, professionals of the field, business-owners and civil society. Meanwhile, the policy councils form part of the policy management structure and their function is to monitor and approve the actions of the executive. The literature points to a number of constraints on the conferences and councils in pursuing their objectives, but it is widely agreed that they are important to democracy (Côrtes, 2009; Moreira and Escorel, 2009; Pogrebinschi and Santos, 2011). Constraints on the councils include the difficulty of the majority in navigating the mechanisms that govern the public administration and the conduct of public policies. That is, there is recognised to be a knowledge gap and councillors are insufficiently informed to take decisions; this has been targeted by numerous capacity-building courses for councillors given by government, universities and civil bodies. Nonetheless, the more active councils do use and produce documents analysing problems in their field of interest.

Over the course of Brazil's history, numerous reforms have been carried out to professionalise the bureaucracy. In the post-1988 period, for the first time, a constitution required public examination as a requirement for entry into the civil service and called for budget and programmatic planning for public policies through multi-year plans. Hiring of personnel can still be framed legally in various different ways, but the introduction of public examinations eliminated a great deal of the clientelism in the civil service. Professionalisation was most extensive at the federal level, but this was not accompanied by most of the municipalities and many states. Numerous problems, such as the lack of regular monitoring and evaluation of civil servants' work, persist at all levels.

The expansion of rights provided for in the Constitution was restricted by the crisis of the 1990s. A far-reaching privatisation programme reduced the number of public enterprises and set up regulatory agencies for a number of areas. Inspired by 'new public management', these reforms produced a profusion of contracts for consultancy, research and studies that indirectly stimulated growth in the policy analysis market, which expanded among public agencies and strengthened partnering and networking outside the state.

The spread of policy analysis after 1988 was also assisted by broader access to higher and postgraduate education, which formed a public that demanded more sophisticated information and analyses. That demand was met by greater specialisation in newspapers, magazines and television coverage. The print press, which had been an important political actor in support of interests and parties since the early decades of the 20th century, came also to reflect the outlooks of public policy specialists in specific columns or articles on sectoral problems. When subscription television operations began in the 1990s, broadcast schedules incorporated environmental, foreign, social, economic, political and so on policy concerns, bringing them to wider audiences and popularising policy analysis in Brazilian culture.

Final remarks

In Brazil, the professionalisation of policy analysis followed the model of development of other countries, in response to the demands of modernisation and the development of a bureaucracy with the technical capacity to produce or commission analyses as input to public policy decision-making. The existence of a modern bureaucracy is a precondition for the emergence of policy analysis, but should not be confused with it, because the professionalisation of policy analysis depends on the availability of technical and intellectual elites with specific sectoral competences able to assure the socially generalised production of knowledge for political decision-making. Although modern bureaucracy and technical and intellectual elites originated in a single process of modernisation of the state and society, the bureaucracy gained competence particularly in relation to policy execution, while the analysts' skills were directed to knowledge production.

Despite the whole process of modernisation since the 1930s, government management based on rational approaches has always been subject to political pressures. For that very reason, to begin with and in parallel with the endeavour to build a modern bureaucracy, it fell to technical elites in insulated structures within the state to guarantee the production of knowledge for policymaking. Even though at the outset the senior members of the bureaucracy were also the first policy analysts and planners, it was precisely the social, institutional and functional differentiation that came with changes in the structure of the state and in relations of governance that enabled policy analysis to be incorporated into the activities of organisations of the state and civil society.

The diffusion and diversification of policy analysis in society only came about with the changes in the morphology of the state and in forms of governance after 1988, when new actors and jurisdictions came into play. Modernisation prepared the ground for meritocracy and professionalisation, while democratisation furnished new rules and institutions for the spread of policy analysis. The different ways different actors took ownership of this field was decisive to the quality of policy analysis in the period after 1988, in a process where greater professionalisation in public administration and civil society organisations combined with state permeability to their demands. Policy analysis outgrew the verticalised structures of the state, took root in society and was incorporated into the new policy arenas.

In a few years, public policy had entered the agenda of professional associations, civil society organisations and social movements, and was spreading in and through the media. Innovations in policymaking, such as the use of deliberation mechanisms and the proliferation of policy networks, stimulated argumentation, participation and interaction, with new styles of policy analysis being integrated into the interplay of democracy and contemporary governance.

The changes in Brazilian society and state that influenced the professionalisation of policy analysis in the period after 1988 are of such a magnitude that they cannot all be adequately described here. That process introduced policy analysis definitively into decision-making in Brazil. The practice of intervening in public policy using appropriately informed, systematised knowledge became widespread in society. Even though policy analysis is not a profession, and neither is there a culture recognising it as an intrinsic component of policymaking, it is doubtless that policy analysis has come to stay.

Notes

1. See: www.plataformabndes.org.br/site/

2. See: www.acendebrasil.com.br/site/sccoes/home.asp

3. See: www.tratabrasil.org.br/

4. See: www.canaldoprodutor.com.br/

5. See: www.inesc.org.br/

6. Recent examples were the discussion over the legalisation of abortion in cases of anencephaly and the demarcation of the Raposa do Sol indigenous reserve.

Acknowledgement

We are grateful to André Costa Lobato, who contributed with data collection for this chapter.

References

Adam, S. and Kriesi, H. (2007) 'The network approach', in P.A. Sabatier (ed) *Theories of the policy process*, Boulder, CO: Westview Press, pp 129–54.

Almeida, P.R. (1998) 'Revista Brasileira de Política Internacional: quatro décadas ao serviço da inserção internacional do Brasil', *Revista Brasileira de Política Internacional*, vol 41, pp 42–65.

Amorim Neto, O. (2011) *De Dutra a Lula: a condução e os determinantes da política externa brasileira*, Rio de Janeiro: Elsevier.

Avritzer, L.A. (2011) *Dinâmica da participação local no Brasil*, Rio de Janeiro: Cortez.

Bardach, E. (1996) *The eight-step path of policy analysis: a handbook for practice*, Berkeley, CA: Berkeley Academic Press.

Bariani, E. (2010) 'DASP: Entre a norma e o fato', in C. Andrews and E. Bariani (eds) *Administração pública no Brasil: Breve história política*, São Paulo: Editora Unifesp, pp 39–62.

Brasil (2012) 'Constituição da República Federativa do Brasil', www.planalto.gov.br/ ccivil_03/constituicao/constituicao.htm

Brooks, S. (2007) 'The policy analysis profession in Canada', in L. Dobuzinsky, M. Howlett and D. Laycock (eds) *Policy analysis in Canada: the state of the art*, Toronto: University of Toronto Press, pp 21–47.

Cheibub, Z. (1985) 'Diplomacia e construção institucional: o Itamaraty em uma perspectiva histórica', *DADOS*, vol 28, no 1, pp 113–31.

Côrtes, S.M.V. (2009) 'Conselhos e conferências de saúde: papel institucional e mudança nas relações entre Estado e sociedade', in S. Fleury and L. Lobato (eds) *Participação, democracia e saúde*, Rio de Janeiro: Cebes, pp 102–28.

D'Araújo, M.C., Farias, I.C. and Hippólito, L. (2005) *IPEA 40 anos: uma trajetória voltada para o desenvolvimento - depoimentos ao CPDOC*, Rio de Janeiro: Editora FGV.

Dryzek, J.S. (2006) 'Policy analysis as critique', in M. Moran, M. Rein and R. Goodin (eds) *The Oxford handbook of public policy*, New York, NY: Oxford University Press, pp 190–203.

Fischer, F. (1980) *Politics, values, and public policy: the problem of methodology*, Boulder, CO: Westview Press.

Geddes, B. (1990) 'Building state autonomy in Brazil, 1930–1964', *Comparative Politics*, vol 22, no 2, pp 217–35.

Gohn, M.G. (2007) *Teoria dos movimentos sociais: paradigmas clássicos e contemporâneos*, São Paulo: Loyola.

Goodin, R.E., Rein, M. and Moran, M. (2006) 'The public and its policies', in M. Moran, M. Rein and R. Goodin (eds) *The Oxford handbook of public policy*, New York, NY: Oxford University Press, pp 3–35.

Gouldner, A.W. (1978) *The future of the intellectuals and the rise of new class*, Nova York: Seabury.

Gouvêa, G.P. (1994) 'Burocracia e elites burocráticas no Brasil: poder e lógica de ação'. PhD dissertation presented at the Instituto de Filosofia e Ciências Humanas, Universidade Estadual de Campinas, p 264.

Hoppe, R. (1999) 'Policy analysis, science and politics: from "speaking truth to power" to "making sense together"', *Science and Public Policy*, vol 26, no 3, pp 201–10.

Howlett, M. and Lindquist, E. (2007) 'Beyond formal policy analysis: governance context, analytical styles, and the policy analysis movement in Canada', in L. Dobuzinskis, M. Howlett and D. Laycock (eds) *Policy analysis in Canada: the state of the art*, Toronto: University of Toronto Press, pp 86–115.

Howlett, M. and Rayner, J. (2006) 'Globalization and governance capacity: explaining divergence in national forest programs as instances of "next-generation" regulation in Canada and Europe', *Governance*, vol 19, pp 251–75.

Ingram, H. and Schneider, A.L. (2006) 'Policy analysis for democracy', in M. Moran, M. Rein and R. Goodin (eds) *The Oxford handbook of public policy*, New York, NY: Oxford University Press, pp 169–89.

Kenis, P. and Schneider, V. (1991) 'Policy networks and policy analysis: scrutinizing a new analytical toolbox', in B. Marin and R. Mayntz (eds) *Policy networks: empirical evidence and theoretical considerations*, Frankfurt: Westview Press, pp 25–62.

Lamounier, B. (1982) 'A Ciência Política no Brasil: roteiro para um balanço crítico', in B. Lamounier (ed) *A Ciência Política nos anos 80*, Brasilia: Editora da UNB, pp 407–33.

Lopes, D., Faria, C.A.P and Casarões, G. (2012) 'Mudanças institucionais no Itamaraty, ethos corporativo e mitigação do insulamento burocrático do serviço exterior brasileiro', in C.A.P. Faria (ed) *Implementação de políticas públicas: teoria e prática*, Belo Horizonte: Editora PUC Minas.

Loureiro, M.R. (1992) 'Economistas e elites dirigentes no Brasil', *Revista Brasileira de Ciências Sociais*, vol 7, no 20, pp 34–69.

Loureiro, M.R. (1997) 'Formação de elites dirigentes no Brasil: o papel das instituições de ensino e pesquisa econômica aplicada', *Relatório de Pesquisa no 18*, Núcleo de Pesquisas e Publicações, Escola de Administração de Empresas de São Paulo, Fundação Getúlio Vargas, p 43.

Lynn, L. (1999) 'A place at the table: policy analysis, its postpositive critics, and the future of practice', *Journal of Policy Analysis and Management*, vol 18, no 3, pp 411–24.

Mayer, I., Bots, P. and van Daalen, E. (2004) 'Perspectives on policy analysis: a framework for understanding and design', *International Journal of Technology, Policy & Management*, vol 4, no 1, pp 169–91.

Melo, M.A. (1999) 'Estado, governo e políticas públicas', in S. Miceli (ed) *O que ler na Ciência Social brasileira, (1970–1995): Ciência Política III*, São Paulo: Editora Sumaré, Anpocs/Capes, pp 59–99.

Moreira, M.R. and Escorel, S. (2009) 'Municipal health councils of Brazil: a debate on the democratization of health in the twenty years of the UHS', *Ciência & Saúde Coletiva*, vol 14, no 3, pp 795–806.

Nunes, E. (1997) *A gramática política do Brasil: clientelismo e insulamento burocrático*, Rio de Janeiro: Jorge Zahar Ed.

Oliveira, A.C. and Haddad, S. (2001) 'As organizações da sociedade civil e as ONGS de Educação', *Cadernos de Pesquisa*, no 112, pp 61–83.

Patton, C. and Sawicki, D. (1993) *Basic methods of policy analysis and planning* (2nd edn), Englewood Cliffs, NJ: Prentice Hall.

Pogrebinschi, T. and Santos, F. (2011) 'Participação como representação: o impacto das conferências nacionais de políticas públicas no Congresso Nacional', *Dados*, vol 54, no 3, pp 259–305.

Radin, B. (2000) *Beyond Machiavelli: policy analysis comes of age*, Washington, DC: Georgetown University Press.

Schwartzman, S. (1981) *O pensamento nacionalista e os "Cadernos do Nosso Tempo"*, Brasília: Editora da UnB, Câmara dos Deputados, Biblioteca do Pensamento Político Brasileiro.

Schwartzman, S., Botelho, A., Alves, S. and Cristophe, M. (2008) 'Estudos de caso: Brasil', in S. Schwartzman (ed) *Universidades e desenvolvimento na América Latina: Experiências exitosas de centros de pesquisas*, Rio de Janeiro: Centro Edelstein de Pesquisas Sociais, Biblioteca Virtual de Ciências Humanas, pp 184–248.

Souza, C. (2007) 'O estado da arte da pesquisa em políticas públicas', in G. Hochman, M. Arretche and E. Marques (eds) *Políticas públicas no Brasil*, Rio de Janeiro: Editora Fiocruz.

Wahrlich, B. (1983) *Reforma administrativa na Era de Vargas*, Rio de Janeiro: FGV.

Weimer, D. (1998) 'Policy analysis and evidence: a craft perspective', *Policy Studies Journal*, vol 26, pp 114–28.

Wildavsky, A. (1979) *Speaking truth to power*, Toronto: Little, Brown and Company.

THREE

Policy analysis styles in Brazil

Christina W. Andrews

Introduction

The evolution of policy analysis in Brazil followed a different path than the one seen in the US, Canada, UK and other developed countries, evolving independently from the Anglo-Saxon intellectual tradition. Up to today, classical authors in the field of policy analysis – such as Harold Lasswell, Charles Lindblom, Theodore Lowi, Yehezkel Dror, James March and Johan Olsen, among others – have not been translated into Portuguese. The only exception is Herbert Simon, who had his book *Administrative Behavior* (Simon, 1972) translated and published in Brazil in 1957 thanks to a cooperation programme between the Brazilian government and the US Agency for International Development (USAID); however, the book is out of print since 1972. Therefore, most policymakers in Brazil did not have contact with the classical books on policy analysis during their academic studies and even later as professionals.

Policy analysis as a specialised field emerged in the early 1950s in the US as a subfield within political science, having as its landmark the publication of the book *The policy sciences: recent developments in scope and method* (Lerner and Lasswell, 1951). In Brazil, during this same period, intellectual and political attentions were focused on economic development strategies. In this context, the works of the United Nation's Economic Commission for Latin American and the Caribbean (ECLAC/CEPAL) became the main intellectual influence in the formulation of public policies in Brazil and throughout Latin America. One important work of this period was Raúl Prebisch's (1950) essay, *The economic development of Latin America and its principal problems*. Thus, while in the US, policy analysis emerged from political science, in Brazil and in other Latin-American countries, policy analysis meant, above all, the analysis of policies aimed at promoting economic development.

This emphasis on economic development lasted for several decades, until it found its limits in the economic downturn of the late 1970s, a period marked in Brazil by the failure of the Second National Development Plan and by the debt crisis (Carneiro, 2002). The 1980s became known as the 'lost decade' due to the long period of recession in Brazil and Latin America that followed the changes in the global economic environment. Throughout the decade, developmentalist policies started to be replaced by macroeconomic adjustment policies, which included privatisation of state companies and financial liberalisation. However, this scenario slowly began to change once again. Despite predomination of neoliberal adjustment in the 1990s, this period was also characterised by the redemocratisation of Brazil,[1] which included the enactment of a new constitution that added social rights to the traditional political rights. This led to a new political status for social policies.

From the end of 1988 onwards, public policies came to be seen as means of assuring access to social rights, acquiring the same importance previously assigned to economic policies. As a consequence, policy analysis finally emerged as a specialised field of investigation in Brazil, moving beyond economic analysis. Because policy analysis emerged in Brazil without having previous contact with the Anglo-Saxon tradition, the methodological styles adopted in the field were influenced by the disciplines historically important in the previous decades. Thus, due to the importance of development policies, policy analysis in Brazil still relies on methods that emerge from economics; in this chapter, we will refer to these methods as the 'economic style'. It includes methods based on measurable performance indicators and also those normally employed in the analysis of infrastructure projects, such as cost–benefit analysis. Thanks to the expansion of the social sciences in Brazil, the methodological repertory associated with the practice of policy analysis was enlarged. In the 1950s, sociology was already a well-established discipline in Brazil (Botelho and Schwarcz, 2009) and from the mid-1960s onwards, political science began to make its mark in the social sciences in Brazil under the influence of North American universities (Forjaz, 1997). In the late 1980s, sociology and political science – as well as anthropology – began providing methodological tools that were then applied to policy analysis; we will refer to these methods as the 'socio-political style'. This style includes a wide variety of methods, which do not necessarily share the same epistemological assumptions. Some of the methods included in this style are associated with positivism, while others stem from the interpretive sociology tradition.

In addition to the two main methodological styles – economic and socio-political – policy analyses in Brazil may also be characterised by the scope of analysis. Policy studies that focus on the broader implications of social policies will be referred to here as the 'macro' approach. For example, in the area of health, macro-level approaches seek to evaluate the impact of the Unified Health System (Sistema Unificado de Saúde; SUS) on society's well-being or its accomplishments regarding stated goals. The micro-level approach has a narrower scope of analysis; it corresponds to the analysis of programmes that deal with specific and localised policy issues or focus on the localised outcomes of policies. Examples of this approach are analyses that investigate the outcomes of educational policies in a given school or that examine the cost-effectiveness of a preventive programme for a specific type of health problem. As will be discussed in more detail in the following section, many policy analysis studies within the micro-level approach have been criticised for their excessive fragmentation and lack of methodological rigour. This type of micro approach is commonly found in academic studies and provides a large amount of the public information on governmental policies. The lack of relevance of such fragmented information could be remediated by meta-analysis studies, but these are very rarely undertaken. The micro approach is also common in the analyses of 'best practices' in Brazil, especially those that focus on local-level policies and programmes.[2] Despite the dissemination of 'best practices', the theoretical debates on this approach are still incipient in the Brazilian context (Andrews, 2008). Finally, the 'meso'-level approach corresponds to policy analyses that focus on specific policies or programmes, but associate their findings to broader policy issues. Studies within this approach may have a narrower focus and may explore a specific outcome, but deliberately seek to relate their findings to an overall analysis of the policy in question. Thus, policy analyses corresponding to this approach hold an intermediate character vis-a-vis the macro and micro policy analysis approaches.

Most studies within the economic style tend to adopt the macro approach. They are often based on analyses of indicators and other quantitative variables and focus on the overall outcome of a given policy. It should be mentioned that these studies also tend to rely on methods used in microeconomics and, as critics have pointed out, these studies often neglect the qualitative aspects of policies. Within the socio-political style, one can find all the three approaches, although the meso and micro approaches are more common.

It is important to keep in mind that the classificatory framework described earlier has a heuristic purpose and is not intended to be a fully developed typology. This framework, therefore, has the purpose of organising the diversity of policy analysis studies undertaken in Brazil in the past 20 years. Such a strategy aims at providing some sense and order in a field that lacks a clear and established tradition. As Brazilian scholars have pointed out, despite recent developments, the field is still characterised by the lack of rigorous application of theories and methods (Souza, 2003). In addition, there is a proliferation of sectoral studies that focus on specific policy areas, foe example, health, education or social assistance. This creates difficulties for the vertical integration of findings, due to the different theoretical and methodological orientations underpinning each policy area. It has also been argued that policy analyses in Brazil tend to focus on specific aspects or stages of policies; the overall analysis is commonly split in studies about agenda-setting, policy formulation, legitimation, management, implementation and evaluation (Souza, 2003). Most policy analysis investigations in Brazil can be best described as a mix of agenda-setting, implementation and evaluation. This may be explained by the lack of assimilation of the idea of the policy cycle, which is the 'bread and butter' of the Anglo-Saxon theoretical tradition.

Another consequence of the lack of theoretical tradition is that the terminology used in policy analysis is problematic in Brazil. Policy analysis studies rarely mention Lasswell's terminology 'knowledge of' and 'knowledge in' (Lasswell, 2000), thus failing to make this differentiation explicit. Despite the intense terminological debates that have taken place in developed countries, it is possible to say that an operational agreement on terminology has been settled. Therefore, in Europe and in the US, the term 'policy analysis' has been associated with the idea of 'knowledge in'. In Brazil, however, the terminological debate is almost non-existent. Terms in use in the Brazilian context have been borrowed from the international academic literature, but because a clear link with the Anglo-Saxon tradition is missing, the terms 'policy analysis' and 'policy evaluation' are often used interchangeably.

In the following sections, the two methodological styles – economic and socio-political – and the three approaches – macro, meso and micro – will be briefly discussed by means of examples of policy analyses undertaken in contemporary Brazil. These examples were drawn from the areas of health, education and social assistance. As mentioned earlier, the expansion of social policies after the enactment of the 1988 Constitution was responsible for the emergence of policy analysis as a field of inquiry in Brazil. Not surprisingly, most policy analysis studies developed in Brazil in the past two decades focus on these three policy areas.

One caveat in necessary here: the cases discussed in this chapter are not statistically representative, although they can be regarded as 'typical'. The selection aims at presenting cases that best illustrate the diversity of styles and approaches found in policy analyses in Brazil.

Socio-political style

One example of the socio-political style that adopts the macro approach in the area of health policy can be seen in the article by Cohn (2009), which discusses the changes in the Brazilian public health system since its conception in the late 1980s. In order for one to understand the methodological approach chosen for the article – the critical essay – it is necessary to briefly present the context that brought about the reform in the Brazilian health system in 1988. Before the enactment of the democratic constitution, only those working in the formal labour market – roughly 50% of the population – had the right to medical assistance in public clinics and hospitals. Although some health services such as vaccination and a few ambulatory services were available to the population at large, the public health system in Brazil was not universal by any means. The struggle for universal health care was part of the overall struggle for democracy in Brazil during the years of the authoritarian regime (1964–85). One of the most important social movements in activity during this period was the Movimento Sanitarista, also called Partido Sanitarista. Composed by union and community leaders, left-leaning health professionals, and progressive intellectuals, this movement defended a public health system founded on the principles of universality, equity, participation and decentralisation (Escorel, 1999). The Brazilian Centre for Health Studies, (CEBES), the movement's think tank, developed studies and proposals that became the intellectual foundation of the public and universal health care system (the SUS) introduced by the 1988 Constitution. The creation of the SUS was regarded by many analysts as 'revolutionary', because it broke away from the corporative approach that previously dominated health care policies in Brazil.

Cohn's article presents a diagnosis of SUS's transformations under the influence of neoliberal reforms introduced in Brazil in the 1990s. The author situates her analysis in the shift from SUS's original principles – universality, equity, participation and decentralisation – to cost control and managerial approaches, which include the outsourcing of public health services. This shift, goes the argument, has not been restricted to actual health policies, but is also noticeable in the production of knowledge in the field. Academic and non-academic studies that once discussed issues such as democracy, the role of the state and structural dimensions related to health/ illness had been replaced by studies adopting a technicist and pragmatic approach. As outsourcing expands within the SUS, the author doubts whether state regulation by itself would be able to adequately guarantee the public interest, because managers of outsourced services are almost exclusively focused on the cost-effectiveness aspects of health care. She is also suspicious of 'family health programmes', which she sees as a conservative attempt to control families, especially the poor. Cohn considers that debates on health reform are increasingly dominated by the technical-scientific dimension, diminishing the attention to SUS's *political* dimension. In sum, her essay is a criticism of recent changes introduced in the Brazilian public health system and of the way policy analysts and academics have been dealing with those changes.

It should be noted here that while in Anglo-Saxon countries, the essay is not the standard 'method' for policy analysis, in Brazil, the essay continues to have an important role in policy analysis and in the social sciences in general. The explanation for this may be found in the predominant social context of the 1920s, when sociology was introduced in Brazil. Before becoming an academic discipline focusing on empirical investigations, sociology was regarded as a tool for policy formulation in the field of education (Almeida, 2008). In Brazil, during the autocratic period from 1938 to 1945, known as Estado Novo, the debates on education shifted from 'education for society', that is, education as a social right, to 'education for the homeland', that is, education as a means for buttressing nationalist feelings in the citizenry. This period witnessed the initial steps in the creation of universities in Brazil, which were then modelled on the French universities. As a consequence of the construction of universities, sociology finally acquired the status of an academic discipline. However, the empirical methods that characterised the discipline in the US did not take hold in Brazil until the 1960s. Meanwhile, the essay remained as the preferred 'method' of Brazilian sociologists for several decades. The now classical book on the cultural character of Brazil, *Raízes do Brasil*, by Sérgio Buarque de Holanda (1995 [1936]), is perhaps the most memorable example of the importance of the essay in the development of the social sciences in Brazil. Despite the assimilation of empirical methods from the 1960s onwards, the essay continues to be widely adopted by Brazilian sociologists, political scientists and policy analysts.

Another method largely used in policy analysis in Brazil is the case study, by far the most common method within the micro approach, but a few policy analysis studies adopt the meso-level approach. One such example is the study by Ribeiro and Costa (2000), which examines the effectiveness of inter-municipal health consortiums. Although most of their analysis is focused on the experience of one specific case, the Consórcio Intermunicipal de Saúde da Microrregião de Penápolis (CISA), their goal has a broader intent. They seek to evaluate the performance of the inter-municipal health care consortiums, focusing on citizens' access to medical specialties, the reduction of idle capacity in hospitals and other aspects of health care provision. Thus, they are concerned with the features that CISA has in common with other health care consortiums, and not with its specific characteristics. Their conclusion, accordingly, is an encompassing one: 'The consortiums, above all, are an innovation because they create unusual parameters of cooperation and coordination of health policy at the local level' (Ribeiro and Costa, 2000, p 217).

However, few policy analysis studies using case studies manage to deal with the meso-level approach. Most studies within the micro approach are case studies, whose methodological purposes have often been misunderstood. The expansion of graduate programmes in the social sciences seems to explain the proliferation of case studies in Brazil, especially in the fields of health and education. Graduate programmes are regulated by the Coordination for Postgraduate Personnel Improvement (Coordenação de Aperfeiçoamento de Pessoal de Nível Superior; CAPES), a federal agency linked to the Ministry of Education. This agency requires that students complete their Masters theses and PhD dissertations within two and four years, respectively; programmes that fail to graduate their students within these time frames are liable to downgrading in their evaluation scores. In the social sciences, one 'solution' to complete research within these short time spans has been the adoption of the case study, a strategy that ended up being inappropriate in many situations.

The misuse of case studies in policy analysis is particularly common in the area of education. As mentioned earlier, in its beginnings, research in the area of education was expected to provide solutions to public policy problems (Almeida, 2008). Nevertheless, the 'policy science orientation' approach that characterised sociology in Brazil slowly began to shift to an academic orientation. In the 1970s, several graduate programmes in the area of education were created, introducing new themes, methodologies and theoretical references (André, 2006). From the 1980s onwards, studies focusing on education using action-research and other qualitative methods in the disciplines of anthropology, history, and philosophy became common. Nevertheless, despite the gains in complexity and diversity favoured by the institutionalisation of research at universities, methodological deficiencies in studies focusing on education began to mount. André argues that this problem was linked to possible defective training in research procedures, intensified by time constraints imposed on Masters and Doctorate programmes in Brazil. Scholars began to note that a growing number of studies in the area of education selected a too-narrow portion of reality, lacked a clear methodological approach or failed to analyse results from a theoretical perspective. In addition, as mentioned earlier, the case study method was often misunderstood. As Alves-Mazzotti (2006) pointed out, many researchers say that they have developed a case study only because they have selected a specific object – a school, a class – without concern as to whether the 'case' in question can contribute to the knowledge base of the field. Moreover, some authors disseminated the belief that case studies are an 'easy' research strategy.

Case studies are also common in the area of social assistance. One example is the study by Rego (2010), which investigated the impact of the Bolsa Família (Family Grant Programme) in the lives of poor women. In this federal programme – as in other Conditional Cash Transfer (CCT) programmes around the world – women are chiefly the recipients of the cash payments and also the ones responsible for assuring that the programme's conditionalities are met.[3] Rego interviewed women from the poorest families included in the programme, women who did not have a regular income and whose lives were a daily struggle for subsistence. Based on the interviews with these women, the author argues that the programme was helping them to get a basic social right: to remain alive. Rego argues that these women, thanks to the Bolsa Família, were allowed to make choices – what to buy for their children or whether to separate from a partner. This aspect of the programme had a positive impact on the subjectivity of the poor women, allowing them to enjoy a concept of citizenship that was previously alien to them. Following the arguments made by Nancy Fraser and others, Rego argues that public policies should not only repair economic and social injustices, but also transform the cultural and educational contexts that impact 'bivalent collectivities', that is, social groups that suffer exclusion not only due to social and economic factors, but also due to gender, ethnicity or cultural affiliation.[4] Thus, the Bolsa Família should be a permanent programme, guaranteeing access to basic citizens' rights, becoming aware of the needs of bivalent collectivities.

Ethnography has also been used for policy analysis in the areas of health, education, race relations and public security. Yet, the use of a method regarded as the turf of anthropology in policy analysis is controversial. Some anthropologists argue that one cannot adopt ethnography as a method while disregarding the theoretical cannons of the discipline. Sarti (2010), for example, argues that there are two anthropology strains claiming authority on health, illness, pain and body: 'medical anthropology' and the 'anthropology of health'. The first strain has an instrumental character, putting itself at the service of biomedical knowledge. She argues that this strain picks one particular interpretation of health and illness in disregard for all the other possible interpretations, becoming a supplementary branch of Western medicine. The anthropology of health, on the other hand, denies any instrumental purpose for the knowledge it produces. Contrary to medical anthropology, this strain is committed to anthropology's relativist tradition. As the argument goes, the anthropology of health, in addition to denying any pre-eminent status to bio-medicine, does not see any value in its accomplishments. Consequently, it has nothing to say about the social distribution of the knowledge produced by scientific medicine. Minayo (1991), on the other hand, takes the point of view that anthropology should aid the analysis and formulation of health policies; thus, it should not disregard the usefulness of the knowledge it produces. She supports this claim with a few arguments. To begin with, anthropology is not intrinsically neutral. In the past, the discipline has served the interests of colonialist policies; this, however, should not lead one to conclude that anthropology itself is responsible for colonialism. In fact, it may serve the interests of disenfranchised groups. 'Scientific medicine' does not necessarily serve one social interest over another, she adds, and should be regarded as an asset belonging to humanity. Likewise, the knowledge and methods of anthropology can – and should – aid the formulation of public policies.

Economic style

Despite the expansion of the socio-political style following the introduction of social rights in the 1988 Constitution, economics has not ceased to be the most important discipline for policy analysis in Brazil. As argued in the introduction of this chapter, this is a corollary of historical factors. In addition to the importance of developmentalism in policy formulation in Brazil, the federal agencies that first started to formulate and analyse public policies were staffed mainly with economists. One paradigmatic example of the focus on economic analysis is the Institute for Applied Economic Research (Instituto de Pesquisas Econômicas Aplicadas; IPEA). This governmental think tank, founded in 1964, states that its mission is 'to produce, articulate and disseminate knowledge to improve public policies and contribute to the planning of Brazil's development' (IPEA, 2010, p 2). The institute was initially linked to the Ministry of Planning, but is now connected to the Secretariat for Strategic Affairs, a department within the president's office. Most of IPEA's intellectual output can be found in a series of Discussion Papers, which have been continuously published since 1979. IPEA increased its output on the analysis of social policies from 2000 onwards; it also started to hire social scientists with advanced degrees in sociology and political science. Nevertheless, most of IPEA's studies can be defined as economic analyses of public policies. Among the Discussion Papers published between 2010 and 2011, only 5% used qualitative methods; the remaining papers were either economic studies or social studies using econometrics and other quantitative methods.

The economic style is also gaining ground in the area of health. In 2008, the Department of Health Economics, Investments and Development (Departamento de Economia da Saúde, Investimentos e Desenvolvimento; DESID), a technical division within the Brazilian Ministry of Health, released a 100-page long brochure to disseminate microeconomic methods for decision-making in health policies, such as cost-effectiveness, cost–utility and cost–benefit analyses (Brazilian Ministry of Health, 2008). Ugá (1995) noted that the use of microeconomics techniques for the evaluation of health policies has divided health professionals into two opposing camps: one expressing 'love' for the quantitative methods and the rationalisation of decision-making, and the other expressing 'hate' for the idea that a human life can be appraised in monetary units. She argues that the two groups fail to correctly grasp the limitations and usefulness of microeconomic methods. Nevertheless, whatever the perspective one holds regarding the application of microeconomic methods in the analysis of health policies, it is necessary to realise that they are here to stay.

A similar debate has been established regarding the presuppositions underlining economics and their implications for the analysis of social policies. While social sciences methods may be used for good or evil, methodological procedures do carry the presuppositions of the theories from which they originated. For this reason, policy analysts should identify the normative presuppositions embedded in theories and methodological approaches. We may illustrate this using the Bolsa Família. This is currently the largest CCT programme in the world, distributing allowances to about 12.5 million families (Brazilian Ministry of Social Development, 2010). Its importance as a social policy has stirred debates and controversies. In their study on the impact of the Bolsa Família on child labour, Cacciamali et al (2010, p 273) argue that one advantage of CCT programmes is that they are easily adaptable to budgetary constraints, because they are not a social right and 'can be suspended at any moment'. This is in sharp contrast to the analysis made by Rego and briefly described in the previous section. For her, the Bolsa Família should become a permanent programme because it can help citizens hold on to the most basic social right of all: life. The paper by Cacciamali and his colleagues follows the principles of human capital theory, that is, they assert that poverty reduction is a means to economic growth; the analysis by Rego, in contrast, asserts the preponderance of social rights.

Two essays published by IPEA illustrate the different views underlining the debate on universal *versus* focused policies. In the first article, Camargo (2003) argues that universal social protection systems, such as the SUS, end up directing fewer resources to the poor because resources are equally distributed between the poor and the well-off. Therefore, in order to make scarce governmental resources more effective, it is necessary to target the poor. Theodoro and Delgado (2003), on the other hand, argue that cash transfer programmes and other targeted programmes are guided by a presupposition that ultimately impedes the overcoming of poverty and inequality. They argue that targeted programmes are only meant to ameliorate the situation of the poor, but do not address the factors generating poverty and inequality in the first place. In these conditions, social policy is reduced to 'poverty and misery management' (Theodoro and Delgado, 2003, p 124).

Human capital theory has also been a controversial theory in the debates over educational policies, in Brazil and elsewhere. As seen earlier, educational policies experienced a shift in their goals during the Estado Novo (1938–45) period in Brazil. In the 1960s, while sociologists migrated to the universities, economists stepped in as the new formulators and analysts of educational policies (Almeida, 2008). Brazil thus became a fertile ground for human capital theory, which was disseminated in the country by the Ford Foundation and the United Nations Educational, Scientific and Cultural Organization (UNESCO). In the US, those were the times when University of Chicago alumni saw their professional skills less appreciated by the Kennedy administration, but were welcome in international organisations, such as the World Bank and the International Monetary Fund (IMF). In the context of the Cold War, many economists in these international organisations were eager to offer an alternative to the works of the ECLAC/CEPAL. Gradually, their studies on educational policies started emphasising the preparation of workers for the market, and they distanced themselves from the previous emphasis on education for citizenship. The methodological style of the studies began to shift accordingly, and the quantitative analysis of educational data became paramount to policy analysis in the field. Economists, properly trained in statistics and econometric methods, finally ascended as analysts of educational policies. After the military coup in 1964, the political influence of neoclassical economists increased. In the 1970s, a debate epitomised the conflicting views on the role of education in Brazil. On one side stood those defending the views of human capital theory, arguing that inequalities in Brazil could be ameliorated through economic development and economic development could be boosted by education; on the other side stood those arguing that inequality was the result of the political context established from 1964 onwards, which included limits on workers' organisation and an economic model that widened the gap between rich and poor. Albert Fishlow, a professor at University of California-Berkeley who visited Brazil several times in the 1970s, defended the view of the latter group, while Carlos Geraldo Langoni, a professor at the University of São Paulo, defended the perspective of the former. After a long war fought with academic papers fired from both sides, the dispute was finally settled in favour of human capital theory. The theory is still evoked in most analyses of educational policies today and is the driving force behind the main educational policy in Brazil, the Fund for the Maintenance and Development of Education and Enhancement of the Teaching Profession (FUNDEF).[5] This programme proved itself to be successful in the promotion of school enrolments, but it did not have a significant impact on income distribution. Not surprisingly, human resources theorists now claim that the poverty/inequality problem is due to a lack of quality in education (Tomlinson, 2005). Nevertheless, in the past 10 years, Brazil experienced a significant reduction in poverty and a small reduction in inequality, but this has been attributed to the Bolsa Família and to the overall improvement in the economy (Hoffmann, 2006), not to an improvement in education. A study involving more than 5,500 municipalities in Brazil showed that the higher is the poverty level in a municipality, the lower is students' performance (Andrews and de Vries, 2013). That family income has a strong impact on students' performance is a fact well-known by policymakers (Coleman et al, 1966). However, educational policies – in Brazil and elsewhere – stubbornly continue to rely on human capital theory.

Final remarks

Policy analysis is still a very young discipline in Brazil and has a long way to go before becoming a field in its own right. At present, it is almost indistinguishable from traditional social science disciplines, sharing with them their methods and theories. Nevertheless, it is possible to draw a few conjectures about the future. Policy analysis in Brazil is likely to expand as a field of inquiry as a consequence of the increasing complexity of Brazilian society, and the demand for sophisticated public policies will therefore continue to grow. In addition, Brazilian scholars are catching up with recent developments in the field.

It is worth noting that the number of undergraduate and graduate programmes focusing on public policies has grown substantially since 2005, especially at the public universities. As to the styles in policy analysis, it is likely that the methods used in economic analysis will continue to be the ones preferred by governmental agencies. Meanwhile, the socio-political style will not lose ground.

Notes

[1.] After a military coup in 1964, Brazil was ruled by authoritarian governments until 1985, when the Congress elected as president the civilian Tancredo Neves, who led the redemocratisation process.

[2.] For an overall analysis of best practices at the local level in Brazil, see Farah (2008).

[3.] Conditionalities include regular school attendance for children under 15 years old, taking vaccines and other health care prevention measures provided by public clinics.

[4.] The author also describes the feelings of humiliation and shame of the men in those poor families for not being able to earn money to support their families. However, she does not discuss how this problem could be addressed.

[5.] FUNDEF was a fund established in 1997, redistributing governmental resources in order to allow local governments to increase school enrolments in primary education (Brazilian National Congress, 1996a, 1996b). It was later expanded to include pre-school and high-school education and has been renamed to FUNDEB (Fundo de Manutenção e Desenvolvimento da Educação Básica e de Valorização dos Profissionais da Educação) (Brazilian National Congress, 2006).

References

Almeida, A.M.F. (2008) 'O assalto à educação pelos economistas', *Tempo Social*, vol 20, no 1, pp 163–78.

Alves-Mazzotti, A.J. (2006) 'Usos e abusos dos estudos de caso', *Cadernos de Pesquisa*, vol 36, no 129, pp 637–51.

André, M. (2006) 'Pesquisa em educação: desafios contemporâneos', *Pesquisa em Educação Ambiental*, vol 1, no 1, pp 43–57.

Andrews, C.W. (2008) 'Best practices in local government', in M.S.D.Vries, P.S. Reddy and M.S. Haque (eds) *Improving local government: outcomes of comparative research*, London: Palgrave/MacMillan, pp 170–92.

Andrews, C. W. and De Vries, M. S. (2013) 'Pobreza e municipalização da educação: análise dos resultados do Ideb (2005-2009)', *Cadernos de Pesquisa*, vol 42, no 147, pp 826-47.

Botelho, A. and Schwarcz, L.M. (eds) (2009) *Um enigma chamado Brasil: 29 intérpretes e um país*, São Paulo: Companhia das Letras.

Brazilian Ministry of Health (2008) *Avaliação econômica em saúde: desafios para gestão no Sistema Único da Saúde*, Brasília: Ministério da Saúde (Série A. Normas e Manuais Técnicos), http://portal.saude.gov.br/portal/arquivos/pdf/livro_aval_econom_saude.pdf

Brazilian Ministry of Social Development (2010) *Relatórios e estatística – Sistema de Informações da SENARC*, Brasília: MDS, www.mds.gov.br/bolsafamilia

Brazilian National Congress (1996a) 'Emenda constitucional No 14', *Diário Oficial*, 13 September, Brasília, www.planalto.gov.br/ccivil_03/constituicao/Emendas/Emc/emc14.htm.

Brazilian National Congress (1996b) 'Lei No 9.424', *Diário Oficial*, 26 December, Brasília, www.planalto.gov.br/ccivil_03/leis/l9424.htm

Brazilian National Congress (2006) 'Emenda Constitucional No 53', *Diário Oficial*, 3 March, www.planalto.gov.br/ccivil_03/constituicao/emendas/emc/emc53.htm

Cacciamali, M.C., Tatei, F. and Batista, N.F. (2010) 'Impactos do programa Bolsa Família federal sobre o trabalho infantil e a frequência escolar', *Revista de Economia Contemporânea*, vol 14, no 2, pp 269–301.

Camargo, J.M. (2003) 'Gastos sociais: focalizar versus universalizar', in Instituto de Pesquisa Econômica Aplicada (ed) *Políticas sociais: acompanhamento e análise*, Brasília: IPEA, pp 117–22.

Carneiro, R. (2002) *Desenvolvimento em crise*, São Paulo: UNESP/UNICAMP.

Cohn, A. (2009) 'A reforma sanitária brasileira após 20 anos do SUS: reflexões', *Cadernos de Saúde Pública*, vol 27, no 7, pp 1614–19.

Coleman, J., Campbell, E., Hobson, C., McPartland, J., Mood, A., Weinfeld, F. and York, R. (1966) *Equality of educational opportunity [summary report]*. Washington (DC): U.S. Dept. of Health, Education, and Welfare, Office of Education.

De Holanda, S.B. (1995 [1936]) *Raízes do Brasil*, São Paulo: Companhia das Letras.

Escorel, S. (1999) *A reviravolta na saúde: origem e articulação do movimento*, Rio de Janeiro: Editora Fiocruz.

Forjaz, M.C.S. (1997) 'A emergência da Ciência Política acadêmica no Brasil: aspectos institucionais', *Revista Brasileira de Ciências Sociais*, vol 12, no 35, pp 101–20.

Hoffmann, R. (2006) 'Transferência de renda e redução da desigualdade no Brasil e cinco regiões entre 1997 e 2004', *Econômica*, vol 8, no 1, pp 55–81.

IPEA (Instituto de Pesquisa Econômica Aplicada) (2010) 'IPEA thinks and researches Brazil', www.ipea.gov.br/portal/images/stories/PDFs/folder_institucional_jul_2010_v9_ingles.pdf

Lasswell, H.D. (2000) 'La concepción emergente de las ciencias políticas', in L.F.A. Villanueva (ed) *El estudio de las políticas públicas*, México: Miguel Angel Porrúa, pp 105–17.

Lerner, D. and Lasswell, H.D. (eds) (1951) *The policy sciences: recent developments in scope and method*, Stanford, CA: Stanford University Press.

Minayo, M.C.D.S. (1991) 'Abordagem antropológica para avaliação de políticas sociais', *Revista de Saúde Pública*, vol 25, no 3, pp 233–8.

Prebisch, R. (1950) *The economic development of Latin America and its principal problems*, New York, NY: ECLA, UN Department of Social Affairs.

Rego, W.D.L. (2010) 'Política de cidadania no governo Lula. Ações de transferência estatal de renda: o caso do Programa Bolsa Família', *Temas y Debates*, no 20, pp 141–55.

Ribeiro, J.M. and Costa, N.D.R. (2000) 'Regionalização da assistência à saúde no Brasil: os consórcios municipais no Sistema Único de Saúde (SUS)', *Planejamento e Políticas Públicas*, no 22, pp 173–220.

Sarti, C. (2010) 'Corpo e doença no trânsito de saberes', *Revista Brasileira de Ciências Sociais*, vol 25, no 74, pp 77–90.

Simon, H. (1972) *Comportamento Administrativo*, Rio de Janeiro: USAID.

Souza, C. (2003) '"Estado de campo" da pesquisa em políticas públicas no Brasil', *Revista Brasileira de Ciências Sociais*, vol 18, no 51, pp 15–20.

Theodoro, M. and Delgado, G. (2003) 'Política social: universalização ou focalização – subsídio para o debate', in Instituto de Pesquisa Econômica Aplicada (ed) *Políticas sociais: acompanhamento e análise*, Brasília: IPEA, pp 117–221.

Tomlinson, S. (2005) *Education in a post-welfare society*, Buckingham: Open University Press.

Ugá, M.A.D. (1995) 'Instrumentos de avaliação econômica dos serviços de saúde: alcances e limitações', in S.F. Piola and S.M.Vianna (eds) *Economia da saúde: conceito e contribuição para a gestão da saúde*, Brasília: IPEA, pp 209–26.

FOUR

Modernisation of the state and bureaucratic capacity-building in the Brazilian Federal Government

Celina Souza

Introduction

The theme of modernisation (of the state, society, countries, the economy and the state apparatus) was the object of intense debate in the 20th century. The search was on to identify the reasons for underdevelopment and to find solutions to the obstacles faced by the so-called 'Third World' countries. According to the diagnosis, the reasons for underdevelopment were endogenous: low schooling, conservative elites, a traditional agrarian structure and a lack of infrastructure. The solution – it was claimed – was modernisation, which would occur by emulating the developed countries' development model and institutions. However, modernisation recipes were criticised in the subsequent decades. Some contended that they were anti-historical and an imposition of the North American model. Others replied that economic and social modernisation would not lead automatically to political modernisation, that is, stable democracies (Huntington, 1968). Confronted with other theoretical frameworks, modernisation and its recipes were the object of criticism but without an evaluation of their role in overcoming some obstacles to Brazil's development.

There are three main types of modernisation, all with impacts on the state's role: first, social modernisation, in which the state is pressured by society to implement changes, that is, a process that develops in the society-to-state direction; second, social modernisation via the state, in which pressures to reform society come from the state, that is, in the state-to-society direction; and, third, modernisation of the state, in which the focus is the efficiency of the government apparatus, its most well-known expression being bureaucratisation, that is, a process that develops in the state–state direction.[1]

Despite the theoretical and empirical production on modernisation, there have never been clear criteria by which changes are actually 'modern'. Modernisation is associated with the idea of progress and of breaking with the past to the extent that the past is identified as an obstacle to development. Margetts (2010), based on the vast literature on the theme, identified three recurrent characteristics: first, elements of economic rationality, or incentives that foster changes by actors and institutions; second, the specialisation of tasks and a professionalisation based on technical and scientific knowledge; and, third, the formal definition of rules and standardisation of procedures. This study focuses on the second characteristic.

The study analyses the modernisation of the Brazilian state (in the state–state sense), associating it with the professionalisation of the federal bureaucracy and following the framework of the literature on state capacity.[2] The study's theme is thus modernisation of the Brazilian state, and the analytical key is bureaucratic capacity-building in the federal sphere, especially through public competition, adding a type of recruitment to those identified by Lindquist and Desveaux (2007), namely, in-house recruitment, in-house think tanks and contracting out. Among the staff in the professionalised bureaucracy recruited by public competition, the study focuses on the career entitled Specialist in Public Policies and Government Management (EPPGG).

I argue that although different administrations and political regimes have used multiple mechanisms to recruit the bureaucracy, the federal executive has always been capable of building bureaucratic capacity to deal with its priorities. Although full of paradoxes, the bureaucratic system has been one of the key elements contributing to the modernisation of the state. Since 2000, however, it has prioritised the professionalisation and qualification of a bureaucracy recruited through competitive selection.

The study is organised as follows. The first part reviews the stages of modernisation of the Brazilian state. The second and third analyse Brazil's bureaucratic capacity-building at the federal level, the various recruitment modalities for the bureaucracy and the consequences for state capacity.[3] The last part concludes.

The Brazilian state: from state-building to modernisation

Since the 1930s, the Brazilian state never stopped being reformed, given its objective of achieving economic and social transformation. These transformations required the creation of new institutions and bureaucratic skills. However, the recruitment of the bureaucracy varied over the decades.

Institution-building in modern Brazil began in the President Vargas era, and in 1936, the Public Service Administrative Department (DASP) was created. Established with the objective of forming a professionalised bureaucracy, the mission of DASP extended beyond: to eliminate the obstacles to development. Evaluations of this experience revealed its successes and failures, especially the resistances by political and bureaucratic groups. In addition, the attempt to select the bureaucracy via public competition obtained mediocre results.[4]

Since then, Brazil's public administration never stopped undergoing reforms, along with the search to establish a professionalised bureaucracy. In President Kubitschek's administration, some attempts were made to resume the DASP proposals, but in the end the strategy was to insulate some of the agencies in charge of the main policies. From that point on, the public apparatus began to grow through the creation of decentralised agencies – autarchies, foundations, public companies, joint capital companies (state–private) – whose proliferation later generated problems of coordination, accountability and control. Different forms of recruitment of the bureaucracy coexisted during this period.

The administrative reform under the military regime was enacted in 1967. It expanded the number of decentralised agencies and the main form of recruitment of the bureaucracy was through private workers' legislation, known as Consolidation of Labor Laws (CLT), hence eliminating tenure in exchange for higher wages and fringe benefits. Evaluations of the results of this reform have concluded that it led to the expansion of government spending. This expansion began to show signs of depletion with the exhaustion of the regime itself. The fiscal crisis, the most visible trait of which was the impossibility of taming inflation, was one of the legacies of this expansionist and fragmented phase of the federal government.

With redemocratisation and the enactment of the 1988 Constitution, public competition became mandatory, ending the differential treatment for civil servants under the decentralised agencies. According to estimates, 400,000 to 500,000 civil servants were granted tenure and full retirement pensions. Another consequence was that some 45,000 civil servants filed for retirement (Gaetani and Heredia, 2002). From 1988 to 1994, the number of federal employees decreased from 705,548 to 587,802, partly due to layoffs by the Collor administration and voluntary resignation programmes, and partly due to the transformation of CLT civil servants into early retirees. Finally, the cost of pension payments increased dramatically (Gaetani and Heredia, 2002).

During the Collor administration and later the Cardoso administration, echoes of the so-called 'New Public Management' began to be heard in Brazil, mainly the downsizing of the state. The tenets were that the Brazilian state was the main culprit behind the fiscal crisis and rampant inflation, that it was a poor manager, that it lacked accountability and that it was prey to clientelism. This diagnosis had three main consequences. First, the extinction of numerous decentralised agencies and the dismissal of 100,000 civil servants during the Collor administration.[5] Second, in 1995, the elaboration of a reform plan during President Cardoso's term, establishing, among other things, what was called strategic state careers. These careers included the EPPGG. Third, reforms in the role of the governments through various constitutional amendments allowing deregulation, a break in state monopolies and the participation of domestic and foreign capital in activities where the state previously played the dominant role.

The diagnosis of an inefficient and spendthrift government was short-lived. Although public competition was restored in 1995, it was not until 2003 that an aggressive policy began to rebuild the federal bureaucracy through public competition, to strengthen the role of policymakers, especially those in charge of fiscal policies, and to strengthen the capacity of agencies in charge of overseeing officials – Accounts Tribunal, Federal Comptroller's Office, Public Prosecutors – as well as the Federal Police. The bureaucratic and institutional strengthening of these agencies highlights a type of modernisation that assigns an important role to oversight. In other words, the state is no longer seen as a mere appendix to economic activities and an inducer of social development, but also as an instrument for strengthening democracy. However, this new state role involves costs and unexpected consequences.

The main tenet of this section is that Brazil continues to pursue state–state and state–society modernisation, while it has incorporated more refined control rules typical of advanced democracies, namely, accountability.

Bureaucratic capacity-building in the federal government

Brazil made numerous attempts at bureaucratic capacity-building, but until the early 2000s, the main option was for various forms of recruitment as a means to reconcile the demands for a professionalised bureaucracy with the needs of different political parties and regimes, as well as the urgency of transforming the country's macroeconomic model and later its social policy. These attempts began with the DASP, as mentioned earlier.

Prior to 1964, Kubistchek's Goals Plan (Plano de Metas) was considered a successful case of state planning, mainly because it was implemented outside the bureaucracy, launching what was called bureaucratic insulation, that is, a strategy to avoid the 'contamination' of pressure groups. The military regime later transferred a large number of public activities to decentralised agencies because of its flexibility to recruit personnel. This strategy shifted the state's main economic activities to these agencies, which also recruited top bureaucrats, leaving other policies to a bureaucracy with limited professionalisation. The 1988 Constitution removed hiring through the CLT, affecting decentralised agencies by assigning them identical rules to those governing the direct public administration. Redemocratisation, combined with unbridled inflation, removed the reconstruction of the bureaucracy from the agenda.

If the 1988 Constitution restored the democratic order, the political environment was still turbulent, and inflation remained uncontrolled. Only in 1994, with the election of President Cardoso, who successfully controlled inflation, did the issue of bureaucracy return to the agenda through the 1995 plan mentioned earlier. The targets were the reconstruction of the bureaucracy, its professionalisation and adjustments to its pay scheme. The proposal concentrated on the strategic careers, encompassing the judiciary, diplomacy, public policies, the police and oversight.

In 1989, the EPPGG career was created to hire professionals with generalist training intended to constitute the upper echelons of the administration. The National School of Public Administration (ENAP) was created to train these professionals.[6] The path to the creation of this new position was slow and faced resistance from political groups and other civil servants. Public competition for this position was quite competitive in the initial phase due to the lack of other equivalent posts that allowed the participation of individuals with any kind of university training. From 1995 to 2010, the group called Gestão (Management) was formed with 3,588 new officials, of which the largest (1,545) were for the EPPGG position.[7] Except for the legal/judiciary careers and the Federal Police, the EPPGG is the highest-paid career position in the government: in December 2010, the starting salary was R$12,960.77 (€5,042,00) a month, and the end-of-career wage was R$18,478.45 (€7,377,00).

In 2003, with the change in the political parties occupying the federal executive, the proposal to strengthen only the strategic core careers was replaced by an aggressive recruitment policy for civil servants, especially those requiring university training. From 2003 to 2010, 206,284 new civil servants were admitted through public competition. The largest contingent went to restoring the faculty of federal universities and for the creation of various new institutions of higher education, followed by the Ministries of Health, Social Security and Finance. With the exception of the Ministry of Finance, most of the positions were not considered strategic by the 1995 plan. However, this does not mean that these careers were not structured. On the contrary, this happened with the Ministry of Foreign Affairs, the legal careers in the executive branch, the Federal Police and the auditors of the Federal Comptroller's Office.[8] However, bureaucratic capacity-building in other policy areas is still incomplete, despite an increase in the number of civil servants.

Tables 4.1 and 4.2 show that the ministries in charge of infrastructure policies maintained a stable staff size, with the exception of Mines and Energy. A remarkable increase was registered in agencies in charge of fiscal policies (Ministry of Finance and Ministry of Planning, Budget, and Management). The number of civil servants

Table 4.1: Number of active federal civil servants in the executive branch according to selected agencies

Ministry	1997	1998	1999	2000	2001	2002	2003	2004	2005	2006	2007	2008	06/09 June 2009
Agriculture	11,703	11,151	10,771	10,696	11,164	11,415	10,973	11,373	11,742	11,409	11,551	11,588	12,076
Development, Industry and Commerce	2,411	2,335	2,580	2,260	2,436	2,401	2,293	2,338	2,328	2,641	2,677	2,780	2,765
Mines and Energy	2,000	2,030	1,872	1,936	1,902	2,104	2,022	2,028	2,351	2,678	2,645	2,957	3,245
Integration	–	–	184	3,905	2,480	2,537	2,469	2,764	2,674	2,667	2,719	2,759	2,723
Transportation	5,235	4,742	4,504	4,796	4,724	4,882	3,878	4,348	4,651	5,337	5,454	5,254	5,508
Cities	–	–	–	–	–	–	207	280	320	430	418	460	586
Culture	2,844	2,695	2,585	2,539	2,508	2,477	2,391	2,589	2,591	2,960	2,976	2,948	2,970
Social Development	–	–	–	–	–	–	–	383	381	522	594	632	682
Environment	8,609	8,322	8,024	5,644	6,409	7,115	7,242	7,894	8,013	8,469	8,559	9,511	8,018
Education	174,996	168,403	165,510	165,595	163,479	165,163	164,870	171,925	173,181	179,449	180,895	188,440	194,548
Health	123,159	116,862	110,804	102,480	104,948	103,634	105,238	103,483	106,079	109,107	106,259	105,621	105,063
Planning, Budget and Management	16,072	14,088	13,164	13,868	13,783	14,079	14,259	12,932	14,550	16,235	16,453	18,076	18,348
Finance	26,207	28,080	26,958	25,331	26,098	26,297	25,622	26,098	26,404	28,672	33,233	33,033	32,882

Source: Workforce Statistical Bulletin of the Ministry of Planning, Budget and Management (MPOG), www.servidor.gov.br/publicacao/boletim_estatistico/bol_estatistico.htm

Table 4.2: Increase in the number of civil servants according to selected government agencies

Ministry	1997	June 2009	Difference 2009 – 1997	Var %
Finance	26,207	32,882	6,675	25%
Planning, Budget and Management	16,072	18,348	2,276	14%
Agriculture	11,703	12,076	373	3%
Development, Industry and Commerce	2,411	2,765	354	15%
Mines and Energy	2,000	3,245	1,245	62%
Transportation	5,235	5,508	273	5%
Integration[a]	3,905	2,723	-1,182	-30%
Environment	8,609	8,018	-591	-7%
Culture	2,844	2,970	126	4%
Social Development[b]	383	682	299	78%
Cities[c]	207	586	379	183%

Notes: [a] Created in 2000; [b] created in 2004; [c] created in 2003.

Source: Workforce Statistical Bulletin of the Ministry of Planning, Budget and Management (MPOG), www.servidor.gov.br/publicacao/boletim_estatistico/bol_estatistico.htm

assigned to the Ministry of Cities and the Ministry of Social Development (MDS) also increased.

There was an increase not only in the federal government's workforce, but also in civil servants with university degrees, from 182,303 in 1997 to 223,404 in 2009, representing 45% of federal employees in 2009. Excluding the faculty of federal universities, federal employees recruited by public competition with university degrees increased from 25.9% in 1995 to 38.58% in 2009. In the absence of studies on the quality of the Brazilian bureaucracy, the increase in the number of civil servants with university degrees can be used as a proxy for growing qualifications. Occupants of politically appointed positions also have high qualifications. During the Lula administration, 97% of the occupants of these positions had university degrees and more than 50% had graduate degrees (D'Araújo, 2007).

What do the increases in the number and qualification of federal employees mean, and what are the consequences for state capacity? Furthermore, what is the significance of the adoption of a new form of recruitment – public competition – which is now the main entry way into public service, in relation to state capacity? The next section seeks to answer these questions.

Various forms of recruitment and their consequences for state capacity

As discussed earlier, since the 1930s, there have been various modalities of recruitment of the bureaucracy. However, for the first time in the history of Brazil's federal bureaucracy, recruitment now occurs predominantly through public competition. Does this mean that previous interpretations about who this bureaucracy is and who it serves have lost their explanatory capacity?

Since Faoro's (1973) study, based on a Weberian approach and first published in 1958, the bureaucracy began to be analysed more as an explanatory variable for explaining the relations between state and society and less as an object per se. Faoro's thesis was that a 'bureaucratic stratum' had always dominated the political and social systems, making Brazil a patrimonial state.

The advent of the authoritarian regime brought growing academic interest in the bureaucratic system, maintaining the same analytical key of the state's prevalence over society. Many of the analyses about that period were influenced by O'Donnell's (1986) bureaucratic-authoritarian model to explain the functioning of authoritarian regimes in Latin America.

The analyses on the role of the bureaucracy in the military regime were numerous, although concentrated on the bureaucracy in charge of macroeconomic and industrial policies. A recurrent interpretation in the analysis on the pre- and post-1964 period is that the bureaucracy in charge of macroeconomic policy was insulated from interests that were contrary to the dominant political and macroeconomic project, while that in charge of social policy was primarily clientelistic. Some of these studies also debated the autonomy of the bureaucracy.[9]

Two important analyses were guided by the challenge of understanding how and why a bureaucratic structure marked by clientelism was able to implement a successful project of state modernisation through industrialisation. Schneider (1991) argued that the Brazilian bureaucracy in the pre- and post-1964 regimes was hardly institutionalised in the sense of formal rules. This bureaucracy was characterised by the circulation of the same cadres among different government agencies, by career advancements and by political appointments. These were the central characteristics of an informal system that, nevertheless, sent signals of institutionalisation to its participants and partially explained the success of industrialisation. If access to government positions was based on clientelism and recruitment was through political appointments, as part of the literature claimed, success would not have been the expected result, but, for Schneider, political appointments combined with the possibility of career advancements explained the success of the industrial policy under both the Kubitschek administration and the military regime.

Using a different methodological approach and with a different objective, Stepan (1978) analysed the various strategies used by the dictatorial regimes in Peru and Brazil as a result of what he called 'new military professionals', whose training included not only traditional military knowledge, but also planning. This group used its power to implement socio-economic reforms in Peru and to further industrialisation in Brazil.

An important contribution to understanding the bureaucracy over the course of the 20th century was by Nunes (1997), convincingly pointing to the plurality of relations between state and society from the perspective of the bureaucracy. These forms materialise in what Nunes called 'four political grammars': clientelism, universalism of procedures, corporatism and bureaucratic insulation.

The studies outlined earlier answer (although only partially) some of the questions raised here. The first is the inclusion of the bureaucracy as one of the explanatory variables in the relationship between the state and society, a typical analytical key for authoritarian periods. Currently, however, this analytical key has limited explanatory capacity, due to the predominance of public competition, making selection of the bureaucracy less penetrable to vested interests or interpersonal relations. The second is the existence of different forms of recruitment in recent decades, a situation that changed since the 1990s. The third is that despite various forms of recruitment, or 'grammars', strategies to implement chosen policies of different administrations and regimes were successful. Finally, the analyses mentioned earlier confirm one of the dimensions identified in the literature concerning state capacity, namely, the unequal implementation of policies between policy areas.

Successful fiscal control allowed the Cardoso administration to rebuild the federal bureaucracy according to the guidelines of the 1995 plan. One central idea was the establishment of efficient management. However, the administration achieved limited success in the adoption of management principles and more in rebuilding the civil service career (Gaetani and Heredia, 2002), although the latter was concentrated on what the 1995 plan defined as strategic careers. The 1995 plan's objectives nevertheless met with resistance and vetoes from the government, the bureaucracy, the courts and Congress.

The formation of a new bureaucracy recruited by public competition was a complex task. Historically, the bureaucracy was recruited by other means. However, and by various mechanisms over time, civil servants achieved tenure and full retirement. Paradoxically, most of the currently existent decentralised agencies always maintained recruitment through public competition. This was the case for the Central Bank, the National Economic and Social Development Bank and Petrobras. In addition, public competition has always been mandatory for the judiciary, for careers in the executive and for the diplomacy.

One of the diagnoses of the 1995 plan was that the provisions of the 1988 Constitution relating to public administration and to civil servants were a step backward in the sense that they increased bureaucratic rigidity. The alternative was to allow the participation of the private sector in providing public services and in hiring via CLT, that is, the option for contracting out some public services to private non-profit organisations with a similar format to the British 'quangos'. However, the Workers' Party (PT) and the Democratic Labor Party (PDT) filed a direct unconstitutionality suit against the law in the Supreme Court. After a series of postponements, the merit of the case only began to be reviewed in 2011, that is, 13 years after the original proposal. The PT's alternative to what is identified as administrative and contractual rigidity was the re-creation of state foundations. However, the bill has been stalled in Congress since 2007.

Another proposal of the 1995 plan was to narrow the gap between the salary paid by the federal government and the private sector for top positions and for positions requiring university training. However, evidence shows that pay levels in the federal bureaucracy are higher than international standards. Whether to attract qualified personnel or due to the fact that a former labour union leader was elected president in 2003, combined with the country's economic growth, the cost of the federal payroll is above the average for Organisation for Economic Co-operation and Development (OECD) countries, but not due to the expansion of the federal workforce. The total number of civil servants at the three levels of government represents a relatively small percentage of all jobs in Brazil. In 2008, it represented some 10–11% of total employment, as compared to an average of 20% in the OECD countries. If one includes state-owned companies, the proportion increases slightly, to some 11–12%, also below the OECD average, some 22%, and lower than in other Latin American countries like Argentina and Chile. The Brazilian federal government now has some 600,000 employees, a similar figure to the mid-1990s (IPEA, 2011). However, while the size of the workforce is comparatively small, the same is not true for its cost: 12% of gross domestic product (GDP), above the OECD average (OECD, 2010). In addition, as of December 2010, the largest percentage (16.7%) of the mean monthly payment to civil servants was in a wage bracket higher than R$8,500 (€3,304).

The 1995 plan's proposal to only professionalise the bureaucracy for strategic careers ended up being unrealistic. Given the low qualifications of civil servants at that time and their declining numbers, the government had to seek other alternatives to count on qualified personnel. However, fiscal adjustment was underway, limiting increases in payroll. The solution was contracting out through UN system agencies operating in Brazil, especially UNESCO (United Nations Educational, Scientific and Cultural Organisation), the United Nations Development Program (UNDP), FAO (Food and Agriculture Organisation) and the World Health Organization (WHO) (OECD, 2010). There is disagreement on the number of such employees, but the estimates reach the thousands. However, this modality was short-lived: it survived from 1995 to 2000, but was extinguished by the intervention of Public Prosecutors, arguing that such a modality violated the constitution, which requires public competition for entering the civil service. As a consequence, and with the election of a new party coalition led by the PT, the vacancies grew and were no longer limited to strategic core careers. Table 4.3 shows the number of new entrants into the civil service through public competition.

As a way of dealing with the complexity of launching public competition, the federal government adopted a further recruitment modality, namely, temporary contracts. These contracts kept growing, starting at some 5,000 in 1995 and reaching more than 12,000 by 2010.[10]

There was also an increase in politically appointed positions, from 70,000 in 1997 to 85,000 in 2010. However, the vast majority are occupied by regular career civil servants (D'Araújo, 2007). The occupants of the so-called Directorate and Higher Assistance (DAS), around 22,000, may be appointed on political grounds but they may also be career civil servants and specialists.

Despite the quantitative growth in the bureaucracy and its increased qualifications, bureaucratic capacity-building in the public sector is still incomplete. This is particularly important in the social and infrastructure areas. There are persistent heterogeneities in the distribution of the professionalised bureaucracy. Despite the priority assigned to social programmes in the governments led by the PT, public competition has still not been launched for 2,400 positions under the Social Policy Development Career, created in late 2010 for the Ministries of Education, Health, Social Development, Agrarian Development, Human Rights, Women, Racial Equality and Employment.

Does the decision to prioritise control and planning careers have repercussions on the state's capacity to implement social and infrastructure policies? Even if these careers are still incomplete, this does not mean that policies are not being implemented. The social inclusion policy has produced important results, as have infrastructure works. However, this bureaucracy still depends on other forms of recruitment and support from other institutions, that is, temporary contracts, politically appointed positions, the participation of IPEA (Instituto de Pesquisa Econômica Aplicada) (a federal think tank) and quite probably the EPPGG.

Table 4.3: Entrants into the federal civil service via public competition, 1995–2010

Job position/career	Number of entrants
Faculty, Federal Universities	52,699
Technical and Administrative Staff, Federal Universities	36,599
General Job Position and Career Plan of the Executive Branch (PGPE)	29,627
Social Security, Health and Labor	13,669
Auditing	11,259
Social Insurance	8,437
Federal Police	7,382
Regulatory Agencies	5,551
Legal careers	5,434
Highway Police	4,790
Science and Technology	4,388
Inspection	4,040
Management	3,588
Environment	2,017
Social Security	1,878
Diplomacy	1,703
Agrarian Reform	1,475
Brazilian Institute of Geography and Statistics	1,084
Federal Penitentiaries	880
National Department of Transportation Infrastructure (DNIT)	865
Oswaldo Cruz Foundation (Fiocruz)	819
Culture	804
Aerial Defence and Air Traffic Control	658
Finance (intermediate level)	656
Infrastructure	632
Agriculture, Fishing and Supply	491
Mining	461
National Fund for Educational Development (FNDE)	401
Securities Exchange Commission (CVM)	378
Military Technology	327
Institute for Applied Economic Research (IPEA)	261
National Institute for Educational Studies and Research (INEP)	194
Superintendence of Private Insurance	164
National Water Agency	77
Other	605
Total	206,284

Source: Workforce Statistical Bulletin of the Ministry of Planning, Budget and Management (MPOG), www.servidor.gov.br/
publicacao/boletim_estatistico/bol_estatistico.htm

In 2011, 9.5% of the EPPGGs were assigned to the Office of the President, 13% to the Ministry of Planning, Budget and Management, 7.9% to the Ministry of Social Development, 7.8% to the Ministry of Justice, and 6.6% to the Ministry of Finance, all led by the PT. This means that the party has been using these cadres to support its flagship programmes.

What are the consequences of the new modality for selecting bureaucratic cadres? Evans (1995) highlights the institutional characteristics of a Weberian bureaucracy: merit-based recruitment through public competition, rules for hiring and firing that replace appointments based on partisan criteria and firing without criteria, and filling top positions in the bureaucracy through internal promotions. In the same vein, Peters (1995) proposes the following indicators for analysing the degree of professionalisation of a bureaucracy: first, recruitment – methods and standards; second, structure of the programmes' administration – internal organisation, variations and reorganisations; third, relations with lobby groups, parties, unions, NGOs and social assistance organisations; and, fourth, control of the bureaucracy, that is, its accountability, responsiveness and relationship to elected officials. Thus, based on both Evans's criteria and Peters's indicators, the Brazilian bureaucracy now displays most of the characteristics of a Weberian, professionalised bureaucracy.

If the replacement of clientelistic practices and the insulation strategy by public competition is a necessary but insufficient condition for the 'modern' democratic state, as argued by Evans (1995), recruitment by public competition also has consequences. These consequences can be divided into two moments. Before competitions are held: first, the time required to launch public competition is at least six months, as compared to one to two months under the CLT; second, procedures for public competition are complex and lengthy, and new careers have to be approved by Congress; and, third, due to the fear of legal appeals, means of selection like interviews, which can evaluate applicants qualitatively, are avoided, meaning that 'the government ends up hiring not whom it needs, but individuals that can meet these rules' (Gaetani, 2007). In other words, while public competition is essential for ensuring the merit system, it also makes the selection excessively homogeneous and closed off to the recruitment of professionals with backgrounds that are more in keeping with the public administration's demands. After entering the career, the civil service regime also brings unexpected consequences. In the EPPGG, for example, the 1995 plan stated that members should not occupy politically appointed positions on the grounds that the career design and payment were similar to the requirements for politically appointed positions (Dos Santos and Cardoso, no date). However, according to a survey by ENAP in 1994 (four years after the first EPPGGs took their positions), 90% were already occupying politically appointed positions (Ferrarezi and Zimbrão, 2006). If, on the one hand, this indicates the high qualifications of these cadres, who very rapidly occupied key positions in the administration, it also demonstrates the difficulties in establishing careers without the need to make use of politically appointed positions because it increases salaries. This phenomenon also characterised the pre- and post-1964 regimes, as shown by Schneider (1991). Another consequence is that civil servants who entered through public competition have created associations to defend their interests, thereby signalling the corporatist grammar identified by Nunes (1997), although this corporatism does not result from constitutional rules, as in the Vargas years. Finally, and as shown earlier, the federal government's workforce has a relatively high cost as compared to the average for OECD countries, thus signalling future budgetary pressures when these federal employees retire.

Final remarks

This study discussed the occurrence of various bureaucratic capacity-building strategies used by different governments and regimes in Brazil. Despite the coexistence of different 'grammars' throughout the years, administrations have always been capable of bureaucratic capacity-building to meet their priorities. The coexistence of a professional bureaucracy with limited institutionalisation and a bureaucracy selected according to clientelistic criteria did not prevent the government from implementing its key policies. Of course, the bureaucracy is only one dimension of state capacity, and numerous other dimensions play important roles in policy results. However, the current bureaucratic system is different from all previous ones due to the predominance of public competition.

In this sense, the system meets several criteria that characterise the 'modern' state, namely, the bureaucracy is now marked by specialisation of tasks, professionalisation and qualification, and it is subject to scrutiny. However, this does not mean that the state lacked the capacity to implement policies in the past; rather, that it is now closer to what the literature calls a democratic state as regards the recruitment and control of its bureaucracy.

The study also showed the changes in the Brazilian state in the last 80 years, moving from a more entrepreneurial state to one also concerned with social inclusion, with the growth of ministries in charge of social policies and better qualifications of its bureaucracy. There was also a change in what was previously identified as the trademark of the bureaucratic system, that is, clientelism. There is now a prevalence of universal procedures and professionalisation and qualification of the bureaucracy via public competition, despite the need for support from other institutions to implement the government's agenda. The greatest change, however, seems to have occurred in the strengthening of the capacity of institutions in charge of bureaucratic control. While this strengthening is an indicator of democratic maturity, it may also mean the prevalence of the means (controls) over the ends (policy results).

Notes

[1] On the different types of modernisation, see Margetts (2010).

[2] State capacity was the object of theoretical and empirical treatment by, for example, Skocpol and Finegold (1982), Evans et al (1985), Mann (1986), Chubb and Peterson (1989), Geddes (1994) and Grindle (1997).

[3] Data on the federal bureaucracy used here were accessed at: www.servidor.gov.br/publicacao/boletim_estatistico/bol_estatistico.htm

[4] In 1943, only 11% of civil servants had been recruited through public competition (Lafer, in Figueiredo, 2010). Although no subsequent data exist, the military regime's option to

recruit the bureaucracy without public competition may indicate that entry without public competition had continued.

[5.] The 274 decentralised agencies existing at the time were reduced to 52, plus 68 subsidiaries (Graef, 2009).

[6.] Both ENAP and the EPPGG career were inspired by a 1982 report by Ambassador Sergio Paulo Rouanet, at the request of DASP (see Ferrarezi et al, 2008).

[7.] This group consists of the following positions: Foreign Trade Analyst, Budgetary Planning Analyst, Financial and Control Analyst, EPPGG, and Middle-Level Positions.

[8.] The auditors from the Federal Comptroller's Office are part of the Management Group under the category of Financial and Control Analyst.

[9.] See, among others, Diniz and Boschi (1978), Draibe (1985), Martins (1991) and Gouvêa (1994). For a review of this literature, see Figueiredo (2010).

[10.] Temporary contracts include high- and middle-level professionals and substitute professors. The latter represent half of these contracts.

References

Chubb, J. and Peterson, P. (eds) (1989) *Can the government govern?*, Washington, DC: The Brookings Institution.

D'Araujo, M.C. (ed) (2007) *Governo Lula: Contornos sociais e políticos da elite do poder*, Rio de Janeiro: CPDOC.

Diniz, E. and Boschi, R. (1978) *Empresariado nacional e estado no Brasil*, Rio de Janeiro: Forense Universitária.

Dos Santos, L.A. and Cardoso, R.S. (eds) (no date) 'A experiência dos gestores governamentais no governo federal do Brasil', paper presented at the fifth International Congress of the Latin-American Center on Administration for Development (CLAD).

Draibe, S. (1985) *Rumos e metamorfoses; um estudo sobre a constituição do estado e as alternativas da industrialização no Brasil: 1930–1960*, Rio de Janeiro: Paz e Terra.

Evans, P. (1995) *Embedded autonomy: states and industrial transformation*, Princeton, NJ: Princeton University Press.

Evans, P., Rueschemeyer, D. and Skocpol, T. (1985) *Bringing the state back in*, New York, NY: Cambridge University Press.

Faoro, R. (1973) *Os donos do poder: Formação do patronato político brasileiro*, São Paulo: Globo.

Ferrarezi, E. and Zimbrão, A. (2005) 'Formação de carreiras para a gestão pública contemporânea: o caso dos Especialistas em Políticas Públicas e Gestão Governamental', paper presented at the International Congress of the Latin-American Center on Administration for Development (CLAD) on State Reform and Public Administration, Santiago, Chile.

Ferrarezi, E., Zimbrão, A. and Amorim, S. (2008) *A Experiência da Enap na formação inicial para a carreira de Especialista em Políticas Públicas e Gestão Governamental – EPPGG: 1988 a 2006,* Brasília: Cadernos Enap.

Figueiredo, A. (2010) 'Executivo e burocracia', in R. Lessa (ed) *Horizontes das Ciências Sociais no Brasil: Ciência Política,* São Paulo: Anpocs, pp 191–216.

Gaetani, F. (2007) 'Interview', http://innomics.wordpress.com/2007/11/23/entrevista-com-francisco-gaetani/

Gaetani, F. and Heredia, B. (2002) 'The political economy of civil service reform in Brazil: the Cardoso years', document prepared for the Red de Gestión y Transparencia del Diálogo Regional de Política del Banco Interamericano de Desarrollo, mimeo.

Geddes, B. (1994) *Politician's dilemma: building state capacity in Latin America,* Berkeley, CA: University of California Press.

Gouvêa, G. (1994) *Burocracia e elites burocráticas no Brasil,* São Paulo: Paulicéia.

Graef, A. (2009) 'A organização de carreiras do Poder Executivo da Administração Federal Brasileira', paper presented at the National Conference on Human Resources, Brasilia.

Grindle, M. (1997) *Getting good government: capacity building in the public sectors of developing countries,* Boston, MA: Harvard University Press.

Huntington, S. (1968) *Political order in changing societies,* New Haven, CT: Yale University Press.

IPEA (Instituto de Pesquisa Econômica Aplicada) (2011) *Burocracia e ocupação no setor público brasileiro,* Brasília: IPEA.

Lindquist, E. and Desveaux, J. (2007) 'Policy analysis and bureaucratic capacity: context, competence, and strategies', in L. Dubuzinskis, M. Howlett and D. Laycock (eds) *Policy analysis in Canada,* Toronto: University of Toronto Press, pp 116–44.

Mann, M. (1986) 'The autonomous power of the state: its origins, mechanisms and results', in J.A. Hall (ed) *States in history,* London: Basil Blackwell.

Margetts, H. (2010) 'Modernization dreams and public policy reform', in H. Margetts, H. Perri and C. Hood (eds) *Paradoxes of modernization: unintended consequences of public policy reform,* Oxford: Oxford University Press, pp 20–33.

Martins, L. (1991) *Estado capitalista e burocracia no Brasil pós-64* (2nd edn), Rio de Janeiro: Paz e Terra.

Nunes, E. (1997) *A gramática política do Brasil: Clientelismo e insulamento burocrático,* Rio de Janeiro: Zahar.

O'Donnell, G. (1986) *Contrapontos: Autoritarismo e democratização,* São Paulo: Vértice.

OECD (Organisation for Economic Co-operation and Development) (2010) *Avaliação da gestão de recursos humanos no governo – Relatório da OCDE,* Brasília: MPOG.

Peters, G. (1995) *The politics of bureaucracy,* London: Longman Publishers USA.

Schneider, B.R. (1991) *Politics within the state: elite bureaucrats and industrial policy in authoritarian Brazil,* Pittsburgh, PA: University of Pittsburgh Press.

Skocpol, T. and Finegold, K. (1982) 'State capacity and economic intervention in the early New Deal', *Political Science Quarterly,* vol 97, no 2, pp 255–78.

Stepan, A. (1978) *The state and society: Peru in comparative perspective,* Princeton, NJ: Princeton University Press.

PART TWO
POLICY ANALYSIS BY GOVERNMENTS AND THE LEGISLATURE

FIVE

Policy analysis and governance innovations in the federal government

José Mendes Ribeiro and Aline Inglez-Dias

Introduction

This chapter analyses how the planning and budget area of the Brazilian federal government goes about the process of identifying issues, setting agendas and conducting internal and external discussions about policy solutions. We address the main features of the production of policy analysis and policy alternatives as employed by the federal government, using the case of the Ministry of Planning, Budget and Management (Ministério de Planejamento, Orçamento e Gestão; MPOG), chosen because of its institutional role in strategic coordination of the state apparatus and its acknowledged political weight within the public administration.

Our study is based on the collection and analysis of documents produced by the MPOG and available on its official site in May 2011. Results indicate that the most prevalent issues related to public sector reform, governance innovations and efficiency and transparency in the federal public sector, all of which are subjects closely associated with the familiar debate on state reform. Many of the discussions in the analysed documents were, however, characterised as dealing with the revitalisation of the state or, in most cases, administrative reform.

It is worth underscoring that our document set was drawn from a period that coincided with the political environment of sharp polarisation among the leading parties that has characterised recent administrations (addressed in other chapters of this book). In this regard, the discussion of alternatives on the MPOG's predominant agenda provides valuable clues about how policy analyses and their internal and external diffusion are processed by one of the key ministries within Brazil's central government.

An examination of this set of documents suggests that authors holding more powerful decision-making positions often produce analyses and solutions that are patently incremental in nature, implying a lower political cost. In contrast, documents produced by authors from intermediate echelons or at a remove from the decision-making centre put forward ideas that entail profound changes, admitted as issues by major decision-makers. Accordingly, documents produced by authors more distant or absent from the power centre deal in solutions with a higher political cost, such as asset reform and financing and provision split.

This picture is consistent with the widespread perception among policy analysts and scholars that politicians and government staff produce alternatives that minimise conflict and are intended to solve issues on the policy agenda only partially. Step-by-step approaches, piecemeal solutions and the diffusion of successful cases hold sway in the technical culture in Brazil, as illustrated in most of the chapters of this book.

This chapter highlights elements of the policy decision-making process, with the intention not of validating or developing a theoretical model, but rather of clarifying some crucial aspects in the case of the Brazilian federal government. Our discussion explores the mechanisms for circulating ideas, the dynamic centres where debate is fostered and where ideas are captured, the activities of senior staff and outside partners, predominant issues, and approval by the upper echelons. Other elements are likewise examined, albeit more superficially, such as issues related to governance and government–society networks.

We begin with a brief discussion of some concepts relevant to policy analysis. We then examine the MPOG's institutional structure and the debate on administrative reform in Brazil. The main results of our document analysis are presented in the form of policy alternatives. In our conclusion, we draw relations between issues, MPOG sectors and the repercussions of policy analyses and studies that are disseminated in the formation of a reform agenda.

The policy decision-making process and policy analysis in support of government decisions

A variety of knowledge fields, each with its own distinct goals, address policy decisions, from philosophy and political science to multidisciplinary approaches encompassing economics, administration, sociology and anthropology, along with subdivisions or combinations of these disciplines. The production of policy analyses for the use of government leaders or political decision-makers has much to do with decision-making mechanisms themselves, notwithstanding efforts to outline the boundaries between analyses and studies, characterised by a wide range of research methods and solutions.

The consolidated notion that the policy decision-making process is primarily an outcome of individual leadership skills can be traced particularly to Machiavelli. Viroli (2000), in his classic biography, emphasises how Machiavelli represented a break with the classical tradition, which saw the alleged good ruler as applying ideal principles of ethics, irrespective of any impact his choices might have on the protection and development of his people. To the contrary, virtuous decisions by leaders involve conflicts among individual and collective interests, whose solutions do not stem solely from atemporal moral principles, but rather from the strategic calculations associated with each type of interest and goal. Individual plans and the strategic plans of rulers are viable and sustainable depending upon the conflicting interests and expectations of different collectivities. This kind of approach fits with a number of traditions in political studies, where we find elements of classical liberalism like ad hoc decision-making, the primacy of actors' will, the competition over ideas and the individualism that has pervaded the utilitarian, teleological tradition in human sciences.

The notion that the policy decision-making process is extremely complex and diversified favours models of analysis where decision patterns are fragile or non-existent. Approaches centred on individual, rational calculation are thus more appropriate when it comes to understanding processes and to identifying tendencies in these environments of high uncertainty. At the same time, a number of methodological designs centred on the role of institutions in constraining individual choices, or designs based on an individual's inability to process the necessary information (bounded rationality), have enjoyed growing prestige in the human sciences in recent decades.

The notion that decision processes often take place in complex environments where their agents are unable to fully comprehend all the available alternatives and information and are limited in their ability to perceive the consequences of their own interests seems well entrenched. Furthermore, interests, information and institutional environments differ when one analyses problems across time. Perceptions and values change, especially when one is dealing with major political issues.

A number of analysts have tried to identify some kind of pattern in this type of policy decision-making process. In this 'muddling-through' environment, Lindblom (1959) emphasises our human incapacity to broadly grasp and comprehend the information we need to guide our choices. Considering that policy alternatives tend to differ marginally, the author posits an incremental decision-making model as a pragmatic approach to decision-making. Lindblom grounded himself – perhaps too much – on what were then minor differences between the projects of the two major political parties in the US, something that is not so clear-cut today. Regardless, his incremental approach gained influence. Many other authors developed models not based solely on rational choice. The observation that decisions about the problems that occur inside organisations with more fluid structures (organised anarchies) are often made outside a rationalist pattern stimulated Cohen, March and Olsen (1972) to formulate their 'garbage can model'. In this model, one often finds circumstances under which, for instance, agents with solutions look for issues rather than the other way around.

Policy decision-making processes are usually not highly structured. Some patterns can be detected, however, and an effort to identify these can facilitate the production of analyses and recommendations and the observation of tendencies. Decisions are often taken in delimited institutional environments and can be identified as feedback loops involving agendas and results (Howlett et al, 2009). In contrast, models more open to societal activism – where formulation and decision stages are hazily defined, as in the formation of advocacy coalitions – have explanatory power in such situations (Sabatier and Jenkins-Smith, 1999). However, in the case of clearly defined institutional environments within the government, where politicians and specialists share the decision-making process with an assortment of interest groups and leaders, theories based on decision-making streams, the action of policy entrepreneurs and windows of opportunity prove quite attractive (Kingdon, 2011). Devised within the US federative environment, the multiple-streams framework, with its policy entrepreneurs, coupling and windows of opportunity, was expanded and developed to fit other institutional environments (Zahariadis, 2003).

The demarcation of boundaries between political science and policy analysis has been studied in applied terms. Policy analysis has been defined through reference to government advisory practices and the way governments appropriate knowledge produced by diverse disciplines. As a professional activity with a well-defined epistemology vis-a-vis evaluation research (Geva-May and Pal, 1999), policy analysis has undergone changes in the US, its classic terrain. Radin (2000) underscores important changes in practices, scientific legitimacy and methodological scope. The emphasis on policy analysis models that were influenced primarily by 1960s' econometrics shifted in the 1990s to a multidisciplinary approach, with different standards for assessing the models' legitimacy. These epistemic changes were the case not only in the field of policy analysis, but in other kinds of policy studies as well. In one influential study, Majone (1989) discusses the logical limits of applying experimental methods from the natural sciences to the study of political phenomena in general and to policy analysis in particular. Policy analysis, in that it uses what data and information are available in any given situation, depends upon the analyst's ability to construct a solid, persuasive argument.

For the purposes of our study, we have adopted the notion that institutions have reasonably consistent decision centres, standards and practices. To understand part of the process of producing and disseminating analyses inside the Brazilian federal government, we have endeavoured to identify such dynamic centres, observe how problems and solutions are disseminated within the government, and explore the circulation of agendas and alternatives.

Ministry of Planning: administrative functions and policy production centres

Brazil has had a Ministry of Planning since 1962, with changes in its name over the years but always focused on central planning, throughout various political and economic cycles. During the course of these cycles, the ministry assumed more salient functions in economic management, for example, following a developmentalist agenda in the 1960s or enforcing macroeconomic adjustment in the 1980s. Down through its history, some of Brazil's top economists have served as minister. Representing a variety of tendencies from Keynesian to neo-classic, they all had one thing in common: advocacy of central planning as a way of ensuring economic development. The ministry has exercised the same powers since 1995, under the title Ministry of Planning and Budget from 1995 to 1999 and the MPOG since then.

In certain periods of well-defined political cycles, administrative functions have been shared with other ministries; this was the case, for example, during implementation of the state reform initiated in 1995 with the creation of the Ministry of Administration and State Reform (Ministério da Administração e Reforma do Estado; MARE). Going farther back in Brazilian history, another moment worth highlighting was the effort to assemble a public administration with a Weberian framework, in the form of the Administrative Department of Public Service (Departamento Administrativo do Serviço Público; DASP), created under Vargas in 1938.

Recent data on the MPOG's structure, expenditures and the professional profile of its staff allow us to analyse its current administrative structure and its capacity for action and devising policy (Brazil/MPOG, 2012). Answering directly to the minister, the 11 sectors with the status of departments (*secretarias*) represent cores of policy administration and implementation. For the purpose of our document analysis, we have defined four of these as dynamic centres of debate and production of analyses and solutions: the Department of Management (Secretaria de Gestão; SEGES), the Department of the Federal Budget (Secretaria de Orçamento Federal; SOF), the Department of Planning and Strategic Investments (Secretaria de Planejamento e Investimentos Estratégicos; SPI) and the Executive Department (Secretaria Executiva) or Office of the Minister (Gabinete do Ministro), the latter two grouped in our study under the designation 'GAB'.

In terms of career personnel and their professional profile, data from the MPOG's statistical report *Boletim Estatístico* (Brazil/MPOG, 2012) shows that the 2012 staff budget was some €1,115,187,970.00, accounting for 3.1% of all outlays for the federal government's civil service. The MPOG has 14,017 active civilian employees, representing 2.5% of total active civil servants. The percentage of MPOG staff who have completed a college education is low, that is, 21.6% (3,032). It should be pointed out that only 3,625 of these staff members are on the MPOG payroll, while the rest are in the employ of foundations tied to the ministry. It is expected that policy formulation and analysis will transpire mainly within the ministry's central core, while the foundations connected to it will basically work through its main heads.

Repercussions of the national debate on public sector reform

In the documents examined from 2011, the issues that stood out involved routine ministerial matters as well as a series of broad-ranging debates. We noted that debates about issues of a political nature leaned heavily towards questions of administrative reform or reform of the state apparatus. Additionally, although the former and current presidents Luiz Inácio Lula da Silva and Dilma Rousseff – representatives of the Workers' Party (Partido dos Trabalhadores; PT) who were elected successively, keeping the PT in power since 2003 – both campaigned against the so-called 'state reform' implemented under Fernando Henrique Cardoso's two administrations, it is clear that this agenda remains in place. A brief summary of the components of the debate will help set the stage for our analysis of the collected documents.

In 1994, following the success of the economic stabilisation plan he spearheaded as Treasury Minister, Cardoso won the presidential elections as candidate for the Brazilian Social Democratic Party (Partido da Social Democracia Brasileira; PSDB). Upon taking office, his agenda combined fiscal adjustment and the privatisation of large state-owned monopolies, on the one hand, with an ambitious project to reform the state apparatus (Reforma do Aparelho de Estado), grounded in the principles of new public management, on the other. The foundations of the project were laid out in the Master Plan for State Reform (Brasil/Presidência da República, 1995), which spawned a number of draft projects put before Congress. The so-called asset reforms (privatisation of state-owned companies) and regulatory reforms (creation of new regulatory agencies) moved along at a brisker political pace than the administrative reform. The Master Plan provided for a state apparatus equipped with a strategic, hierarchical core of a normative and bureaucratic nature (with tinges of managerialism in some sectors) and a broad, diversified 'non-state public sphere' based chiefly on Britain's experience of the 1990s. The political process thus launched sought at one and the same time to solidify fiscal adjustment, foster asset reform and tackle the chronic problem of inefficiency in the Brazilian public sector, long afflicted by political patronage.

The Brazilian literature on patrimonialism and corporatism as integral elements of the country's political system and their impacts on public administration is vast. Nunes (1993) analyses the intimate ties between patrimonialism, corporatism and procedural universalism, in the Weberian sense, that have configured the actions of government leaders and reformers for decades. The model announced in 1995 represents a combination of innovative proposals for the para-state sector and markets (privatisation, regulatory agencies, result-based management), along with an updated version of a Weberian bureaucratic administration for the central government core. A number of collections of articles are representative of these debates and of hopeful expectations about the reform (Bresser-Pereira and Spink, 1998; Bresser-Pereira et al, 1999). Reactions to and criticisms of the proposed reforms were heard from wide swathes of opposition parties and unions (Santos, 2000). A multitude of analyses were offered, from those highlighting the advances associated with the reform cycle (Abrucio, 2007), to those underscoring instead the limitations that became evident (especially those derived from the environment of fiscal adjustment that pervaded the Cardoso administration), the effects of public job-cutting and the need to modify the incentive structure within the public administration (Rezende, 2009).

Contrary to what one might imagine given the strong political polarisation between the PT and PSDB that has reigned since the mid-1990s, the documents analysed herein pertaining to the second year of the Rousseff administration show that the original administrative reform agenda is still with us, with some adaptations. Coordinated by the MPOG, the continuation of this debate in new terms resulted in an important document, in which the ministry addressed the matter of a comprehensive administrative reform meant to solidify the intermediary sector between the state and society and submitted this document to Congress (Modesto, 2009). We also observed that the MPOG has led the debate on modernisation of the state and on innovations in governance at the federal level.

Formation of policy alternatives in the political environment of federal government planning

The ministry has made a plethora of documents available on its site,[1] many of which are highly pertinent to our study. Except for list-serves restricted to staff, which deal with specific issues like information technology, we can state that the hundreds of unrestricted open-access documents that are available reflect both the more active sectors in policy production as well as the most prevalent content. We have excluded documents that are merely informative in nature, those dealing with administrative services, calendars of events, bulletins on financial implementation or other texts that do not speak to a specific political debate or contain highly relevant information. The documents included in the analysed sample refer mainly to the periods of the Lula (2003–10) and Rousseff (2011 to present) administrations. To varying degrees and in different ways, many of these documents can be seen to relate to issues from the state reform agenda that headlined Cardoso's two administrations.

Our analysis identified content that was considered either one of the most important themes or a secondary one, among others. We developed criteria for defining an author's influence vis-a-vis his position in relation to the federal administration. After selecting documents available on the site, we used additional criteria to determine inclusion in the final group to be analysed, the main ones being: ministry departments (*secretarias*) that issued documents on public policy; strategic programmes, such as the public administration (*Gespública*) portal; the public–private partnership portal (*portal parcerias público-privadas*); and government programmes with direct ties to the administrative structure.

Additionally, we identified the most robust centres of activity within these departments and strategic programmes, that is, those whose actions affect the ministry and other areas of government as well. The main centres and issues include: the monitoring of macroeconomic policy and the forum of debate on public–private partnerships (PPPs), centralised in the Advisory Office on Economic Affairs (Assessoria de Assuntos Econômico; ASSEC); regulation of foreign financing and loans from international agencies, by the Department of International Affairs (Secretaria de Assuntos Internacionais; SEAIN); monitoring of the performance of state-owned companies and their major investment programmes, by the Office for the Coordination and Governance of State Companies (Departamento de Coordenação e Governança das Empresas Estatais; DEST); policies of managerial modernisation and reform of the public sector, led by the Department of Management (SEGES), and an agenda of solutions related to performance-based administration, handled through a special forum (*Gespública*; SEGES); monitoring of pluriannual plans (PPAs) – the main tool of government planning – centralised within the Department of Planning and Strategic Investments (SPI), which also plays the role of technical unit for the Mercosur regional development fund; and the Department of Human Resources (Secretaria de Recursos Humanos; SRH), responsible for the administration of the permanent federal civil service, which is an important source of statistical data and analysis on federal public employment, in addition to debates on incentives and evaluations of the public service sector.

As to the decision-making status of the authors of these documents, the criterion for determining their degree of influence was proximity to the decision-making centre, represented by the minister of the MPOG, with declining influence in other federal public bodies, state-owned companies, sub-national bodies and, lastly, foreign public and private entities. By focusing the criterion on the central government, we excluded the influence of leaders in the more general political scenario, which varies in ways detached from their roles in the public or private sector and which requires further research. Official documents issued by the MPOG were assigned greater influence, while monographs or theses, even those by ministry specialists, were considered equivalent to outside products, like those by consultants.

While the present study is not concerned with establishing a more detailed picture of decision-making streams, the observed hierarchies and horizontal governance mechanisms reveal the presence of non-random processes of public policy analysis. We have treated these levels as decision-making environments with a greater or lesser proximity to the MPOG decision-making centre.

Traditional horizontal governance mechanisms (markets and contracts) are also not an object of this study. However, the MPOG does display horizontal mechanisms in the form of joint bodies like the Foreign Financing Commission (Comissão de Financiamentos Externos; COFIEX), among others. There are highly active networks within the internal and external communities that develop content, management solutions and open-access software, which have the ability to produce standards of conduct in information technology within federal institutions. This results in a highly dynamic picture wherein the ministry is a relevant institution in the production of agendas and alternatives in Brazil. Our study sought to observe only a portion of these activities, with the focus on debates enjoying more government sanctioning.

We analysed reforms on a gradient from greatest political impact (asset reform) to least (civil service career plans) while also analysing their relation to author influence, lending us a notion of the penetration and impact of these issues as alternatives within the political debate. We classified the author's degree of influence as 'high' (MPOG and senior staff), 'medium' (other federal executive and control bodies, other branches of government, state-owned companies, public universities and sub-national public entities) and 'low' (Brazilian non-governmental environments, including think tanks, non-governmental organisations [NGOs] and consultants).

The documents were analysed in terms of content, origin, author's political influence and relationship to the daily operations of the federal government and public sector reform agenda, in terms of the characteristics of the Lula and Rousseff administrations. Following careful classification, we validated 994 documents produced from 1997 to 2011. However, the total number of documents related to the Cardoso government available on the site is quite small (14 from 1997 to 2001). Starting in 2002 – year one of Lula's first administration – the total number of documents per year rises steadily, from 24 in 2002 to 215 in 2009. We note a steady reduction from the year Rousseff took office: a validated total of 199 in 2010 and only 23 during the first five months of 2011, based on our study's criteria. Projections suggest a cooling down in the debate on routine government tasks concerning reform processes, which may reflect greater political centralisation in the hands of the president, as evidenced in the privatisation of major airports, and a consequential decrease in political initiative on the part of her ministers. This affirmation meshes with media reports, although this cannot be taken as any kind of firm evidence.

The documents in our data set are predominantly analytical in nature (80.3%), in part reflecting the kind of filter we used to determine their inclusion. The remainder are predominantly descriptive, serving to disseminate standards or results (14.2%) or consisting of bulletins or communiqués that were deemed relevant (5.5%).

Looking at the top echelons of the MPOG, we observe that the documents on the site came from sectors that lead in the exercise of regular ministry tasks and those more involved with political reform processes. The management area (SEGES), the main actor in managerial reform, accounts for 42.4% of the documents. This is followed by the planning area (SPI), with 23.9%; budget and finances (SOF), with 15.8%; and the minister's office (GAB), with 12.5%. The documents were classified according to the main issue presented or analysed in their pages.

By studying the distribution of these issues across key sectors, we can identify the most dynamic poles in the production of analyses or dissemination of ideas within the ministry. As shown in Table 5.1, an analysis of the key issue addressed in each document reveals that one group stands out as displaying the most predominant issues. PPAs, public budgeting and governance in the public sector are the predominant issues in over 100 documents, demonstrating that the ministry is focused on its main institutional attributions.

The subject of PPAs is almost wholly sustained by the SPI (at 98.8%). This performance-based planning tool is a legacy of President Cardoso's state reform; all federative spheres are to apply it to their budgets and its indicators are to be monitored by control agencies and released to the public. The documents offer ample discussions on how pluriannual planning has had an impact on public administration quality and on MPOG mechanisms for driving implementation in Brazil. The SPI's specialised areas are vital centres for analysis of this policy.

Another specialised area that concentrates heavily on one issue is the SOF, which accounts for 73.6% of all documents related to the public budget, followed by the GAB itself (23.3%). Similarly, the SEGES ranks highest by far in the debate on governance mechanisms in the public sector (88.0%).

Table 5.1: **Predominant document issues, by MPOG sector (May 2011), absolute and relative (%) values**

Predominant issue	SEGES	SOF	SPI	GAB	Others	Total
Pluriannual plan	none	none	162 (98.8)	2 (1.2)	none	164 (100.0%)
Public budgeting	5 (3.1)	120 (73.6)	none	38 (23.3)	none	163
Public sector governance	110 (88.0)	6 (4.8)	1 (0.8)	6 (4.8)	2 (1.6)	125
State reform	72 (87.8)	none	2 (2.4)	8 (9.8)	none	82
Public bureaucracy and processes	27 (34.2)	4 (5.0)	10 (12.7)	27 (34.2)	11 (13.9)	79
Studies released	49 (62.0)	23 (29.1)	none	5 (6.3)	2 (2.5)	79
Public investments/competitiveness	4 (6.0)	1 (1.5)	59 (88.1)	1 (1.5)	2 (3.0)	67
Human resources/tertiarisation	40 (67.8)	1 (1.7)	non90e	14 (23.7)	4 (6.8)	59
Management contracts/quango/state foundation	54 (98.2)	none	none	1 (1.8)	none	55
Quality in the public sector	48 (100.0)	none	none	none	none	48
Government bulletins	2 (7.4)	2 (7.4)	2 (7.4)	none	21 (77.8)	27
Public–private partnerships	3 (12.0)	none	none	22 (88.0)	none	25
Foreign relations	7 (33.3)	none	2 (9.5)	none	12 (57.2)	21
Total	421 (42.4)	157 (15.8)	238 (23.9)	124 (12.5)	54 (5.4)	994

The distribution of the other issues across sectors reinforces the notion that policy analyses, studies and debates within the MPOG match up with the specialised centres within each department and with their institutional competences. Thus, the vast majority of documents addressing state reform (87.8%) are produced by the public management area. Other leading issues by SEGES likewise fall within its realm of competence, such as human resources and tertiarisation (67.8%), management contracts and organisational innovations like *organizações sociais* (roughly equivalent to quasi-autonomous non-governmental organisations [quangos]) and public state-owned foundations (*fundações estatais de direito público*) (98.2%), and public sector quality (100.0%). Public investments, competitiveness and development policies are addressed primarily by the SOF (88.1%). Documents dealing with PPPs are concentrated in the GAB, through the ASSEC (88.0%), accessible through a specific link since the issue is administered by a managing committee that encompasses not only the MPOG, but also the Executive Office of the President (Casa Civil) and the Ministry of the Treasury.

In addition to the high degree of departmental specialisation in policy debates within the MPOG, another facet that stands out in these documents is the steady presence of issues related to the public sector reform agenda. In 233 documents (23.4%), the theme of state reform, as introduced by President Cardoso, was found to be either a leading or secondary issue, in the latter case, generally serving to legitimise the key point at issue. The import of the continuation of this debate becomes apparent if we redefine Cardoso's state reform under the more general connotation of public sector reform, including issues not emphasised under the former and thereby extending into the Lula and Rousseff administrations. This keeps the total number of documents roughly the same (236), indicating – as suggested by a reading of the documents – that the debate on state reform as launched under Cardoso's presidency provides discursive support for public sector reform under Lula and Rousseff. What emerges is the apparent entrenchment of a long cycle of reforms aimed at greater public sector efficiency, based on the separation of strategic centres and para-state sectors, which dates back to Decree Law no 200 of 1967.

Table 5.2 shows the distribution of issues related to public sector reform among the analysed documents. A total of 236 of them addressed the subject, with several dealing with more than one of the issues. The enhancement of institutional governance mechanisms in the public sector was the most prevalent issue on this agenda, addressed in 121 documents. Next came the tertiary sector (108) and regulatory agencies (72). Although civil service reform was dealt with in only 48 documents, it was this issue that was behind the government's submission to Congress of a wide-ranging draft bill based on the MPOG debate. The theme of privatisation was not as common (25 documents), currently less about the integral transfer of public assets to the private sector and more about their transfer to intermediary concessionary regimes or PPPs.

Table 5.2: **Issues related to public sector reform, by predominant or secondary content, and degree of author or institution influence (n = 236)**

Issue	Influence			
	Low	Medium	High	Total (100.0%)
Public sector governance	18 (14.9%)	66 (54.6%)	37 (30.6%)	121
Tertiary sector	25 (23.2%)	62 (57.4%)	21 (19.4%)	108
Regulatory agency	11 (15.3%)	55 (76.4%)	6 (8.3%)	72
Civil service reform	5 (10.4%)	21 (43.8%)	22 (45.8%)	48
Privatisation	1 (4.0%)	19 (76.0%)	5 (20.0%)	25

When we compare issues with author influence, certain factors involving the political costs of reforms emerge. The participation of the highest echelon of influence (the MPOG and its senior staff) is more intense when addressing civil service reform (45.8%), outranking the medium level of influence (43.8%), which comprises other sectors of the federal government, universities and sub-national governments. Another issue where the MPOG core participates actively is public sector governance (30.6%). These two issues have a lower political cost as they affect property ownership and public employment less. In contrast, the medium level of influence generally has the most to say about privatisation (76.0%), which is associated with a high political cost.

Table 5.3 illustrates further details about the types of authors and issues found in these documents. For purposes of classification, we chose the predominant issue among the various ones under focus in each document, and then grouped these by

Table 5.3: **Predominant document issue by authors' legal nature, absolute and relative (%) values**

	Foreign private	Brazilian private	Sub-national public	Foreign public	Federal public	Total
Pluriannual plans	none	none	none	none	164 (100.0)	164 (100.0%)
Public budgeting	none	12 (7.36)	none	5 (3.07)	146 (89.57)	163
Public sector governance	3 (2.40)	13 (10.40)	7 (5.60)	11 (8.80)	91 (72.80)	125
Public bureaucracy and processes	1 (1.27)	1 (1.27)	1 (1.27)	1 (1.27)	75 (94.94)	79
Investments/competitiveness	none	1 (1.49)	1 (1.49)	5 (7.46)	60 (89.55)	67
Human resources/tertiary sector	2 (3.39)	1 (1.69)	none	3 (5.08)	53 (89.83)	59
State reform	9 (10.98)	3 (3.66)	49 (4.88)	28 (34.15)	38 (46.34)	82
Management contracts/quangos/ state foundations	none	6 (10.91)	12 (21.82)	none	37 (67.27)	55
Studies released	6 (7.59)	20 (25.32)	7 (8.86)	9 (11.39)	37 (46.84)	79
Quality in the public sector	1 (2.08)	8 (16.67)	11 (22.92)	none	28 (58.33)	48
Government bulletins	none	none	none	none	27 (100.0)	27
Foreign relations	3 (14.29)	none	none	4 (19.05)	14 (66.67)	21
Public–private partnerships	11 (44.00)	1 (4.00)	6 (24.00)	4 (16.00)	3 (12.00)	25
Total	36 (3.62)	66 (6.64)	49 (4.93)	70 (7.04)	773 (77.77)	994

the authors' or institutions' administrative status, allowing us to observe the main links between authorship and preferred issues.

In proportional terms, authors and institutions associated with the federal public administration focused heavily on issues such as PPAs (although this type of planning is also mandatory for sub-national entities), public budgeting, public sector governance, investment and development policies, organisational innovations (like quangos), and international relations. Although the federal public sector is the dominant source for our document set (77.77%), there is selectivity among issues. While the sub-national public sector accounts for the smallest share of the documents, it does have a presence, especially in discussions about organisational innovations (quangos, PPPs) and service quality. The foreign private sector displays a preference for issues like state reform and PPPs, while the Brazilian private sector is represented more in 'studies released', some through prizes, especially in the form of consultant reports and authors of monographs.

Final remarks

Our analysis does not seek to validate theories on policy decision-making, but does shed light on some important elements of the production of policy analysis in a vital sector of the federal administration and in some of the more salient channels of debate and dissemination of ideas, which reveals aspects of how ideas circulate and are appropriated by the central government. The study has endeavoured to identify some of the mechanisms by which issues and alternatives circulate within the federal government, through the MPOG and its more constant partners. Aspects of the transformation of debated ideas into government agenda were observed in regards to at least two items: administrative reform and the privatisation of airports. In the case of administrative reform, we captured how the debate transpired during the period under study through its formalization as a government agenda and the draft bill now in public consultation to be submitted to Congress. In the case of the privatisation of federal airports, we noted an organised debate, especially within the PPP forum, particularly the bid processes held in late 2011.

This study has not endeavoured to establish definitive causal relations between debates waged and decisions made. However, the case of public consultation about the new public administration model, coordinated by the MPOG, with the involvement of a commission of renowned specialists, shows how an internal debate was taken up by the presidency of the republic, edited in a book with government support and submitted to public debate. In the case of the recent privatisation of federal airports, the relationship between the debates expressed in these documents and central government decisions is more tenuous; yet, we may be looking at an inversion here, as compared with the case of administrative reform. It is likely that the discussion of PPPs was a response to the Office of the President's interest in finding solutions for the airport crisis, which has been the target of much national political debate. Opportunities for the emergence of this agenda also derive from upcoming global events, such as the 2014 World Cup, to be held in 12 of Brazil's state capitals, and the 2016 summer Olympics, to be hosted by Rio de Janeiro.

In addition to reflecting departmental specialisation, issues are generally distributed among author profiles in conformity with an identifiable logic. The sharp predominance of government authors and institutions and federal institutions indicates that the political debate occurs among peers within the federal administration and their regulatory entities. The private sector is called on to fill in specific gaps, while sub-national public entities contribute by disseminating successful experiments.

Agenda-setting processes and the range of alternatives presented here, as identified in the analysed documents, display similarities with what has been observed in stream theories on the policy decision-making process. Specialised staff members and senior outside consultants, private institutions that are formal or informal partners, and sub-national institutions debate through networks or seminars. The channels for the diffusion of ideas within the MPOG comprise specialists and senior staff who produce alternatives. Under certain circumstances, windows present themselves and more active leaders manage to link specialists with politicians and issues, forming a policy stream. Although we have not discussed how the issues addressed in the documents became part of the government agenda, mechanisms of an incremental nature are a relevant part of the process.

At the highest echelons, author influence tracks with lowest political cost, although the weight of medium-level echelons is quite strong. This shows that public sector areas like universities, sub-national governments, regulatory agencies and audit courts are the most active sectors in the production of ideas. These bodies enjoy greater independence from the federal government, along with high status in the public eye. Another aspect highlighted here is the persistence of administrative reform as an issue, shifting from a broad-ranging reform of the state under the two Cardoso administrations (1995–2002) to an incremental reform under Lula and Rousseff.

This incipient analysis of processes of debate within the realm of the federal government, using the MPOG as a case example, opens the way for deeper studies aimed at understanding the current set of mechanisms for consolidating policies in the sphere of government decision-making.

Note
[1] See: www.planejamento.gov.br

References

Abrucio, L.F. (2007) 'Trajetória recente da gestão pública brasileira: um balanço crítico e a renovação da agenda de reformas', *RAP*, special edition, pp 67–86.

Brasil/MPOG – Ministério do Planejamento, Orçamento e Gestão (2012) *Boletim Estatístico de Pessoal*, vol 17, no 190.

Brasil/Presidência da República (1995) *Plano Diretor da Reforma do Aparelho de Estado*, Brasília: Imprensa Nacional

Bresser-Pereira, L.C. and Grau, N.C. (eds) (1999) *O público não-estatal na Reforma do Estado*, Rio de Janeiro: Editora FGV.

Bresser-Pereira, L.C. and Spink, P. (eds) (1998) *Reforma do Estado e administração pública gerencial*, Rio de Janeiro: Editora FGV.

Bresser-Pereira, L.C., Wilheim, J. and Sola, L. (eds) (1999) *Sociedade e Estado em transformação*, São Paulo/Brasília: Editora UNESP/ENAP.

Cohen, D., March, J.G. and Olsen, J.P. (1972) 'A garbage can model of organizational choice', *Administrative Science Quarterly*, vol 17, no 1, pp 1–25.

Geva-May, I. and Pal, L.A. (1999) 'Good fences make good neighbours: policy evaluation and policy analysis – exploring the differences', *Evaluation*, 5(3), pp 259-77.

Howlett, M., Perl, A. and Ramesh, A. (2009) *Studying public policy: policy cycles and policy subsystems*, Toronto: Oxford University Press.

Kingdon, J.W. (2011) *Agendas, alternatives and public policies* (2nd edn), Boston, MA: Longman.

Lindblom, C.E. (1959) 'The science of muddling through', *Public Administration Review*, vol 19, no 2, pp 79–88.

Majone, G. (1989) *Evidence, argument, and persuasion in the policy process*, New Haven, CT: Yale University Press.

Modesto, P. (ed) (2009) *Nova organização administrativa brasileira*, Belo Horizonte: Editora Fórum.

Nunes, E. (1993) *A gramática política do Brasil*, Rio de Janeiro: Jorge Zahar Editora.

Rezende, F.C. (2009) 'Desafios gerenciais para a reconfiguração da administração burocrática brasileira', *Sociologias*, no 21, pp 344–65.

Sabatier, P.A. and Jenkins-Smith, H. (1999) 'The advocacy coalition framework', in P.A. Sabatier (ed) *Theories of the policy process*, Boulder, CO: Westview Press, pp 117–66.

Santos, L.A. (2000) *Agencificação, publicização, contratualização e controle social: possibilidades no âmbito da Reforma do Aparelho de Estado*, Brasília: DIAP.

Zahariadis, N. (2003) *Ambiguity and choice in public policy: political decision making in modern democracies*, Washington, DC: Georgetown University Press.

SIX

Policy monitoring and evaluation systems: recent advances in Brazil's federal public administration

Rômulo Paes-Sousa and Aline Gazola Hellmann

Introduction

This chapter discusses the evaluation function as part of the policy analysis field in Brazil. Policy evaluation refers here to the endeavour to obtain relevant, systematic knowledge about policy contexts, decision-making, programmes, teams, publics, outcomes, impacts and consequences (Sabatier, 1995; Dobuzinskis et al, 2007; Wollmann, 2007). Policy analysis refers to either an interdisciplinary or applied field within the social sciences and is explored extensively in previous chapters of this book.

As an object of study of policy analysis, the evaluation function is important because: first, it runs through and influences the whole government policy cycle, through ex ante evaluations, monitoring and ex post evaluations,[1] with performance-monitoring activities being regarded as a type of evaluation that occurs together with policy implementation (Wollmann, 2007, pp 393–5); and, second, it also contributes directly to the production of the valid knowledge characteristic of policy analysis.[2]

This chapter has three goals, taking Brazil as a case. First, it will review the contribution of evaluation studies to the interdisciplinary field of policy analysis. Second, it describes in general terms the process of institutionalisation of policy and programme monitoring and evaluation (M&E) functions in the federal government. Finally, it aims to investigate M&E experiences in some Brazilian federal government agencies, specifically: the Office of the President (PR), the Ministry of Planning, Budget and Management (MP), the Ministry for Social Development and the Fight against Hunger (MDS), the Ministry of Health (MoH) and the Federal Court of Audit (TCU).

The methodology used comprises a literature review, including official documents, and semi-structured interviews of key actors at these agencies. The final section points to some of the political, normative, technical and budget challenges facing the policy evaluation function in Brazil's federal administration.

Policy analysis in Brazil: the place of evaluation

Policy evaluation, whether as a systematic practice in government or as an object for academic research and teaching, is new in Brazil. Until the late 1990s, what predominated were sectoral evaluations carried out by civil servants and focusing on policy formulation and decision-making processes (Cepik, 1997; Melo, 1999; Dulci, 2010). Since the 2000s, however, there has been a marked increase in evaluation activities not only by governmental agencies, but also by other important actors, such as international organisations, civil society interest groups and universities. Four factors explain this increase.

First of all, the 1988 Constitution assigned a more leading role in social policy to the democratic state, particularly at the federal and municipal levels. The 20 years of dictatorship (1964–84) were followed by initial efforts to build legitimacy for, and improve the efficiency and productivity of, government action in the context of public spending cuts that characterised the 1990s. Reorganisation of the Brazilian state during the 2000s established the issues of transparency and effectiveness firmly on the agenda. The increase in evaluation thus resulted from the increase in social public spending itself and the corresponding attention paid by society to the effectiveness and efficiency of public policies (Faria and Filgueiras, 2007).

The second factor is the recent expansion of undergraduate and postgraduate degrees with policy study majors offered by Brazilian universities. This is an important factor because:

> The scarcity of 'post-decision' studies seems to be explained not only by fragile institutionalisation of this field in Brazil, as a result of which public policy analysis continues to gravitate around analytical issues more traditionally valued by Political Science, but also by the weakness of the Public Administration field of studies in Brazil. (Faria, 2003, p 22)

Growth in a new curriculum better coordinated with research made it possible to overcome the historical dispersion and discontinuity of projects in this field and to improve synergy between the academic fields of the social sciences, public administration, economics and other relevant areas (Melo, 1999; Silva and Costa, 2002).

The third factor, new information and communication technologies (ICTs), has affected government M&E activities as information systems have become increasingly sophisticated and the cost of public access to important information flows has diminished. The construction and management of information systems and governance of public agencies' technological and informational resources have created new conditions and posed new challenges for evaluation of government policies, programmes and actions (Rodrigues, 2009; Cepik and Canabarro, 2010).

The fourth factor was the series of incentives offered by international organisations for monitoring policy-related initial conditions, implementation processes and impact. Naturally, those incentives include requirements by agencies, such as the World Bank (WB) and the Inter-American Development Bank (IDB), making funds transfers conditional on the development of M&E protocols in order to assess policies' implementation risks associated with the loan operations (Faria, 2005, p 99). However, modalities of international support for the development of M&E have been diverse and constitute an explanatory factor in some cases in Brazil.

In 2002, Brazil's MoH introduced the Extension Project in Family Health (Projeto de Extensão de Saúde da Família; PROESF), which was designed to improve the quality of health care. This was funded by a WB loan under a bilateral agreement calling for baseline studies of health care to evaluate the prior context in Brazil.

Another example is the Evaluation Brazil Programme (Programa Brasil Avaliação; BRAVA), a WB project offering technical assistance to Brazil's federal government, which ran from 2005 to 2009. Its lead partner was the M&E Technical Chamber

(Câmara Técnica de M&A; CTMA), a committee drawn from the main government agencies interested in the subject. Among BRAVA's goals, Borges et al (2011, p 9) highlight the following: to develop an M&E policy and methodologies for the federal government; to prepare result management systems (RMS); and to promote the use and circulation of information produced by M&E.

As a result and expression of all four factors, the Brazilian Monitoring and Evaluation Network (Rede Brasileira de Monitoramento e Avaliação; RBMA) was set up in 2008 with support from representatives of diverse institutions, ranging from international agencies (for example, IDB, WB and United Nations Development Program [UNDP]), federal agencies (for example, the MDS, Presidential Secretariat for Strategic Affairs [SAE/PR] and TCU) and state bodies (for example, the SEADE Foundation, São Paulo; João Pinheiro Foundation, Minas Gerais; and the Ceará, Rio Grande do Sul and Bahia state governments), to third sector organisations (for example, Ecofuturo Institute, Itaú Social Foundation, Unibanco Institute).

In April 2011, the RBMA launched the monitoring and evaluation journal *Revista Brasileira de Monitoramento e Avaliação*, with support from the MDS Secretariat for Evaluation and Information Management (SAGI/MDS) and the SAE/PR. Although the RBMA's members come from Brazil's 26 states and the Federal District, 48% are civil servants and only 3% come from study and research centres (Borges et al, 2011), indicating that academics still need to incorporate the evaluation function as one of their study objects, and to dialogue with the knowledge it produces.

Institutionalisation of the evaluation function in the Brazilian state

Until the 1980s, M&E activities in Brazil were limited basically to accounting audits. In 1982, the TCU introduced the concept and practice of operational auditing, with features similar to the performance auditing carried out since 1972 by the US Government Accountability Office. Operational audits, besides ascertaining institutional compliance with fiscal responsibility requirements, also evaluate more systematically the efficiency and efficacy of programmes, projects and activities conducted by the agencies and bodies under TCU jurisdiction. In this respect, operational auditing may be considered an important type of policy evaluation (Brasil Tribunal de Contas da União, 2000; Araújo, 2008; Serpa, 2010).[3]

From 1988 onward, following the proclamation of Brazil's new federal constitution, government action came to be organised into Multi-Year Plans (PPAs) and the Budget Guidelines Act (Lei de Diretrizes Orçamentárias; LDO). The Constitution required the legislature, executive and judiciary to maintain integrated internal control systems to evaluate the fulfilment of goals set in the PPA and execution of government programmes and budgets (Brasil, 1988). However, the first PPA drafted after the 1988 Constitution (1991–95) was not supported by a government plan to coordinate it with the annual budget. In addition, it was not revised, because there was no organised system to monitor the dynamics of policy implementation that would make it possible to incorporate policy changes and adapt interventions (Garcia, 2000, pp 9–12).

The Real Plan for Economic Stabilisation (1994) and the State Reform Steering Plan (1995) redefined the policy M&E context in Brazil. In August 1996, in the context of the second PPA (1996–99), the federal government launched the programme

Brazil in Action (Brasil em Ação), 42 priority actions were pursued under a special monitoring and management regime deigned to guide budgeting, identify priorities, detect implementation problems, develop information bases for attracting investors and facilitate public–private partnerships. To each action the programme assigned a manager with authority and certain means to interact with all other actors involved either in implementing the actions planned or in monitoring and evaluating those activities. Where Brazil in Action innovated most, however, was that it was supported (at least conceptually) by a customised management information system (Silva and Costa, 2002, pp 40–41). Nonetheless, it was not until the third PPA, Advance Brazil (Avança Brasil) (2000–03), that this kind of management organisation was extended to all federal government programmes.

From the 2000s on, therefore, federal government M&E rules and parameters continued to improve significantly in relation to the PPAs Brazil for All (Brasil de Todos) (2004–07), Development with Social Inclusion and Quality Education (Desenvolvimento com Inclusão Social e Educação de Qualidade) (2008–11) and Brazil without Extreme Poverty (Brasil sem Miséria) (2012–15). Since then, the challenges have tended to be less normative and conceptual than material, organisational and informational, as well as relating to qualified personnel to carry out monitoring and evaluations appropriately.

In 2001, the Management and Planning Information System (Sistema de Informações Gerenciais e de Planejamento; SIGPLAN) was launched, providing basic information for preparing the government's annual evaluation report. However, SIGPLAN depends on the quality of the information and how often it is input by managers, and still affords poor interoperability with other federal government systems, such as the Planning, Budget and Management Ministry's Integrated Budget Data System (Sistema Integrado de Dados Orçamentários; SIDOR) or the Finance Ministry's Financial Administration System (Sistema de Administração Financeira; SIAFI). Moreover, some sectoral systems for highly capillary, nationwide public policies, such as the Education Ministry's Integrated Monitoring, Execution and Control System (Sistema Integrado de Monitoramento, Execução e Controle; SIMEC) or the Healthcare Action Planning, Monitoring and Evaluation System (Sistema de Planejamento, Monitoramento e Avaliação de Ações em Saúde; SISPLAN), are more sophisticated, offering more detailed and accurate information than used by SIGPLAN. This also poses a challenge for interoperability (Cunha, 2006; Mesquita and Bretas, 2010).

In 2004, the creation of the MDS marked an important milestone in the institutionalisation of M&E functions in Brazil. The new institution reorganised three existing federal agencies, merging national social assistance, food and nutritional security policies with the nascent conditional family cash transfer programme (Bolsa Família). Decentralised implementation of 21 programmes (involving the federal, state and municipal governments), plus significantly increased investments in social protection, required that the ministry introduce a new M&E framework. The result was the Secretariat of Evaluation and Information Management (SAGI), an innovation in Brazilian public management as it was the first secretariat exclusively for M&E functions and, above all, because it ranked at the same hierarchical level as decision-making secretariats (Vaitsman et al, 2006, pp 17, 63).

Lastly, the Planning Ministry introduced the National Public Management and De-bureaucratisation Programme (Programa Nacional de Gestão Pública e Desburocratização; GESPÚBLICA) to improve public services while increasing competitiveness in Brazil. Its actions feed into the three processes of management evaluation, de-bureaucratisation and improved public services.

As shown in Table 6.1, institutionalisation of M&E activities progressed gradually and cumulatively in Brazil's federal public administration, starting with operational audits in the 1980s, then managerial monitoring in the 1990s and strategic evaluation from 2000 onward.

Table 6.1: **Implementation of the evaluation function in Brazil**

Predominant concept of public administration	Type of evaluation	Important events for M&E
1980s Bureaucratic	Operational audits	1970: Evaluation of Graduate Programmes; Accounting Audit 1980: Yellow Book translated and operational audits begin 1988: Federal Constitution 1991–95: First PPA
1990s Managerial	Managerial monitoring	1995–99: PPA Brazil in Action 1995: State Reform Plan 1998: Decree 2829, 28 Oct 1998 (links programmes and PPA) 2001: SIGPLAN created
2000s Strategic	Strategic evaluation	2000–03: PPA 'Go Brazil' 2004–07: PPA 'Brazil for All' 2004: SAGI created by MDS 2005: GESPÚBLICA 2008–11: PPA 'Development with Social Inclusion' 2009: 'Citizens' Charter' 2012: Access to Information Act 2012–15: PPA 'Brazil without Extreme Poverty'

While highlighting the overall, common process by which M&E activities were institutionalised in Brazil's federal public administration, it is important to recognise that these practices are very diverse and seek different goals. Accordingly, the next section of this chapter describes examples to illustrate that diversity and some possible determinants.

Monitoring and evaluation in Brazil: five experiences in the federal government

In systematic comparative studies, the various experiences of M&E in one country or even different countries can be classified by their position in the state hierarchy, staff qualification, size, level of systematisation in the demand for evaluation and funding for evaluation. The following examples from Brazil may contribute to posing new research problems on the issue of evaluation in the policy analysis field in Brazil.

The Office of the President

The PR is structured into 13 core agencies, most with ministerial status, in addition to a special advisory agency and the presidential cabinet, plus over eight national councils and commissions. The annual report on the government's actions, drafted by the Office of the Chief of Staff, is based essentially on data gathered by SIGPLAN. This section will mention three salient M&E experiences ongoing in agencies of the presidency.

The first is the Presidential Cabinet's Information and Decision-Making Support Office (Gabinete-Adjunto de Informações e Apoio à Decisão do Gabinete Pessoal do Presidente da República), which was set up in 2003 to monitor the president's decisions and commitments, give a sense of continuity to government decisions, and provide reliable technical information for the president to use on visits, in speeches and at interviews.

The system involved following all meetings at the PR and identifying commitments made by the president. The team also systematised all presidential commitments made in meetings, speeches and interviews, and reported to the relevant ministries and agencies. For each sector, an official was appointed to manage the institutional responses to presidential commitments (Conti, 2008).

The team later used the Federal Government Priority Actions Monitoring System (Sistema de Acompanhamento de Ações Prioritárias do Governo Federal; SIGOV), developed with UNDP support. That system, however, was not integrated with other systems that structured the government, such as SIGPLAN and SIAFI. From 2003 to 2010, over 3,000 commitments were monitored and circulated through presidential reports, memorandums and resolutions. When President Dilma Roussef took office in 2011, she maintained the Information and Decision-Making Support Office.

The second case is the Information Organisation Committee (COI). In 2006, three areas of the Brazilian Presidential Office (the Cabinet, the Chief of Staff and the Institutional Relations Secretariat) joined forces to organise information received from the ministries and standardise demands on them, so as to avoid duplicate requests. A system allowing authorised personnel remote information access was developed to support COI workflows.[4]

The third example is the Growth Acceleration Programme (Programa de Aceleração do Crescimento; PAC). Between 2007 and 2010, the executive secretariat of the PAC Executive Board (Grupo Executivo do Programa de Aceleração do Crescimento; GEPAC) was provided by the Office for Communication and Monitoring (SAM) of the Chief of Staff of the Presidency. GEPAC's duties included: monitoring PAC physical and financial targets and identifying critical problems and constraints. Twelve thematic situation rooms were set up to support the PAC monitoring structure. Their bi-weekly meetings could call on databanks, referential information architectures and a specific PAC monitoring system (SIsPAC). The quarterly PAC reports and annual PPA evaluation reports have trigged numerous outside and in-house evaluations by non-governmental actors.

Ministry of Planning, Budget and Management

Introduced in 2004, the Multi-Year Plan Monitoring and Evaluation System (Sistema de Monitoramento e Avaliação do Plano Plurianual; SMA) integrated an M&E commission (CMA) (representing the core government agencies: Ministry of Planning, Presidential Chief of Staff and Presidential Office) and sectoral technical teams in M&E units (UMAs) installed in each ministry or agency with the PPA's programme and project leaders. The SMA promoted standardisation of methods and procedures and fostered M&E best practices, representing a major advance in the ministry's strategic planning.

The new structure used the SIGPLAN to organise and integrate the PPA management network. Launched in 2001, the SIGPLAN reflected the regulatory features of the current management model: results orientation, de-bureaucratisation, shared use of information, prospective focus and social transparency. However, increasingly intensive use of the system as a PPA managerial tool revealed that it was not being accurately and appropriately fed by managers, and thus failed to assure precise, reliable programme information. As a result, senior government officials ceased to consult SIGPLAN (hence, the introduction of the Presidential Cabinet's Information and Decision-Making Support Office).

Soon afterwards, the various ministries' Planning and Budget Offices (Subsecretarias de Planejamento e Orçamento; SPO) responsible for integrating the Monitoring and Evaluation System (SMA; led by the Ministry of Planning) became overloaded with other administrative duties, severely undermining the M&E function. That especially affected ministries whose programmes did not require beneficiary co-responsibility or were not part of the PAC. In many cases, information flows became less robust and were maintained only to comply with the SIGPLAN monitoring protocol.

Similarly, the SIsPAC was not intensively used. It covered a large number of actions, but with little in-depth information – each PPA comprised approximately 5,000 actions by all government agencies and the PAC alone comprises around 2,600 projects. As a result, the federal government made a top priority of monitoring PAC projects.

Even so, both systems – SIGPLAN and SIsPAC – could offer more to managers if they were integrated and coordinated with actions to develop the M&E capabilities of managers tasked with policy execution (Mesquita and Bretas, 2010).

Ministry for Social Development and the Fight against Hunger

The MDS SAGI introduced new possibilities for organising and implementing M&E methodologies and interactions with policy managers. Vaitsman et al (2006, p 44) report that the SAGI developed 'its own institutional evaluation model, including routine procedures for the evaluation cycle, from defining the problem to developing terms of reference for research, contracts, follow-up, publicity and regular publication of results'.

The SAGI implemented a Monitoring and Evaluation System consisting of two independent and organised subsystems grounded in distinct (monitoring and evaluation) procedures (Rodrigues, 2009). Also, the SAGI's role included commissioning evaluation services, a strategy that yielded gains of scale, diversity and quality. From the outset, the SAGI partnered with the Brazilian Geography and Statistics Institute (Instituto Brasileiro de Geografia e Estatística; IBGE) to conduct nationwide household (and institutional) surveys, as well as experimenting with different types of evaluation studies, such as panel and anthropological case studies (Vaitsman et al, 2006, p 44). From 2004 to mid-2012, the SAGI commissioned or conducted more than 120 evaluation studies.

One innovative M&E procedure was to store all micro-data from studies commissioned or conducted by the SAGI in one public institution. The data was then made available through the internet for academics and other interested parties, permitting meta-evaluation and other fully independent impact studies.

Ministry of Health

Together with the Ministry of Education, the MoH has one of the longest traditions in programme monitoring and evaluation in Brazil. At the MoH, secretariats and specialised agencies conduct and commission evaluation studies, often through special departments.

At the Health Surveillance Secretariat (Secretaria de Vigilância em Saúde; SVS), for instance, the Health Situation Analysis Department (DASIS) coordinates information systems, produces health situation analyses as part of the National Health Promotion Policy and makes technical contributions to the M&E of a number of programmes. The Secretariat for Science, Technology and Strategic Materials (Secretaria de Ciência, Tecnologia e Insumos Estratégicos; SCTIE) evaluates the National Health Science and Technology Policy and national pharmaceutical care and drugs policies. Finally, prominent, routine M&E activities at the Healthcare Secretariat (Secretaria de Atenção à Saúde; SAS) include those of its Basic Healthcare Department and the National Health Services Evaluation Programme (Programa Nacional de Avaliação dos Serviços de Saúde; PNASS).

Another important measure is designed to unify M&E methods and procedures across the MoH administrative structure. The Executive Secretariat coordinates the initiative, with the MoH Health Situation Room as the hub of the process. The Health Situation Room's purpose is to provide information to support decision-making, management, professional practice and knowledge generation. This process plays a strategic role in government actions in the Unified Health System (Sistema Único de Saúde; SUS) by providing material for trend and sectoral evaluations through its four modules: socioeconomic; basic and specialised care; morbidity and mortality; and health care management. Specifically, the health care management set of monitoring indicators is integral to Brazil's Health Pact, providing technical support for resource allocation, management processes, decentralisation and social oversight.

Federal Court of Audit

In Brazil, operational or performance audits are carried out by both the TCU's Government Programme Inspection and the Secretariat Evaluation (Secretaria de Fiscalização e Avaliação de Programas de Governo; SEPROG). SEPROG has a small but skilled team and a clearly defined theoretical framework. However, it lacks a standardised inspection schedule. The current schedule combines routine procedures with occasional demands from other secretariats. That is, there is no institutional scheduling methodology, and scheduling may be strongly influenced by personal or sectoral views.

In one of the recent audit experiences, the SEPROG highlighted the MoH's use of risk analysis methodology. This initiative has generated a two-year-long inspection schedule, during which operational audits were conducted in the areas of oncology, popular pharmacies and transplant centres.

The SEPROG revealed that the lack of systematised information was the key difficulty in performing audits. Inspections of wastage, for instance, revealed that information on assets sold at public auction is incomplete. In other cases, it has shown that information provided by agencies and data gathered during inspections and investigations were inconsistent. Although operational auditing is institutionalised and therefore considered legitimate and useful by governmental agencies audited, there is increasing concern to improve integration among the auditing, monitoring and evaluation functions.

Final remarks

In Brazil, policy M&E activities can be observed to be increasingly institutionalised. Investments, particularly in infrastructure and social concerns, have increased significantly and services have substantially expanded in coverage and improved in quality, heightening the need for policy M&E. Brazil's government has developed an unprecedented set of tools for results management, policy impact studies and promoting an institutional culture of M&E.

This process, however, is far from linear and uniform. Accordingly, this chapter has also highlighted specific examples within Brazil's federal public administration. As a Policy analysis research object, M&E functions should be addressed via several types of comparative studies between different Brazilian ministries, state and municipal governments, and Brazil and other countries. It would also be important to compare government practices with how other actors (for example, international bodies and interest groups) perceive and perform evaluation.

Finally, in conclusion, let us reiterate that knowledge produced through policy evaluation also relates more broadly to policy analysis: both are types of knowledge that can be seen as part of a more general process of producing more professional, enlightened and transparent ways to rule (Vaitsman and Paes-Sousa, 2011). Increasing the state's capacity and expanding democracy in the digital age entail requirements of their own and there is often a tension between them (Sabatier, 1995), but they are both challenges of our times that cannot be renounced.

Notes

[1.] There are many ways to classify evaluation activities (cf Ala-Harja and Helgason, 2000; Kusek and Rist, 2004). This chapter considers three types: evaluation before programmes are decided on and implemented (*ex ante*), evaluation during implementation (*ongoing*) and evaluation of policy outcomes and impacts (*ex post*). Following Wollmann (2007: 393–5), performance-monitoring activities are considered a type of evaluation concomitant with policy implementation.

[2.] For support regarding the ethical and political division between policy evaluation and policy analysis, see Geva-May and Pai (1999). For the role of knowledge and the political dimension of policy evaluation, see Faria (2003, 2005). For a brief introduction to research on policy evaluation, see Arretche (1998) and Wollmann (2007).

[3.] Although accounting audits are not considered monitoring and evaluation activities as such (Wollmann, 2007, p 393), they were important as forerunners of democratic transparency and fund accountability practices. Operational auditing is a type of continuous evaluation similar to the institutional performance and effectiveness monitoring of operations, information systems, administrative methods and the organisations themselves, as well as the appropriateness and timeliness of strategic decision-making (Araújo, 2008).

[4.] See: http://wikicoi.planalto.gov.br

References

Ala-Harja, M. and Helgason, S. (2000) 'Em direção às melhores práticas de avaliação', *Revista do Serviço Público*, vol 51, no 4, pp 50–58.

Araújo, I.P.S. (2008) *Introdução à Auditoria Operacional* (4th edn), Rio de Janeiro: Editora FGV.

Arretche, M.T.S. (1998) 'Tendências no Estudo sobre Avaliação', in E.M. Rico (ed) *Avaliação de políticas sociais: uma questão em debate*, São Paulo: Cortez, pp 29–39.

Borges, A.H., Pinho, J., Azevedo J.P., Newman J.L., Wenceslau, J., Joppert, M.P. and Carvalho, S.N. (2011) 'A Rede Brasileira de Monitoramento e Avaliação: um relato do processo de sua criação e desenvolvimento', *Revista Brasileira de Monitoramento e Avaliação*, vol 1, no 1, pp 4–17.

Brasil (1988) 'Constituição da República Federativa do Brasil', www2.camara.qov.br/atividadeleqislativa/leqislacao/Constituicoes Brasileiras/con stituicao1988.html/constituicaotextoatualizado ec29.pdf

Brasil Tribunal de Contas da União (2000) *Manual de Auditoria de Natureza Operacional*. Brasília: TCU, Coordenadoria de Fiscalização e Controle, www.lapiedad.orq.ar/base/cap5 archivos/Brasil.pdf

Cepik, M. (1997) 'Informação & Decisão Governamental: Uma Contradição em Termos?', IMAP, Anais do Seminário Informação, Estado e Sociedade. Prefeitura de Curitiba, pp 27–44.

Cepik, M. and Canabarro, D. (2010) *Governança de TI: transformando a administração pública no Brasil*, Porto Alegre: WS Editor.

Conti, M.S. (2008) 'Azia, ou o dia da caça', *Revista Piauí*, no 28, http://revistapiaui.estadao.com.br/edicao-28/o-primeiro-e-o-terceiro-poder/azia-ou-o-dia-da-caca

Cunha, C.G.S. (2006) 'Avaliação de políticas publicas e programas governamentais: tendências recentes e experiências no Brasil', www.scp.rs.qov.br/upload/Avaliacao de Politicas Publicas e Programas Gover namentais.pdf

Dobunskis, L., Howlett, M. and Laylock, D. (2007) *Policy analysis in Canada: the state of the art*, Toronto: University of Toronto Press.

Dulci, O.L. (2010) 'Avaliação de programas sociais: desafios e potenciais na construção de um sistema de informações', *Cadernos de Estudos Desenvolvimento Social em Debate*, no 13, pp 221-37.

Faria, C.A.P. (2003) 'Idéias, conhecimento e políticas públicas: um inventário sucinto das principais vertentes analíticas recentes', *Revista Brasileira de Ciências Sociais*, vol 18, no 51, pp 21-29.

Faria, C.A.P. (2005) 'A política da avaliação de políticas públicas', *Revista Brasileira de Ciências Sociais*, vol 20, no 59, pp 97–110.

Faria, C.A.P. and Filgueiras, C.A.C. (2007) 'As políticas dos sistemas de avaliação da educação básica do Chile e do Brasil', in G. Hochman, M. Arretche and E. Marques (eds) *Políticas Públicas no Brasil*, Rio de Janeiro: Editora FIOCRUZ, pp 327–67.

Garcia, R.O. (2000) 'A reorganização do processo de planejamento do governo federal: o PPA 2000-2003', Texto para discussão no 726, p 45, Brasília: IPEA.

Geva-May, I. and Pai, L.A. (1999) 'Good fences make good neighbours: policy evaluation and policy analysis: exploring the differences', *Evaluation*, vol 5, pp 259–76.

Kusek, J. and Rist, R. (2004) *Ten steps to a results-based monitoring and evaluation system: a handbook for development practitioners*, Washington, DC: World Bank.

Melo, M.A. (1999) 'Estado, governo e políticas públicas', in S. Miceli (ed) *O Que Ler na Ciência Social Brasileira (1970–1995). Ciência Política, v III*, São Paulo: Ed. Sumaré, pp 59–100.

Mesquita, C.S.F. and Bretas, N.L. (2010) *Panorama da Interoperabilidade no Brasil*, Brasília: SLTI-MP.

Rodrigues, R.W.S. (2009) 'A centralidade da informação no campo das políticas públicas', in Ministério do Desenvolvimento Social e Combate a Fome (ed) *Concepção e gestão da proteção social não contributiva no Brasil*, Brasília: MDS–UNESCO, pp 287–303.

Sabatier, P. (1995) 'Political science and public policy', in S. Theodoulou and M. Cahn (eds) *Public policy: the essential readings*, Upper Saddle River, NJ: Prentice Hall.

Serpa, S.M.H. (2010) 'Para que avaliar? Identificando a tipologia, os propósitos e a utilização das avaliações de programas governamentais no Brasil', Masters Thesis, Programa de Pós-Graduação em Administração, Universidade de Brasília (UnB).

Silva, P.L.B. and Costa, N.R.A. (2002) *Avaliação de Programas Públicos: reflexões sobre a experiência brasileira*, Relatório Técnico, Brasília: IPEA-BID, p 60.

Vaitsman, J. and Paes-Sousa, R. (2011) 'Avaliação de programas e profissionalização da gestão pública', *Revista Brasileira de Monitoramento e Avaliação*, vol 1, no 1, pp 18–35.

Vaitsman, J., Rodrigues, R. and Paes-Sousa, R. (2006) *O sistema de avaliação e monitoramento das políticas e programas sociais: a experiência do Ministério do Desenvolvimento Social e Combate à Fome do Brasil*, Policy Papers no 17, Brasil: UNESCO.

Wollmann, H. (2007) 'Policy evaluation and evaluation research', in F. Fischer, G. Miller and M. Sidnay (eds) *Handbook of public policy analysis: theory, politics, and methods*, Boca Raton, FL: CRC Press, pp 393–402.

SEVEN

Privatisation and policy decision-making in Brazil

Licinio Velasco and Armando Castelar Pinheiro

Introduction

In one of the most sweeping privatisation programmes in history, Brazil has transferred control of more than 100 state-owned enterprises (SOEs) to the private sector, thereby raising tens of billions of dollars in revenue, which has helped control spiralling public debt. These results are even more impressive in view of the considerable degree of mistrust that existed in both the Brazilian state and society at the time – as it does to this day – of the market's ability to foster development.

In that respect, privatisation was pursued in Brazil not for ideological reasons, but rather as an instrument of economic policy intended to solve the (mainly macroeconomic) problems that plagued the country. That is, although the privatisation process reached its peak during the administration of Fernando Henrique Cardoso, it had begun in the 1980s and evolved over time as society gained confidence in the techniques used to divest enterprises to private investors.

The privatisation process features prominently in public policy analysis in Brazil for a number of reasons: its size and duration; its structurally adverse, but conjuncturally favourable, political and economic context; and the extent to which its success hinged on the autonomy and initiative of a specific public agency, the National Economic and Social Development Bank (Banco Nacional de Desenvolvimento Econômico e Social; BNDES). As will be shown, the BNDES's role was decisive, even though to some extent fortuitous. The rather accidental way the BNDES engaged with the process influenced its own rules and mode of implementation, which in turn were fundamental in assuring the programme's survival at more critical moments.

This chapter will examine: first, how the privatisation process took place in terms of its motivations, historical process and implementation; and, second, the role played by the BNDES. It is structured into five sections. The second section discusses the historical context and how, from a policy rejected ideologically by a country accustomed to state leadership in the economy, privatisation came to be accepted as the best instrument to solve a variety of economic problems. The third section examines the macroeconomic motivations that dominated the dynamics of this process, as well as the political constraints that had to be overcome and which helped shape privatisation in Brazil. The fourth section discusses how historically the BNDES engaged in this process and the role its peculiar technical and administrative structure played in shaping implementation. The final section summarises the main conclusions and speculates briefly as to future prospects.

In addition to analysing the privatisation process in different cycles of government, this chapter considers the role of the BNDES as a strategic agent and the development and strengthening of sectors of the bank with the capacity to identify problems and produce solutions. The bank's participation in the protracted process examined here has incremental and competence-development characteristics that were passed on from administration to administration. The processes analysed in this study suggest that the bank's gain in organisational capacity accompanied privatisation outcomes and also that the sectors and staffs involved in producing solutions operated in the traditional sphere of policy analysis.

The beginnings of privatisation: the pragmatism of Figueiredo and Sarney

The earliest discussions of privatisation in Brazil date from the mid-1970s. The deteriorating economic conditions and the decision by the government that took office in March 1974 to reduce private sector influence on decisions about how to allocate public savings led to the first objections to increased state participation in the economy. The government responded to this movement by proposing to strengthen domestic private companies through tax and credit subsidies, but without restricting the expansion of state enterprises, and much less considering their sale. On the question of privatisation, the government noted that it would not attack the essence of the development problem: filling the 'gaps' in the production structure (Pessanha, 1981, p 122).

It was seen as harmful to Brazil's interests to do more than strengthen private firms. The government continued to prioritise industrialisation via the 'occupation' of what were considered 'strategic' sectors, which domestic private companies were not equipped to do and from the 'national security' standpoint, it was not desirable to allow foreign companies to do. Accordingly, it remained to be done by state enterprises.

In the late 1970s, Brazil's macroeconomic situation worsened once again and the economic policy priority became to control inflation and the external deficit. Rapid expansion of the entrepreneurial state came to be inconsistent with the goal of stabilisation. On the other hand, the idea of privatisation began to permeate government discourse more seriously, although practical consequences were lacking. Also in 1979, the government set up the Special Secretariat for Oversight of State Enterprises (Secretaria Especial de Controle das Empresas Estatais; SEST) for the purpose of restraining the growth of state enterprises.

This brought about a change in public policy objectives and instruments imposed by macroeconomic imbalance, which deprived the government of degrees of freedom. Since the state enterprises were responsible for a great deal of domestic investment and consumption, it would be almost impossible to stabilise the economy without some form of control over their spending. Privatisation would be no help; what was more, divestment of large SOEs was still regarded as a byword for denationalisation of the economy.

Not until 1981 did privatisation formally enter the economic policy agenda. In July of that year, Brazil's president set up the Special Committee on Destatisation (Comissão Especial de Desestatização; CED), and established a set of rules for the transfer, conversion and disposal of enterprises controlled by the federal administration.

The CED identified 140 SOEs that could be privatised in the short term, 50 of which were initially shortlisted for sale. However, only 20 SOEs were sold, one leased and eight incorporated with other public institutions, generating revenue of only US$190 million. Together these enterprises totalled US$274 million in assets and employed less than 5,000 workers. In the same period, six private companies on the verge of bankruptcy had been incorporated by the BNDES in the so-called 'hospital operations'.

In the democratic period, under the Sarney administration (March 1985 to March 1990), privatisation continued with the same institutional structure centred on the CED and at the same pace, although the rhetoric was more aggressive. In all, 18 companies were sold, another 18 transferred to state governments, two were incorporated into other federal institutions and four were closed down. Most of these companies were small or medium-sized and engaged in sectors dominated by private enterprise. The assets of the SOEs privatised during this period totalled US$2.5 billion, and these companies employed a total of 27,600 people. Overall, privatisations during the Sarney administration generated revenue of US$533 million.

In the 1980s, privatisation policy remained largely disconnected from the major national issues, focusing rather on small businesses where there was no justification for state ownership. Crucial in this context was the relative autonomy enjoyed by the groups responsible for managing this process in the federal bureaucracy. Prominent here was the BNDES, which regarded privatisation as a means to improve the financial health of its subsidiary, the National Economic and Social Development Bank Equity S.A. (Banco Nacional para o Desenvolvimento Econômico e Social Participações S.A.; BNDESPAR), whose 'hospital operations' had left it holding numerous problematical companies that were a drain on its capital and managerial resources. In an article published in the newspaper *Folha de São Paulo*, Marcio Fortes, president of the BNDES at the close of the Sarney administration, expressed the issue as follows:

> Actually, privatisation was not such a central policy. It was the BNDES that needed first to generate revenue from its own assets and second to obtain liquidity for its normal activities. Then, thirdly, its own internal administration was greatly hampered by the build-up of management acts necessary daily, because the bank owned or controlled more than 25 highly complex enterprises. (Fortes, 1994)

Privatisation under Collor, Franco and Cardoso: macroeconomic considerations first

From 1990, when the Collor government took office, privatisation became a central component of economic policy and more strongly linked to macroeconomic management. This prominence resulted from several factors: domestic and international political changes, reorientation of economic development strategy, worsening performance by public enterprises and macroeconomic policy needs.

The emphasis on risks to national security, and of denationalising the economy, lost importance during this period. To a large extent, this shift can be credited to democratisation and the departure of the military, together with the end of the Cold War, which fostered a more open international environment. The end of

East–West conflict eased the pressure to keep industries such as telecommunications, oil and electricity under state or national control for strategic reasons. The same process occurred in countries of the Organisation for Economic Co-operation and Development (OECD), especially in Western Europe.

The development strategy changed, the focus shifting from capital accumulation – presented as a concern to 'occupy empty spaces' – to an approach directed more to increasing efficiency and productivity. Consequently, the very existence of SOEs as an instrument of economic policy began to lose meaning. For that very reason, the National Destatisation Programme (Programa Nacional de Desestatização; PND) was launched simultaneously with trade liberalisation and deregulation of the economy.

The declining performance of SOEs also helped generate support for privatisation. In the second half of the 1980s, management positions in SOEs began to be allocated on a party-political basis, leaving them, with few exceptions, top-heavy and particularly inefficient. Some of these companies were brought to the edge of bankruptcy, as occurred with the iron and steel enterprise, Companhia Siderúrgica Nacional (CSN), and the aeronautical enterprise, Empresa Brasileira de Aeronáutica S.A. (Embraer). To accommodate rising payroll and current costs, investment in these companies was reduced. The enterprises' public image deteriorated.

However, it was the weak performance of the economy in the late 1980s that provided the strongest driving force to overcome the inertia and broaden the scope of privatisation. On the one hand, this was because the government lost leeway in conducting interventionist policies, which forced it to pursue more liberal, market-oriented strategies and, on the other, because of the increased need to control spending by SOEs at a time when these enterprises needed to invest heavily to modernise and expand output.

Not only did the Treasury lack funds to invest and implement a sustained industrial policy, but investment financing for state companies dried up for another less obvious reason: as the public sector banks account for almost all long-term credit in Brazil and as, for political and legal reasons, they were unable to execute the guarantees offered by these enterprises, the SOEs did not bother to pay their debts, becoming bad credit risks.

As a result, in the mid-1980s public banks were prohibited from granting loans to SOEs. It therefore became necessary to privatise these enterprises so that they could borrow and thus finance their investments. As private companies, they could offer their creditors collateral assets that could be executed in case of default. That was the common ground that permitted a tacit coalition between those who believed that the state should remove itself permanently from business activities and those who saw privatisation as a necessary evil.

On the original rationale for the PND, it was organically dependent on the stabilisation programme launched at the start of the Collor government, which explains the new government's decision to privatise quickly and regardless of the context of macroeconomic instability. This synergy did not materialise due to problems in both privatisation and stabilisation programmes. The PND started out with excessively optimistic goals in terms of revenue and time frame, which proved unachievable in view of the SOEs' poor financial situation and the complexity of their stockholder agreements.

It was not until late 1991 that the first enterprise was sold through the PND. It was also at that time that the savings in *cruzados novos* retained by the Central Bank began to be returned to savers, so that they could hardly be used as privatisation currency. Thus, although revenue from privatisation was in fact used to reduce public debt, the symbiosis originally designed to exist between the PND and the stabilisation programme had to be abandoned, and other types of public debt were used as privatisation currency.

With the failure of the Collor plan, the government came to rely on the PND as proof of its commitment to structural change. This meant that the programme was maintained, even after Collor was impeached and succeeded by Itamar Franco, who had publicly come out in opposition to privatisation as Vice-President. Nonetheless, rising inflation and slow growth reduced the already depressed levels of domestic and foreign investment, severely limiting the scope of privatisation.

In all, 33 enterprises were privatised during the administrations of Fernando Collor and Itamar Franco (1990–94), generating total revenue of US$8.6 billion and transferring US$3.3 billion in debt to the private sector. Almost all the enterprises privatised were in the manufacturing industry, concentrated mostly in the petrochemical, steel and fertiliser sectors. The enterprises selected for sale had in common the fact that they belonged to relatively competitive sectors.

From 1995, the scope of privatisation expanded greatly to cover infrastructure sectors and included more prominent SOEs, such as Companhia Vale do Rio Doce. In total, the 80 privatisations concluded in the period 1995–98 yielded revenue of US$60.1 billion and transferred US$13.3 billion in debt to the private sector. Two almost simultaneous movements led to that expansion: the end of public sector monopolies in infrastructure sectors and state governments' decision to pursue privatisation programmes of their own.

Several factors contributed to these two movements. First, in the past, failure to control inflation had limited governments' political prestige and ability to pursue a bold privatisation programme. The success of the Real Plan in stabilising prices gave the Cardoso administration the political strength necessary to amend the Constitution to allow private sector participation in telecommunications and the distribution of piped gas, as well as to facilitate its expansion in mining and electricity.

Second, to maintain price stability the government needed to impose fiscal discipline, which restricted its ability to finance the major investments needed by state enterprises in order to increase output at the pace required by renewed economic growth. Also, for fiscal reasons, as discussed earlier, economic policy limited SOEs' access to domestic and external financing. One of the main objectives of privatisation during this period was to increase investment in privatised enterprises, particularly in infrastructure sectors.

Third, the states saw privatisation as an important source of financing that would enable them to reduce their debt and, in some cases, expand spending. In addition, renegotiation of states' debts to the federal government involved a requirement that states amortise part of the principal at the outset, which could be done with proceeds from the sale of their assets, that is, through privatisation. An additional stimulus was given by the states' contracts with the BNDES, which enabled them to anticipate these revenues by taking out loans secured against income from future privatisations.

Fourth, prices had stabilised and perceptions of risk and market growth potential had changed for the better, as reflected, for example, in increased foreign direct investment, all of which helped boost the value of SOEs, making privatisation more attractive.

Fifth, the success of privatisations conducted between 1991 and 1994, reflected in the increased efficiency of and investment in the privatised enterprises, helped attract support for the programme, in that it highlighted the problems with SOEs and the prospects for these companies to grow in private hands.

For a number of reasons, the privatisation process slowed almost to a halt during Fernando Henrique Cardoso's second term (1999–2002). Three key reasons explain its decline in importance and pace: first, popular support for the government faded significantly after the (maxi) devaluation of the *real* in January 1999, eroding the political capital it needed to push through a programme that always faced opposition from considerable portions of society; second, the fiscal adjustment programme that had just started and the fall in the trade deficit due to devaluation greatly diminished the role of privatisation in controlling public debt and external financing; and, third, as privatisation had advanced in previous years, so the sectors that remained under state ownership were generally those that were harder to transfer to the private sector, particularly through the institutional apparatus underpinning the PND.

Nevertheless, some important privatisations were carried through in the second Cardoso administration, notably, the sale of the São Paulo State bank, Banespa. Also, during this period, the models for private sector concessions were refined, including sectors such as ports and highways, and would later serve the Lula administration as a framework. Without the strong connection with macroeconomic imperatives, however, privatisation was not to regain the importance it had enjoyed in the 1990s.

The National Economic and Social Development Bank and the implementation of privatisations[1]

The foregoing sections described the necessary conditions for privatisation to occur in the Sarney, Collor, Franco and Cardoso administrations; however, that is not to say that they were sufficient to permit implementation. To understand that implementation means, to a large extent, understanding the role of the BNDES.

The BNDES was set up in 1952 for the purpose of financing industry and infrastructure projects. In addition to this form of support, in 1974, the bank was authorised to capitalise domestic private companies through temporary minority shareholdings, and set up subsidiaries that operated in the areas of capital assets, commodities and consumer goods. In July 1982, the successor to these subsidiaries, BNDESPAR, was constituted as a wholly-owned subsidiary of BNDES, concentrating share subscription activities in a single institution.

Accordingly, it is important to note that, in addition to its traditional functions that enabled it to train technical staffs in project evaluation, as of 1974, through its equity participation activities, the BNDES also acquired capacity in company appraisals.

The economic crisis that assailed Brazil's economy in the late 1970s and early 1980s forced the Bank to bail out a number of domestic private groups whose investments matured during the crisis. To the extent that these groups were unable to pay off the BNDES financing, it was converted into capital, with the Bank gaining a controlling interest as a result. The BNDESPAR was tasked with conducting the privatisation of these companies. This function would be consolidated in later administrations as, progressively and adaptively, the BNDES system was structured organisationally to play a role in support of a broader policy of privatisation.

Sarney period: March 1985–March 1990

The Inter-ministerial Privatisation Council (Conselho Interministerial de Privatização) was set up in 1985, and later replaced by the Federal Destatisation Council (Conselho Federal de Desestatização). As shown earlier, however, this did not mean that privatisations were in fact a priority on the public agenda in the Sarney administration, but functioned more as a response to the new international context and to diffuse demands for an end to state ownership.

Nevertheless, decrees passed after 1985 introduced innovations that gave visibility to the programme, including the requirements that: sales should be conducted through public mechanisms on stock exchanges; the enterprises should be evaluated by private consultancy firms; and the sale process should be monitored by audit firms to ensure transparency and compliance with law.

Of the 18 privatisations during the Sarney period, 11 involved companies controlled by the BNDES. Another two, of enterprises belonging to the state-owned steel-holding SIDERBRAS, were also conducted by BNDESPAR under contract as privatisation agent (SIDERBRAS decided to avail itself of BNDESPAR's institutional support, given its experience in evaluating companies, which by then qualified it beyond question to manage privatisation processes). Of the total funds raised in sales of state assets in the period, 98% were obtained, directly or indirectly, through management by BNDESPAR.

On a view similar to that of the BNDES president at the time, Schneider (1991, pp 29–31) argues that privatisations during this period resulted much more from the actions of the BNDES than from those of the Conselho Federal de Desestatização. Indeed, the BNDES committed to the privatisation programme believing that it constituted a mechanism for recovering the economic and financial capacity it needed to play its development role. More than 50% of the amount it disbursed in the period 1982–85 was concentrated in enterprises controlled by BNDESPAR, mostly to fund the subsidiaries' current spending, while sidelining the investments in minority shareholdings for which it had originally been set up.

Not without reason, from 1986 on, BNDESPAR's annual action plans advocated the sale of its subsidiaries. Funding for these companies began to be released more selectively, and disbursements to them were progressively cut back until they became negligible in 1989, which, from 1988 onwards, contributed to reversing BNDESPAR's own negative results.

Another important aspect is that BNDESPAR acted as a *privatisation agent* for the SIDERBRAS group. This policy helped offset BNDES liabilities, since the bank held credit with the SIDERBRAS system. These privatisations operated on the same logic as the others in that they involved enterprises in notoriously difficult situations in which the BNDES held equity. The expectation was to find new controllers who could put the enterprises to rights and improve the quality of the credit, replacing non-executable state debtors with executable private ones.

In summary, during the Sarney administration, the BNDES's interest in recovering the freedom of action necessary for it to fulfil its role in support of domestic private companies decisively favoured the implementation of privatisation in this period, while qualifying the bank to manage the PND in the next administration.

Collor period: March 1990–December 1992

Privatisations entered the public agenda explicitly under Collor when the PND was set up by law. The BNDES was chosen to manage the programme not only for its prior experience, but also because it was a public institution with expertise, through BNDESPAR, in company evaluation. The PND allowed debts of SOEs under National Treasury responsibility to be accepted as a form of payment, provided that such debts were converted into Treasury-certified securities, which would then be freely negotiable with third parties interested in acquiring shares through the PND.

This form of financing privatisation enhanced the opportunities envisaged by the BNDES during the Sarney administration, when it received the delegation to sell off enterprises of the SIDERBRAS group. From its exposure to the steel industry – one of the main generators of such debts, given the insolvency of the SIDERBRAS holding and many of its enterprises – the BNDES held credits totalling the equivalent of approximately US$1.7 billion. Ultimately, this value represented the steel industry's potential default with the BNDES, which had been masked by serial rescheduling.[2]

In summary, the BNDES's role progressed from privatisation agent for SIDERBRAS to manager of the PND, while it also took on the function of financing investors through the sale of its certified securities. This strengthens the argument of organisational competences acquired progressively and associated with a capacity for strategic analysis. On the other hand, the question arose of how to gain support for the programme. Collor took office without either a party base or organised support from segments of society. The votes he won granted diffuse support for the anti-statist discourse of his election campaign, without that necessarily meaning that they would convert into support for anti-state intervention sentiments, to be expressed as privatisation policy. In short, Collor did not in fact hold a *neoliberal mandate* (Schneider, 1992, section II).

Moreover, privatisations do not qualify as an easy-to-implement reform, because they involve uncertain benefits to society and concentrated costs for beneficiaries of the status quo, facilitating collective action by the segments affected. Observation of models for implementing privatisation in other countries revealed that no models were appropriate to just any country or historical context. Two experiences will serve as examples:

- UK: large-scale share sales at fixed prices, giving no priority to the amount that might be raised by selling control in the companies; and
- France: directed privatisation, with the government structuring groups of shareholders to acquire control of the companies.

As, at that time, privatisation in Brazil was connected with the expectation of reducing public debt, neither was appropriate: the British model because it entailed low sale values, and the French model because it required a capacity for intervention that the Brazilian state did not have at the time (Diniz, 1995, pp 401–3).

As a rule, privatisation processes during the Sarney period followed a model by which control was sold in the form of single blocks of shares, as justified by the fact that most of the enterprises privatised had no history of profitability or an economic scale offering the prospect of shared equity control. Not only was this a one-winner model, but it also induced outcomes in which these winners were the leading companies in the sectors of the enterprises being sold.

This revenue-maximising model, although compatible with one of the objectives of the PND, nonetheless went against the general view in the literature, which recommends expanding the number of winners as a way of gaining support for implementing reform policies. Schneider's observation that the Collor administration was not in fact neoliberal, plus the greater visibility of a programme of the magnitude of the PND, were also indicators of the importance of a sale model that would allow there to be more winners.

The BNDES tackled this issue by selecting a lead case that would allow the model to be modified while signalling a choice that represented a break with the past in an effort to build up business confidence. That lead case was to be Usiminas, a company of substantial size that was technologically up to date and the only profitable business in the iron and steel industry.

The model of sale adopted for Usiminas did not define in advance how control of the company should be formatted on conclusion of the sale. The government's block of shares was offered with no requirement for a strategic investor with experience in the industry or any specification of minimum quantities to be purchased. Basically, all that was required was advance proof of the ability to pay. The outcome of the auction could be, at one extreme, acquisition of the block of shares by a single buyer or, at the other, broadly pulverised share control. The new model thus filled the gap identified by the literature in that it permitted a greater number of beneficiaries, but with no guarantee that this would occur.

Indeed, the structure of voting capital in Usiminas, after sale, proved to be formatted completely differently from hitherto existing patterns in Brazil. Investors with what, in theory, were divergent interests became involved in unprecedented shared ownership. The final share structure comprised industrial companies, financial institutions and state pension funds, with the major shareholder holding only 15% of the voting capital. The model's success was proven repeatedly in the Collor and Franco periods for almost all equity sales of significant value, generating a broad spectrum of shareholding formats similar to those that occurred in the Usiminas sale.

What is fundamental is that this model was formatted at a crucial time, early in the implementation of the PND, for the privatisation of a company of acknowledged importance, thus cementing an unprecedented coalition of support from potential investors. Once this supporting coalition was formed, the BNDES, as programme manager, gained the leeway to seek flexibilities in the model with time.

Itamar Franco Period: December 1992–December 1994

After Collor's impeachment, Itamar Franco took office as president in an atmosphere of strong mistrust of the policies implemented during the previous period. Attitudes to the PND were no different, and a substantial review was to be expected. From the outset, major privatisation auctions suspended included Ultrafertil, a fertiliser enterprise belonging to the Petrobras Group, and the emblematic national iron and steel enterprise, CSN. In addition, a Joint Parliamentary Committee of Inquiry was installed to investigate facts resulting from execution of the National Destatisation Programme.

At the close of the Franco administration, however, surprising results came to light. Holding to the course charted by the previous administration, the PND had carried out 17 privatisation processes, raising a total equivalent to US$4.7 billion. Franco had outperformed the Collor administration, which was really unexpected for a president not identified with liberalising positions. Among the companies auctioned were Ultrafertil and CSN, each sold for almost exactly the previously stipulated minimum price. Apart from the episode that led to the postponement of the Ultrafertil and CSN auctions, the programme made no substantial changes in course. The final report by the parliamentary commission of inquiry supported the continuation of the PND.

The *Usiminas model of sale* continued in place, providing the support network that had sustained the PND during the Collor period. This coalition triumphed over other forces calling for the PND to be discontinued or its brief reviewed. On the other hand, the state's lack of intervention capacity also showed in its inability to alter the previous policy for want of the political resources to captain a reconfiguration of alliances.

Fernando Henrique Cardoso period: January 1995–December 2002

When Cardoso took office, there was less opposition to the policy of privatisation, because the Brazilian state's capacity for governance had increased, as reflected in the election of a president supported by a clearly defined parliamentary coalition. Privatisation of public services was to provide the opportunity to make changes in the *Usiminas model*. The change is not difficult to explain technically. On the one hand, the existence of a controlling group defined and constituted in advance met the requirements of the regulatory agencies.[3] On the other, given the scarcity of domestic capital on which to draw for the amounts involved in these privatisations, sale in a single block would attract foreign capital by reducing investor uncertainty as to the funds to be mobilised and the partners they would have to work with.

From the implementation standpoint, this change was possible not only because privatisation no longer bore the stigma of a move away from the concept of the state as the main driving force behind development, which society was used to, but also because the government now had the support of society as the users of public services that were notoriously inadequate, which offset the loss of support resulting from modification of the *Usiminas model*.

Three important privatisation processes from this period are discussed in the following. The privatisation of Companhia Vale do Rio Doce (CVRD) involved the first significant change to the *Usiminas model* and took place amid intense controversy, with a profusion of lawsuits filed to halt the auction. Some features of this privatisation help understand this fact: the sale was made in a single block, the maximum number of shares that could be purchased by companies in the steel and mining sectors was restricted, and the new controllers were required to include previously defined provisions in their articles of incorporation. This meant a smaller number of winners and a break with the concept of non-interference underlying the *Usiminas model*. By opting for directed privatisation, the government lost the support of investors unused to being excluded in advance from negotiations with previously formed groups.

Unlike the situation with public services, there was no compensatory support from society, which in this case would benefit only diffusely from privatisation of a company that was perceived as an efficient SOE. Not surprisingly, then, privatisation of CVRD encountered strong resistance. On the other hand, despite all the difficulties, the very fact that the government had privatised a flagship company such as CVRD signalled a governance capacity acquired during the Cardoso period for this type of public policy.

Although the PND law delegates to the executive, several bills were introduced in the Senate to stop the privatisation process. As CVRD's activities were concentrated significantly in certain states of the federation, even senators of the governing coalition from these states were willing to support bills sponsored by the opposition. This was prevented only because the government was able to negotiate with the Senate Committee on Infrastructure to arrive at a privatisation that took into account the demands of the legislature and society. The bases of this negotiation were structured and incorporated by the BNDES into the call for expressions of interest in the sale of the company, as part of the obligations to be assumed by the new controlling group (Velasco, 2005, ch 4).

The government's commitment to privatising CVRD was also connected with the goal of maintaining exchange rate stability, on which the Real Plan rested. It signalled a commitment to market reforms, allowing greater volumes of external funds to be raised for other critical projects on its agenda, such as privatisation of the telecommunications industry.

Privatisation of Telebras, the state telecommunications holding, derived from the overall divestment of the sector by the state, as framed by three federal laws: EC 8 – a constitutional amendment that flexibilised the state monopoly of telecommunications; Law 9295/96 – on rules for operating mobile telephony services; and LGT (Lei Geral das Telecomunicações) – a law setting up the regulatory agency for the sector and stipulating conditions for restructuring and privatising the Telebras system.

The constitutional amendment and Law 9295 marked the start of privatisation of the sector, allowing the Ministry of Communications to call for tenders for concessions of B Band mobile telephony, which was not owned by Telebras. The Telebras system was restructured by splits that resulted in 12 state holdings: three grouping the wireline telephony operators, eight the A Band mobile operators, and one a long-distance carrier. The sale of these holdings yielded the most significant privatisation revenues, equivalent to US$18.9 billion (US$26.6 billion including the B Band sales).

The BNDES, like the PND before it, was chosen by the Ministry of Communications to implement the privatisation of the 12 holdings, and the model of sale was constructed to meet the ownership restrictions of the LGT law. In privatisations at the state level, the role the BNDES played was to support the Ministry of Finance's policy of restoring public finances to health through the State Restructuring and Fiscal Adjustment Programme.

During 1997 and 1998, most states renegotiated their debts, transferring a significant portion to the federal government. Those renegotiations contained clauses stipulating that part of the amortisation would be covered by revenues from state privatisations. At the states' discretion, the BNDES supported these privatisations technically and financially under cooperation agreements, playing the role of manager – as under the PND – and advanced funding to be reimbursed from sales. One illustration of how the BNDES adapted organisationally to play its role in support of the privatisation policy is that it set up a special department to conduct these state privatisations.

Final remarks

In his 1979 inaugural speech, President Figueiredo supported the privatisation of state enterprises that were not necessary for national security, a key concern to an authoritarian regime during the Cold War, but whose influence declined in subsequent years. In 1981, the government formally inaugurated the privatisation process in Brazil by setting up the Federal Destatisation Commission. The Figueiredo administration and all the governments to follow would engage in privatisation. The process grew steadily, reaching its peak in the first term of Fernando Henrique Cardoso (1995–98). From Cardoso's second term on, the programme lost importance, but was never completely abandoned.

The longevity of the privatisation process in Brazil, and its dynamics in terms of the sectors covered and models used, resulted from two main factors. First, the programme has always been approached pragmatically as the best solution to specific problems, from fostering macro-stability to permitting public financing. Accordingly, it was no coincidence that privatisation gained in intensity when its relation to macroeconomic policy became more central.

Three main macroeconomic objectives led to the privatisations of the 1980s and 1990s:

- From the Sarney administration onwards, advancing privatisation came to signal a commitment to reforms, a way of indicating to the foreign investors and multilateral organisations who financed Brazil's external deficit that groups committed to responsible macroeconomic policy retained a significant degree of influence in the government.
- When privatisation reached infrastructure sectors, it came to be seen as the only way to raise investment in critical sectors.
- The privatisation of large state enterprises went on to generate considerable volumes of revenue, which was used almost entirely to pay off debt, thus helping to improve the quality of fiscal indicators, whose trajectories at the time were verging on the unsustainable. In the first Cardoso administration, foreign investment driven by privatisation also helped finance a significant portion of the external deficit.

Fiscal adjustment measures and exchange devaluation at the beginning of Cardoso's second term made privatisation less important to ensuring macroeconomic adjustment. This occurred simultaneously with a change in the profile of the remaining SOEs, whose potential for generating revenues and attracting foreign investors, given the regulatory framework in place at the time, was not as strong as in the telecommunications sector.

The second key element was the role played by the BNDES, which was managing not only the PND, but also the processes conducted by the states and the Ministry of Telecommunications. The bank's engagement in the privatisation process was also pragmatic, but its concentrated stock of public expertise on how to sell SOEs not only made it an enabler of the process, but also created an institutional inertia that helped it to carry the process forward in politically more troubled times.

Privatisation in Brazil thus constitutes an important case where a public agency plays a central role in implementing a policy of major national impact. The factors that contributed to this included not only the historical circumstances outlined earlier, but also the model of governance of the bank's activities, which affords it a fair degree of political and operational independence. In fact, it could be argued that this process became bidirectional: while the BNDES's autonomy in terms of fund availability, technical quality and administrative flexibility enabled it to carry privatisation further than would have been possible for agencies of the direct administration, the autonomy granted to the bank at moments when it was not in the government's interest to associate too directly with the PND created a culture of autonomy and a technical reputation in civil society that would later lead to this autonomy being extended to other BNDES activities.

These factors contributed to further privatisations, even under presidents who had previously opposed the programme, such as Itamar Franco, Lula da Silva and, most recently, Dilma Rousseff. Noteworthy are the privatisations of banks and highways conducted under the Lula administration, and under Rousseff, the private airport concessions driven by mounting demand for air transport in Brazil and the notorious difficulties faced by the public sector in conducting airport infrastructure expansion projects. The airport concessions currently ongoing are being conducted by the Department of Civil Aviation, reporting to the presidency and unsurprisingly led, at the time of this study, by staff recruited from the BNDES.

Under Lula da Silva, in a process of organisational adaptation to government priorities, the BNDES has set up an area designed to promote the structuring of infrastructure projects to be supported by the bank, with private sector participation, in sectors previously occupied predominantly by the state, such as airports and ports. That area can currently be said to fulfil the institutional role played by BNDESPAR in previous administrations, of supporting the reconfiguration of state-managed economic activities.

Notes

[1] For a detailed account of part of the arguments of this section, see Velasco (1996, 2010).

[2] This value can be compared as a percentage of total BNDES disbursements in 1988, 1989 and 1990: US$5.4 billion (31.5%), US$4.3 billion (39.5%) and US$2.6 billion (65.4%), respectively.

[3] ANEEL (Agência Nacional de Energia Elétrica – ANEEL LIGHT S.A), the electric power sector regulatory agency, was set up in December 1996 after privatisation of LIGHT, an electricity distributor, which had retained the same structure as the Usiminas model.

References

Diniz, E. (1995) 'Governabilidade, democracia e reforma do estado: o desafio da construção de uma nova ordem no Brasil dos anos 90', *Dados*, vol 38, no 3, pp 385–415.

Fortes, M. (1994) 'Integração competitiva e privatização', *Jornal A Folha de São Paulo*, 19 October.

Pessanha, C.F. (1981) 'Estado e economia no Brasil: a campanha contra a estatização', Masters Thesis, Rio de Janeiro, IUPERJ.

Schneider, B.R. (1991) 'A política de privatização no Brasil e no México nos anos 80: variações em torno do tema estatísta', *Dados*, vol 34, no 1, pp 21–51.

Schneider, B.R. (1992) 'A privatização no governo Collor: triunfo do liberalismo ou colapso do Estado desenvolvimentista?', *Revista de Economia Política*, vol 12, no 1, pp 5–18.

Velasco, L., Jr (1996) 'A política de privatizações e a reforma do Estado no Brasil: uma análise do período 1985/96', Masters Thesis, IUPERJ.

Velasco, L., Jr (2005) 'A política pública de privatização no presidencialismo de coalizão brasileiro', PhD dissertation, IUPERJ.

Velasco, L., Jr (2010) 'A privatização no Sistema BNDES', *Revista do BNDES*, no 33, pp 307–82.

EIGHT

Production of policy-related information and knowledge in Brazil: the state government agencies

Cristina Almeida Cunha Filgueiras and Carlos Alberto Vasconcelos Rocha

Introduction

Particularly since the mid-20th century, there has been a growing trend worldwide to value knowledge as the bedrock of public decision-making. It is thus increasingly necessary for public decision-makers to have access to the results of good research. This need is reflected in a consensus on the idea that public policy analysis can contribute to offering solutions to collective problems. Accordingly, there is growing appreciation for research on this subject, and mounting demand for professional qualification in public bureaucracies.

The need to produce knowledge for public decision-making has loomed large in the state-building process in a number of countries – and Brazil was no exception. Activities to produce knowledge bearing on public policies, especially under the authoritarian regime installed in 1964, were conducted only in specific institutions of state. As Brazil had adopted a federative system, such institutions were initially set up by the federal government, and only later spread to various state governments. During the 1980s, public policy analysis began to become established in the universities, in theory, offering the prospect of producing research that was more critical of the government and greater freedom in selecting theories and methods (Melo, 1999).

This chapter examines the presence in the policy analysis field in Brazil of state government agencies that produce policy-related information and knowledge. The chapter takes a broad view of public policy analysis, spanning both studies from the 1960s, which embodied generalist approaches related to the agenda of the developmentalist state and to government planning, and studies produced from the 1980s on, focusing on specific policy areas and subjects connected with reform of the state (Melo, 1999). Our point of departure is that the role played by state agencies, although differing in importance in the context of the Brazilian federation, is both considerable and under-researched. This chapter will discuss the context in which these institutions emerged and their nature, their institutional format, general aspects of their evolution, and salient features of their role in producing and spreading information and knowledge about conditions in the state and about government activities.

Emergence and evolution of state policy analysis agencies

The federative system has fundamental implications for policymaking. In such a system, decision-making authority is distributed among the territorial spheres of government. The decision-making process is affected by various factors; among them, the distribution of technical capability across levels of government. The case of Brazil must be examined in view of the fact that it is a federation and that policy decision-making prerogatives are distributed across a variety of territorial governments that make up the nation-state.

Another important aspect to be considered as regards the central theme of this study is that modernisation came later to Brazil than to the developed countries. That means that public decision-making incorporated technical analyses in the manner and to the extent possible in a late-developing country. This chapter will argue, however, that the Brazilian case is reasonably synchronous with those of the developed countries as regards the process of laying down the technical groundwork for public decision-making. The transformation of the Brazilian state, which intensified significantly from the 1960s onwards, occurred simultaneously with that of countries such as the US and Canada. The fact that processes of the same kind occurred simultaneously in countries with different degrees of development is explained partly by the fact that 'States are increasingly embedded in an international marketplace of state expertise centred in the academies and related institutions in the United States' (Dezalay and Garth, 2002, p 198). This general trend, however, is nuanced by the specific characteristics of each case. In Brazil, therefore, specific domestic traits account partly for the way policy analysis emerged, as we will endeavour to show below.

This chapter, as mentioned earlier, focuses on state governments. The Brazilian federative system was established in the 1891 Constitution, and Brazilian federalism is currently characterised by the existence of three autonomous levels of government. There are 27 intermediate governments, called states (including the Federal District), and some 5,560 local governments, called municipalities, all with formal political and administrative autonomy, and therefore prerogatives with regard to policy decisions. As federative entities, municipalities enjoy a status similar to that of the Union and the states, thus constituting a threefold federation, which is not very common in the international context. In addition, Brazilian federalism does not reflect ethnic, linguistic and religious divisions, as occurs in some countries. However, the role of regional elites is undeniably important to understanding its politics.

Over time, the dynamics of Brazilian federalism has produced moments of more assertive central government power alternating with others when the power of the intermediate governments grew. During the two authoritarian periods of the past century (1937–45 and 1964–85), the central government undermined the power of the intermediate bodies. At the same time, it endeavoured to ensure that public decisions were produced on a logic of technical rationality, which it did by insulating certain bureaucracies, especially those responsible for promoting policies relating to economic growth and to addressing, however inadequately, the social problems of urban workers (Santos, 1987). Steadily, especially from the 1960s onwards, this protection of the technical core of the state expanded as a means of neutralising the pork-barrel approach, which was functional for purposes of political and electoral competition, but irrational in terms of the stated objectives of public policies. Today, as a result, a considerable portion of the policies addressing economic and social goals have been formulated 'in restricted decision-making arenas dominated by bureaucrats' (Loureiro, 2010, p 108). All the same, it should not be forgotten that the bureaucracy's power as a policymaker has always depended on support or delegation from political players.

With the authoritarian regime imposed by the military in 1964, government planning became systemic in Brazil. The federal government applied itself to preparing long- and medium-range planning, to specifications set out by technicians vested with decision-making power. In this way, state and municipal policies came to be decided by the central government, creating a situation where the sub-national governments were politically and financially highly dependent on the Union. This centralisation of decision-making power led to the states replicating the same institutional structure as at the federal level. In the planning sector, several states, following the pattern set by the central government, created decentralised government agencies, insulated from the logic of political competition. They went on systematically to train a technical staff who enjoyed better labour conditions and pay than the rest of the public administration (Fundação João Pinheiro, 2001; Reis Veloso, 2005). Paradoxically, the central government-induced strengthening of state bureaucracies, pursued for the purpose of providing administrative support for the implementation of federal policy guidelines, also paved the way for some states to embark on projects of their own in any leeway left by central government control.

The characteristics and specific conditions that account for the creation of each state public policy analysis agency, and the role attributed to each of them, varied according to the context and conditions in each state. Common traits and trends can be identified, however. Two defining moments can be distinguished in the way that the state agencies were formed: when the agencies were first set up; and then their adaptation to the changes in the environment they had to submit to in the last quarter of the 20th century. State policy analysis agencies were set up mainly between 1969 and 1978, although there had been some previous endeavours, particularly with a view to collecting and circulating statistics.[1] At a later stage, from the mid-1980s onwards, these agencies had to adapt to the changes underway in Brazil, in the process of political democratisation, and in the world, with the advent of so-called globalisation, and more specifically with the spreading influence of neoliberal principles.

As regards the period during which the state policy analysis agencies were first set up, three factors account for their spread: central government inducement, the state governments' own development strategies and support from international institutions. First and foremost, state policy analysis institutions emerged in the 1960s in connection with the central government's strategy of institutionalising a national planning system, especially as of 1964, when the Planning Ministry and the Institute for Applied Economic Research (Instituto de Pesquisa Econômica Aplicada; IPEA) were set up at the federal government level. In an authoritarian, centralist context, the federal government sought to set up its own agencies and, at the same time, worked to reproduce its endeavour to endow the policymaking process with more technical underpinning in the states. In the 1970s, the IPEA became a reference for the creation of research agencies in Brazil's more developed states. The IPEA, whose mission was institution-building, was one of the major forces behind the propagation of institutionalised state centres for the production of knowledge about public policies through technical and financial support made available to state governments.

Parallel to these central government incentives, the second factor was that certain state governments detected, relatively autonomously, the need to formulate their own economic development policies, and set strategies to reposition themselves to meet the structural changes that the Brazilian economy was undergoing. For that purpose, they began to organise planning systems that attempted to reproduce, on a sub-national scale, the institutional set-up for planning at the federal government level. Accordingly, some states – mostly in the South and Southeast – drew up their own economic and social development strategies, and built institutions to provide the corresponding knowledge and informational support.[2]

The effort expended by some states to set their own policies, even in a context where the central government sought to lay down policy guidelines for the whole country, are connected with the growing regional inequalities within Brazil. In the Brazilian model of industrialisation, São Paulo State was the central dynamo of economic development, heightening its economy's importance over those of the other states of the federation. Accordingly, states like Minas Gerais, Paraná and Rio Grande do Sul attempted to foster conditions for their economic development, and established rules of their own in the gaps in central government dominance.

The states of the North, Northeast and Midwest – Bahia being one of the exceptions – did not have the necessary material and technical base or sufficient internal incentive to develop their own policy analysis agencies. In fact, the development strategies for the first two regions were set by the central government's regional development agencies, respectively the North Development Superintendency (Superintendência de Desenvolvimento do Norte; Sudam), and the Northeast Development Superintendency (Superintendência de Desenvolvimento do Nordeste; Sudene), whose existence seems to have discouraged states from investing in their own institutions. Although São Paulo was Brazil's most developed state, and therefore the best equipped to develop technical institutions to support policymaking, such agencies would not be set up there until the mid-1970s. From then on, they occupied a prominent place among institutions of this type in Brazil. In fact, the central government's plans prioritised economic development in São Paulo State, which consolidated as the dynamic hub of the Brazilian economy. Since São Paulo's interests were considered a priority of central government planning, it can be assumed that there was no urgent need for the state to set up policy analysis agencies of its own.

A paradoxical dynamics was thus set up, in which certain states – those with a higher level of development – would submit to central government planning while, at the same time, striving to attain goals of their own, with a view to improving their standing in the national federative context. That paradox was reflected in the objectives of the state research institutions, which had been created both to support the central government's policies and to cater to the specific economic and social objectives of their respective states.

The third factor that explains the institutionalisation of state policy research agencies relates to the international sphere and is connected largely with the dynamics of relations between the state and universities. As mentioned earlier, the field of public policy studies consolidated in Brazil, at different periods, as a result of the work of established researchers in various institutional settings, that is, universities and government agencies with a specific remit on the subject. The relationship between universities and state agencies that produce knowledge for policy purposes is, to some extent, complementary, given that knowledge and personnel circulate between the two spheres. A number of researchers have worked for both, alternately or simultaneously. Therefore, the establishment of government agencies to produce knowledge about public policy depended, to a certain extent, on the development of a field of public policy studies in the universities, which helped to produce and spread knowledge, and to train personnel.

In that respect, the endeavour to provide scientific grounding for policy decisions benefited strongly from implementation of a national system of postgraduate studies in Brazil, which boosted supply of researchers, both generally and in the political science field specifically. International agencies, particularly the Ford Foundation, funded the setting up of research institutions and granted scholarships for Brazilian researchers to pursue their studies at centres of excellence in the US. The numerous institutions that received Ford Foundation support for the pioneering purpose of training researchers and an elite from the public bureaucracy included several federal universities and autonomous research centres such as the Getúlio Vargas Foundation (Fundação Getúlio Vargas; FGV) and the Brazilian Analysis and Planning Centre (Centro Brasileiro de Análise e Planejamento; CEBRAP). There were thus international agencies helping to build up an intellectual elite, to US standards of academic production, and that elite went on to influence policymaking in Brazil (Forjaz, 1997, p 3).

Universities and state policy analysis agencies thus constituted the two institutional spheres where knowledge on public policy matters was produced and circulated – although each had its own specific emphasis. The government agencies were not simply set the goal of generating knowledge; first and foremost, they were to provide support for government decision-making. The process behind the creation of the IPEA illustrates this difference: it was clear to Reis Veloso, one of its founders, that 'research must be policy-oriented, and not simply academic, because there is no wish to duplicate the academic research carried out in the universities' (Reis Veloso, 2005, p 39).

While, in the early days, at the time those agencies were being set up in the late 1960s and through the 1970s, those agencies were a priority for state governments, there came a second stage, starting in the 1980s, where their importance waned because of a series of factors relating to two almost simultaneous processes: Brazil's political democratisation and the worldwide changes characterised by globalisation and neoliberalism. During the 1980s, a strong movement for political democratisation in Brazil produced trends in favour of restoring true federalism by decentralising political, fiscal and administrative matters towards the states and municipalities. In such a context, where these levels of government were reasserting their power, one might expect moves to strengthen state research agencies as a means of consolidating the increased autonomy achieved in policy decision-making prerogatives. However, the opposite occurred: government policy analysis institutions were hit by a crisis. That this tendency for the research agencies to weaken took hold can be explained by two reasons combined.

First, during the authoritarian periods, the states would obey decisions issued by the central government whose content was highly technical. During the democratisation process, however, they became more resistant to granting decision-making power to technocrats. The reintroduction of democracy brought greater legitimacy to elected governments, in other words, the primacy of political concerns was asserted over technical content. In addition, the existing collaboration between state agencies and the federal government was disrupted to a certain extent by the reassertion of the states' power in dealings with central power. In the new context, the state agencies had to redefine the basis on which they worked, in which they were really not very successful.

In parallel with the democratisation process, a series of events at the international level changed the context surrounding policy planning and analysis activities. In the last quarter of the 20th century, events such as the crisis in capitalism, characterised by economic deceleration and fiscal crisis in most countries, the end of the Cold War, and the globalisation process confronted states with the challenge of 'redefining their very reason for being, as well as their relations with other institutions' (Wilheim, 1999, p 22). The developmentalist outlook that had prevailed since the 1930s, which defined state planning as a means to compensate for 'market flaws', started to be strongly questioned. Concepts based on the virtues of the logic of the market became predominant.

In the early 1990s, both central and state governments in Brazil were deep in fiscal crises and caught up in an escalating process of performance deficit. The policy planning and analysis institutions started to lose substance and effectiveness. As a survival strategy, these institutions started to incorporate marketing mindsets. Some agencies became more aggressive in selling consultancy services, even operating in other states of the federation, which heightened competition in the policy analysis market that was taking shape.

In short, the 1980s marked the start of a period where the existence of public institutions in general was precarious and fraught with crisis, which was also to impact the policy analysis agencies. Certain events in the first decade of the 2000s, however, signalled a revaluation of production in the public sector policy analysis field. In the central government specifically, the IPEA has been taking a steadily more prominent place in the production and distribution of knowledge about Brazilian public policies. In the states, it is generally not yet clear whether their policy analysis agencies are recovering.

The state agencies: an overview

In the second half of 2010, a survey identified 16 policy analysis agencies belonging to 15 states and the Federal District (see Table 8.A1 in the Appendix). In Acre, Alagoas, Amapá, Amazonas, Mato Grosso, Mato Grosso do Sul, Rio Grande do Norte, Rondônia, Roraima, Santa Catarina, Sergipe and Tocantins – nearly half of Brazil's states – no state agencies were identified. In several, however, a sector of the state planning department was found to fulfil part of the basic function performed by state agencies in other states, especially as regards producing and systematising statistical data and geographic information.[3] However, as our study focused on autonomous policy analysis agencies, these states were not included among the agencies identified.[4] What follows is a panorama of the institutions surveyed, giving both their objectives and their activities and fields of operation.

The institutions examined are strikingly diverse in origin and trajectory. Differing political and economic scenarios affected or strongly influenced agencies' trajectories and operations. Each institution has its own defining moments, which reveal periods of flourishing activity and others of contraction, whether in institutional organisation or the menu of services and products offered. The state agencies' activities vary in significance, with a small number of them achieving a more prominent presence that extends beyond the sphere of their state and makes them regional or national references.

Over the whole period considered, there is constant fluctuation and instability among state agencies as a whole. Many of these institutions resulted from mergers of other agencies, while others have either been reformulated or extinguished. It is common for their functions to be changed and/or their structure reorganised, due either to some specific change in the planning area of the state government, or to broader administrative reform in the public administration.

Of the 16 agencies identified at the state level, five – State Data Analysis System Foundation (Fundação Sistema Estadual de Análise de Dados; Fundação SEADE) (São Paulo); Maranhão Socioeconomic and Cartographic Studies Institute (Instituto Maranhense de Estudos Socioeconômicos e Cartográficos; IMESC) (Maranhão); Siegfried Emanuel Heuser Economics and Statistics Foundation (Fundação de Economia e Estatística Siegfried Emanuel Heuser; FEE) (Rio Grande do Sul); Rio de Janeiro State Statistics, Research and Civil Service Training Centre (Centro Estadual de Estatística, Pesquisa e Formação de Servidores Públicos do Rio de Janeiro, Fundação; CEPERJ)[5] (Rio de Janeiro); and Pernambuco State Planning and Research Agency (Agência Estadual de Planejamento e Pesquisas de Pernambuco; CONDEPE) (Pernambuco) – were found to have originated in statistics bureaus. These bodies were responsible for various types of survey, mainly regarding the economy, but, with time, they began to address more diverse subjects, coming to cover social, demographic and geographic information.

The Bahia state government agency (Bahia Economic and Social Studies Superintendency [Superintendência de Estudos Econômicos e Sociais da Bahia; SEI]) founded in 1955, is the oldest of the institutions surveyed. In another seven states, agencies were set up between the early the 1960s and the first half of the 1970s, as mentioned earlier. Apart from SEI, only one was created before the military government of 1964: the Pará Economic Development Council (Conselho de Desenvolvimento Econômico do Pará), which dates from 1961, and would later give way to the Pará Economic, Social and Environmental Development Institute (Instituto de Desenvolvimento Econômico, Social e Ambiental do Pará; IDESP). The other agencies were founded during the military government and, to begin with, were associated with state economic development banks – that was the case with the João Pinheiro Foundation (Fundação João Pinheiro; FJP) (Minas Gerais) and the Paraná Economic and Social Development Institute (Instituto Paranaense de Desenvolvimento Econômico e Social; IPARDES) (Paraná) – or with economic development and planning agencies, as occurred with the Piauí Economic and Social Research Centre Foundation (Fundação Centro de Pesquisa Econômicas e Sociais do Piauí; Fundação CEPRO) (Piauí) and IDESP (Pará).

As already mentioned, there are Brazilian states in all the regions that never set up agencies of this kind. There are signs of federal government inducements to set up planning agencies in these states. These were unsuccessful, however, either because existing central government regional development agencies already performed the knowledge production function in those regions, or because material and technical conditions in certain states were precarious. In the North region, the only state with an institution for public policy analysis is Pará.

The state-level policy analysis agencies generally address a variety of subjects relating to economic, social, political and cultural conditions in the state, doing research and producing information as an input to policy decision-making, and to support the development of government measures, plans and programmes. Each agency tends to emphasise whatever specific issues are most problematical in their state.

Agencies also work with a broad range of kinds of information. This generally includes their producing economic and social indicators, calculating indicators of industrial activity, and calculating the Gross Domestic Product (GDP) of the state and its municipalities, just to mention some of the commonest examples. In addition to basic statistics, a number of agencies produce specific indices relating, for instance, to the performance of their municipalities or the performance of specific economic sectors. However, no evidence was found of such information actually being used by decision-makers and public administrators.

Economic and social concerns have been the most addressed since the agencies were set up. However, other thematic areas came to be included as objects for diagnoses, studies and research as they gained importance on national or each state's policy agendas. Salient here are matters relating to the environment, tourism, culture and urban development. There are also policy assessment studies, many conducted in order to meet contractual requirements by international agencies, such as multilateral development banks.

Also deserving of mention are the intergovernmental cooperation endeavours in which state agencies take part in studies coordinated by national bodies, such as IPEA and the Brazilian Geography and Statistics Institute (Instituto Brasileiro de Geografia e Estatística; IBGE). These initiatives highlight the fact that state agencies deal not only with issues specific to each state, but also with public policies that are national in scope, thus contributing to the development of knowledge about Brazil in general.

One group of institutions in Southeast Brazil (the Administrative Development Foundation [Fundação do Desenvolvimento Administrativo; FUNDAP], FJP and CEPERJ) and one in the South (IPARDES) have a School of Government as part of their structure, offering specialisation and postgraduate courses in the fields of planning, administration and public management. Also, a large number of these institutions run policy-related seminars, workshops and events designed to update and circulate their studies among a variety of publics (civil servants, academics and private sector personnel).

Evidence of intergovernmental cooperation efforts undertaken since the late 1990s can be seen in the partnering and exchange among state agencies, and between them and their national counterparts, which materialised in the founding of the National Association of Planning, Research and Statistics Institutions (Associação Nacional de Instituições de Planejamento, Pesquisa e Estatística; ANIPES). This body reflects its members' interest in positioning themselves in a broader sphere than each state of the federation. It brings together the main agencies working in this field in Brazil and 'is a key link in the chain of production and dissemination of official government statistics, and of studies and surveys conducted by state and municipal planning, research and public statistics institutions and agencies' (Carvalho and Figuerôa, 2009, p 6). With a view to publicising its members' output, the association founded a public statistics newsletter (*Boletim Estatísticas Públicas*), which has become a key source for consultation on this type of public agency.

Final remarks

This chapter addressed the subject of state-level policy analysis institutions in the context of Brazilian federalism. These agencies emerged in a process of growing awareness worldwide of the fact that policymaking should be guided by premises grounded in technical and scientific knowledge.

The information collected to support the analysis presented here revealed a heterogeneous set of institutions that, in a way, expresses Brazil's regional differences.

An example of this is that 11 out of 27 states did not institutionalise agencies for public policy analysis. Even though all the existing institutions perform activities within the same range of functions, they differ significantly in the quality of the research and services they produce. In addition, the specific characteristics of each agency are shaped by its dependence on political and economic conditions, and on relations within the state apparatus, especially the planning sector.

We have demonstrated that the emergence of the state-level agencies responded, on the one hand, to support and inducement from the federal government and international bodies and, on the other, to certain states' specific development strategies directed at improving their standing in the context of Brazil's federal system. These agencies emerged in the context of an authoritarian regime in the late 1960s and during the 1970s, when planning played an important role in the federal government's developmentalist strategy. With time, however, the surrounding conditions changed, impacting policy analysis institutions with changes in organisational format, objectives and priority areas of study and analysis.

In the 1980s, with the international economic crisis and ascendancy of neoliberal principles, public authorities made fewer investments in the administrative apparatus, and the conviction that planning capability was a strategic development resource weakened. During that same period, with the ongoing process of political democratisation, political considerations were given pride of place over technical concerns, which were considered characteristic of the authoritarian regime. In that context, the agencies' importance within the state apparatus declined.

During the 1990s, however, the democratisation process and implementation of reform of the state towards decentralisation and participation led to increased demand for statistics, information and surveys on public policies. In that light and as a condition for their survival, in the course of the following decade, policy analysis institutions had to rethink their modus operandi and their portfolio of services and products. Thus far, the results have varied. At the federal level, national planning institutions have been reinvigorated and the federal government is making major investments in applied research. At the state level, various different institutional solutions have been proposed. However, the outcomes of these efforts are not yet clear and, once again, various different strategies, efforts and results are to be observed among Brazil's state governments.

Notes

[1.] Noteworthy, however, is the pioneering case of Bahia State, where an Economic Planning Commission (Comissão de Planejamento Econômico) was set up in 1955. The commission's duties included conducting studies, research and analyses, and it was the precursor of state bodies that would later give rise to the current Bahia Economic and Social Studies Superintendency (Superintendência de Estudos Econômicos e Sociais da Bahia; SEI). The Appendix itemises state policy analysis agencies. For further related information, see Filgueiras and Rocha (2011).

[2.] Brazil is divided administratively into regions: the South and Southeast, comprising the most economically and socially developed states, and the North, Northeast and Midwest.

[3.] In Brazil, statistical data are produced and circulated by state and federal agencies. The Brazilian Geography and Statistics Institute (Instituto Brasileiro de Geografia e Estatística; IBGE) is a federal body that coordinates the national statistics system (Jannuzzi and Gracioso, 2002).

[4.] That choice is based on evidence that the existence of autonomous policy analysis agencies reflects the importance state governments give to knowledge production for policy decision-making. It is not usual for sectors within the structure of planning secretariats to carry out policy research. The exception considered by this study was the Economic and Social Studies Superintendency of the Bahia State Planning Secretariat (Superintendência de Estudos Econômicos e Sociais da Bahia; SEI), because of the importance of its activities. On the other hand, this study considered two policy analysis agencies in São Paulo State. This study did not include state government institutions engaged exclusively in specific policy areas, but rather focused on agencies dealing with a broad range of subjects.

[5.] Rio de Janeiro State deserves special mention here. The CEPERJ was created as a result of a merger of two institutions. The first is the Rio de Janeiro State Civil Service School Foundation (Fundação Escola do Serviço Público do Estado do Rio de Janeiro; FESP), which resulted from the transformation of the Guanabara State Civil Service School (Escola de Serviço Público do Estado da Guanabara), Guanabara being the former name of Rio de Janeiro State until 1960, when the federal capital was moved to Brasilia. The second institution is the Rio de Janeiro Information and Data Centre Foundation (Fundação Centro de Informação e Dados do Rio de Janeiro; CIDE), which, since the late 1980s, has been responsible for providing data and information about conditions in the state.

References

Carvalho, C.V. and Figueroa, E.S.B. (2009) 'Anipes 10 anos: função social, entraves e desafios', *Boletim Estatísticas Públicas*, no 5, pp 6–15.

Dezalay, Y. and Garth, B. (2002) 'Dollarizing state and professional expertise: transnational processes and questions of legitimation in state transformation, 1960–2000', in M. Likosky and J. Perkovich (eds) *Transnational legal process*, Oxford: Oxford University Press.

Filgueiras, C.A.C. and Rocha, C.A.V. (2011) 'As agências estaduais e a produção de informação e conhecimento sobre políticas públicas no Brasil', report presented to the Escola Nacional de Saúde Pública/FIOCRUZ, Belo Horizonte.

Forjaz, M.C. (1997) 'A emergência da Ciência Política no Brasil: aspectos institucionais', *Revista Brasileira de Ciências Sociais*, vol 12, no 35, pp 101–20.

Fundação João Pinheiro (2001) *Projeto Reposicionamento Estratégico*, Belo Horizonte, Fundação Joao Pinheiro.

Jannuzzi, P.M. and Gracioso, L.S. (2002) 'Produção e disseminação da informação estatística: Agências estaduais no Brasil', *São Paulo em Perspectiva*, vol 16, no 3, pp 92–103.

Loureiro, M.R. (2010) 'Democracia e políticas públicas', in F. Lopez and F. de Sá e Silva *Mesa Redonda 7º Encontro da Associação Brasileira de Ciência Política*, Recife: Instituto de Pesquisa Econômica Aplicada, pp 109–40.

Melo, M.A. (1999) 'Estado, governo e políticas públicas', in S. Miceli (ed) *O que ler na ciência social brasileira (1970–1995). Ciência Política* (2nd edn), São Paulo: Editora Sumaré: ANPOCS, pp 59–100.

Reis Veloso, J.P. (2005) 'Entrevista', in M.C. D'Araújo, I.C. Farias and L. Hipólito (eds) *IPEA 40 anos: uma trajetória para o desenvolvimento*, Rio de Janeiro, IPEA.

Santos, W.G. (1987) *Cidadania e justiça: a política social na ordem brasileira* (2nd edn), Rio de Janeiro: Campus.

Wilheim, J. (1999) 'Por que reformar as instituições?', in L.C. Bresser Pereira, J. Wilheim and L. Sola (eds) *Sociedade e Estado em transformação*, São Paulo: Editora Unesp, pp 15–22.

Appendix

Table 8.A1: Policy analysis agencies in the states and Federal District

State	Agency	Year founded	Role within the structure of the state government
North			
Pará	Pará Economic, Social and Environmental Development Institute (*Instituto de Desenvolvimento Econômico, Social e Ambiental do Pará*; IDESP)	2007	Autarchy under the Government Secretariat
Northeast			
Bahia	Bahia Economic and Social Studies Superintendency (*Superintendência de Estudos Econômicos e Sociais da Bahia*; SEI)	1995	Planning Secretariat
Ceará	Ceará Economic Research and Strategy Institute (*Instituto de Pesquisa e Estratégia Econômica do Ceará*; IPECE)	2003	Autarchy under the Planning and Management Secretariat
Maranhão	Maranhão Socioeconomic and Cartographic Studies Institute (*Instituto Maranhense de Estudos Socioeconômicos e Cartográficos*; IMESC)	2006	Autarchy under the Planning and Budget Secretariat
Paraíba	Paraíba Municipal and State Development Institute (*Instituto de Desenvolvimento Municipal e Estadual da Paraíba*; IDEME)	1988	Planning and Management Secretariat
Pernambuco	Pernambuco State Planning and Research Agency (*Agência Estadual de Planejamento e Pesquisas de Pernambuco*; CONDEPE/FIDEM)	2003	Autarchy under the Planning and Management Secretariat
Piauí	Piauí Economic and Social Research Centre Foundation (*Fundação Centro de Pesquisa Econômicas e Sociais do Piauí*; Fundação CEPRO)	1971	Planning Secretariat
Midwest			
Goiás	Statistics, Research and Information Superintendency (*Superintendência de Estatística, Pesquisa e Informação*; SEPIN)	1978	Planning and Development Secretariat
Distrito Federal	Federal District Planning Company (*Companhia de Planejamento do Distrito Federal*; CODEPLAN)	1966	Urban Development and Environment Secretariat

State	Agency	Year founded	Role within the structure of the state government
Southeast			
Espírito Santo	Jones dos Santos Neves Institute (*Instituto Jones dos Santos Neves*; IJSN)	1975	Autarchy under the Economy and Planning Secretariat
Minas Gerais	João Pinheiro Foundation (*Fundação João Pinheiro*; FJP)	1969	Under the Planning Secretariat
Rio de Janeiro	Rio de Janeiro State Statistics, Research and Civil Service Training Centre (*Centro Estadual de Estatística, Pesquisa e Formação de Servidores Públicos do Rio de Janeiro*; Fundação CEPERJ)	2009	Under the Planning and Management Secretariat
São Paulo	State Data Analysis System Foundation (*Fundação Sistema Estadual de Análise de Dados*; Fundação SEADE)	1978	Under the Economy and Planning Secretariat
São Paulo	Administrative Development Foundation (*Fundação do Desenvolvimento Administrativo*; FUNDAP)	1974	Under the Public Administration Secretariat
South			
Paraná	Paraná Economic and Social Development Institute (*Instituto Paranaense de Desenvolvimento Econômico e Social*; IPARDES)	1973	Autarchy of the State Planning and General Coordination Secretariat
Rio Grande do Sul	Siegfried Emanuel Heuser Economics and Statistics Foundation (*Fundação de Economia e Estatística Siegfried Emanuel Heuser*; FEE)	1973	Under the Planning and Management Secretariat

Note: No state-level policy analysis agencies were identified in the states of Acre, Alagoas, Amapá, Amazonas, Mato Grosso, Mato Grosso do Sul, Rio Grande do Norte, Rondônia, Roraima, Santa Catarina, Sergipe and Tocantins.

NINE

Policy analysis at the municipal level of government

Marta Ferreira Santos Farah

Introduction

Public policy literature has increased in Brazil over recent decades, as have local government studies. However, in both fields, there is a lack of research on how policy analysis contributes to policy formulation, implementation and evaluation at the local level of government. This gap results partially from the fact that policy analysis has not become a clearly defined professional and academic field in Brazil, unlike what has occurred in the US.

However, even if one considers policy analysis to be *the generation and mobilisation of knowledge for the resolution, by government of relevant public problems* – even though such activities may not be given this designation (public policy) and therefore do not constitute a clearly delimited field – the gap is still there.

The research agenda regarding public policy and local government in Brazil has emphasised other subjects, reflecting the societal and the governmental agenda. Prominent topics include: democratisation of policymaking at the municipal level of government, with emphasis on new mechanisms for participation and new institutional arrangements, such as policy councils and participatory budget; the *recognition of difference* by social policies, bringing to analysis the inclusion of gender, ethnic and age concerns of public policies through the implementation of policies for women, the indigenous population, the black community and children and adolescents; and issues such as popular control of policymaking, the structuring of integrated and decentralised policy systems, and intergovernmental relations in a federative context.

These subjects reflect the main challenges that were being faced (and still are) by Brazil during its turnaround from an authoritarian to a democratic state, and from a centralised to a decentralised state. Even though policy analysis was absent from the research agenda on public policies and local governments, that is not to say that there were no processes of generating and mobilising knowledge as input to local government public policies, but rather that this subject was not being problematised.

This chapter intends to contribute to the study of public policies at the local level of government, centring the discussion on policy analysis understood as the *generation and mobilisation of knowledge for the formulation, implementation and evaluation of public policies or government programmes*. The chapter offers a panorama of the evolution of public policies at the municipal level of government in Brazil, from the early initiatives in the local sphere, deriving from municipal governments' *identification of important public problems*, through to the establishment of decentralised social policy systems after 1988. Taking local policies as a reference, it endeavours to determine what kind of knowledge they rest on and to identify the actors and institutions involved in generating and mobilising this knowledge as a basis for policymaking or implementation. It also attempts to highlight connections between the process of knowledge generation and mobilisation and the political and institutional context in which public policies are formulated and implemented.

Urban problems and the first local interventions

In Brazil, the first government measures to address local problems date from the late 19th century. Those measures focused on urban problems relating to the growing cities, especially those involved in the coffee economy. Up until the 1930s, government action was primarily indirect through legislation on housing issues in Brazil's major urban centres, particularly Rio de Janeiro, then capital of the republic. Tenements, seen as places where tramps and rogues would get together, as loci of vice and focal points for the spread of epidemics, were the target of the first governmental measures on housing. These consisted in laws prohibiting the construction of tenements, recommending their closure or demolition, and introducing incentives for the construction of hygienic housing complexes (Bonduki, 1982; Blay, 1985).

Even at that time, legislation was preceded by studies carried out by commissions set up specifically for this purpose. In 1893, the São Paulo Municipal Chamber installed a Committee to Examine and Inspect Workers' Housing and Tenements in the Santa Efigênia District, with the purpose of describing the living and housing conditions of workers and tenement dwellers (Blay, 1985, p 64 et seq). Based on its diagnosis of the situation, the Commission then forwarded proposals for actions, recommending the prohibition of new constructions of tenements and the adoption of hygienic measures in existing housing. It also recommended the introduction of building and occupation guidelines for workers' housing. Similar committees were set up at the same period in other regions of Brazil, such as the sanitation commissions in Rio de Janeiro and Recife.

Physicians and engineers played a central role in the definition of urban and housing problems and in formulating and selecting policy alternatives (Valladares, 2000). Those were the main players in the process of state intervention at the local government level at that moment. At the same time, they were the decision-makers – frequently the municipal mayors, as was the case of Pereira Passos, Mayor of Rio de Janeiro at the start of the 20th century, who led a major urban intervention in that city – and those responsible for enunciating the problem and proposing policy alternatives.

At that time, it was they who were responsible for mobilising knowledge to address public problems. Technically based knowledge was generated either at the few universities then existing in Brazil, or more often abroad and then brought to Brazil through contact between the elites and leading international centres.

Developmentalism and urbanism

With the National-Developmentalist period that followed the Revolution of 1930, the Brazilian state took on the role of promoting development by direct intervention in the economic and in the social spheres. This was an important period for public policies – understood as a coordinated set of state actions directed to solving public problems and implementing collective projects.

State intervention by the federal government demanded major institution-building efforts. That endeavour included setting up new centres for education and knowledge generation. New universities, colleges and research institutes were founded; among them, in São Paulo, the Escola de Sociologia e Política (School of Sociology and Politics) in 1933 and the Universidade de São Paulo (University of São Paulo) in 1934 (Motoyama, 2004) and, in Rio de Janeiro, the Fundação Getulio Vargas (Getulio Vargas Foundation) in 1944 (Farah, 2011). These institutions were part of the developmentalist effort and the national project that framed government actions in that period.

The changes in Brazilian society, largely resulting from the developmentalist drive led by the federal government, had a strong impact on local conditions, especially in the large towns and cities. In the 1940s and subsequent decades, there was an increase in the process of urbanisation, with impacts in housing and transport problems in the major urban centres.

Solutions adopted by low-income families themselves, such as self-construction and *favela* shanty towns, entered the public and governmental agenda as public problems (Maricato, 1979; Mautner, 1981; Taschner, 1990). *Favelas*, which gained notoriety both in Brazil and abroad, are a good illustration of the relevance of urban problems on municipal and national agendas. *Favelas* were seen as strongholds of rogues and tramps, as the locus of disorder – and the *favelas* of Rio de Janeiro were the most conspicuous, because of the city's strong symbolic presence even after 1960 when it ceased to be the capital of Brazil.

In addition to the housing problem, other themes entered the municipal agenda, particularly the subject of urban planning in response to the process of intense growth in the larger towns. Disorderly urban growth began to be conceived and analysed as a problem, resulting in interventions to 'bring order' to urban development (Villaça, 1999).

Disorganised growth in large towns and the housing problem prompted a series of studies and surveys designed to learn the characteristics of the cities and of their populations and 'gauge the magnitude of the problem', to provide input to governmental interventions.

At first, municipalities were not ready for this challenge. Accordingly, the studies and surveys were carried out either on the initiative of the universities or autonomous institutions being set up at the time, or at the request of municipal governments. Thus, for instance, the São Paulo School of Sociology and Politics, with direct participation from Donald Pierson of the emerging Chicago school of sociology, conducted studies of workers' standards of living and of ethnic groups, with the purpose of identifying 'ethnic encystments' (Mendoza, 2005).

In 1956, the São Paulo city government commissioned a study of the city of São Paulo to underpin urban planning in the municipality. The survey was conducted by the Society for Graphic and Mechanographic Analysis Applied to Social Complexes (Sociedade para Análise Gráfica e Mecanográfica Aplicadas aos Complexos Sociais; SAGMACS), set up and coordinated by the French Dominican priest Joseph Lebret (Ambrogi, 2008). At that time, the São Paulo municipal administration already included the City Government Department of Urbanism, set up in 1947, as a specialised structure able to mobilise this kind of knowledge as an input to the formulation of alternative courses of action.

The first systematic surveys of Rio de Janeiro's *favelas* date from the 1940s. Those studies signalled a turning point in how *favelas* were treated: accurate information started to be considered key to defining government action (Valladares, 2000). There was a new concern to generate and mobilise knowledge as an input to policymaking for the *favelas*, so as to characterise and gauge the problem in order to formulate alternative courses of action.

Based on these studies and on conceptions about the *favela* problem, *favela*-related policies were introduced in Rio de Janeiro (Valla, 1985). There was a lack of continuity in those policies, reflecting conflicting conceptions about the problem itself (*favela*) and about alternative policies. The two main alternatives being proposed at that time were the eradication and the urbanisation of the *favelas* (Santos, 1984).

Also in the 1950s, policy for *favelas* became impregnated with populist practices based on exchanges of favours and on local politicians' efforts to win electoral support (Leeds and Leeds, 1977, p 206). This grammar of relationship between the state and society (Nunes, 1997) undermined the process of mobilising knowledge as an input to policymaking (Leeds and Leeds, 1977, p 206). Administrators and technicians were immersed in a complex environment where government action was hampered by the exchange of favours. On the one hand, technicians in the public administration would mobilise data from 'scientific' surveys of *favelas*; on the other hand, they mobilised less formal knowledge, obtained through direct contact with *favela* dwellers and their leaders – and that knowledge too was a basis for proposing courses of government action.

In the period starting in 1930, there was thus a diversification of the actors involved in the process of enunciating the public problems and proposing solutions at the municipalities. Physicians and engineers, the leading players under the Old Republic, were joined by urbanists, architects, social scientists, social workers, educators and other professional categories that were then being established in Brazil, as public problems became more diverse and as new universities and education centres were set up as part of the developmentalist project. Although the latter was a national project, it had local repercussions, which contributed to the emergence of new problems and the presence of new players and institutions.

Planning, centralised intervention and the urban question

The military regime that took power in 1964 endeavoured to base governmental action on rational planning techniques insulated from politics, as a counterpart to the clientelist and populist practices typical of the period from 1930 to 1964, and particularly the 1950s. In the effort to distance itself from clientelism, it also eliminated democratic participation in the process of policy formulation. The military period was also notable for centralisation, primarily at the federal level. Municipalities' scope of action was greatly reduced.

Urban problems, such as housing, sanitation and urban transport, worsened during that period, especially in large towns. That resulted partly from the government's developmentalist actions themselves, and was one face of economic growth (Camargo et al, 1975). On the other hand, that period was marked by the acknowledgement of urban problems. The urban question, especially metropolitan issues, came to be central to the military regime's characteristic development project. In order to deal with those problems, it set out federal public policies (at that time, they were not termed public policies, but were recognised as government policies), which conceived the urban problem and efforts to address it as part of the development project. Government intervention sought to ensure the conditions for economic growth and, at the same time, 'social peace' (Farah, 1996). To that end, government action in the housing, sanitation and transportation sectors, and others, became strategic.

In the 1960s, the National Housing Bank (Banco Nacional da Habitação; BNH) and Housing Finance System (Sistema Financeiro da Habitação; SFH) were founded, centralising housing finance and policy. Funding mechanisms – both voluntary, under the Brazilian Savings and Loans System (Sistema Brasileiro de Poupança e Empréstimo; SBPE), and compulsory, from the Time of Service Guarantee Fund (Fundo de Garantia por Tempo de Serviço; FGTS) – were also set up, along with housing programmes tailored to different segments of the population, including low-income groups (Maricato, 1979; Azevedo, 1988). As occurred in the housing sector, structures for governmental funding and action were also put in place at the federal level for sanitation and urban transport projects.

In order to carry these policies through, state institutions equipped themselves technically, reinforcing their role as specialised bureaucracies informing the decision-making process with scientific knowledge that was supposedly neutral and rational. The government, the universities and 'backup' government institutions also established research centres on urban issues, which provided input to policy formulation and implementation, and evaluated government programmes.

Even though that period was characterised by policy centralisation at the federal government level, policy implementation entailed setting up state and municipal bodies to apply the policies. For housing, for instance, state and municipal housing companies were established to execute housing policy at the localities. Another characteristic of the period was policy standardisation: the local agents' role was merely to apply centrally defined policies.

From the mid-1970s, urban social movements grew up nationwide, but particularly in the largest towns and cities (Boschi, 1982), exposing the unmet needs of low-income city populations in areas such as health, education, transportation, sanitation and housing. These movements would highlight the exclusionary nature of public policies and express demands for new policies.

The search for policy alternatives occurred with the collaboration of a variety of actors. Members of the federal bureaucracy responsible for policy, researchers at universities and research centres, members of social movements, and members of state and municipal bureaucracies engaged with policy implementation. By then, it was already possible to identify an informal network of 'public policy analysts' who discussed the problem – at times, redefining it – and alternative solutions.

Support from federal and state institutions was fundamental in enabling municipalities to implement federal programmes. During the re-democratisation process of the 1980s, the BNH, through its Research and Applied Research Department (Departamento de Pesquisas e Pesquisas Aplicadas; DEPEA), hired several institutions to provide input to policy formulation, decision-making and implementation through diagnostic studies and analyses of policy alternatives, and to evaluate programmes already in place. That action was designed particularly to support state and municipal governments (Informe DEPEA, 1986). It was clear a concern, then, with the lack of municipal capacity. Accordingly, the BNH supported capacity-building programmes such as the Programme of Technical Assistance to the Integrated Plan to Support Municipalities (Programa de Assistência Técnica ao Plano Integrado de Apoio ao Município; PROMUNICIPIO), developed by the

Brazilian Administration Institute (Instituto Brasileiro de Administração; IBAM) for the purpose of supporting municipal administrations in improving their technical and operational capabilities and in planning and preparing projects to upgrade housing, urban infrastructure and community facilities.

Just before the 1988 Constitution, it became clear that public policies designed since 1964 were insufficient to deal with urban problems and social issues. The 'system' itself had become flexible, and sought alternatives to standardised solutions and to centralised policy.

Redefining the role of municipalities and expanding the municipal agenda

Brazil started its transition to democracy in the late 1970s, and decentralisation was one of the flagships of that process. The pro-decentralisation attitude was reflected in the redefinition of Brazilian federalism in 1988: the 1988 Constitution recognised municipalities as federative entities, alongside the Union and the states. The new Constitution broadened the range of competences of the municipalities, and also increased local government participation in shared fiscal resources (Afonso and Silva, 1995). The municipal agenda underwent a process of redefinition, now to include public problems in the social domain, such as education, health and social assistance. At the same time, urban issues no longer held centre stage on the national agenda, as reflected in the 'dismantling' of housing finance structures, which displaced housing from its position at the centre of the municipal agenda.[1] The municipalities' new role did not mean, however, that policymaking had been transferred to them. Decentralisation is more complex than that (Kugelmas and Sola, 1999; Franzese and Abrucio, 2009).

If the BNH and SFH can be considered the paradigm of the public policy regime of the authoritarian period; the Unified Health System (Sistema Único de Saúde; SUS) can be considered the paradigm of the democratic period. This system resulted from a process of mobilisation, debate and discussion of alternatives, extending over more than a decade, among health sector stakeholders led by public health physicians (Moreira and Escorel, 2009). With the SUS, national health policy came to be organised less centrally and more hierarchically, under the coordination of the federal government, with the three government levels acting in complementary and coordinated fashion.

On the SUS model, policies are largely formulated at the federal level of government. Unlike the BNH/SFH model, however, the municipality is not a mere executive agent of federal policies. It is responsible for managing and implementing federal programmes, with the participation of local civil society. The concept of this new system includes an articulation between local policies and federal programmes, implemented at the local level. There is some tension between policymaking at the federal level and policy implementation at the municipal level, which is intrinsic to the new paradigm: the SUS and the unified systems created in other policy areas inspired by it provide for the municipalities to become increasingly autonomous in policy management. Since implementation 'reformulates the formulation', local administrations permanently redefine policy, thus influencing federal policy itself.

In the 1990s and early 2000s, the municipal level of government was a veritable laboratory of innovation in Brazil. Between 1996 and 2006, a programme developed by

Fundação Getulio Vargas and the Ford Foundation, with the support of the National Bank on Economic and Social Development (Banco Nacional de Desenvolvimento Econômico e Social; BNDES) that rewarded innovative initiatives by sub-national governments, built up a database of over 8,000 experiences from all over the country, more than 80% of which originated in municipalities (Spink, 2000; Farah and Spink, 2008). Some of these innovations occurred in areas where there had been no systematic public policies in the previous period, as in the case of policies with a gender approach and environmental policy (Fujiwara and Jacobi, 2001; Farah, 2006a).

One of the characteristics of public policies pursued by local governments after democratisation consisted in setting up new institutional channels for participation, such as policy management councils and participatory budgets. That characteristic resulted both from guidelines issued at the federal level and from initiatives taken locally. On the one hand, the 1988 Constitution and complementary legislation call for councils to be set up at the various levels of government, as a mechanism for including civil society in discussion of policy alternatives and in the control of government actions. On the other hand, local governments were an important locus for policy democratisation, where policies and programmes were designed and implemented for the first time. Such is the case of the participatory budget (Sugiyama, 2004) and the formulation of policy alternatives based on participatory processes (Spink, 2000; Dagnino, 2002; Simielli, 2008).

This innovation movement at the localities occurred during the 1990s and early 2000s, driven by alliances between government and non-government players around a political project directed to reducing inequality and democratising the policy regime in Brazil. The Workers' Party (Partido dos Trabalhadores; PT) played an important role at the start of this process, which quickly outgrew the party, however. The key component of this movement, as already mentioned, was the inclusion of new actors, new voices, in policymaking process. Little attention was given at first to the technical or scientific grounds for decision-making. In fact, just as centralisation was criticised, so the policy regime of the authoritarian period was also criticised for its technocratic foundations, which framed 'closed' decisions, insulated from politics.

Notwithstanding the democratic emphasis of the new policy regime, however, constructing new policy alternatives also involved mobilising systematic, technically grounded knowledge. Given the diversity of sectors where local governments came to act following democratisation, mobilising that knowledge involved a wide variety of actors and institutions. The process involved epistemic communities in the fields of health, education and social assistance, as well as members of bureaucracies at all levels of government (especially in medium-sized and large municipalities, which had benefited from capacity-building during the previous period). Other participants included members of political parties, social movements and non-governmental organisations (NGOs) engaged in a diversity of issues on the public agenda: women, youth, disability, race, children and adolescents, housing, and local development. Local leaders and the members of the local bureaucracy would often belong simultaneously to sectoral epistemic communities and to political coalitions for a new democratic governance, thus helping not only to define the problem (or 'translate' it to the local level), but also to develop alternative policies (or adapt a federal policy locally).

In this process, local stakeholders allied with supra-local actors, which influenced local agendas and the formulation of policy alternatives. For specific technical expertise, specialised institutions were mobilised; as in the previous period, these were mainly state-level universities and research institutions.

Meanwhile, the new institutions – policy councils, forums, participatory budgets and municipal, state and national policy conferences (Farah, 2001; Cortes, 2002; Dagnino, 2002; Wampler and Avritzer, 2004) – functioned as channels for the inclusion of new actors in the diagnosis of public problems and in the study of alternative policies. They concentrated diverse types of knowledge in open public spaces, and offered the opportunity for debate and argumentation on proposals for action and policies.

After the mid-2000s, the federal government presence in municipal activities underwent a redefinition. Federal programmes, some of them inspired by municipal innovations of the 1990s,[2] gained importance. In this way, while local initiatives had at first been a prominent source of inspiration for the design of federal programmes, at a later stage, federal government inducement of local action grew stronger. Through this inducement, the federal government seeks to coordinate and equalise the process of development and the extension of public services and public policies.

In several policy areas, the federal government established programmes to which municipalities may adhere. The possibility of access to federal funding – conditional on compliance with centrally defined rules – serves as an incentive to adhesion. A large number of Brazil's 5,500 plus municipalities are, however, unprepared to meet access requirements in several sectors. The lack of preparation is more evident in smaller municipalities in less-developed regions (Souza, 2002).

This unpreparedness consists partly in a lack of technical and professional capacity in preparing diagnoses and alternative courses of action, adapting the programmes to local specificities, which are typical elements of 'policy analysis'. This bottleneck is surmounted in several ways, including: resorting to private consultancies; getting support from state government agencies; direct support from NGOs; drawing inspiration from measures developed elsewhere (Farah, 2006b); capacity-building courses offered by different kinds of institutions; federal programmes' preparing 'manuals' providing guidelines for local action;[3] and mobilising practical expertise that is not structured as scientific knowledge, and generally emerges from the experience of local government and non-government actors.

Inducement to mobilise knowledge to comply with federal government rules is leading policies to be redesigned at the municipal level of government, in a process that has significantly expanded the number of actors informing government action at the local level.

Final remarks

This chapter presented an overview of 'policy analysis' at the municipal level of government in Brazil. Based on the observation that Brazil, unlike the US, lacks an established disciplinary field and professional activity specialised in policy analysis, this chapter examined the generation and mobilisation of knowledge in support of municipal measures directed to solving public problems, and highlighted the actors and institutions engaged in that process.

By reconstituting the actions of government at the municipal level, it was possible to identify the public problems that have risen up the municipal agenda since the late 19th century. The local agenda, which originally centred on the urban question, became more complex and diversified, especially after democratisation and the 1988

Constitution, as competences and funding were transferred to the municipal level of government.

The chapter also showed how the array of actors and institutions involved in responding to local public problems also changed substantially over time. New institutions were set up to support the mobilisation and generation of knowledge, and a diversification of the types of actors engaged in the process of knowledge mobilisation as an input to policymaking emerged.

After the reconstitution of municipal policies in Brazil over time made in this chapter, it is possible to establish a dialogue with policy analysis typologies, such as those of Radin (2000) and of Mayer, Van Daalen and Bots (2004), as revisited by Howlett and Lindquist (2007). The first model these typologies of policy analysis is the rational, neo-positivist model of the 1960s and 1970s, which draws on empirically based quantitative methods. In Radin's typology, a second, 'postmodern' model contrasts with the former type in that it is sensitive to the social construction of the problem, and to policy-related discourse and the politics of policy. The typology of Mayer, Van Daalen and Bots, on the other hand, identifies several types of 'policy analysis' based on factors such as the actors the analyst interacts with (clients, actors without a voice in the political process) and the type of intervention by the analyst (as an independent actor in the discussion, facilitator, 'advocate' of interests or process manager). This typology identifies the following styles of policy analysis: rational, client advice, argumentative, interactive, participatory and process.

In Brazil, the activity of generating and mobilising knowledge as an input to municipal policies did not become established in the first style – the rational model. At certain points, it did, however, enjoy the support of systematic, scientifically and empirically based research generated in an environment 'insulated' from politics. There was some effort in that direction in the 1950s, but it was particularly during the military period that 'rationalisation' of the policy process intensified. That period, however, also featured a systematic endeavour to 'eliminate politics' and towards centralisation, leaving the municipality – this chapter's object of analysis – to a role as simply the executor of policies laid down by the federal government.

From the late 1980s onwards, as a result of the decentralisation process, local governments needed to mobilise and generate knowledge to inform their policies. That process, however, was built up on a template that challenged the insulated, technical decision-making typical of the previous period's policy regime, and therefore distanced itself from the rational model. In that process, different elements of the various styles mentioned by Mayer, Van Daalen and Bots found expression: knowledge generation or mobilisation for clients; 'analysts' participating as independent actors; as advocates for causes of traditionally 'voiceless' stakeholders; as agents facilitating discussions between players; and as process managers, the analysts acting as network managers.

However, even though these affinities can be discerned, I do not believe that the trajectory examined in this chapter can be interpreted in the light of such typologies. First, in Brazil, policy analysis did not take shape as an independent discipline or professional activity. 'Analysis' itself is often not even a clearly differentiated activity in the policymaking process, but occurs diffusely as part of other activities, such as decision-making (in the process of policy formulation) and implementation. Accordingly, there is no clearly differentiated policy analysis stage or actor, the 'policy analyst'. Nonetheless, there is knowledge generation and mobilisation *for* public policies – and that process of generation and mobilisation takes place with the participation of diverse actors both internal and external to the government. Moreover, since Brazil's re-democratisation, one fundamental feature of the process has been the integration among scientific knowledge and the practical expertise mobilised by diverse actors for different policies.

Notes

[1.] It was only recently that housing policy was reintroduced in the agenda, to a great extent associated with the goal of creating jobs. The My House, My Life Programme highlights this change in 2009.

[2.] Examples include: the Family Grant, inspired by the School Grant from the Federal District and by the Minimum Income from the municipality of Campinas; and Family Health, inspired by the Family Doctor from Niterói.

[3.] For example, several ministries publish guidebooks, which provide guidelines to municipalities for adhering to federal programmes and forms for the assessment of the municipal administration of programmes from several sectors, which are conditions for gaining access to resources.

References

Afonso, R.B.A. and Silva, P.L.B. (eds) (1995) *A federação em perspectiva: ensaios selecionados*, São Paulo: Fundap.

Ambrogi, I.H. (2008) 'A cidade e a escola: diretrizes de uma rede escolar instituída nos anos 50 na cidade de São Paulo', *Anais do XIX Encontro Regional de História: Poder, Violência e Exclusão*, ANPUH/SP – USP, São Paulo, 8 to 12 September, Cd-Rom.

Azevedo, S. (1988) '22 anos de política de habitação popular. (1964–1986): criação, trajetória e extinção do BNH', *Revista de Administração Pública*, vol 22, no 4, pp 107–20.

Blay, E. (1985) *Eu não tenho onde morar: vilas operárias na cidade de São Paulo*, São Paulo: Nobel.

Bonduki, N. (1982) 'Origens do problema da habitação popular em São Paulo 1886–1918', *Espaço & Debates*, no 5, pp 81-111.

Boschi, R.R. (ed) (1982) *Movimentos coletivos no Brasil urbano*, Rio de Janeiro: Zahar Editores.

Camargo, C.P.F, Cardoso, F.H., Mazzucchelli, F., Moisés, J.A., Kowarick, L., Almeida, M. H.T., Singer, P.I. and Brant, V.C. (1975) *São Paulo 1975: Crescimento e Pobreza*, São Paulo: CEBRAP/Comissão de Justiça e Paz da Arquidiocese de São Paulo/ Edições Loyola.

Cortes, S.M.V. (2002) 'Construindo a possibilidade da participação dos usuários: conselhos e conferências no Sistema Único de Saúde', *Sociologias*, vol 4, no 7, pp 18–49.

Dagnino, E. (ed) (2002) *Sociedade civil e espaços públicos no Brasil*, São Paulo: Paz e Terra.

Farah, M.F.S. (1996) *Processo de trabalho na construção habitacional: tradição e mudança*, São Paulo: Annablume.

Farah, M.F.S. (2001) 'Parceria, novos arranjos institucionais e políticas públicas no nível local de governo', *Revista de Administração Pública*, vol 35, no 1, pp 119–44.

Farah, M.F.S. (2006a) 'Gender and public policies', *Revista Estudos Feministas*, vol 12, no 1, pp 47–71.

Farah, M.F.S. (2006b) 'Dissemination of innovations: learning from sub-national awards programmes in Brazil', in A. Alberti and G. Bertucci (eds) *Innovations in governance and public administration: replicating what works* (1st edn), New York, NY: United Nations (UNDESA), pp 75–84.

Farah, M.F.S. (2011) 'Administração pública e política pública', *Revista de Administração Pública*, vol 45, pp 813–36.

Farah, M.F.S. and Spink, P. (2008) 'Subnational government innovation in a comparative perspective: Brazil', in S. Borins (ed) *Innovations in government: research, recognition, and replication*, Cambridge/Washington, DC: Ash Institute for Democratic Governance and Innovation, Harvard University/Brookings Institution Press, pp 71–92.

Fujiwara, L. and Jacobi, P. (2001) 'Programa de proteção de mananciais: consórcio das Bacias dos Rios Piracicaba e Capivari', in M. Farah and H. Barbosa (eds) *20 Experiências de Gestão Pública e Cidadania*, São Paulo: Programa Gestão Pública e Cidadania.

Franzese, C. and Abrucio, F.L. (2009) 'A combinação entre federalismo e políticas públicas no Brasil pós-1988: os resultados nas áreas de saúde, assistência social e educação', in Cibele Franzese, Claudia Anjos, David Ferraz, Fernando Luiz Abrucio, Gabriela N. Cheli, Geysa Maria Bacelar Pontes Melo, Jeni Vaistman, Júnia Laoerira Dutra Nehmé, Lauseani Santoni, Matilde Gago da Silva, Monica Rubio, Pablo Yanes, Sonia Nahas, Paulo de Martino Jannuzzi, Rômulo Paes Sousa, *Reflexões para Ibero-América: avaliação de programas sociais*, Brasília: ENAP, See: www.enap.gov.br/files/Caderno_EIAPP_Programas_Sociais.pdf

Howlett, M. and Lindquist, E. (2007) 'Beyond formal policy analysis: governance context, analytical styles, and the policy analysis movement in Canada', in L. Dobuzinskis, M. Howlett and D. Laycock (eds) *Policy analysis in Canada*, Toronto: University of Toronto Press, pp 86–115.

Informe DEPEA (1986) *Cadernos de Saúde Pública*, vol 3, pp 387–9.

Kugelmas, E. and Sola, L. (1999) 'Recentralização/descentralização: dinâmica do regime federativo no Brasil dos anos 90', *Tempo Social. Revista de Sociologia da USP*, vol 11, no 2, pp 63–83.

Leeds, A. and Leeds, E. (1977) *A sociologia do Brasil urbano*, Rio de Janeiro: Zahar Editores.

Maricato, E. (1979) *Autoconstrução, a arquitetura possível: a construção capitalista da casa e da cidade*, São Paulo: Alfa-Ômega.

Mautner, Y. (1981) 'A cria rebelled', Masters thesis, FAU-USP, São Paulo.

Mayer, I.S., Van Daalen, C.E. and Bots, P.W.G. (2004) 'Perspectives on policy analyses: a framework for understanding and design', *International Journal of Technology, Policy and Management*, vol 4, no 2, pp 169–91.

Mendoza, E.S.G. (2005) 'Donald Pierson e a escola sociológica de Chicago no Brasil: os estudos urbanos na cidade de São Paulo (1935–1950)', *Sociologias*, vol 7, no 14, pp 440–470.

Moreira, M.R. and Escorel, S. (2009) 'Conselhos Municipais de Saúde do Brasil: um debate sobre a democratização da política de saúde nos vinte anos do SUS', *Ciência e Saúde Coletiva*, vol 14, no 3, pp 895–905.

Motoyana, S. (ed) (2004) *Prelúdio para uma história: ciência e tecnologia no Brasil*, São Paulo: EDUSP.

Nunes, E. (1997) *A gramática política do Brasil: clientelismo e insulamento burocrático*, Brasília/Rio de Janeiro: ENAP/Jorge Zahar.

Radin, B.A. (2000) *Beyond Machiavelli: policy analysis comes of age*, Washington, DC: Georgetown University Press.

Santos, C.N.F. (1984) 'Em trinta anos passou muita água sob as pontes urbanas', *Espaço & Debates*, vol 4, no 11, pp 28–41.

Simielli, L.L.R. (2008) 'Sobral: defining public policies with basis on citizen participation – Brazil', in R. Kadalie (eds) *Learning from innovations: community participation and public service*, São Paulo: Programa Gestão Pública e Cidadania.

Souza, C. (2002) 'Governos e sociedades locais em contextos de desigualdades e de descentralização', *Ciência e Saúde Coletiva*, vol 7, no 3, pp 431–42.

Spink, P. (2000) 'The rights approach to local public management: experiences from Brazil', *Revista de Administração de Empresas*, vol 40, no 3, pp 15–24.

Sugiyama, N.B. (2004) 'Political incentives, ideology and social networks: the diffusion of social policy in Brazil', paper delivered at the 2004 Meeting of the Latin American Studies Association, Las Vegas, Nevada, 7–9 October.

Taschner, S.P. (1990) 'Habitação e demografia intra-urbana em São Paulo', *Revista Brasileira de Estudos de População*, vol 7, no 1, pp 3–34.

Valla, V.V. (1985) 'Educação, participação, urbanização: uma contribuição à análise histórica das propostas institucionais para as favelas do Rio de Janeiro, 1941–1980', *Cadernos de Saúde Pública*, vol 1, no 3, pp 282–96.

Valladares, L. (2000) 'A gênese da favela carioca: a produção anterior às ciências sociais', *Revista Brasileira de Ciências Sociais*, vol 15, no 44, pp 5–34.

Villaça, F. (1999) 'Uma contribuição para a história do planejamento urbano no Brasil', in C. Deak and S.R. Schiffer (eds) *O processo de urbanização no Brasil*, São Paulo: Editora da Universidade de São Paulo.

Wampler, B. and Avritzer, L. (2004) 'Participatory Publics: Civil Society and New Institutions in Democratic Brazil', *Comparative Politics*, vol 36, no 3 (April), pp. 291-312.

TEN

The role of the Brazilian legislature in the public policy decision-making process

Fabiano Santos

Introduction

Analyses of public policy decision-making process in Brazil in the years following the enactment of the 1988 Constitution generally emphasise lawmaking initiatives by the executive. When such studies involve the legislature, they take a predominantly pessimistic tone, contending that interaction between policymakers does not occur under favourable conditions for the formulation and approval of an agenda focused on issues with a broader public interest. Nevertheless, and after intense debate in the 1990s, the more pessimistic view gave way to a nuanced perspective in which the National Congress appears as one of the main political actors in defining crucial stages in the decision-making process concerning major public policies.

However, Brazilian legislative studies still virtually agree on the lack of rules and procedures capable of spawning the development of expertise and training of Congress members for public policy formulation and implementation. In other words, the Brazilian Congress still needs to develop informational mechanisms for its lawmaking work. This chapter examines the public policy decision-making process in the Brazilian Chamber of Deputies, within which, it is argued, it is possible to detect institutions that play informational roles, more specifically, the Chamber's standing technical committees and its staff structure (with particular emphasis on the Consultoria Legislativa or Legislative Consulting Body). The chapter further argues that it is essential to grasp the nature and dynamics of these institutions in order to understand how the public policy decision-making process operates in the Brazilian legislature.

The chapter is organised in four sections, in addition to this introduction and a conclusion. The next or second section maps the recent literature, showing how the legislature is seen as a central component in the analysis of public policies in democratic Brazil; the third examines in greater detail the informational perspective applied to the Brazilian case; the fourth defines the study's more general characteristics and explains the decision to focus on the advisory structure of the Chamber of Deputies; the fourth discusses the results of interviews with legislative advisors and consultants, a group of highly influential public employees in analysing bills under review by the legislature. The conclusion provides a more general commentary on the study's findings and its impacts on the current discussion of the legislative branch and public policies in Brazil.

Literature

There are two traditions in the area of legislative studies. The first, with a functionalist extraction, seeks to identify the role or roles of the legislature in a given country. The second, developed from the neo-institutionalist approach, verifies the career objectives of congressmen and the rules by which they interact with their colleagues and other political actors in order to explain relevant phenomena for legislative life, such as party discipline, lawmaking output and greater or lesser predominance of the executive, among others.

A functionalist look at the Brazilian Chamber of Deputies would define it as reactive.[1] For the current chapter's purposes, it is relevant to highlight that this type of legislature is characterised by the delegation of policy initiatives to the executive, especially for the more central policies on the agenda. The agenda's definition and order of priority by which bills are reviewed are transferred to the administration and later negotiated with the members of Congress that lead the majority party or coalition. Concerning the Brazilian legislature, Amorim Neto and Santos (2003) observed that out of a total of more than 2,000 bills passed from 1985 to 1999, only 336 were initiated by members of Congress. They also found that although the latter bills were important for various groups and sectors of society, they did not affect the country's economic and social status quo, and were more targeted interventions on specific issues pertaining to the lives of ordinary citizens. Meanwhile, the budgetary process, essential to public policy implementation, is also organised so as to favour priorities set by the dominant partisan coalition in government, while intervention by members of Congress in this area is basically marginal (Figueiredo and Limongi, 2002).

A more recent and hegemonic tradition in political science is known as the neo-institutionalist approach. Its application to the area of legislative studies produced fundamental results for understanding the role of the National Congress in the decision-making process.

Studies in this area, which initially focused mainly on the US Congress, are subdivided into three major perspectives: distributive, partisan[2] and informational. The first postulates that the organisation of Congress serves the interests of its members' electoral reproduction.[3] Assuming that winning votes is a positive function of the representatives' capacity to meet interests rooted in the district from which they are elected, they will seek to specialise in public policy issues with a strong impact on that same district. A system of highly specialised committees and regimental instruments that hinder amendments to bills negotiated within this system are the mechanisms by which the Congressional decision-making process satisfies the desideratum of distribution of visible benefits to voters.

The partisan perspective contends that political parties play two important roles: they serve as a vehicle for voters to make their decisions and as a mechanism for coordinating the behaviour of members of Congress once elected.[4] In other words, politicians derive benefits from the parties' existence, facilitating their action as candidates and signalling their stances on public-interest issues and their legislative work by backing their decisions on bills coming up for vote on the floor. An especially relevant role falls to the party leadership: they are responsible for disciplining the conduct of a party delegation in Congress, preventing members' parochial interests from jeopardising the party's collective image. They are also responsible for preventing conflicts of interest and opinion within the party's congressional representation from leading to its electoral and political discredit. In a word, the role of the party leadership is to harmonise the individual and collective interests within a single congressional coalition.

Finally, the informational perspective, common in the partisan approach, begins with a critique of the foundations and central proposals of the distributive perspective. Briefly, where the latter sees particularism, the informational approach finds collective efficiency (see Gilligan and Krehbiel, 1987; Krehbiel, 1990; Brady and Volden, 1998). For example, the organisation of Congress through committees expresses more the members' demand for expertise than the distribution of parochial benefits – a demand deriving from the attempt to reduce the uncertainty that necessarily pervades public policy formulation and implementation. The chapter's next section provides a more detailed discussion of the empirical premises and implications of the informational argument.

The recent literature on the Brazilian Congress has revealed the coexistence of distributive and partisan elements in the members' lawmaking behaviour (see Figueiredo and Limongi, 1999; Pereira and Mueller, 2000; Amorim Neto and Santos, 2003; Carvalho, 2003). Indicators like opinion polls, lawmaking output, budgetary process and party discipline reveal at least two fundamental points: there is broad recognition of the importance of building a personal reputation with voters, that is, the task of political representation in Brazil is strongly anchored in the politician's individual figure; however, the room for individual action by the representative is limited in Congress, meaning that legislative activity – its organisation and decision-making process – is centred in the party leadership, particularly in the parties forming the administration's allied congressional base. Bills of special interest to the administration are frequently sent directly to the floor through special review instruments such as Provisional Measures (executive decrees) and requests for fast-track review, thereby downplaying the work of standing committees.

Thus, public policies originating in Congress have a dual stamp and a deficiency – although they are always consistent with the agenda reached by consensus among the leaders of the parties that comprise the coalition supporting the executive, somehow they end up being affected by the members' need to distribute benefits of a more parochial nature. The deficiency relates to the scarce informational input in the bills that reach the floor for a final vote.

The informational basis of legislative activity in the Brazilian Chamber of Deputies

Recent analyses have applied informational models to various aspects of congressional dynamics in Brazil, with good theoretical and empirical results (see especially Santos and Almeida, 2011). Such models begin with a scenario in which the representative needs to choose a public policy p from a one-dimensional space. Each policy p is associated with an outcome x, also defined in a one-dimensional space. However, the legislators do not know the relationship between p and x, but only that for each value of the former, there is a probability distribution for the latter's values. By way of simplification, an additive relationship is defined between policies and their outcomes, such as $x = p + \omega$, where ω is a parameter whose value is not known for certain in advance.[5] From a substantive point of view, ω can be conceived as the expression of exogenous factors vis-a-vis the legislative decision.

The legislature can acquire information on ω and thus reduce its uncertainty and corresponding informational loss by 'consulting' actors that detain information on the policy's effects. One assumes two fundamental actors in the Brazilian political dynamic: the executive and the system of technical committees in the legislature (hereinafter, simply the 'committee'). In general, the executive is highly informed about ω and can easily claim that it possesses more information than the committee and Congress as a whole. However – and this is the crux of the issue for this chapter's purposes – the committee has the means to gather relevant information.

Due to the informational asymmetry between the executive and legislature, the former is naturally the principal proponent of public policies, and whenever it proposes a policy, it is actually issuing a recommendation to the latter. The question is under what conditions the government, when it proposes a policy, shares all the information it has on its consequences, or, on the contrary, whether it hoards essential elements for legislative decision-making. According to Santos and Almeida (2011), the decision by the executive to reveal information depends on the degree of convergence of interests and preferences between it and the majority inclination in the legislature concerning policy p. In other words, the greater the convergence of preferences between the executive and the majority of Congress concerning p, the less the need for the latter to turn to an alternative data production source – in the case of the informational perspective, the committees – in order to obtain additional information; therefore, the less is committees' role during the process of public policymaking. On the other hand, in a scenario in which the administration is the proponent of policies, the existence of significant divergence between the executive and the legislature is a fundamental condition for the committee system to be called on to play its role.

Santos and Almeida (2011) also seek to identify the conditions under which the standing committees would have incentives to act, given the institutional context of which the Brazilian Congress is a part. Assuming a high degree of uncertainty in the legislature concerning policy p, even after observing the recommendation by the executive, the former could mobilise two distinct types of committees: one that is 'opposition-leaning' in nature and the other more 'pro-government'.[6] A committee is considered 'opposition-leaning' when the majority of members take an opposite view to that of the executive, given the majority position of Congress on a policy. That is, when the executive is more inclined towards one end of the one-dimensional space vis-a-vis the central tendency in the legislature concerning policy p, an opposition committee will be positioned (in relation to p) at the opposite extremity vis-a-vis this same central tendency. Otherwise, the committee is considered 'pro-government'.

Pro-government committees do not have major reasons to produce information, because their members know that the executive has an incentive to divulge all the information that benefits them. Opposition-leaning committees, on the contrary, have a strong incentive to produce additional and different information from that revealed by the executive. The legislature, aware of this incentive and anxious to reduce its own uncertainty, provides the conditions for the committee to play its role as an informational agent. Obviously, for the legislator, the effectively informative committee is the 'opposition-leaning' one: based on the nature of its participants, it is the only type of committee that is capable of revealing information that is strategically omitted by the executive.

If one accepts the line of reasoning developed by Santos and Almeida (2011), the conclusion is that the system of standing committees in the legislature plays a relevant informational role regarding the public policy decision-making process. This role increases in proportion to the divergences between the executive and the congressional majorities concerning the set of public policies submitted to Congress by the administration, and the greater the oppositional nature of the committee in charge of examining this set of policies. In other words, the ordinary lawmaking process, when supported by opposition committees, allows the floor to make a more informed decision and thus to reduce potential losses resulting from its disinformation.

Some empirical results have confirmed hypotheses that stem naturally from the theory. So-called Provisional Measures (executive decrees) and fast-track proposals have been reviewed, amended and passed at higher rates when the agendas of the administration and the congressional majority are more convergent. Rapporteurs for bills have been selected according to the same logic: opposition rapporteurs of bills submitted by the administration are more common when the distance is greater between the positions of the executive and legislature. In short, there is great room for investigating how members of the Brazilian Congress use the existing informational institutions in the legislature.

Staff structure of the Brazilian Chamber of Deputies: overall characteristics

Let us suppose that the executive decides to send an important set of bills to Congress, a kind of package of measures involving sensitive areas for various interests and social groups. Let us suppose that the administration requests fast-track treatment for the bills in this policy package. Let us further suppose that Congress is not entirely aligned with the administration on various issues in the package. Thus, and according to the informational logic, members of Congress will react to the executive's use of extraordinary review mechanisms, such as fast-track and provisional measures, a reaction whose most evident empirical and institutional manifestation is to mobilise the committee system. In other words, Congress will distribute the bills to 'opposition-leaning' committees whose expertise is pertinent to the various facets of the package, in addition to allocating time and resources for them to produce additional and alternative information vis-a-vis the initial policy recommendation by the executive.

At this juncture, the fundamental question is the following: how is the Chamber of Deputies structured to deal with the challenge of developing arguments and identifying evidence that are distinct from those embedded in the package? How can Congress induce changes in the proposed policies in order to draw the decisions closer to the preferences and interests of the congressional majority? Answering these questions means shifting the analysis to the staff structure of the Chamber of Deputies, since it is mobilised by committee members when seeking alternative information to that furnished initially by the executive.

The administrative structure of the Brazilian Chamber of Deputies is highly complex, including some 15,000 employees, a General Directorate, a General Secretariat (reporting to the Steering Board) and units subdivided into five agencies, which in turn multiply into a further 14 small bodies. In terms of the distribution of professional support staff for the House, there are two major groups: the agencies consisting of employees per se, like the Department of Committees (DECOM), advisory bodies to the party leaders, employees linked to the General Secretariat of the Steering Board and institutional consulting bodies (the Legislative Consulting Body [CONLE] and the Budgetary Consulting Body); and the ad hoc advisory bodies, freely appointed, as requested by members of the Steering Board and the party leaders (the so-called Special Nature Positions [CNEs]), in addition to the Parliamentary Secretariat, also consisting of appointed members, with the difference being that the appointments are made by individual members of Congress.

Table 10.1 illustrates the important weight of the Parliamentary Secretariat within the overall congressional advisory structure. However, the staff professionals comprising the Secretariat do not have functions related to examining public policies. They work in the offices of Congress members and help organise their terms of office.[7] Most of this large and complex structure actually focuses on internal administrative activities and support for the members' terms of office. The congressional employees that are trained and authorised for policy analysis are basically those in the DECOM, the Party Leadership Advisory Body and CONLE. In other words, these comprise the staff structure per se.

Table 10.1: **Chamber of Deputies staff (as of 31 August 2011)**

Career employees	3,373
Special Nature Positions (CNEs) (freely appointed)	1,291
Parliamentary Secretariat — without permanent contracts	10,227
Parliamentary Secretariat — requisitioned	539
Total	15,430

Source: Directorate of Administrative Coordination (Legislative Consulting Body, Chamber of Deputies).

Table 10.2 illustrates the significant investment made by the Chamber of Deputies in staff training for public policy analysis.[8] All the members of CONLE (a centralised structure whose function is to support the staff working directly with members of Congress to draft reports, bills and amendments) have university degrees. Nearly 50% have graduate degrees (77 have Masters' degrees or PhDs). There is naturally a wider variation in the staff statistics from DECOM and the offices of the party leaders, which include all types of professionals, from support personnel with less training to more specialised public policy experts. Even so, there is a significant contingent of advisors with university diplomas and with some expert training. The figures are lower for Masters' degrees, and there are few or no PhDs.

A superficial reading of the numbers does not allow any inference concerning the greater or lesser degree to which the committees call on these advisors for support. A simple calculation would indicate that each standing committee (of which there are now 20) is supported by an average of 15 advisors (counting the total professional staff assigned to the DECOM, namely, 312). This is no negligible figure, considering how many have graduate degrees. Still, the standing committees are not the only ones to analyse policies under review in the House. A major share of legislative activity involves the special or ad hoc committees, created to examine specific bills. In addition,

Table 10.2: **Educational level of the Chamber of Deputies staff training for policy analysis**

Educational level	DECOM	Party Leaders	CONLE
Complete PhD	0	1	23
Complete Masters' degree	18	14	54
Complete specialisation	102	100	59
Complete university	119	85	28
Complete primary	7	13	
Complete secondary	39	44	
No information	17	42	
Total	312	299	164

Source: Directorate of Administrative Coordination (Legislative Consulting Body, Chamber of Deputies).

and specifically relevant for the purposes of our argument, a significant contingent of expert advisors also works with the party leaders. As shown in the chart, the latter rely on 299 advisors, the vast majority of whom have university diplomas, and one third of whom with at least specialist degrees. More important still is a large contingent of PhDs and Masters among the CONLE staff. This is definitely the internal body that is best prepared to develop informational work, as foreseen under the informational theory applied to the case of the Brazilian legislature.

One can naturally imagine that advisors assigned to different positions also undergo distinct pressures. Those in the CONLE would be more exposed to forces and demands from individual members of Congress when compared to party leadership advisors, whom one would suppose would be called on to defend the party line when analysing specific bills.

The interviews discussed in the following aim precisely to identify the incentives or underpinnings behind the work by congressional advisors in the Brazilian legislature. In short, the study's aim, based on interviews with key actors in the Chamber of Deputies' advisory structure, is to measure the degree to which the congressional advisory structure serves as an informational mechanism for members of Congress as a whole.

Informational work of the Brazilian Congress in public policy review

The study consisted of applying an open questionnaire to high-performance, high-pressure legislative advisors and consultants on the analysis of public policy bills and other matters in the Chamber of Deputies. The notion is that such staff members are perfectly prepared to conduct informational work as required by the committees. Five interviewees were selected, categorised as follows: one employee of the General Secretariat of the Chamber of Deputies' Steering Board; one legislative consultant specialised in constitutional issues who advises the Committee on Constitution, Justice and Citizenship (CCJC); one legislative consultant specialised in educational affairs who routinely provides support to the Committee on Education, Culture and Sports (CECD); one advisor to a major party with a centre-right profile; and one advisor to a major centre-left party.

These specific staff members were selected for the following reasons. In the institutional structure of the Chamber of Deputies, the main body that initiates the review process and later determines a bill's destination is the General Secretariat of the Steering Board. The Secretariat processes all the bills that require decisions by Congress. The General Secretariat is responsible for determining which committee (or, frequently, how many and which committees) should assess the merit and adequacy of a given bill. Importantly, sending a bill to one or more committees is not politically neutral, because when a bill or amendment is reviewed by three or more standing committees, the Chamber's standing orders require the creation of a special committee for the final decision.

The next most important body in the legislative decision-making process is the CCJC. This is a standing committee, but all the bills reviewed by the Chamber pass through it. Without its approval, nothing can be passed either on the floor or by way of conclusive recommendations by the standing committees. Although, technically speaking, the CCJC is only responsible for ruling on the constitutionality and legislative rules of order used in drafting the bill, a body with such a prerogative obviously brings considerable weight to bear on the Chamber's overall legislative behaviour.

The committee system in the Chamber of Deputies also uses various permanent bodies for substantive public policy assessment. In the social area, in addition to the Committee on Labor, Health and Human Rights, the CECD plays an outstanding role and was chosen for one of the interviews. As shown in the discussion from the literature, the committees' work is sometimes interrupted by the party leaders, when (in coordination with the executive) the bills under review are sent to the floor before the rapporteur's report reaches a vote in the committee. However, this does not mean that the relevance of the substantive committees is entirely cancelled out during the course of the decision-making process. Various amendments are commonly drafted inside the committees, in addition to hearings, depositions and debate on the most polemical points around various matters under review.

Yet, if the parties (through their leadership) are the main entities dealing with the decision-making process, especially for bills that are in the administration's interest, it is necessary to examine how their technical support staff (in other words, their advisory structure) conducts its activities. The advisory structures of two major parties were chosen, namely, the Democrat Party (DEM; centre-right) and the Workers' Party (PT; centre-left).

The basic questionnaire (see the Appendix), which includes 10 questions, focused on the process of receiving bills and distributing them to various levels or individual members of Congress with a view towards producing final policy reports. The aim was to measure the advisors' degree of autonomy in performing their work and the main sources of external lobbying. Minor variations were made in the questionnaire based on the distinct nature of the interviewees.

What was expected of the interviews? Basically, a description of the expert advisor's work during the examination of relevant bills, namely, those aimed at significant changes in the country's status quo. In general, a change in the legislation is the beginning of any public policy decision-making process, especially when the objective is to alter given social conditions that are considered undesirable. The interviews also aimed to detect external constraints on the advisors' work. Finally, it was important to examine potential convergences and disparities between the different advisors in the nature of such constraints.

The overall picture emerging from the study highlighted at least three main points of consensus: first, that the legislature actually experiences significant informational disadvantages in relation to the executive in the examination of public policies; second, that the parties themselves and lobbying impact the work of the General Secretariat of the Steering Board, and naturally also the advisory structure of the party leadership; and, third, that although the Legislative Consulting Body is institutionally bound to the Chamber and its individual members, in practice, its work is almost entirely devoted to the committees. Other specific points from the various interviewees include the following:

- The first fundamental question pertains to the criteria for sending relevant bills to the committees, or to retrieve them. We learned from the interview with the expert advisor to the Steering Board that this decision is based on technical criteria, according to explicit orientation under the Chamber's bylaws. According to this same interviewee, the Speaker of the Chamber, who is ultimately responsible for the decision, follows the advisors' recommendations. Still, pressure is brought to bear to distribute the bills to the specific committees, and such pressure comes from the chairpersons of the standing committees, but also sometimes from congressional groups and coalitions. As for retrieving bills from the committees and referring them to the floor or to some ad hoc committee, there is no order from the Steering Board's advisors concerning the substance of the matter. The advisors limit themselves to informing on deadlines and recommending extensions under specific circumstances. There is also a recommendation in the case of complex bills whose content directly affects more than three standing committees.
- The interview with the consultant who works in an area close to that of the CCJC raised the following central points: first, any member of Congress, and not only the rapporteurs for bills under review, can request assistance from consultants at any time (especially for drafting separate votes, but also for accompanying debates and votes); second, however, most of the demand comes from the rapporteurs; third, the consultant's work is essentially technical, autonomous and backed mainly by his or her own research, with no additional consultation with external agents; and, fourth, the turnaround time for the consultants' work is dictated by the members of Congress that request it.
- The consultant belonging to the substantive public policy areas added the following points to the two previous interviews: first, the consultants' work essentially affects the drafting of reports, but consultancy on amendments to bills coming up for vote is also requested; second, when there is a shortage of time and an excess demand, there is an order of priorities in the consultants' work. For example, fast-track bills (awaiting a report to the congressional floor) and bills with a broader scope (like those reviewed by special committees) end up being prioritised; third, the consultants can recommend hearing the opinion of external groups through public hearings; and, fourth, agreements between party leaders and fast-track reviews end up altering the pace of the bill review process.

- The advisors to party leaders painted a significantly different picture from that presented by the previous consultant, with the following highlights: first, the so-called Technical Advisory Body for Party Representatives issues reports and proposes amendments mainly for the most important bills on the agenda, and the degree of importance is defined by the party leaders, for example, the DEM assigned top priority to the provisional measures under review; and, second, it is common to consult with actors from outside the legislature, such as non-governmental organisations, press organisations, interest groups and social movements.

Final remarks

The study's results confirm the basic assumptions extracted from the application of informational theory to the case of the Brazilian Chamber of Deputies. The executive's informational advantage was emphasised by the consultants and advisors interviewed here, who are directly involved in public policy bills under review in the legislature. Meanwhile, the structure assembled in the CONLE, where a major share of the staff hold graduate degrees, gives Congress some degree of expertise for endogenously generating information. And this is precisely the essence of the work by these advisors, according to interviews with them.

The CONLE is structured to meet individual or collective demands by members of Congress. It is thus legitimate to ask whether the congressional committees benefit from the consultants' work, and whether such work primarily expresses the representatives' need to specialise in the distribution of benefits to more restricted regions and groups. However, this was not the picture that emerged from the consultants heard by this study. According to these advisors and consultants, although the work by the CONLE can be requisitioned at any time by members of Congress who are interested in producing amendments, its daily operations are characterised by supporting rapporteurs in drafting reports.

In clear contrast with the work by advisors to party leaders (namely, to seek backing for increasing the efficiency of party strategies in their political confrontations in the Chamber), the consultants' work is to generate information ('hard data') for generating reports and expert opinions to be examined by the committees. This work is done autonomously, with the exception of consultations with experts hired to expound their knowledge in public hearings.

So, what emerges from the preceding discussion? Basically, that the standing committee system in the Brazilian legislature does indeed play a relevant informational role in the public policy decision-making process. When the divergence between the executive and the congressional majorities on a given policy is sufficiently great and there is an 'opposition' committee in charge of examining the bill, the Chamber of Deputies has the necessary advisory structure to oppose the recommendations issued by the executive.

Notes

[1] In the functionalist structural literature, a legislative branch can be transformative, active or reactive. On this line of analysis, see Polsby (1968), Packenham (1970), Loewenberg and Patterson (1979) and Mezey (1985).

[2.] For an interesting discussion on this literature, see Limongi (1994).

[3.] The main studies along this line are Mayhew (1974), Ferejohn (1974), Fiorina (1977), Shepsle (1979), Weingast and Marshall (1983) and Cain et al (1987).

[4.] The most important studies in this tradition are Kiewiet and McCubbins (1991), Rohde (1991), Cox and McCubbins (1993) and Sinclair (1995).

[5.] The most common assumption, which we share, is that ω is the realisation of a uniformly distributed random variable based on [0,1]. For a discussion of the implications of this assumption, see Bendor and Meirowitz (2004).

[6.] For a more detailed analysis of the committee's reasons for producing information, see Chapter Two, this volume.

[7.] The Parliamentary Secretariat involves the staff professionals that work directly in the offices of members of Congress. They are hired directly by the Deputies and can work both in Brasília and in the home states. For a description of this class of civil servants, see: www2.camara.gov.br/a-camara/estruturaadm/depes/portal-da-posse/secretariado-parlamentar

[8.] Concerning investment in staff training, see the website of the Chamber of Deputies and specifically the link to the Center for Human Resources Training (CEFOR) (www2.camara.leg.br/a-camara/estruturaadm/cefor/contatos).

References

Amorin Neto, O. and Santos, F. (2003) The inefficient secret revisited: the legislative input and output of Brazilian deputies', *Legislative Studies Quarterly*, vol 28, no 4, pp 449–79.

Bendor, J. and Meirowitz, A. (2004) 'Spatial models of delegation', *American Political Science Review*, Vol 98, Issue 02, pp 293-310.

Brady, D.W. and Volden, C. (1998) *Revolving gridlock: politics and policy from Carter to Clinton*, Colorado, CO: Westview Press.

Cain, B., Ferejohn, J. and Fiorina, M. (1987) *The personal vote: constituency service and electoral independence*, Harvard, MA: Harvard University Press.

Carvalho, N.R. (2003) *E no início eram as bases: geografia política do voto e comportamento legislativo no Brasil*, Rio de Janeiro: Revan.

Cox, G. and McCubbins, M. (1993) *Legislative leviathan: party government in the house*, Berkeley, CA: University of California Press.

Ferejohn, J. (1974) *Pork barrel politics: rivers and harbors legislation 1947–1968*, Stanford, CA: Stanford University Press.

Figueiredo, A.C. and Limongi, F.G.P. (1999) *Executivo e legislativo na nova ordem constitucional*, Rio de Janeiro: Fundação Getulio Vargas Editora.

Figueiredo, A.C. and Limongi, F.G.P (2002) 'Incentivos eleitorais, partidos e política orçamentária', *Dados*, vol 45, no 2, pp 303–44.

Fiorina, M.P. (1977) *Congress: keystone of the Washington establishment*, New Haven, CT: Yale University Press.

Gilligan, T. and Krehbiel, K. (1987) 'Collective decision-making and standing committees: an informal rationale for restrictive amendment procedures', *Journal of Law, Economics, and Organization*, no 3, pp 287–335.

Kiewiet, D.R. and McCubbins, M.D. (1991) *The logic of delegation: congressional parties and the appropriations process*, Chicago, IL: The University of Chicago Press.

Krehbiel, K. (1990) *Information and legislative organization*, Ann Arbor, MI: The University of Michigan Press.

Limongi, F. (1994) 'O novo institucionalismo e os estudos legislativos: a literatura norte-americana recente', *BIB – Boletim Informativo e Bibliográfico de Ciências Sociais*, vol 37, pp 3–38.

Lowenberg, G. and Patterson, S. (1979) *Comparing legislatures*, Boston, MA: Little Brown.

Mayhew, D.R. (1974) *Congress: the electoral connection*, New Haven, CT: Yale University Press.

Mezey, M.L. (1985) 'Functions of legislatures in the third world', in G. Lowenberg, S. Patterson and M.E. Jewell (eds) *Handbook of legislative research*, Cambridge, MA: Harvard University Press.

Packenham, R. (1970) 'Legislatures and political development', in A. Kornberg and L.D. Musolf (eds) *Legislatures in developmental perspectives*, Durham, NC: Duke University Press.

Pereira, C. and Mueller, B. (2000) 'Uma teoria da preponderância do poder executivo: o sistema de comissões no legislativo brasileiro', *Revista Brasileira de Ciências Sociais*, vol 15, no 43, pp 45–68.

Polsby, N. (1968) 'The institutionalization of the US House of Representatives', *American Political Science Review*, vol 62, pp 144–68.

Rohde, D.W. (1991) *Parties and leaders in the post-reform House*, Chicago, IL: The University Press.

Samuels, D.J. (2003) *Ambition, federalism, and legislative politics in Brazil*, New York, NY: Cambridge University Press.

Santos, F. and Almeida, A. (2011) *Fundamentos informacionais do presidencialismo de coalizão*, Curitiba: APPRIS.

Shepsle, K.A. (1979) *The giant jigsaw puzzle*, Chicago, IL: The University of Chicago Press.

Sinclair, B. (1995) *Legislators, leaders and lawmaking: the US House of Representatives in the post reform era*, Baltimore, MD: The Johns Hopkins University Press.

Weingast, B. and Marshall, W. (1983) 'The industrial organization of congress; or, why legislatures, like firms are not organized as markets?', *Journal of Political Economy*, vol 96, no 1, pp 132-63.

Appendix: Basic questionnaire

1. Is the work by the consultant (or advisor) only requisitioned by the rapporteur to respond to the need to issue an opinion or report, or can it be requested by other committee members and in a wider variety of circumstances?

2. What internal criterion does the committee use to allocate the consultants' (advisors') time to a given public policy, that is, the criterion to support demands by members of Congress?

3. Do members of Congress other than the rapporteur have the habit of requesting this advisory support?

4. Does the rapporteur always request such advisory support, or does it depend on the policy?

5. Does the work by the consultant (or advisor) focus exclusively on constitutional aspects of the bill, or is the bill's substance also assessed?

6. Is the consulting (or advisory) body encouraged to seek backing from outside agents, such as other contacts inside Congress (for example, party leaders) and extramural agents (like the federal, state and municipal executive branches, as well as interest groups, non-governmental organisations, and so on)?

7. Or is the consulting (advisory) work essentially autonomous, extracted entirely from the consultants' (or advisors') own research and points of view?

8. In general, what degree of investment in information do consultants (advisors) make in a given public policy? In your assessment, is it consistent with the analogous work in the executive?

9. In general, what is the response to the consulting (or advisory) structure when drafting reports and opinions? Is there a return on this investment in terms of the policy's final profile?

10. What can interrupt (or speed up) the research work by the consultants (or advisors) for the CCJC concerning a specific public policy?

PART THREE

PARTIES, COUNCILS, INTEREST GROUPS AND ADVOCACY-BASED POLICY ANALYSIS

Brazil's National Council for Social Assistance and the policy community supporting social assistance as a right

Soraya Vargas Côrtes

Introduction

In the past 20 years, forums with societal participation – such as participatory budgets and policy councils and conferences – have been introduced in Brazil in practically all areas of government (Dagnino, 2002; Santos and Avritzer, 2002). The policy councils are most conspicuous because they have become widespread across the country. They are present in municipalities and states of the federation, in addition to the 32 councils and two national commissions operating at the federal level (Brasil, 2010c). They promote the democratisation of the state and democratic governance at the various levels of government (Boschi, 1999; Dagnino, 2002; Santos and Avritzer, 2002; Côrtes, 2006). However, the institutional history of the respective policy area and the activities of sectoral policy communities endow them with other functions beyond those usually mentioned in the literature. The communities are formed on the basis of relationships between actors in existing networks in specific policy areas (Heclo, 1978). They involve a limited and relatively stable number of members who share beliefs, values and a certain view of what the policy outcomes should be (Rhodes, 1986). The analysis of this chapter focuses on the strategies used by a policy community that supported social assistance as a citizens' right. In the late 2000s, as a result of those strategies, the Unified Social Assistance System (Sistema Único de Assistência Social; SUAS) was set up and the institutional roles of the National Council for Social Assistance (Conselho Nacional de Assistência Social; CNAS) were redefined.

In the 2000s, social assistance ceased to be an aggregate, relatively disorganised set of actions pursued by 'charitable' individuals or organisations – referred to as philanthropic –and become one of the most important policy areas in Brazil (Vaitsman et al, 2009). This is expressed in the fact that, between 1995 and 2009, it was the social area that expanded most, as indicated by federal social spending, which grew by 1,250%. Over that same period, as a percentage of gross domestic product (GDP), social spending rose from 0.08% in 1995 to 0.75% in 2004 and 1.08% in 2009 (IPEA, 2011).

The institutional framework that organises this area has its origins in Brazil's 1988 Constitution, which enshrined the right of the needy to assistance, and the principles of 'political–administrative decentralisation' and 'public participation' (Brasil, 1988, Art 204). After 1993, supplementary legislation and federal administrative measures introduced: councils and conferences at the federal, state and municipal management levels; exclusive national, state and municipal funds to support assistance;

mechanisms for fund transfers from the federal to state and municipal levels of management; federative intermanagerial coordination commissions; and municipality responsibility for implementing the policies in their territories. In 1997 and 1998, Basic Operational Norms (NOBs) stipulated the main features of, and funding and federative coordination mechanisms for, the sector. The process culminated when NOBs were issued in 2004 to set up the SUAS (Brasil, 2004) and, in 2005, to regulate the new system (Brasil, 2005).

Social assistance, financed basically from federal funds (Brasil, 2007), offers social services through a network of government, philanthropic and private providers. The government's capacity to administer the recently established system is not yet well developed. In 2009, there were municipal social assistance councils in 99.3% of municipalities and almost all of them (99.8%) had some kind of administrative structure responsible for the area. That same year, however, only 70% of municipalities had a government department dealing exclusively with social assistance; in a quarter of them, policies were conducted by the first lady; and in 54% of them, the local manager did not have higher education (IBGE, 2009).

Social assistance is designed for the underprivileged. For those of a liberal ideological bent, only a few – children or people with disabilities, for instance – deserve support. The rest should make a livelihood in the market. Associated with this conception is the view that attributes the function of providing succour to the needy primarily to voluntary charitable organisations. In Brazil, organisations connected with Christian churches, especially the Catholic Church, were chiefly responsible for this type of social care (Menezes, 2010). To others, such as those behind the SUAS, below certain thresholds of income and access to goods and services, all citizens are entitled to social assistance. The area's growing relative importance is due partly to the strategic actions of a policy community that supported this latter view and whose members, from 2004 onward, took the helm of social assistance policy.

The CNAS was set up in 1994 at the start of the process of structuring a national social assistance policy. Like similar forums in other areas, the CNAS is a neo-corporatist intermediary organisation introduced by the Brazilian state and stands at the apex of a chain of state and municipal councils and periodical conference processes. In the course of the 2000s, the CNAS issued crucial resolutions to regulate the SUAS, which was being structured at that time. In 2009, thanks to the enactment of Law 12.101 (Brasil, 2009b), the council was deprived of the function it had played up until then, of accrediting beneficent social assistance organisations, and thus granting them tax exemptions. The CNAS's transition to its new role was now complete.[1]

There are three sections to this chapter. The first discusses the concepts of 'neo-corporatist intermediary organisations' and 'policy communities', which are fundamental to understanding the CNAS's role in this area. The second examines the participating actors and how the council operates. The third section examines that community's actions and how the forum's institutional role has changed.

Neo-corporatist intermediary organisations and policy communities

The CNAS is a 'neo-corporatist intermediary organisation' (Streeck and Kenworthy, 2005: 15–17) recognised and set up by the government, which has strong influence over it (Côrtes and Gugliano, 2010). Established from the top down, the national forums form the upper level of a major inter-organisational array of intermediary institutions, which interact with societal intermediary organisations belonging to the lower level, formed from the bottom up. Participation by representatives of diverse interest groups – business, philanthropic, professional and other civil society associations – does not mean the state 'licensing' the organisations they represent, as in state corporatism; however, it undoubtedly does grant them 'recognition', and therefore legitimates these representatives with regard to their organisations' members, as in neo-corporatism (or 'societal corporatism'). Accordingly, representatives who sit on the councils are seen as leaders who can influence policies. Meanwhile, they undertake to comply with decisions taken there and become responsible for executing the policies through their organisations (Côrtes and Gugliano, 2010).

In Brazil, a developmentalist state took an active part in organising civil society by imposing corporatist arrangements (Rodrigues, 1990; Schmitter, 1971). In the 1990s, the state structured new forms of governance by setting up neo-corporatist intermediary organisations, particularly public policy councils. In countries with highly unequal socio-economic structures, such as Brazil, neo-corporatist mechanisms for representing interests can open the decision-making process to social groups that lack the capability to find proper representation in the pluralist sphere (Santos, 2001).

In 'executive-dominant' political systems, such as Brazil's (Figueiredo and Limongi, 2009), participation by neo-corporatist intermediary organisations in the government decision-making process is favoured by their proximity to the core group of decision-makers in the federal executive. This group has strong influence on the process of choosing among solutions to problems placed on the government agenda (Heclo, 1978, p 2006). On the councils, societal stakeholders influence government decision-makers, while the latter commit representatives of societal organisations to implementing decisions taken at these forums. This is one of the chief reasons the CNAS became so important during the introduction of the SUAS in the 2000s. However, both the perception that the council could favour policy implementation and the decision to work through it depended on the activities of a policy community that interconnected societal and state stakeholders to that end.

The notion of policy community (Heclo, 1978; Jordan and Richardson, 1979; Rhodes, 1986) helps to understand how policy-related decision-making takes place. Policy communities comprise state and social actors, and support a certain view as to desirable policy outcomes. State actors are individuals or groups that hold senior office in government bodies, while the concept of societal actor refers both to social actors, from civil society, and market actors associated with the market economy (Cohen, 2003). The communities are made up of individuals and groups who hold positions in the state and societal spheres, and participate in policy networks, endeavouring to affect decision-making processes that have become highly segmented in that policies are formed by myriad interconnected and interpenetrating government and societal organisations (Jordan and Richardson, 1979). Their strategies are built up in processes closed to other communities and to the general public (Rhodes, 1986). They may be called 'iron triangles', 'issue niches', 'policy subsystems', 'issue networks' or 'advocacy coalitions', but 'whatever the name one gives to these communities of specialists operating out of the political spotlight, most issues most of the time are treated within such a community of experts' (True et al, 2007, pp 157–8). When they become policy decision-makers, members of a community act so that the chosen solutions to problems on the government agenda are suited to their policy values and outlook.

The functioning of the CNAS, a neo-corporatist intermediary organisation that went through far-reaching changes in 2010, is examined in the following. Due chiefly to the actions of the policy community advocating for social assistance as a right, it lost its traditional notarial role of accrediting organisations as 'charities' and consolidated a role as a producer of norms that guided the institutionalisation of the SUAS nationwide.

Working dynamics of the National Council for Social Assistance: dominance of federal government representatives

In 2010, the council comprised a plenary, permanent and temporary commissions, working parties, an executive secretariat, and a steering group termed the 'joint chair' (Presidência Ampliada) (Brasil, 2009a).[2] It also had three adjudication chambers, responsible for the remaining applications for certificates of charitable purpose, which the CNAS ceased to issue as of November 2009 (Brasil, 2010a).

The most important body was the *plenary*, which had 18 full members, each with one deputy member (see Table 11.1). It met monthly for two or three consecutive days to analyse and discuss proposals for the area and to produce resolutions. There were also *permanent commissions* on policies, councils, financing and norms, as well as *working parties* and *temporary commissions* comprising and coordinated by council members. Their purpose was to discuss agenda topics in detail and to inform plenary decisions with their analyses. The *executive secretariat*, reporting directly to the council chair and functionally linked to the Ministry for Social Development and to Combat Hunger (Ministério do Desenvolvimento Social e Combate à Fome; MDS), was responsible for managing the support structure for forum activities. The *steering group* – the 'joint chair' – was responsible for setting agendas for the meetings. It was elected by council members during the plenary assembly. Most council management and representation functions were concentrated in the chair.

Originally, the government was over-represented in the plenary, because legislation stipulated parity between 'government' and 'civil society' representatives (Brasil, 1993a, Art 16). The 'government' group comprised representatives from the federal, state and municipal levels of management, while council members from organisations of providers, social service beneficiaries and professionals and workers made up the 'civil society' segment. As Table 11.1 shows, in 2010, seven out of nine government representatives came from federal agencies; that is, they alone accounted for 39% of council members. Also, in 2010, most issues discussed by the plenary were introduced by federal managers or entered the agenda because the government had taken measures with major impact on how the area and council itself operated (Brasil, 2010a).

Once a topic entered the agenda, it went through the process of deliberation that preceded plenary decision-making. Often, prior agreements were reached during party and commission work, during seminars involving participants from public agencies and civil society organisations, during the work of the joint chair, and in ministry offices. Council members who led council decision-making processes sought actively to build agreements. Plenary decisions were usually reached by consensus (A.S., 2011; G.J., 2011; P.L., 2011).

Table 11.1: Composition of the National Council for Social Assistance by type of state and societal representative, 2010

State representatives	Government	Ministry of Social Development and to Fight Hunger (four representatives), Ministry of Social Security, Ministry of Planning, Ministry of Budget and Management, and Ministry of Education **National Forum of State Social Assistance Secretaries** **National Board of Municipal Social Assistance Managers**	
Societal representatives	Private social assistance service providers[a]	JANUARY TO MAY 2010 Brazilian Federation of Young Men's Christian Associations	JUNE TO DECEMBER 2010 Camillian Social Union Brazilian Union for Education and Teaching
	Social assistance professionals and workers	National Federation of Psychologists	
		JANUARY TO MAY 2010 National Federation of Social Assistants National Federation of Workers in Beneficent, Religious and Philanthropic Organizations	JUNE TO DECEMBER 2010 CUT National Confederation of Social Security Workers
	Workers (non-social assistance)		JUNE TO DECEMBER 2010 Central Union of Brazilian Workers
	Associations of people in a situation of social vulnerability		JUNE TO DECEMBER 2010 National Movement of Street Population
	Entities representing people with diseases or disabilities	National Federation of Associations to Value People with Disabilities	
		JANUARY TO MAY 2010 Brazilian Association for the Blind National Federation of Associations of Parents and Friends of the Mentally Disabled	JUNE TO DECEMBER 2010 Brazilian Association for Autism
	Churches	JANUARY TO MAY 2010 Methodist Church Association Brazilian National Conference of Bishops	JUNE TO DECEMBER 2010 Brazilian Spiritist Federation

Note: [a] Although such organisations represented 'philanthropic' service providers, they are identified as 'private' here because they operated on the educational, health or social assistance services and goods markets.

Source: Brasil (2010c)

Who were the council members who led the council's decision-making process? Considering the level of involvement in plenary assemblies as a significant indicator, state and social stakeholders participated significantly. However, Figure 11.1 shows that federal government representatives spoke most at all stages of meetings.[3] They intervened more than other participant types during analysis of the topics, and they spoke even more during the decisive stage of discussions when final recommendations were given for decisions to be made. Non-members were more active during the analysis process, since they were guest experts invited to provide technical input to inform the council members' decision-making process. Of the social stakeholders, two types of participant were most active: church representatives and representatives of social assistance professional and workers associations. Council members from private

Figure 11.1: **Words spoken by participant type by stage in plenary meetings, National Council for Social Assistance, 2010**

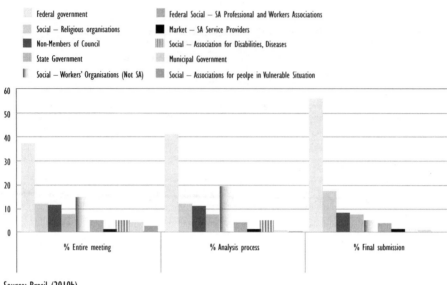

Source: Brasil (2010b)

service provider organisations formed the fourth most active group at all three stages of discussion, excluding interventions by non-members.

Participation by different groups of council members varied with the issue on the agenda, except for federal government representatives, who intervened more at all stages of meetings. In 2011, during discussions that led to approval of Resolution NOB-RH/SUAS regulating SUAS work teams (Brasil, 2011), most interventions came from representatives of social assistance professional and workers associations, especially psychologists and social workers. In fact, they were even more active than the federal government representatives (4,433 and 1,105 words recorded in the minutes, respectively). During debate of NOB/SUAS 2010 (Brasil, 2010a), which – among other things – introduced new mechanisms for municipalities to qualify for the different levels of managerial autonomy and expanded government regulation of social assistance services, interventions by representatives of social assistance professional and workers associations were surpassed in volume only by those of federal government council members (1,626 and 3,829 words, respectively). When the CNAS addressed Federal Law 12.101 (Brasil, 2009b), which relieved the forum of responsibility for accrediting charitable organisations, participation by Church representatives was exceeded only by that of council members from the federal management (2,100 and 12,990 words, respectively).

The process that led the CNAS's institutional role in the area to change during the 2000s can be better understood in the light of two key features of the dynamics underlying its workings. The first is the hegemony of federal government representatives in the council, as expressed in their intense involvement in plenary meetings at all stages. Also, as social assistance policy became more important, so programmes, projects and norms issuing from the federal government often entered the council agenda. However, these federal managers were not content just to set the CNAS agenda. There was deliberate action designed to direct the council's activity and alter its institutional role.

The second characteristic is the dynamics of alliances and conflicts among groups of councillors, reflected both on the council and in the social assistance area at the time. On the one hand were representatives of the federal administration and often council members from social assistance professional and workers associations; on the other were Church groups in coalition with private social assistance service providers. These two groups were the most active on the council. Representatives of social assistance professional and workers associations defended their corporate interests, as in the discussion of Resolution NOB-RH/SUAS. However, the most active councillors in this group not only identified with the government project to set up the SUAS, they also formed part of the policy community in favour of reform (G.J., 2011). The second alliance rested on the close connection between private providers and religious organisations. This is reflected in the CNAS plenary's composition in 2010: the three organisations representing private providers belonged to Christian Churches – the Brazilian Federation of Young Men's Christian Associations (Federação Brasileira das Associações Cristãs de Moços), the Camillian Social Union (União Social Camiliana) and the (Marist) Brazilian Union for Education and Teaching (União Brasileira de Educação e Ensino) (see Table 11.1). The tensions between the two groups emerged particularly whenever the former advocated a larger state role in organising and regulating the SUAS, while the latter resisted what they often regarded as excessive government intervention.

Despite the conflicts, the federal managers of this community pushed through their reform project. Legal and administrative regulation in the area was traditionally sparse, and municipal managers did not interfere much in how private and philanthropic providers delivered their services. Providers unused to having their actions subject to public oversight mechanisms were not the only ones to resist change, municipal managers accustomed to clientelist practices and to social work assigned to first ladies, and now compelled to take on new responsibilities and organise social goods and service provision on technical criteria, also resisted the changes (F.L., 2012; G.J., 2011). The reform endeavour was successful for several reasons. One decisive factor, however, was the work of the reformist policy community, which took advantage of opportunities created by Lula's rise to the presidency, with Patrus Ananias as Minister of Social Development, and the CNAS facing allegations of corruption, to speed up consolidation of the SUAS in line with the principles they supported and to change the CNAS's institutional role.

The policy community supporting the right to social assistance and the National Council for Social Assistance's changing institutional role

The Lula government, which began in 2002, placed the issue of social inequalities and poverty right at the centre of the government agenda. However, it was not until 2004, when Patrus Ananias took over the MDS, that proposals from the policy community supporting the right to social assistance actually became government policy and its members took federal management office (A.S., 2011; F.L., 2012). Once the window of opportunity opened and the problem was firmly on the government agenda, the solutions chosen were those advocated by the reformist policy community. From then on, the process of forming the social assistance system begun in the 1990s picked up pace. In 2004 and 2005, respectively, the MDS launched the National Social Assistance Plan (Plano Nacional de Assistência Social) (Brasil, 2004) and NOB-SUAS (Brasil, 2005), which instituted the SUAS and set out its basic operating rules. The two measures were published as CNAS resolutions rather than as ministerial orders, in itself an indication of the central role the council played in the area at the time.

The new decision-makers regarded the CNAS as a hub from which to radiate the regulatory norms that would organise the system that was taking shape (A.S., 2011). In several municipalities, there were no government agencies addressing social assistance exclusively or municipal managers persuaded that it was a citizens' right (G.J., 2011). The council stood at the apex of a chain of state and municipal participatory forums that was able to take its decisions to the states and municipalities. Also, since administrative capability in the area was limited and the CNAS was very powerful within the system, the shortest and quickest route to ensure implementation of the SUAS organisational guidelines was considered to be to 'govern' through council resolutions. One of the leading CNAS members, a federal government representative, explains the strategy in the following interview excerpt:

> 'We needed to make rapid changes in the federal government, changes in the area, to implement the SUAS, change rulemaking in the area. If we had to do this through bureaucratic regulations, decrees and legislation, it would take too long.… So we put together a whole project and implemented the SUAS as we went along, through National Council Resolutions, even before making it [SUAS] law.' (A.S., 2011)

Getting proposals approved was relatively easy, because federal managers and their allies were in the majority on the council. However, for those resolutions to be considered legitimate meant exercising the art of persuasion (Goodin et al, 2006) so that council members would commit to implementing council decisions in their home organisations. It was essential to convince individuals, including those who initially opposed the proposals. Federal managers actively pursued this aim, as illustrated by the following interview excerpt: 'Usually when the Council drafts a Resolution there is enough consensus. Everybody knows it's going to pass.… Not that the interests aren't different. They are different, but council members need to exhaust all capacity to create agreements' (A.S., 2011).

Consensus built within the CNAS rested on a support base of individuals, groups and organisations that, whether in the government, professional associations, unions or even private provider associations, shared a belief in social assistance as a citizens' right. Liberal conceptions critical of this notion were not significant either on the council or at the decision-making core of the federal government (Brasil, 2010a; G.J., 2011). Arguments for assistance as charity to be given to the deserving figured in party-political clashes in legislatures, in some municipal and state governments, and in the media (B.L., 2010; A.S., 2011; P.L., 2011). Disagreement on the council related to how far the government should regulate services provided by philanthropic or private providers.

Religious and private provider organisations agreed that social assistance is a citizens' right and that publicly funded service provision should expand. However, they were opposed to the government extending its control over service organisation and provision. They considered the federal government's role to be policymaking and system coordination and they argued that the non-governmental service providers' complementary role in policy execution stipulated in the legislation was not being duly respected by government (P.L., 2011).

The process of transforming the council into a source of rules to structure the SUAS more quickly nationwide and to increase the government's control over the system gathered even more momentum when the reformist policy community saw a window of opportunity to neutralise resistance from religious and private service provider organisations: Operation Pharisee, organised by Brazil's Federal Police in 2008, yielded evidence that organisations providing hospital, educational and social assistance services had bribed CNAS members to facilitate certification of charitable institutions. This fraud, which gained major media coverage, had allegedly resulted in tax evasion of over £1.3 billion (*Estadão*, 2008). The operation weakened the political position and public image of religious social service provider organisations (A.S., 2011).

Federal managers regarded CNAS certification of charitable purpose as one of the hindrances to enacting supplementary legislation to regulate philanthropic activities (Brasil, 1993a, 1993b, 1998), because it prevented effective technical and administrative oversight of compliance with the legal requirements for the issue and maintenance of such certificates. In 2009, with the main opponents to the change politically weakened, and after intense and conflictive debate in the area (A.S., 2011), they were able to pass Federal Law 12.101 (Brasil, 2009b). The law transferred the prerogative of granting certificates of charitable purpose in the social assistance, health and education fields from the CNAS to the bureaucracies of the social development, health and education ministries, respectively.

Religious and private provider organisations accepted that the council would no longer be the accrediting body and that criteria for awarding and maintaining certification would become stricter. However, they did not agree that evaluation of the charitable status of health care and education service providers should be transferred to the ministries of health and education. They insisted that, regardless of the field in which the service is provided, the not-for-profit nature of the organisation made it a charitable social assistance institution. They argued that the accreditation process should not be moved out of the field (P.L., 2011) – a field where historically they had been more predominant (A.S., 2011; G.J., 2011). According to a council member representing the federal managers on the CNAS:

> 'With its proposal, the government managed to make it clear that schools belong to the education field. That sort of thing may sound ridiculous; I mean, making it clear that a hospital belongs to the health field.... This is one of the parts that most bothers the most conservative sectors on the national council, and not just the conservatives.... This issue keeps threatening to crop up.' (A.S., 2011)

Despite the resistance, the reformist policy community pushed through measures to organise the SUAS according to the principles it stood for, and brought about the change in the council's institutional role. From being a 'registry office' that issued certificates of charitable purpose, the council became a source that issues and circulates rules for organising and managing the system. Such rules were embodied in council resolutions addressing: parameters for the accreditation of charitable social assistance organisations; NOB/SUAS 2010, which introduced new mechanisms for qualifying municipalities at the different levels of management and expanded government regulation of service providers, along with other measures to further the integration and federal management of the system; NOB-RH/SUAS, which regulated work teams in the system; definition of social assistance, advisory and rights advocacy, and protection organisations; definition of social assistance benefits; social oversight of the family allowance programme (Programa Bolsa Família); and the scope of the National Fund for the Elderly (Fundo Nacional do Idoso) (Brasil, 2010a). These decisions' importance and unquestionable impact on the consolidation of the SUAS – as a decentralised, hierarchised system coordinated by the federal government, with federative and participatory management mechanisms, and offering social services and goods through qualified professionals and workers – demonstrates the success achieved by the policy community that defended social assistance as a right of Brazilian citizens.

Final remarks

The CNAS, set up in the 2000s as an neo-corporatist intermediary organisation open to participation from societal representatives, favoured democratic governance of the social assistance field. In that period, the council was an important source of regulation for the SUAS, which was then consolidating and expanding rapidly. The strategic actions of a policy community that had supported social assistance as a citizens' right since the 1980s contributed to establishing the SUAS and to institutionalising this new role for the council.

Members of that community took advantage of successive windows of opportunity to submit proposals to political decision-makers to solve the issue of 'marked social inequality and poverty'. Those proposals were placed at the centre of the political and governmental agenda during the Lula administration, which began in 2002. When Patrus Ananias took over the MDS in 2004, he proved amenable to their proposals. From 2004 onward, the MDS and the council passed legal and administrative rules that established and organised the SUAS according to principles supported by the reformists.

Conflicts that occurred within the council reflected disagreements relating mainly to the level of government control over the system. On one side were federal government representatives, often allied with council members from social assistance professional and workers associations; on the other were religious and service provider organisations – the former wanting to expand government control over the emerging system, and the latter wanting to maintain their historical freedom of action.

The reformist policy community took advantage of a new window of opportunity that opened up in 2008 when Operation Pharisee publicly exposed illegal connections between certain council members and organisations granted charitable purpose accreditation, and thus entitled to substantial tax exemptions. As a result, legal and administrative measures deprived the forum of its prerogative of accrediting and overseeing 'charitable' organisations, which was then transferred to government authorities in the social assistance, health and education fields. From then on, the council consolidated its role as a source of rules on the organisation of the social assistance system in Brazil. Its participants became co-responsible for compliance with CNAS decisions within their organisations and in their home municipalities and states, and accordingly committed to implementing policies established at the federal level of management.

The reformist policy community and the CNAS took shape as a collective actor and a neo-corporatist intermediary organisation that participated actively in the process of setting up the SUAS. This policy community developed the arguments, produced the technical solutions to issues that arose in the course of implementing the new system and devised strategies to advance their project. The council stated the rationale for the changes: it was the main arena for the process of persuading stakeholders involved in social service management and provision and, above all, it produced analyses and rules that propagated from the federal to the local level, making it possible in fact to implement the SUAS nationwide. In that light, the activities of the reformist policy community and council were decisive to building a social assistance system organised according to the principles of the universality of the right of the needy to assistance, administrative decentralisation, public sector oversight of how goods and services are provided, and social participation. That system, from the outset, has fostered social inclusion for millions of Brazilian citizens.

Notes

[1.] The research on which this chapter is based focuses on the year 2010 – when Federal Law 12.101 was enacted – but is not restricted to it. We have analysed: relevant acts and ministry regulations; resolutions and other documents issued by the Council itself; information available from the Council and Ministry for Social Development and to Combat Hunger (Ministério do Desenvolvimento Social e Combate à Fome; MDS) websites; and minutes of 11 CNAS plenary meetings. We also used in this study transcripts of interviews with two very active council members, one a civil society and the other a federal government representative, in addition to two MDS managers and one state manager, the last three very much involved with the SUAS construction process.

[2.] The CNAS was located in set of meeting rooms in an office building in Annex A of the Ministry of Labour.

[3.] Interventions made by the Council's president were not taken into account. Because of its prominent role in conducting sessions, its inclusion in one of the groups might have biased results, artificially increasing the number of interventions of the segment to which the president belonged.

References

A.S. (2011) Interview conducted on 10 October, Brasília, transcribed, Arquivos GPPS/UFRGS.

B.L. (2010) Interview conducted on 19 June, Porto Alegre, transcribed, Arquivos GPPS/UFRGS.

Boschi, R.R. (1999) 'Descentralização, clientelismo e capital social na governança urbana: comparando Belo Horizonte e Salvador', *Dados*, vol 4, no 42, pp 655–90.

Brasil (1988) *Constituição da República Federativa do Brasil de 05 de Outubro de 1988,* Assembléia Nacional Constituinte (www.senado.gov.br/legislacao/const/).

Brasil (1993a) *Lei 8.742 de 7 de Dezembro de 1993 – Dispõe sobre a organização da assistência social e dá outras providências,* Congresso Nacional (http://legis.senado.gov.br/sicon/).

Brasil (1993b) *Decreto 752, de 16 de fevereiro de 1993. Dispõe sobre a concessão do Certificado de Entidade de Fins Filantrópicos, a que se refere o art. 55, inciso II, da Lei no 8.212, de 24 de julho de 1991, e dá outras providências* (http://legis.senado.gov.br/sicon/).

Brasil (1998) *Decreto 2.536, de 6 de abril de 1998. Dispõe sobre a concessão do Certificado de Entidade de Fins Filantrópicos a que se refere o inciso IV do art. 18 da Lei no 8.742, de 7 de dezembro de 1993, e dá outras providência* (http://legis.senado.gov.br/sicon/).

Brasil (2004) *Plano Nacional de Assistência Social,* November, Brasília: MDS.

Brasil (2005) *Norma Operacional Básica – NOB/SUAS – Construindo as bases para a implantação do Sistema Único de Assistência Social,* July, Brasília: MDS.

Brasil (2007) 'Financiamento da Assistência Social no Brasil', MDS, *Caderno SUAS,* vol 2, no 2 (www.mds.gov.br/assistenciasocial/secretaria-nacional-de-assistencia-social-snas/cadernos/caderno-suas-2-2013-financiamento-da-assistencia-social-no-brasil/caderno-suas-2-2013-financiamento-da-assistencia-social-no-brasil).

Brasil (2009a) *Resolução No 70 de 17 de agosto de 2009. Altera o Regimento Interno, o Manual de Procedimentos e arquiva os processos com diligências não cumpridas pelas respectivas entidades,* CNAS (www.mds.gov.br/cnas/legislacao/legislacao/resolucoes/arquivos-2009/resolucoes-normativas-de-2009/).

Brasil (2009b) *Lei No 12.101, de 27 de novembro de 2009. Dispõe sobre a certificação das entidades beneficentes de assistência social; regula os procedimentos de isenção de contribuições para a seguridade social; e dá outras providências,* Congresso Nacional (http://legis.senado.gov.br/sicon/).

Brasil (2010a) 'Atas de reunião', CNAS (www.mds.gov.br/cnas/Eventos_CNAS/reunioes-ordinarias/reunioes-do-cnas/reunioes-ordinarias/atas/Atas%20de%202010/atas-de-2010/).

Brasil (2010b) 'Ata da reunião No 178', CNAS (www.mds.gov.br/cnas/Eventos_CNAS/reunioes-ordinarias/reunioes-do-cnas/reunioes-ordinarias/atas/Atas%20de%202010/atas-de-2010/).

Brasil (2010c) 'Secretaria Geral da Presidência da República. Secretaria Nacional de Articulação Social', *Conselhos Nacionais,* Brasília: Presidência da República (www.secretariageral.gov.br/.arquivos/arquivos-novos/Livro_Conselhos_peq.pdf/view).

Brasil (2011) *Resolução No 17, de 20 de junho de 2011. Ratificar a equipe de referência definida pela NOB-RH/SUAS e Reconhecer as categorias profissionais de nível superior para atender as especificidades dos serviços socioassistenciais e das funções essenciais de gestão do SUAS,* CNAS (www.mds.gov.br/cnas/Entidades%20Certificadas/deliberacoes/arquivos/2010/).

Cohen, J.L. (2003) 'Sociedade civil e globalização: repensando categorias', *Dados,* vol 46, no 3, pp 419–59.

Côrtes, S.M.V. (2006) 'Foros participativos y gobernabilidad: una sistematización de las contribuiciones de la literatura', in C.W. Lubambo, D.B. Coelho and M.A.B.C. Melo (eds) *Diseño institucional y participación política, experiencias en el Brasil contemporâneo,* Buenos Aires: Clacso, pp 15–37.

Côrtes, S.M.V. and Gugliano, A.A. (2010) 'Entre neocorporativos e deliberativos: uma interpretação sobre os paradigmas de análise dos fóruns participativos no Brasil', *Sociologias*, vol 24, pp 44–75.

Dagnino, E. (2002) 'Sociedade civil e espaços públicos no Brasil', in E. Dagnino (ed) *Sociedade civil e espaços públicos no Brasil*, São Paulo: Paz e Terra, pp 9–15.

Estadão (2008) 'Prejuízo com esquema de falsas filantrópicas chega a 4 bilhões', 13 March.

Figueiredo, A. and Limogi, F. (2009) 'Poder de agenda e políticas substantivas', in M. Inácio and L. Rennó (eds) *Legislativo brasileiro em perspectiva comparada*, Belo Horizonte: Editora UFMG, pp 77–104.

F.L. (2012) Interview conducted on 14 March, Brasília, transcribed, Arquivos GPPS/UFRGS.

G.J. (2011) Interview conducted on 11 October, Brasília, transcribed, Arquivos GPPS/UFRGS.

Goodin, R., Moran, M. and Rein, M. (2006) 'The public and its policies', in R.E. Goodin, M. Rein and M. Moran (eds) *The Oxford handbook of public policy*, Oxford: Oxford University Press, pp 3–35.

Heclo, H. (1978) 'Issue network and the executive establishment', in A. King (ed) *The new American political system*, Washington, DC: American Enterprise Institute for Public Policy Research.

IBGE (Instituto Brasileiro de Geografia e Estatística) (2009) 'Munic 2009' (www.ibge.gov.br/home/presidencia/noticias/noticia_visualiza.php?id_noticia=1612&id_pagina=1

IPEA (Instituto de Pesquisa Econômica Aplicada) (2011) '15 anos de gasto social federal notas sobre o período 1995 a 2009', *Comunicado do IPEA*, no 98, Brasília: IPEA.

Jordan, G. and Richardson, J.J. (1979) *Governing under pressure*, Oxford: Martin Robertson.

Menezes, F.C. (2010) 'O serviço social e a "responsabilidade social das empresas": o debate da categoria profissional na Revista Serviço Social & Sociedade e nos CBAS', *Serviço Social & Sociedade*, vol 103, pp 503–31.

P.L. (2011) Interview conducted on 6 September, Porto Alegre, transcribed, Arquivos GPPS/UFRGS.

Rhodes, R.A.W. (1986) *The national world of local government*, Oxford: Allen and Unwin.

Rodrigues, L.M. (1990) *Partidos e Sindicatos*, São Paulo: Ática.

Santos, B.S. and Avritzer, L. (2002) 'Introdução: para ampliar o cânone democrático', in B.S. Santos (ed) *Democratizar a democracia. Os caminhos da democracia participativa*, Rio de Janeiro: Civilização Brasileira, pp 39–82.

Santos, M.H.C. (2001) 'Que democracia? Uma visão conceitual desde a perspectiva dos países em desenvolvimento', *Dados*, vol 44, no 4, pp 729–71.

Schmitter, P.C. (1971) *Interest conflict and political change in Brazil*, Stanford, CA: Stanford University Press.

Streeck, W. and Kenworthy, L. (2005) 'Theories and practices of neocorporatism', in T. Janoski (ed) *The handbook of political sociology*, Cambridge: Cambridge University Press, pp 441–60.

True, J.L., Jones, B.D. and Baumgartner, F.R. (2007) 'Punctuated-equilibrium theory: explaining stability and change in public policy making', in P.A. Sabatier (ed) *Theories of the policy process*, Boulder, CO: Westview Press.

Vaitsman, J., Andrade, G.R.B. and Farias, L.O. (2009) 'Proteção social no Brasil: o que mudou na assistência social após a Constituição de 1988', *Ciência & Saúde Coletiva*, vol 14, no 3, pp 731– 41.

TWELVE

Brazil's response to the HIV/AIDS epidemic: integrating prevention and treatment

Elize Massard da Fonseca and Francisco I. Bastos

Introduction

Brazil's response to the HIV/AIDS epidemic has been viewed worldwide as one of its most successful policies. This chapter discusses the crucial and evolving role of civil society organisations (CSOs) in the Brazilian response to the AIDS epidemic. Specifically, we explore the responsibility of civil society in shaping AIDS public policy during the late 1980s and 1990s, and these groups' evolving and increasing participation on two key issues for HIV/AIDS prevention and treatment: first, policies and interventions aiming to reduce illicit drug-related harms; and, second, initiatives to inform the debate on intellectual property that could hinder the availability of AIDS drugs in the 2000s.

Many different policies could be highlighted in the broad context of the Brazilian response to HIV/AIDS, but our choice of these two aspects is far from incidental. Policies aiming to reduce illicit drug-related harms have been a focus of constant debate in Brazil and elsewhere, for instance, the debate in the US Congress over re-enactment of the federal ban on syringe and needle exchange programmes, which was repealed in the early years of the Obama administration.

Similarly, patent protection for drugs to treat AIDS has also been the subject of discussions that have sometimes degenerated into litigation and panels between Brazil and other countries and firms. At the time of writing, civil leaders from Brazil, together with CSOs from Colombia, Peru and Ecuador, have submitted a formal complaint against the European Union for repeated seizures of AIDS drugs and precursors moving through European harbours during shipment from India to Latin America.

For the purpose of this chapter, these two policy cases illustrate the evolving capability of CSOs to influence government decisions: in the former case, as service providers and pressure groups; and, in the latter, by closely informing decision-makers about highly technical aspects of pharmaceutical regulations. Note that these are two facets of interest group participation. Prevention initiatives such as needle exchanges demand legitimacy, while intellectual property is a much more information-intensive arena. AIDS patient groups in Brazil have been able to adjust their capabilities and engage in both respects in an unprecedented example of civil society engagement in a national HIV/AIDS response.

This chapter draws on documentary research, key-informant interviews and the authors' direct experience in collaborations in the public health field in Brazil and abroad. Numerous studies explain the development of Brazil's AIDS policies (for example, Nunn et al, 2009), but little is known about the evolution of CSO participation in influencing AIDS and pharmaceutical policymaking in Brazil. This analysis complements previous studies on the AIDS movement in Brazil by providing original data on advocacy for the rights of people who misuse illicit drugs and on pharmaceutical regulation, but also by demonstrating how the preferences of interest groups evolved in their interaction with government.

Two methodological disclaimers are important. First, this chapter does not take account of decisions by the National AIDS Commission (CNAIDS) (a working group to deliberate on scientific guidelines for AIDS in Brazil). Although CSOs have five seats on this commission, there is little evidence that the CNAIDS's decisions have had any major impact on the timing and direction of the macro-politics surrounding the AIDS policies under analysis. Thus, this chapter relies on well-established arguments of the role of CSOs in Brazil and expands these through inductive investigation. Second, our intention in this chapter is not to pin down the mechanisms of policy influence, such as advocacy coalitions (Sabatier and Jenkins, 1993). Presenting qualitative evidence from doctoral research on lobbying and pharmaceutical regulation in Brazil (Fonseca, 2011), this chapter offers a narrative of how AIDS advocacy has evolved in Brazil. A series of papers will be published expanding on this analysis. Therefore, this chapter aligns with the 'atheoretical case study' type (Lijphart, 1971). As Brazil is a crucial case for the study of CSOs on AIDS policy, this description is important for information-gathering on these phenomena in Brazil and for identifying avenues for further investigation.

AIDS in Brazil

AIDS incidence has stabilised in recent years in Brazil, with about 30,000 new cases registered a year. Nationwide, mathematical modelling reveals an estimated 600,000 people living with HIV infection in Brazil, with estimated national mean seroprevalence of less than 0.5%. Those figures have been fairly stable since 2000. There has been a marked reduction in incidence in large metropolitan areas, but a continuous though relatively modest spread of the epidemic to less industrialised regions of the country, as well as to small- and medium-sized municipalities (Carvalho et al, 2011), due to the less than optimal implementation of measures successfully adopted in Brazil overall.

An ongoing challenge is to reduce, or prevent the increase, of transmission in vulnerable populations, such as gay men, illicit drug users and commercial sex workers. HIV and other sexually transmitted infection (STI) infection rates remain high in these populations. However, there has been a substantial decline in the epidemic among injecting drug users. This decline is likely to have resulted: from saturation, observed in a segment that, in Brazil, is relatively small; from illicit drug users moving to non-injecting modes (for example, crack); and from the impact of prevention measures, such as needle exchange programmes.

Treatment has been a success and mortality has decreased strongly, despite persistent gaps, most of them preventable, and in this regard constituting key issues to be tackled by renewed efforts to manage AIDS better in Brazil (Veras et al, 2011). The sustainability of free access to antiretroviral (ARV) treatment is examined often, because those in treatment will accumulate treatment failures, adverse events and metabolic changes that will require attention. So far, Brazil has tackled this challenge with a well-structured treatment programme and a broad portfolio of drugs, combining first-line generic drugs produced locally at low cost, second-line drugs produced through compulsory licence and drugs under patent protection acquired internationally with negotiated discounted pricing.

Collaboration and conflict: prevention strategies and the role of civil society

CSO and gay activism played a key role in shaping the Brazilian response, particularly during the 1980s. Initially, the federal government largely ignored AIDS. The epidemic was viewed as a problem of gay men and other marginalised groups, rather than a general public health threat. In response, CSOs and the São Paulo State Health Secretariat filled the AIDS education void by campaigning for more effective prevention strategies. Newly formed AIDS CSOs played a key role in the development and implementation of most prevention programmes targeting hard-hit populations (for example, sex workers).

Because there were no effective treatments for PLWHA (people living with HIV/AIDS), contracting HIV was associated with social stigma. The social consequences of contracting HIV were just as dire as the health consequences. It was in this social context that Brazil's first AIDS programmes developed. Based in São Paulo, these programmes were grounded in a human rights-based approach and focused on including vulnerable populations in programme implementation, countering stigma and discrimination, educating the general population about HIV risks, and preserving the human rights and civil liberties of PLWHA. CSOs and public servants in São Paulo used political activism to kindle public policy debate about HIV/AIDS and the mass media to broadcast their messages.

CSOs pressed for local (municipal) prevention campaigns, initially in the larger metropolitan cities. In 1985, a partnership among gay men, human rights activists and health professionals launched the first AIDS non-governmental organisation (NGO) in Brazil, the AIDS Prevention and Support Group (GAPA). GAPA soon became a key model, fostering the development of similar NGOs in other cities throughout the country. In Rio de Janeiro, researchers, health professionals and gay activists founded the Brazilian Interdisciplinary AIDS Association (ABIA) in 1986 and in 1989, the first self-identified HIV-positive advocacy group, Grupo Pela VIDDA (Grupo pela Valorização, Integração e Dignidade do Doente de AIDS), was launched.

Productive collaboration between CSOs and the government alternated with periods of dissent and occasional conflict. These latter included the political turmoil that culminated in the impeachment of President Fernando Collor de Mello, the protests against health budget cuts introduced by President Fernando Henrique Cardoso in his first term and the litigation filed by ABIA and other NGOs against agreements reached between Brazil's Ministry of Health (BMoH) and drug companies over the costs of some ARVs during President Luis Inácio Lula da Silva's first term.

One of GAPA's main contributions to AIDS activism was the installation of a legal assistance service for PLWHA. For example, GAPA sued companies for discriminating against PLWHA and governments for failing to provide drugs to treat AIDS. According to Nunn (2008, pp 50–1), human rights were an overarching frame for this activism. The 'rights' language would not just shift the stigma of 'victim' away from these patients, but would also legally justify their demands within the constitutional right to health care for all citizens. These court decisions had long-term impacts on public policy by outlawing discrimination and forcing governments to provide drugs to PLWHA (Scheffer et al, 2005).

In 1993, a new era commenced when Brazil received a major World Bank (WB) loan for work on AIDS.[1] The federal government had set up a National AIDS Programme (NAP) in 1985, but initiatives to respond to the AIDS epidemic at the central level were underfunded until the 1993 loan agreement with the WB (although the official agreement began in 1994, Brazil received funding from the WB a year earlier to prepare the proposal) (Galvao, 2000). Civil society representatives and health professionals helped design the WB loan agreement and many were later invited to join the National Coordination on HIV/AIDS as staff members (Nunn, 2008, p 61). This placed them in an advantageous position to participate in developing Brazil's response and formally institutionalised collaborations between the Brazilian NAP and CSOs. The loan included funding for CSO projects, ranging from capacity-building and advocacy events (for example, the annual gay parade), through to preventive interventions with vulnerable populations.

The main results from this funding were that partnering between the public health sector and CSOs expanded and prevention activities were scaled up. Between 1998 and 2001, a total of 1,681 projects, involving 686 CSOs, were financed with total spending of US$30 million (Brasil, 2002); and between 2003 and 2007, US$107.3 million was invested in CSOs (Brasil, 2008). Interestingly, the fact that the federal government provides core funding for most CSOs and that there are close links between CSOs and the BMoH (with a high rate of key personnel commuting between the government and the organisations) may have had an impact on these institutions' autonomy.

While this funding may have fostered vibrant AIDS advocacy in Brazil, it also drew criticism from CSO insiders for silencing their militancy. The dissatisfaction of some activists with this new role of HIV/AIDS CSOs was reported by (Biehl, 2004). Biehl provides rich evidence of several activists being frustrated, not with the government response, but with the 'industrialisation of non-governmental work' and the 'depoliticised mission of NGOs'. Their concerns were that the close collaboration with the government had reduced activists' street and legal advocacy. For instance, stronger demands should be made for more beds at university hospitals.

Paulo Teixeira, former director of the NAP, responded to the critique by arguing that CSOs (AIDS advocacy groups) also have the right to use a fraction of public funds (Biehl, 2007, p 106). Nevertheless, collaboration between CSOs and the BMoH has yielded fruitful results and is usually acknowledged as an important component of the successful Brazilian response to the AIDS epidemic.

The case for people who misuse drugs: the challenge and the response

Up to the present decade, IDUs (injecting drug users – mainly cocaine users) have had a negligible role in the HIV/AIDS epidemic in the less industrialised areas in Northeast Brazil, with the exception of the state of Bahia (Dourado et al, 2006), the southernmost state of this region. However, IDUs have played a central role in the HIV/AIDS sub-epidemic in the industrialised Southeast, especially in the state of São

Paulo, and, in the later 1990s, along the southern coast extending from São Paulo to Brazil's southernmost border (Hacker et al, 2006).

In order to respond quickly to the synergy of cocaine trafficking/consumption and the HIV/AIDS epidemic, Brazil has included harm reduction strategies in its public health agenda since the mid-1990s. Purchase and possession of injecting equipment are legal in Brazil and there were no prescription or paraphernalia laws as exist in the US.

These initiatives were launched in Brazil by a small group of local activists, in opposition to BMoH policy at the time and, above all, in outright opposition to the prevailing drug abuse legislation approved during the military dictatorship (1964–85). That legislation defined any measure other than the permanent pursuit of abstinence as condoning and even encouraging illicit drug consumption. Enforcement resulted in activists and health professionals being arrested and prosecuted and their material (clean needles and syringes) confiscated and destroyed.

With time, state laws were passed with a view to protecting activists and health professionals from being charged and prosecuted, beginning with the approval of the São Paulo State law 42.927/1998. State legislation was helpful in implementing programmes designed to reduce illicit drug-related harms, but faced two major caveats. First, in Brazil, as in most federative countries, legal matters relating to issues that may affect national security, such as policy on illegal drugs, are regulated at the federal level (Fonseca and Bastos, 2012). Despite the regulated environment offered by state laws, nothing actually changed (in the strict legal sense) until the first, still tentative, reform of the drug law by President Cardoso and, later on, after the comprehensive drug law reform during President da Silva's government. Second, the new state laws did not have any immediate impact on local police forces' everyday procedures. Confiscation of drug users' materials continued, as well as now less-explicit but nonetheless intimidating actions against outreach workers in the field.

Despite these difficulties, needle exchange programmes (NEPs) grew steadily. By November 2006, approximately 150 NEPs were operating in Brazil (more than in any other middle- or low-income country), the vast majority funded by the BMoH and state or municipal health secretariats, but implemented by CSOs (Fonseca et al, 2006). Studies suggest that NEPs in major urban areas have successfully reduced rates of needle-sharing and HIV prevalence (Bastos et al, 2005). However, many NEPs lack managerial capacity, proper stock management and stable, well-trained staffs, resulting in less than optimal outcomes in some settings.

Recent analyses have shown that IDUs and non-injecting drug users have benefited much less than other individuals living with HIV/AIDS and/or viral hepatitis, as a result of less than optimal referral, late entry into treatment, stigma and so on (Malta et al, 2011). The management of HIV-positive cocaine users remains a challenge. There are several reasons for this, including the dynamic nature of cocaine dependence, the limitations of most drug treatment centres and HIV referral units in Brazil, which lack well-trained, motivated staff (Somaini et al, 2011).

In all, a coalition of activists and a committed cadre of health professionals, as well as institutions such as the Brazilian Association of People Working with Harm Reduction (ABORDA), have been pivotal in advocating more pragmatic health policies, as well as drug policy reform. Much has still to be accomplished in terms of proper management and support for people who misuse illicit drugs, especially in view of the recent increase in crack cocaine use in Brazil.

With the dramatic decline of injecting drug use all over the country and the substantial increase in smoked crack cocaine, the fate of harm reduction in Brazil now stands at a crossroads. In recent years, the role of IDUs in the AIDS epidemic has been very small – closer to negligible in some regions, such as Rio de Janeiro State, where it corresponds to less than 1% of new AIDS cases reported to the State Health Secretariat. This pronounced change in the drug scene all over the country demands a thorough renewal of initiatives successfully implemented in the last 25 years. From the perspective of a text being written in 2012, the new paths to be taken are far from clear, but the commitment of civil society, activists and a substantial minority of health professionals who have been working in this field for decades suggests that new ideas and initiatives will emerge to meet the new challenges posed by extensive crack cocaine use and the associated harms and risks.

Informing government decisions: the evolving role of AIDS activism and the provision of care for people living with AIDS

Brazil's policies of promoting free and universal access to AIDS drugs in the late 1990s created a budget challenge for the BMoH, which was obligated by law to provide drugs, but had an insufficient budget to finance AIDS treatment. Also at that time, Brazil's civil society networks began collaborating with global networks that had rallied around a global social movement to promote more widespread access to AIDS treatment. In 2001, Brazil publicly challenged pharmaceutical companies over the high costs of HIV drugs, and threatened to produce generic ARVs locally if companies did not lower the prices of their AIDS drugs (Nunn et al, 2007).

The question of access to AIDS drugs, especially as regards intellectual property rights and the discussion around patents, now forms part of both the Brazilian government and CSO agendas (Reis et al, 2009). In 2001, the Working Group on Intellectual Property (GTPI) of the Brazilian Network of the Integration of Peoples (REDRIP) was founded. ABIA was one of the main AIDS CSOs involved in this new network (Reis et al, 2009).

The creation of the working group demonstrates that AIDS activism in Brazil has evolved. This patient advocacy group has not just participated in prevention activities or pressuring government for access to ARVs, but has actively informed pharmaceutical regulatory debates. This section analyses this new capability of AIDS activism, how this came about and its implications for pharmaceutical regulation that affects the provision of AIDS drugs. More abstractly, this provides important lessons on the evolution of interest group preferences by demonstrating how the content of AIDS activism has changed over time.

The GTPI was set up jointly by the international NGOs Oxfam and Action Aid and several local CSOs, such as IBASE (Instituto Brasileiro de Análises Sociais e Econômicas) and GAPA. Its members include organisations working with people living with HIV/AIDS, human rights and consumers' rights. At first, the GTPI's primary concern was to consolidate different organisations and empower their political actions around intellectual property matters (GTPI, 2010). In 2003, an internal decision by REBRIP tailored the group's focus to access to drugs and intellectual property issues, which had previously included seeds and biodiversity issues as well. Initially, the working group's core aim was to engage in traditional advocacy initiatives, such as to disseminate the implications of intellectual property issues for public health and make this complex/technical topic more accessible to other Brazilian NGOs by, for instance, preparing seminars and workshops to empower leaderships on the issue.

In the mid-2000s, however, the GTPI expanded its activities and has been assisting the Brazilian government (executive, legislature and judiciary) in (re)designing pharmaceutical regulatory rules. It is difficult to pin down exactly when this participation in regulatory affairs began. Based on field research, our interpretation is that this evolution of AIDS activism relates to the current generation of highly skilled activists participating in these CSOs. Furthermore, as previously mentioned, WB and BMoH funding fostered the institutional capacity of CSOs in Brazil. With its expertise on different aspects of pharmaceutical regulation, GTPI has been able to mobilise extensive support from other CSOs, but has also collaborated more closely with the government in the regulatory process in this sector. This process has required constant learning on how to act in regulatory lobbying, as the following sections demonstrate.

Pipeline mechanism

A review of newspaper articles published in the 2000s showed that GTPI began voicing their concerns over the pipeline mechanism issue in 2006 (Reis and Chaves, 2006); that is, as regards retroactive patent protection for drugs registered outside Brazil and not yet commercialised in the country. Their concern is that of the 1,182 pipeline patents requested by innovator pharmaceutical firms, four were for ARV drugs and 18 have been on the list of exceptional drugs provided by Brazil's Unified Health System (Jurberg, 2008; Terto et al, 2009).

AIDS activists have been participating as *amicus curia* (to assist court decisions) in several law suits. In November 2007, for instance, the GTPI presented Brazil's Prosecutor General with a petition claiming the unconstitutionality of articles in the Patent Act that refer to the pipeline mechanism. It requested that the Prosecutor General file a Direct Action of Unconstitutionality (ADI) with the Supreme Court (given that civil society cannot file the procedure by itself) (Reis et al, 2009). The ADI is a judicial instrument that allows federal authorities to review the constitutionality of a law or normative act. If their request is accepted by the Supreme Court, the legislation on the pipeline mechanism can be removed from the legal system. The GTPI claims that the pipeline mechanism is unconstitutional for four reasons: first, drugs granted pipeline patents in Brazil were already in the public domain (in other words, they were already generic commodities), contradicting the principle of novelty; second, it violates the principle of reasonability and proportionality as the patent is granted without analysing material requirements (Brazil's patent office [INPI] does not assess these applications, as the patent is approved on the basis of international patent office reports); third, it violates the principle of equality as it differentiates between national and foreign products – while Brazilian industries have to go through the INPI, foreign applications are submitted only in their originating countries; and, fourth, it violates social interests as it allows a monopoly of knowledge that was already in the public domain, unnecessarily increasing expenditure on medications.

In 2008, the GTPI's claim gained the support of the BMoH. In addition, the Brazilian Prosecutor General brought the case before the Federal Supreme Court, challenging the constitutionality of the pipeline mechanism on the grounds that it does not respect the principle of novelty. If accepted by the Supreme Court, this could invalidate the patent of 565 drugs protected under this rule. By 2009, 11 pharmaceutical associations and NGOs had filed requests to participate as *amicus curia* in the litigation, but only one application (from Interfarma, which represents the interests of research-based firms) was accepted.

TRIPS Plus agenda: polymorphs and second use

In 2007, representatives of the GPTI learned through the press that Brazil's patent office (INPI) was revising its patent standards. The INPI invited representatives of the pharmaceutical sector and the Brazilian health surveillance agency (ANVISA) to discuss options for reformulating Brazil's patent standards. AIDS activists complained that these meetings were held in closed sessions, excluding participation by civil society on the grounds that only pharmaceutical sector experts should be admitted. In contrast, the INPI argued that resistance to hearing the NGOs was due to their inexperience in conducting public consultations and apologised for its clumsy behaviour (Avila, 2007). While the INPI claims that this is a strictly technical matter, HIV/AIDS activists highlight the political component of this decision (Reis et al, 2009, p 41).

The relevance of this event is twofold. First, it shows the importance of the AIDS activists who drew attention to the politics of the patent application process, hitherto seen to rest on methodological decisions neutral to the various different interests on the issue. Second, it also demonstrates how these activists are claiming their right to inform the government on crucial public health topics, rather than just lobbying for access to drugs. The INPI's initial reluctance to allow them to participate in technical meetings shows how these activists were regarded as less able to contribute to the debate. Accordingly, they had to claim their right to collaborate in these discussions.

AIDS activists have monitored virtually all government discussions on this topic. In addition, the GTPI has been participating in legislative activities. The group wrote a complementary legal opinion supporting approval of Bill 2511/2007, which proposes to eliminate patents on second medical use and polymorphs, and quoting other countries that have taken similar decisions (for example, India and Argentina). The GTPI has also educated members of Congress on the international guidelines provided by the World Health Organisation, which do not recommend patent protection for second use and polymorphs (Reis et al, 2009). This highlights how these activists have gained space and legitimacy to voice their demands on technical aspects of pharmaceutical regulation.

Procedure to register pharmaceutical patents in Brazil

The group has also been active on drug patent registration procedures in Brazil (the prior consent mechanism), that is, the INPI and ANVISA have authority to review patent applications. In November 2009, the GTPI was invited, together with other representatives of research-based pharmaceutical industries, to a public hearing in Congress to debate Bill 3709/2008 (which discussed the role of prior consent). The GTPI argued strongly that prior consent should remain unaltered as this institutional arrangement was important in order to keep patent examination standards high and thus avoid underserved patents (Chaves, 2009).

Other agendas

The following paragraphs summarise two events in which the NGOs collaborated with the government in intellectual property discussions that could impact the market for ARV drugs.

Tenofovir and Kaletra pre-grant opposition

In December 2006, the GTPI filed a request with the INPI opposing patent applications for two ARV drugs: a second patent application for Kaletra (Abbott) and another for Gilead's Tenofovir Disoproxil Fumarate. Pre-grant opposition is an administrative mechanism under Article 31 of Brazil's Patents Act that allows any interested parties to provide documents and information to assist patent examination. The intention was thus to clarify why the INPI should not grant these two patent applications.

The arguments opposing these patents were different in each case. The case against Tenofovir Disoproxil Fumarate relates to Gilead's applying for a patent of an active ingredient that is used to treat HIV infections. AIDS activists argued that the only active ingredient that acts on the virus is Tenofovir, while the Disoproxil assists in fostering the availability of Tenofovir, and Fumarate helps stabilise the drugs. The patents on Tenofovir and Disoproxil had expired 15 and nine years prior to this new grant application. The activists also argued that the use of Fumarate salt is a chemical practice known since 1963. Together, these arguments reinforced the fact that Gilead's application did not meet patentability requirements under Brazilian law (Article 8 of the Patents Act). In 2008, the BMoH declared Tenofovir of public interest, which expedited the INPI's review of the application (Ministério da Saúde, 2008). Gilead's application was denied in 2008 and its appeal was denied in 2010 on similar grounds argued by the GTPI. In the case of Kaletra, Abbott had requested a second patent on this drug (divisional patent application, which splits the uses of a single invention into separate patents). The first patent was granted as a pipeline mechanism and AIDS activists argued that, according to the Patents Act, there is no legal provision for divisional applications under the pipeline mechanism and, accordingly, the INPI should deny the patent request (Reis et al, 2009).

Particularly interesting in both these cases is the CSOs' capacity to collaborate with the INPI in the patent approval process, providing information and supporting a decision that is highly technical, rather than just using pressure or media fanfare to express their criticism.

Efavirenz compulsory licence

Efavirenz (EFV) was commercialised in Brazil by Merck and used by nearly half of AIDS patients in need of treatment in 2007. Merck had a long tradition of negotiating prices with the Brazilian government and had reduced its price by more than 50% since 2001 (Nunn et al, 2007). However, as EFV became a convenient treatment choice (for example, fewer pills), more patients were put into treatment in 2003 and 2004. The Brazilian government demanded a price reduction of EFV from US$1.59/daily dose to US$0.65/daily dose, given that other countries such as Thailand were paying much lower prices than Brazil for EFV and that much less costly generic drug versions of EFV were available from Indian companies.

After several meetings with Merck, the Minister of Health decided to declare EFV of public interest (the first step to issuing a compulsory licence) in 2007. The compulsory public interest licence meant that Brazil could produce these drugs locally for non-commercial purposes, but would still pay 1.5% in royalties for using them (*Valor Econômico*, 2007). The NGOs supported the government at every step of this negotiation (GTPI, 2007). The NAP informally consulted the AIDS activists during the process. That meeting examined several alternative approaches to securing a compulsory licence under Brazilian law, looking at the possibilities and constraints of each and voicing the civil society perspective. The compulsory licensing of EFV is important in two keys respects. First, it further demonstrates the participation of NGOs in intellectual property discussions and their role in supporting government decisions with scientific information and legitimation. Second, it illustrates the fact that their advocacy had evolved beyond demands for access to drugs to monitoring the regulatory bottlenecks.

Final remarks

In sum, CSOs have been pivotal in terms of advocacy, policymaking and monitoring AIDS policies over the years. Their role has been highly dynamic and has moved well beyond the traditional role of mobilising activists, organising demonstrations and holding the government accountable for its constitutional responsibilities (for example, to provide care through the national health service network at no cost at the point of delivery).

Like some of their international counterparts, Brazilian CSOs have engaged in broad networks. These networks have been key to more pragmatic policies targeting disenfranchised populations, such as illicit drug users. Despite their long-standing activism, they have been strongly marginalised, preventing their initiatives from having sustained, far-reaching impact on public policies. In this regard, broad coalition-building to include current and former illicit drug users, activists, health professionals and policymakers has been key in the implementation of various measures to reduce drug-related harms.

Unlike most international initiatives, Brazilian CSOs have developed a unique competency and scientific literacy on the complex regulations, standards and procedures related to drug licensing and have had a role in recent decisions in this field that goes well beyond that achieved by other local or national organisations. Despite their local/national basis, Brazilian coalitions, such as the GTPI, have had an influence on public policies comparable to major transnational organisations, such as Oxfam International (actually, a coalition of 15 different institutions to relieve poverty and promote sustained development worldwide) and have been working in close cooperation with major global players such as Médecins sans Frontières.

While, on the one hand, financial support from the WB and the BMoH was important to fostering CSO advocacy and capacity-building, on the other, these CSOs have slowly learned how to act in regulatory advocacy. It is thus plausible to conclude that CSOs in Brazil have influenced HIV/AIDS policy, but were in turn influenced by the political process with which they have interacted. Future studies should investigate the mechanisms of the CSOs' acquisition of new preferences, as opposed to arguments that see political actors as having fixed, instrumental preferences.

It is not clear whether the proactive role of Brazilian CSOs can be sustained in years to come in a context of economic crisis, shrinking budgets (including the international aid allocated by major donors) and deep political change. Whatever the prospects for the future, Brazilian CSOs working in the HIV/AIDS field have very meaningful experience in their recent history to share with other countries and societies worldwide.

Note
[1.] Brazil received WB loans between 1993 and 2012, with a matching grant of 50% of the loan funding.

Acknowledgements

The authors would like to thank the editors for the valuable comments on the manuscript. Elize Fonseca was funded by the São Paulo State Research Foundation (FAPESP).

References

Avila, J. (2007) 'Audiencia Publica: debate acerca de patentes pipeline e acesso a medicamentos', Comissão de Direitos Humanos e Minorias, Camara dos Deputados, No 2159/07.

Bastos, F., Bongertz, V., Teixeira, S., Morgado, M. and Hacker, M. (2005) 'Is human immunodeficiency virus/acquired immunodeficiency syndrome decreasing among Brazilian injection drug users? Recent findings and how to interpret them', *Memórias do Instituto Oswaldo Cruz*, vol 1, no 100, pp 91–6.

Biehl, J. (2004) 'The activist state: global pharmaceuticals, AIDS and citzenship in Brazil', *Social Text*, vol 3, no 22, pp 105–32.

Biehl, J. (2007) *Will to live: AIDS therapies and the politics of survival*, New Jersey, NJ: Princeton University Press.

Brasil (2002) 'Response: the experience of the Brazilian AIDS Programme', www.aids.gov.br/sites/default/files/resp_ingles.pdf (accessed 22 February 2012).

Brasil (2008) 'Resposta: a experiência do Programa Brasileiro de AIDS', www.aids.gov.br/sites/default/files/resposta_2008.pdf (accessed 22 February 2012).

Carvalho, B., Cardoso, L., Damasceno, S. and Stefani, M. (2011) 'Moderate prevalence of transmitted drug resistance and interiorization of HIV type 1 subtype C in the inland North State of Tocantins, Brazil', *AIDS Research and Human Retroviruses*, vol 10, no 27, pp 1081–7.

Chaves, C. (2009) *Audiência Pública – PL 3709/08 – CDEIC – Câmara dos Deputados – Posição do Grupo de Trabalho sobre Propriedade Intelectual da Rede Brasileira pela Integração dos Povos*. Brasilia: Federação Nacional dos Farmacêuticos.

Dourado, I., Veras, M., Barreira, D. and De Brito, A. (2006) 'Tendências da epidemia de AIDS no Brasil após a terapia anti-retroviral', *Revista de Saúde Pública*, vol 40, pp 91–7.

Fonseca, E. (2011) 'Reforming pharmaceutical regulation: a case study of generic drug policy in Brazil', PhD thesis, Department of Social Policy, University of Edinburgh, Edinburgh, UK.

Fonseca, E. and Bastos, F. (2012) 'Os tratados internacionais anti-drogas e o Brasil: políticas, desafios e perspectivas', in M. Jorge and S. Alarcon (eds) Álcool e Outras Drogas: Diálogos sobre um mal-estar contemporâneo, Rio de Janeiro: Ed Fiocruz.

Fonseca, E., Ribeiro, J., Bertoni, N. and Bastos, F. (2006) 'Syringe exchange programs in Brazil: preliminary assessment of 45 programs', *Cadernos de Saúde Públicaa*, vol 22, pp 761–70.

Galvao, J. (2000) *AIDS no Brasil: a agenda de construção de uma epidemia*, Rio de Janeiro: Abia.

GTPI (Working Group on Intellectual Property of the Brazilian Network of the Integration of Peoples) (2007) 'Nota a imprensa: licenca compulsoria para o Efavirenz', *GTPI*, 5 May.

GTPI (2010) 'Apresentacao do GT Propriedade Intelectual', 3 August, www.rebrip. org.br/_rebrip/pagina.php?id=655

Hacker, M., Leite, I., Renton, A., Torres, T., Gracie, R. and Bastos, F. (2006) 'Reconstructing the AIDS epidemic among injection drug users in Brazil', *Cadernos de Saúde Pública*, vol 22, no 4, pp 751–60.

Jurberg, C. (2008) 'Challenge raised to constitutionality of Brazilian pipeline patents', Intellectual Property Watch, www.ip-watch.org/weblog (accessed 22 January 2008).

Lijphart, A. (1971) 'Comparative politics and the comparative method', *The American Political Science Review*, vol 65, no 3, pp 682–93.

Malta, M., Cavalcanti, S., Gliksman, L., Adlaf, E., Hacker, M., Bertoni, N., Massard, E. and Bastos, F. (2011) 'Behavior and major barriers faced by non-injectable drug users with HBV/HCV seeking treatment for hepatitis and drug addiction in Rio de Janeiro, Brazil', *Cien Saude Colet*, vol 16, no 12, pp 4777–86.

Ministério da Saúde (2008) 'Declaração de interesse público – Tenofovir. Ministério da Saúde', Portaria No 681 de 8 de abril de 2008.

Nunn, A. (2008) *The politics and history of AIDS treatment in Brazil*, New York, NY: Springer.

Nunn, A., Fonseca, E., Bastos, F. Gruskin, S. and Salomon, J. (2007) 'Evolution of antiretroviral drug costs in Brazil in the context of free and universal access to AIDS treatment', *PLoS Medicine*, vol 11, no 4, p 305.

Nunn, A., Fonseca, E., Bastos, F. and Gruskin, S. (2009) 'AIDS treatment in Brazil: impacts and challenges', *Health Affairs*, vol 28, no 4, pp 1103–13.

Reis, R. and Chaves, C. (2006) 'O reexame das patentes pipeline no Brasil', *Valor Econômico*, 7 November.

Reis, R., Vieira, M. and Chaves, C. (2009) 'Access to medicines and intellectual property in Brazil: a civil society experience', in R. Reis, V. Terto Jr and M. Pimenta (eds) *Intellectual property rights and access to ARV medicines: civil society resistance in the global South: Brazil, Colombia, China, India, Thailand*, Rio de Janeiro: ABIA.

Sabatier, P. and Jenkins, S. (eds) (1993) *Policy change and learning: an advocacy coalition approach*, Boulder, CO: Westview Press.

Scheffer, M., Salazar, A. and Grou, K. (2005) *O remédio via Justiça: um estudo sobre o acesso a novos medicamentos e exames em HIV/AIDS no Brasil por meio de ações judiciais*, Brasília: Ministério da Saúde, Secretaria de Vigilância em Saúde, Programa Nacional de DST e AIDS.

Somaini, L., Donnini, C., Raggi, M., Amore, M., Ciccocioppo, R., Saracino, M., Kalluppi, M., Malagoli, M., Gerra, M. and Gerra, G. (2011) 'Promising medications for cocaine dependence treatment', *Recent Patents on CNS Drug Discovery*, vol 6, no 2, pp 146–60.

Terto, V., Jr, Pimenta, M. and Reis, R. (2009) *Questions and answers about pipeline patents: how do they affect your life?*, Rio de Janeiro: ABIA.

Valor Econômico (2007) 'Governo anuncia hoje quebra de patente de remédio anti-AIDS', 5 May.

Veras, M., Ribeiro, M., Jamal, L., McFarland, W., Bastos, F., Ribeiro, K., Barata, R., Moraes, J. and Reingold, A. (2011) 'The "AMA-Brazil" cooperative project: a nation-wide assessment of the clinical and epidemiological profile of AIDS-related deaths in Brazil in the antiretroviral treatment era', *Cadernos de Saúde Pública*, vol 27, no 1, pp S104–13.

THIRTEEN

Media and policy analysis in Brazil: the process of policy production, reception and analysis through the media

Fernando Lattman-Weltman

Introduction

In the specific political context of contemporary democratic States,[1] policies are produced as the result of actions and interactions among highly differentiated, specialised and largely autonomous institutions, such as governments and parliaments, and their technical agencies.

The implementation and success of most of that policy output – practically all of it and in practically all cases – depends on its being favourably received and treated by journalists and the mass media, those individual and collective actors who, in an open and democratic society, occupy the strategic position of mediators of information in the so-called public domain.

This chapter intends to provide a (synthetic, but comprehensive) overview of the specific communicational variables that enter into and impact the process of policies' being publicly received and analysed by the media, in its many forms and properties, in contemporary Brazil. For that purpose a brief account is given of the ill-fated proposals advanced in Brazil at the beginning of the first Lula government (2003-2007) to set up a National Council of Journalism and an Agency for Brazilian Cinema and Audiovisual Production.

Processes like these are certainly not restricted to Brazil, so the theoretical framework underlying the analysis is intended to have a wider heuristic validity.

Nonetheless, even brief study of a specific case of policies' being received problematically in the contemporary Brazilian context will – it is believed – illustrate the theory's potential, as well as serving as a stimulus and starting parameter for comparative studies in other contexts.

Conjunctural dynamics, policy formulation, implementation and analyses, and the media

A typical policy production process usually brings to mind a certain agenda of problems or interests, a specific cycle in which institutional responses are prepared for such an agenda, and a particular configuration of actors and/or sectors inside and outside the main deliberative political bodies, interested in giving these policies a, once again specific, direction and shape. In this first approximation to the subject approach it makes little difference how such political projects originate: whether 'demanded' by important or influential sectors or 'discovered' or 'appropriated' more or less opportunely (or opportunistically) by some 'professional' politician. What most often does matter is that, once the project's actual existence is given (or 'verbalised' or 'manifested'), it enters onto the political agenda as a salient fact, appropriate 'gravitationally' to draw the attention of the leading actors (or players) and/or those most directly interested in the matter (or issue).

Once the issue has been presented in the form of a policy proposal, it is not difficult to delineate the set of State and 'civil society' actors, especially those with greater power of veto, directly interested and active in the discussion and in the endeavour to steer the policy at issue (Tsebelis, 2009). Thus, given the stakeholders' different institutional prerogatives, the number of different substantial votes they can count on – whether in parliaments or elsewhere, in primary electoral contexts – and any other resources they can marshal and use, it is possible to have a reasonable idea of the correlation of forces in action, and relatively early in the discussion. Especially in historical contexts of relative constitutional stability, the institutional and party political configuration of political forces and their familiarity with civil society and its organisations can make the power game relatively predictable, along with its stages and the key contenders' main strategic options.

That is unless, of course, any of the forces in action intervenes to upset the balance of available information stocks, the semantic structures of reference, or – as always seems possible in a context of 'structural change in the public sphere'[2] – such forces are able to again re-configure the hazy outlines of the grey zone reigning on the boundaries between things public and private, which are essential to polyarchy.

That is, more than any other polyarchic institution, the media – on their own account or used by other political forces – can, if not actually alter the balance of power in a given scenario of policy debate and deliberation (and any other debate or dispute), at least expand (or reduce) policy transaction and implementation costs by framing the issues from certain angles or – with the 'proper' focus – bringing out behaviours and practices of the contenders that can leave them suddenly vulnerable to attack by opponents. The media are often in a privileged position to alter, if not the balance of power itself, at least some of the important symbolic resources at the contenders' disposal. This they can do through mechanisms by which they affect, firstly, the whole 'symbolic economy': a contingent, symbolic configuration of premises and evidences – 'facts' and versions – that somehow give meaning to a given society's collective experience, in time and space and, even if contradictorily, serves its members as a common frame of reference. This is a kind of narrative script, the unpredictable outcome of interaction among various discursive 'investors', which, broadly speaking, defines what is at stake in the public arena at each moment, and what the most important issues are – sometimes also defining their chief moral meanings – and who the leading and supporting players are in the drama (or comedy).[3]

Accordingly, when the expression 'symbolic economy' is used so as better to characterise the process of shaping the references that give form and meaning to a collectivity's average perception of its own public experience in a given historical context, the intention is to emphasise the following dimensions of the process: 1) its social character, that is, the way that such configurations are the unforeseen and unforeseeable results of collective discursive interactions, however with the participation of an indefinite number of particular actors and groups; 2) the unequal nature of the discursive resources and investments brought to bear by each of these actors and groups, as well as the characteristic uncertainty of the outcomes they may secure there (however great their particular resources), including, of course, the media themselves, which to a point operate with privileges on this trading floor as the main 'broker' or 'advertising agency'; 3) the simultaneously contingent – or, to be more exact, largely random – and nonetheless binding nature of the configurations of the symbolic economy. These are contingent (and almost random), because they result from interactions that occur only once (in the 'here' and 'now') with no possibility of being systematically reproduced, just as the interactions in a game with several players acting simultaneously produce results that are non-reproducible and largely path-dependent on the actual interactions. They are binding, because once produced and (reasonably) stabilised in their meanings (until new change sets in), from that point on they exert their referential and parametric effects on all participants in the same economy.[4]

In this regard, the operation of this Public Discourse Market (PDM, Lattman-Weltman, 1994) should be considered from the wider perspective of a political economy involving very diverse actors and sub-systems. Indeed, in the first place, the PDM comprises – besides the media themselves, of course – all a given society's main discursive investors, that is, all the individual and collective actors capable of formulating arguments with some exchange value (and some utility) for any collective discussion on the market, and making them at least minimally public. Secondly, and obviously, this PDM includes the public itself that consumes such goods and products, or better still, such discursive 'assets' (or 'liabilities').[5]

The case of the investors of such discourses and their consumer public, therefore, relates to the whole universe that Communication Theory usually differentiates by the notions of 'senders' and 'receivers', or even 'sources' and 'publics', and which Schumpeterian political theory refers to roughly as election 'entrepreneurs' and their 'clienteles'.[6] In the specific and strategic case of the media, however, a concrete analysis of their interference in the overall process of policymaking or policy analysis will often also have to take account of the specific variables of the Communication Market (CM), that is, the set of communication media and vehicles acting in a given polyarchy, and their relative penetration and influence on the PDM.

Before that, however, it is important to consider the general ways in which the media as a whole interfere in the processing of the topic in hand here.

Typical forms of media interference: visibility and publicity

There are three typical mechanisms by which the media, more than any other players, exert their strategic influence on the symbolic economy, and thence on the processes of democratic policy discussion and diffusion:

1. *Agenda-setting:* as pointed out by several studies,[7] the media interfere with the contingent process that defines what themes are important for the wider public agenda. Whether the reasons are editorial – limitations of space or time, commercial strategy constraints and so on – or more properly political and/or ideological, the fact is that all and any medium – even web portals – tends to select or at least hierarchically rank its information content and to follow some strategy for drawing and directing the attention and interest of its consumer public. Given their growing everyday importance to citizens as sources of general information,

this naturally tends to reduce and/or hierarchise the field of issues and subjects offered primarily, and with greater regularity and naturality, to their consumers' imagination and interest, endowing that information with greater legitimacy, precisely by approving it for Publicness.[8]

Depending, of course, on inequalities and fractures in actual specific Communication Markets (CMs), the efforts of political actors to alter the contextual content of the agenda may be more or less successful through political communication strategies and tactics that seek to benefit from 'noise' in the global communication process, or from power niches, or political resources less prone to the massification of information, or even from alternative (and segmented) channels of communication.[9] However, there is really no escaping the more generalised and restrictive impositions of mass public agendas, especially when the intention is to influence the vote of the absolute majority of an electorate of continental proportions, or get support for the implementation of policies that depend on this diffuse, often intangible and elusive – but nonetheless active – thing called 'public opinion'.

2. *Framing:* another strategic resource manipulated with privilege by the media – and which obviously works in permanent interaction with the agenda-setting process – is the so-called power to frame, that is, the prerogative not only to define what is news, but also how; the power to determine a particular focus, certain associations of sense, a certain meaning for each event, version or subject[10]. Accordingly, the subjects that gain public visibility and value by their presence – and differentiated hierarchical weight – in the newscasts, and thus on the agenda, are themselves subject to framing in order to tell a certain story about the realities, one with certain implications for the political process, and not necessarily other stories (depending, as we have seen, on the contingent impositions or 'quotations' on the PDM). Certainly, one single narrative can often contain contradictory versions and scripts that are capable of producing quite different receptions for the same transmission (as consumption of art and fiction constantly shows us). Even in news coverage that is richer and potentially more polysemous, however, there are strong homogenising mechanisms operating that – even when sincerely committed to ideals of the highest objectivity (or precisely because of that) – tend to try to reduce the potential diversity of perspectives in any rendering to one single, empirically consistent script of events or chain of plausible events.

Therefore, political agents, policy-makers – whenever they depend, one way or another, on more favourable contexts of reception to get policy implemented – will not only have to submit to the constraints of the public agenda, or use whatever breaches or shortcuts this may afford them, in order to advance their own agendas. They will have to do so taking into account also the specific ways in which the issues they are interested in are framed on such agendas. They will have to contend then not only with the relative and 'publicly-attributed' importance of their agendas, but also with the favourable or adverse meanings and associations with which that same 'public domain' has previously framed their issues.

3. *Panoptical effects:* however, no effect resulting from the privileges of the media as regards the reproduction of Publicness – and the production of accountability – seems more visible and politically influential than the ability to expose public figures in practices considered morally inadmissible or simply illegal. As seen earlier, when fulfilling its self-defining functions of 'guardian' or 'watchdog' of the public democratic interest, the mass media thus interfere directly in the political capital

of public figures – careful of their reputations – by operating like the panopticon proposed in the 19th century by the English philosopher Jeremy Bentham (and analysed by Michel Foucault, in the 20th century context). In Bentham, the panopticon was a model of building designed to be applied to closed institutions – such as mental asylums and prisons – with the intention of affording a small group of guards simultaneous control of the largest possible number of patients or inmates. Most important, however, was to design it so the inmates could not know exactly when they would be under scrutiny by the guard. Foucault typically explored the internalisation of the control procedure: given that guards could watch inmates' behaviour at any time without their knowing exactly when, the panopticon's institutional success is achieved when inmates – led to suppose that that the guard indeed knows everything they do – start to control themselves (when the guard could in fact abandon his/her control post).

Anyway, regardless of the actual conditions under which it operates its unique panoptic resources, this capacity of the media makes itself felt by nearly all public actors and thus, indirectly, can also interfere with the processing, the timing and the definition of the contingent limits on political deliberation about policies, and affect the balance of power that surrounds or confines its participants and formulators. This can happen independently of any specific policy content – and sometimes even with no relation even to its political implications. However, it does so solely and exclusively as a result of the inevitable connections and competitions among political parties, or power struggles that involve the concrete actors involved in deliberating on and implementing policy proposals. That is to say, what a policy proposes is not the only important factor; just as decisive (or even more so) to its fate may be what agent or party proposes it (or opposes it, one way or another). In this way, the reputation of such personages and institutions – whether or not affected by the great media panopticon – also comes to be an important variable in the complex and multivariate political game surrounding the fate of policies.[11]

Thus far, therefore, we have talked generically about 'media' and emphasised the general ways they interfere in the process of policymaking and analysis. Indeed, agenda-setting, framing, and panoptical effects make themselves felt more strongly precisely because of the all-pervasive way they operate, that is, involving interaction among, and simultaneous action by, a number of communication vehicles.

Now we will examine how the factors and variables responsible for the political and ideological diversity typical of polyarchy operate when duly 'filtered' – or rather, processed – by the media machinery of re-signification or reproduction.

Strategic variables of media intervention in policy-related political cycles

One of the most recurrent problems in analysing the media's role in polyarchic political dispute is precisely the difficulty of ascertaining how far one can properly speak of The Media as a unit, or whether the mediums or vehicles should be referred to separately in all their diversity. Indeed, when speaking of a symbolic economy, the tendency is to emphasise the collective dimension of the media vehicles and the more general outcomes of their interactions, both amongst themselves and with their public. When what is involved are specific, substantive political disputes, which in polyarchies – by definition – involve different actors and interests in different or opposing positions, a minimally plural CM should include vehicles that will seek to interfere in different and equally contradictory ways in the PDM, regardless of through what mechanism.

It is easier to understand and deal with this problem of the dialectic between univocality and plurivocality by – even if only analytically – distinguishing at least three basic levels of signification in the overall media output: (1) one first, more general and comprehensive, 'meta-institutional' level relates to normative premises that make sense of the overall working of the political system and its institutions, and prescribes the values that should guide their action (for example, defence of the basic principle of social equality); (2) at a second, 'contingent public agenda' level, the more general principles are translated, at each conjuncture, into more concrete issues (continuing the previous example might see the general demand for social equality being reproduced in debates over specific income redistribution policies); (3) and lastly, at an even more concrete and contingent 'actor personification' (or 'soap-operisation') level, both the meta-institutional principle and the issue convert into, or give rise to, specific dramas with heroes, villains and supporting cast (the example might now find expression in detailed articles on, for example, the misuse of funds earmarked for income redistribution, and following flesh-and-blood characters, either denounced as corrupt or revealed as victims of corruption, and so on).

Thus, while nearly all media vehicles may tend to share the same characteristic premises of the more generic, comprehensive – and abstract – level of signification, greater diversity should be seen in their coverage of the related issues – with more frequent omissions and differences in agenda-setting and framing – and finally even greater likelihood of differences in how they tell the 'soap opera stories' and define each character's narrative – or moral – functions. Now, it is as a result of such differences in levels of signification that public dispute becomes much more frequent – as do the complaints and criticisms of political interference by media vehicles – around the content of the third (most personified) level than around coverage of the issues and, even more so than on the essential plane of the normative and meta-institutional prescriptions. This is not only because the political 'soap operas' are easier to assimilate,[12] but also because they affect directly the political capital and the strategies and tactics of the actors in dispute.

Going back to our dialectic, however, it is important to stress that the similarities and dissonances among media vehicles in how they deal with these three levels of narrative – but especially at the latter two – may be caused by the greater or lesser influence of a series of variables with the potential to draw them closer together or separate them more widely. These range from: (1) ideological and party political variables involving not only political groups and programmes but also (and particularly) the classic dynamics of the confrontation between incumbency and opposition – as certain vehicles identify with such factions and their outlooks; (2) through important sociological and/or socioeconomic variables, that is, in line with very concrete connections between communication vehicles and specific social groups and economic interests; lastly, to (3) variables typical of the CM, relating to the differing editorial projects that separate and oppose different vehicles (and are often distinguished by the rhetorical strategies adopted by journalists and media vehicles in order to differentiate themselves and mark out their specific, and equally differentiated, communities of readers/listeners/spectators/web surfers).

We will now look at how such variables, whether structural or contingent, can operate in a specific case of policy intermediation by the media – by no coincidence, an example where the very institutional conditions of media operations were at stake.

Visibility and expectations of the media agenda: a paradigmatic case of an unsettling policy agenda

For some time now Brazil's social communication system has had regulatory problems. Since Brazil's democratisation in the 1980s the country had continued with statutes inherited from the last dictatorship (1964-1985) and only very recently retired (such as the Press Act enacted in 1967, which was revoked in 2009), coexisting with new constitutional principles relating to communication, established in 1988 but not duly regulated by supplementary law, or simply not put into effect.[13]

With the election of the Workers' Party (Partido dos Trabalhadores, PT) to the federal executive in the 2002 elections, the time seemed to have arrived when long-standing demands in sectors of the social movement allied with the party's broad, diverse base would be implemented. This was the backdrop to the emergence, in the early years of the first Luiz Inácio Lula da Silva government (2003-2007), of policy projects designed to broaden and qualify public intervention in the communication field. The first proposed a national or federal Board of Journalism, a kind of corporative (non-State) body with the role of 'licensing, representing and defending journalists, and setting ethical and disciplinary standards for the profession of journalism'.[14] The second set up the Brazilian Cinema and Audiovisual Agency (Agência Nacional do Cinema e do Audiovisual, Ancinav), a regulatory agency for the audiovisual production market – including television.

As is widely known, these proposals were relentlessly criticised by the major Brazilian media and their representative bodies – on the argument that they represented unconstitutional threats to freedom of speech. The proposal for a Board of Journalism was the first to be shelved by the government because of its poor reception. After a great deal of debate, the Ancinav project met the same fate towards the end of 2004. Even though it is still possible to find strong sympathy for these policy initiatives among organised sectors of society, and even among the main institutions and parties with power of agenda and veto – starting with the federal government itself – it is highly unlikely that anything similar will be put forward again (at least in the near future).

Well, how is such an efficient informal veto produced? What role did the media actually play in the process? In what respect can the theories and concepts mentioned above help grasp the context and fate of these policy proposals?

It would be easy to explain the failure of this agenda in the light of the theory of Tsebelis (2009), for example, had it succumbed to a stalemate resulting from different preferences of status quo amongst the main institutions and parties acting, with power of veto, in those four years of Brazil's political life, that is, the federal government, the congress and, 'within' them, the majority coalition supporting the president, led by the PT (or, also in the legislature, a cohesive opposition). In the first place, however, this 'clash' never happened: the executive had hardly submitted its proposals when it had to back down in view of the reaction. Above all, however, it is hard to imagine that the Lula government could not have had them approved one way or another, given the institutional characteristics of relations between our executive and legislative, and the parliamentary majority at his disposal at the time, in the early years of a highly popular first term of office. Only a very radicalised climate of opinion or a strongly polarised political conjuncture could widen the gap between the more powerful contenders and make the issue a subject for struggle and legislative uncertainty.[15] A problematical occasion that could have triggered such a struggle did in fact arise a few years later,[16] but by then the proposals to set up the Board of Journalism and Ancinav had been struck off the agenda.

The real veto, as it were, to these policy proposals was actually produced in the first year of the Lula administration, via the informal resources of the media.

Firstly, as regards the power of *agenda-setting* mentioned above: policy proposals like these can never figure prominently in the most influential media coverage, nor be subjects for conspicuous attention and reaction, until such time as they gain sponsorship by important political actors (those that hold institutional power of agenda and veto). This seems to have been precisely the case with the attempts to set up a board to oversee journalists' activities and a regulatory agency on audiovisual production, which had long been called for by Brazilian civil society actors, but had never caused much concern in the mainstream media. Once actually embraced by sectors of the governing party as possible changes in the status quo, not only did they become 'news', but also a matter for political controversy, of actual struggle for power and, in this case, even taking on strategic proportions – even risk – for the media itself as an institution.

However, once entered onto the public agenda thanks to the political and institutional prerogatives of other players, another battle begins involving precisely the senses of the *framing*: as the issue was imposed by its political qualities, it will be on their meanings that all interested investors will have to ponder and act. This is especially true of those who have the privilege of mediating the larger collective process of attributing sense to the discursive contexts underlying such disputes. After all, what do such policy proposals mean? In whose interest are they? Who proposed them and who combats them? With what intentions? What benefits and advantages or, conversely, what risks and losses do they entail for particular sectors and, last but not least, for the so-called greater good of society? What is at stake with such measures?

With the overall script thus arranged, with its meanings and leading characters – in other words, its frame – all of these actors are subject to the so-called *panoptical effects*. Indeed, as public figures who care about their reputations, such actors already were – by definition, and at least potentially – under the spotlight of publicness and the visibility it confers. Now, however, their identities also start to suffer new pressures resulting from their involvement in the issue, in the disputes of power and over meanings initiated by the discussion over the policies. Their actions start to have strategic importance and they will literally start to be watched with new eyes, with new attention – for better or for worse.

Brief analysis of this whole process will disclose the three interrelated narrative levels mentioned earlier: 'meta-institutional', 'contingent public agenda', and '*soap-operisation*'.

Indeed, given the longevity of this agenda of demands in the communication field (and of other, even bolder demands) and its historical welcome by many among the PT grassroots (or sympathisers), plus the more or less articulate (but certainly intense and to a point justified) series of fears over how the party would behave once it had attained the central seat of power in Brazil, as soon as such policy proposals were made public the 'soap opera' script was given for almost all Brazil's main private media communication vehicles unanimously: the proposals aimed to allow the State (now duly 'staffed' by PT members) to interfere politically in Brazilian journalistic and audiovisual markets, so as to privilege the party's hegemonic intentions, or to serve the possibly unspeakable purposes of other groups allied to or protected by it. On a broader and more impersonal level, however, the movement is regarded as part of a larger ideological agenda – which is equally worrying for the mainstream media, their spokespersons and related interest groups – involving a return to certain 'statist' and 'interventionist' traditions that had their (controversial) place in our recent past, but whose economic and social dysfunctions are considered now to have been denounced and targeted by a costly effort to reform Brazil's political institutions in our even more recent past. According to that script, any new communications regulation agenda is regarded as an out-of-context, 'ideological' reaction. Finally, an older, broader and deeper meta-institutional confrontation was considered to underlie the struggle, one expressed in the clash between truly democratic values – entrenched in the uncompromising defence of freedom of speech – and authoritarian positions taken from time to time in our history in the name of the popular interest and the supremacy of the greater value of social equality.

On the other hand, just reverse the signs and arguments and you get a good idea how the 'counter-hegemonic' narrative is constructed, as favoured by sectors of the PT, or close to the party, in confronting the media's predominant framing of such communication policy proposals in Brazil: defence of the supreme right to plural public information in a context of political advances by the social movement in the struggle against centuries of inequality, in a face-to-face combat with the forces of privilege and privatisation of the public sector in Brazil (represented in this case, obviously, by the media itself, and by the interests groups related to it – including, of course, the opposition parties).

That is, the PT's rise to power – and, therefore, to control of agenda and veto positions that are strategic in Brazil's political system – has thus provided abundant material to support the thesis that a policy proposal's success (or failure) simply often depends much more on who proposed it and when, than on any other variable.[17] In many cases, to put forward their agendas, the PT and its government can count on specific channels of communication established in the course of its history with various organised sectors of Brazilian 'civil society'. On the other hand – and the case of the media agenda is exemplary – they are also confronted by inflamed reactions when their actions so much as hint at confirming equally longstanding suspicions with regard to the Brazilian left's historical commitment – or lack of it – to the institutions of representative liberal democracy. Throughout the Lula administration (2003-2011), the first-ever PT government, in the contemporary Brazilian political imagination (inside and outside the party, for it and against it) these ambiguities were associated paradigmatically with the purported existence of a notorious 'Plan B', a supposedly more radical version of a PT government more consistent with former images and rallying cries of the party, but to this day not put into practice, by either Lula in his two terms of office or (even more improbably) by the current president.

Another contextual factor seems to have contributed to predisposing the mainstream media adversely in its reception and framing of any policy proposals put forward by the federal government for the communication sector. It is no coincidence that, at the time, the Latin American political and institutional panorama across the continent reverberated to the clashes between leaders such as Hugo Chavez in Venezuela, Nestor

Kirchner in Argentina and Rafael Correa in Ecuador and some of those countries' main communication vehicles. That those events were received as examples of institutionalised threats to freedom of expression in Latin America (or threats on the way to being institutionalised) could have had no other effect – and they were even more disturbing to the media, because they were often accompanied by expressions of sympathy towards those leaders from President Lula (even if for other reasons), but above all from high-ranking members of the PT.

Therefore, whatever the specific arena for regulatory debate, regardless even of how diversified the sets of different strategic actors involved in each terrain of confrontation and negotiation (on issues as different as, for example, maintaining the Press Act, requiring a bachelor's degree to become a journalist, (de)regulating technological convergence in the field of telephony and cable TV content, and so on), in such a tense context, everything tended (and still does) to degenerate into ideological radicalisation – which certainly raises significantly the transaction costs of any substantial policy proposal.

The fate of recent policy proposals to regulate the media in Brazil can thus be understood in the light of the premises outlined above as a typical case where: (1) the media's reception of this policy agenda as in fact constituting one single, ideologically consistent agenda contributed greatly to making it unworkable, because as a result the number of actors with interests at variance with it (and frequently antagonistic to it) and mobilised to interfere in the fate of the proposals in question was systematically expanded; (2) once – and however – the purported unity (or univocality) of this agenda was established, the difficulties involved in implementing it were heightened still further, in that they were framed in terms of a prevailing symbolic economy characterised by a burden of mistrust of the Brazilian State and its history of interference in the communication sector, a process aggravated, as seen above, by purported, more or less diffuse, radical intentions attributed to the party in power and to the organised social sectors connected with it.

Therefore, by examining the case of a policy in which the media itself had a special interest, I believe it is easier to perceive the scope and potential for interference by this singular institution in the policy implementation process.

Even though the media do not enjoy veto and agenda prerogatives – which, in a polyarchy, belong to other institutions – the media's privileges in relation to the more or less contingent configurations of the overall symbolic economy enable it to interfere directly or indirectly in the transaction costs inherent to processing and concluding, to whatever term, all cases of policies.

Notes

[1.] From here on referred to as 'polyarchies', according to Dahl's classical interpretation (1997): regimes that perform well on the basic items of institutionalised political competition and popular participation.

[2.] This is the title of the famous Habermas book (1985) where he proposes his historical concept of 'bourgeois public sphere': an ideal space for debate and decision where all participants are free and enjoy equal conditions to argue and do not suffer, as a result, any kind of coercion or constraint, which would ideally allow rational dialogue subject to the intrinsic qualities of the arguments, rather than to the speaker's strategic weight, authority or power.

[3.] The concept is developed and applied in Lattman-Weltman (1994) and Lattman-Weltman et al (1994).

[4.] Clearly a thorough analysis of any specific configuration of such a symbolic economy in a given space time context will certainly find in it elements – long-term narrative constructions, deeply-rooted rationales and preconceptions, and so on – that cannot be treated as strictly 'contingent' (and neither as exactly random). What is always and definitely contingent (and, so to speak, 'new') is the form these configurations take in each instance, as a result not only of new narrative content, but especially as a result of the frequent changes in the correlation of forces. It is because of that, for example, that we say that, despite its typical regularities, each election is a case in itself. The two themes are elaborated on in Lattman-Weltman (2006 and 2009).

[5.] In the exact sense of objects endowed only with exchange value – such as papers and shares on a securities market – for use in trading (Lattman-Weltman, 1994).

[6.] According to a classic passage from his book, Capitalism, Socialism and Democracy, where Schumpeter characterises democratic political leaders as true electoral entrepreneurs, who are even responsible for formulating the political agendas with which they not only attract their voter-consumers but actually mobilise them, actualising certain political agendas that otherwise could exist only in theory or, if preferred, only in 'latent' form (Schumpeter, 1984).

[7.] The classic reference on agenda-setting is the paper by McCombs and Shaw (1972).

[8.] Many of the hopes vested in the internet and its democratising potential derive exactly from the expectation that its distinctive interactive properties will allow it to surmount such visible limitations on interaction in the so-called traditional media. On the internet, see Barros Filho et al (2007) and Gomes and Maia (2008).

[9.] This is what seems to have happened recently in some Brazilian electoral contexts: see Fausto Neto et al (2003), and Lima (2007).

[10.] The concept originates from the sociological studies of Goffman (1974). A good example of the concept's empirical application in relation to the media in politics is given by Aldè (2004).

[11.] On the media's strategic importance in burnishing or tarnishing the reputations of public figures, see Thompson (2002).

[12.] And certainly more suited to the linguistic resources of the most popular 'reading contracts' of mass communication: audiovisuals (Lattman-Weltman, 2009).

[13.] This is the case, for example, of Article 221 of the 1988 Constitution that defines the principles to which the production and programming of radio and television broadcasts are subject in Brazil.

[14.] See the Bill instituting the board on the website of the Brazilian Federation of Journalists (Federação Nacional dos Jornalistas, Fenaj) at www.fenaj.org.br/cfj/projeto_cfj.htm.

[15.] On relations between executive and legislative in Brazil after 1988, see, for example, Figueiredo and Limongi (1999).

[16.] This was the 2005 '*mensalão*' crisis ('big monthly payoff' in Brazilian Portuguese) in which the PT was accused of paying federal congressmen of parties in the alliance supporting the government to vote in favour of bills in the government's interest. The allegation was that these payments were made on a monthly basis – hence the name – through an influence-brokering network steered from within the government by José Dirceu, then leader of the Labour Party and First Secretary for political relations in the Lula Government. The official version – given by the government and the PT – claimed that such an arrangement never existed, but that rather there was an illegal scheme to finance electoral campaigns, as also practiced by other parties.

[17.] On such party-political factors conditioning how policies are received, see for example Weir (1992).

References

Aldè, A. (2004) *A construção da política: democracia, cidadania e meios de comunicação de massa*, Rio de Janeiro: Editora FGV.

Barros Filho, C., Coutinho, M. and Safatle, V. (2007) 'O uso das novas mídias na campanha presidencial de 2006', in V.A. Lima (ed) *A mídia nas eleições de 2006*, São Paulo: Perseu Abramo.

Bentham, J. (2000) *O Panóptico*, Belo Horizonte: Autêntica.

Dahl, R.A. (1997) *Poliarquia: participação e oposição*, São Paulo: EDUSP.

Fausto Neto, A., Verón, E. and Rubim, A.A.C. (2003) *Lula presidente: televisão e política na campanha eleitoral*, São Paulo/São Leopoldo: Hacker Editores/Unisinos.

Figueiredo, A. and Limongi, F. (1999) *Executivo e legislativo na nova ordem constitucional*, Rio de Janeiro: Editora FGV.

Foucault, M. (1991) *Vigiar e punir*, Petrópolis: Vozes.

Goffman, E. (1974) *Frame analysis*, New York, NY: Harper and Row.

Gomes, W. and Maia, R. (2008) *Comunicação e democracia: problemas e perspectivas*, São Paulo: Paulus.

Habermas, J. (1984) *Mudança estrutural da esfera pública*, Rio de Janeiro: Tempo Brasileiro.

Lattman-Weltman, F. (1994) 'Imprensa e sociedade: a economia do discurso público', *Arché Interdisciplinar*, vol 3, no 8, pp 117-33.

Lattman-Weltman, F. (2006) 'Mídia, denuncismo e política: nova espiral da velha novela moral brasileira', *Democracia Viva*, no 32, pp 8-14.

Lattman-Weltman, F. (2009) 'O Rio nas Cruzadas: Comunicação, Democratização e Usos da Internet numa Eleição Carioca', *Revista ECO-POS*, vol 12, no 3, pp 24–37, www.pos.eco.ufrj.br/ojs-2.2.2/index.php?journal=revista&page=article&op=view&path%5B%5D=301&path%5B%5D=334

Lattman-Weltman, F., Ramos, P.A. and Carneiro, J.A. (1994) *A Imprensa faz e desfaz um Presidente*, Rio de Janeiro: Nova Fronteira.

Lima, V.A. (ed) (2007) *A mídia nas eleições de 2006*, São Paulo: Perseu Abramo.

McCombs, M. and Shaw, D.L. (1972) 'The agenda-setting function of mass media', *Public Opinion Quarterly*, vol 36, no 2, pp 176-87.

Schumpeter, J.A. (1984) *Capitalismo, socialismo e democracia*, Rio de Janeiro: Zahar.

Thompson, J. (2002) *O escândalo político*, Petrópolis: Vozes.

Tsebelis, G. (2009) *Atores com poder de veto: como funcionam as instituições políticas*, Rio de Janeiro: Editora FGV.

Weir, M. (1992) 'Ideas and the politics of bounded innovation', in S. Steinmo, K.A. Thelen and F. Longstreth (eds) *Structuring politics: historical institutionalism in comparative analysis*, Cambridge: Cambridge University Press.

FOURTEEN

Parties and public policy: programmatic formulation and political processing of constitutional amendments

Paulo Fábio Dantas Neto

Parties and constitutional change

The conviction that political parties play an important part in the performance of the democratic institutions established in the 1988 Constitution has taken root firmly in the political science produced in Brazil. Their role in coalitional presidentialism (Abranches, 1996) is seen as evidence that they have consolidated as pillars of the institutional structure of Brazilian democracy and as key actors in systemic processes of political interaction. In the literature on Brazilian political parties, the focus has shifted away from these institutions falling short of normative models (Fleischer,1981; Mainwaring, 2001; Mainwaring and Scully,1995; Mainwaring and Shugart, 2002; Mainwaring and Torcal, 2005) towards their actual role in the political system (Panebianco, 1988; Mair, 2003; Kinzo, 2005; Melo, 2010). Instead of revealing Brazil to be an 'anomaly' or symptomatic of the generalised 'crisis' in the party-form, the emphasis is on its shrinking horizontal representativeness and increasingly robust systemic functions. Today, parties are regarded as more important in the competitive dimension than in the participatory dimension of polyarchies. Rather than exceptional, Brazil is exemplary.

In exploring this territory, the intention of this chapter is to identify party-political contributions to the intense activity directed to amending the Constitution throughout the 1990s and with less momentum in the following decade. By early 2012, there had been 76 amendments – 70 isolated constitutional amendments (ECs) and six Constitutional Review Amendments (ECRs) enacted during the 1993–94 Constitutional Review. These numbers, confirm suggestions in the literature of: a certain instability in the Constitution, as in the expression 'interminable constitution' (Arantes and Couto, 2008); predominantly consensus-oriented negotiations during the Constituent Assembly (Souza, 2008); and scheduled postponement suited to government needs (Melo, 2002, 2005). The amendments established markers for the institutionalisation of public policies.

Parties' role in coalitional presidentialism suggests that they are more important in the production of constitutional amendments involving the political system or 'systemic' areas managed by the executive. Of the 76 amendments, the 37 that fall into this category relate to changes to the political system and public administration (9), the economic order (9), tax and social security systems (11) and fiscal policy (8). Together with another 11 social policy-related amendments, they form a body of 48 amendments covered by this discussion of political parties' contributions to proposals for constitutional change and to ensuring their successful passage through parliament.

In order to observe the parties as formulators or critics of policies, the amendments are compared with the party documents that preceded them and with positions taken by party members. The parties' parliamentary contribution to the political process (politics) is observed in terms of their involvement in the progress of the Proposed Constitutional Amendments (PECs) that resulted in the amendments.

Since the 1990s, the presidency has been disputed primarily between the Brazilian Social Democracy Party (Partido da Social Democracia Brasileira; PSDB) and the Workers' Party (Partido dos Trabalhadores; PT). Melo (2010) explains that this is because, over the cycle of presidential elections, both have been able to establish themselves as alternatives in policy terms. Accordingly, they are the chosen focus of this analysis along with, for comparative purposes, the Liberal Front Party (Partido da Frente Liberal; PFL), renamed the Democrats (DEM) in 2007, and the Brazilian Democratic Movement Party (Partido do Movimento Democrático Brasileiro; PMDB), which have been the PSDB's or PT's key allies over the period. In terms of numbers of congressional representatives, these parties were the most important during the period.

Parties considered and the 1993–94 Constitutional Review

In 1979, the Brazilian Democratic Movement (Movimento Democrático Brasileiro; MDB), the party in parliamentary opposition to the regime installed by the 1964 coup, became the PMDB, which inherited its composition as a political front. In the 1980s, it was Brazil's most important party, and, until recently, the largest in Congress. It no longer holds the political centre ground and has become a federation of interests of regional elites, focusing on state elections (Melo, 2010).

The PT also emerged in 1979. Its specific features have led it to be considered unprecedented in Brazil's political history (Meneguello, 1989), following Duverger (1980), who correlates mass parties with left-wing ideology. It gradually transferred the strength it had gained in civil society to political society by gaining mandates in municipal governments, Congress, state governments and finally the presidency. It has headed the executive since 2003 with the support of heterogeneous coalitions.

The PFL (today the DEM) appeared in 1985 as a dissenting offshoot from the Social Democratic Party (Partido Democrático-Social; PDS), which was formerly National Renewal Alliance (Aliança Renovadora Nacional; ARENA), the government party under the military regime. During the 1990s, the coalition with the PSDB around a liberal reform programme made the party a 'fish firmly in the water' (Cantanhede, 2001). It has gone into decline over the past decade.

The PSDB was founded in 1988 by left-wing dissidents from the PMDB. The split occurred, programmatically, because the core of the PMDB was judged to be an obstacle to Brazil's economic and political modernisation. Pragmatically, though, leaders constrained by the influence of the then governor of São Paulo State in the PMDB were looking for political leg-room. The PSDB gained the presidency in 1995 promising a monetary stabilisation plan. It held office for eight years under strong opposition from the PT and other left-wing parties.

Enactment of the 1988 Constitution provided for Constitutional Review, which took place in 1993 and 1994. Documents show that the PFL and PMDB took diametrically opposed positions on the review, the first bent on making it broader, the second on confining it to limited adjustments.[1] The PT shared the PMDB's mistrust of liberal revisionism, but was uncomfortable supporting the Constitution it had rejected in 1988. Meanwhile, the PSDB concurred with the PFL, but until the advent of the Real Plan was wary of allying with former figureheads of the dictatorship. It is from this perspective that the leading roles played by the PFL and PMDB until 1994 should be framed. The PFL formally proposed 74 amendments to the Review Congress. The PMDB, meanwhile, proposed a review focusing on federative topics (decentralisation and municipalisation), but did not regard the Constitution as a threat to governability. Rather, in the 1992 *Carta de Brasília* (*Letter from Brasília*), the party feared that wide-ranging review 'could distort the Constitution's guiding principles'.

The only constitutional topic that gained the attention of all four parties simultaneously was the economic order and, within it, the state's role in the economy. Two debates proceeded in parallel: one, more ideological than programmatic, between the PT and PSDB, focused on general guidelines; the other, between PMDB and PFL, connected the revisionist's broad agenda with government activities. On balance, however, party-political production during that period shows that in Congress, inertia prevailed over revisionist drive. Of the six ECRs enacted, only two had really substantial repercussions, and none was proposed by parties. Outside the Constitutional Review, four amendments were made between 1992 and 1994. Things would be different during Fernando Henrique Cardoso's two terms.

Constitutional revisionism unbound (1995–2002)

Considerable institutional change took place after Fernando Henrique Cardoso became President of Brazil. The 1994 election legitimised a reform agenda designed to extend the fiscal adjustment begun by the previous government and to reaffirm the primacy of the market. At the outset, the focus was on altering the chapter on the economic order, and then on addressing the federative design, the social security and tax systems, fiscal policy instruments, and the structure of public administration.

Of the leading parties, only the PT took up a position of systematic opposition. It took this stance from Fernando Henrique Cardoso's (FHC's) first term of office by contesting the constitutional reform agenda. When reforms to the economic order began to advance and were then followed by EC16/97, allowing the president to be re-elected, the confrontation turned more radical, reaching a peak during the second term. A resolution passed during the PT's second Congress (1999) called on workers to 'occupy the centre' in national politics. Its diagnosis showed a Brazil in crisis caused by the PSDB's economic policy, which the PT proposed to solve by terminating the agreement with the International Monetary Fund (IMF), a precondition for introducing food security and minimum income programmes. Solutions to the crisis would thus entail simultaneously attacking the government's economic policy and the president's 'mandate'. In social movements influenced by the PT, this guideline echoed in the rallying cry 'FHC Out!', which revealed an ambiguous strategy embodying two alternatives: disputing the 2002 elections and wagering on an institutional crisis.

The breadth of the FHC government's parliamentary base was decisive to advancing the reform agenda. Political consensus achieved during the first term ensured successful reform of the chapter on the economic order and the introduction of specific constitutional tax and fiscal policy instruments. The second term was not enough, however, to complete the reform quickly, as the PSDB had hoped. The idea of a sweeping tax reform, including redesign of the federation, was shelved for the future and the administrative and social security reforms were only partly accomplished. This can be seen by comparing 23 of the 35 amendments enacted between 1995 and 2002 with party documents from the same period.[2] The subject matter of all 23 amendments shows the greater importance of the economic order and tax and fiscal issues. Seven revised the chapter on the economic order; six reformed systemic areas, if only partially (two addressed the political system, one the public administration, two the tax system and one the social security system); five instituted temporary constitutional instruments to support current fiscal policy; and five were concerned with social policy.

Review of the economic order – particularly delimiting the state's role in the economy – sparked denser debate and a larger number of amendments. In particular, EC06/95 (ending the distinction between Brazilian companies with national and foreign capital), EC08/95 (ending the state telecommunications monopoly) and EC09/95 (flexibilising the government oil monopoly) affected substantial interests and historical ideological controversies that resonated strongly with public opinion.

Most of the amendments were concentrated in 1995, early in the first FHC administration. Party formulations on constitutional topics, with the exception of the PFL's *Programme for reform of the state*, came later and therefore did not affect the content of the amendments. The PFL was also the only party that had previously produced substantial proposals on the economic order along the lines of those that now formed part of the government agenda. In the 1993 proposals for the Constitutional Review and in the 1994 document, the programmatic orientation was to redefine the relationship between state and economic order through proposals for amendments addressing the following concerns: 1) free access to the market and free exercise of economic activity; 2) elimination of restrictions on foreign capital; 3) prevention of abuse of economic power; and 4) de-monopolisation. The second point was addressed directly in EC 6 and the fourth in ECs 5, 8 and 9. The PFL had proposed an article prohibiting monopolies, except in nuclear affairs, with separate proposals emphasising the oil, piped gas and telecommunications monopolies, in terms that would be established in the PECs submitted in 1995.

The PFL line continued unchanged from the start of the FHC administration through to the party programme approved in its 1995 convention. A document from the National Executive Commission, then another from the National Convention, were already discussing reducing government intervention in the economy, in terms that gave outright support for the PECs already enacted or pending in relation to the chapter on the economic order. That position was reflected in massive support from the party's members in Congress for all these proposals.

The PMDB's new programme of 1996 suggests various counterpoints. While admitting that reform of the state was crucial, it alerted against 'the neoliberal avalanche that intends to destroy the Brazilian State in the name of domestic adjustment and hypothetical entry into modernity'. Reaffirming the previous programme, it emphasises: that the state is an 'incontestable instrument of national sovereignty' and the monopoly principle 'determines the extension and limits of the State's role'; that economic policy instruments grounded in the sovereignty principle and under state control 'continue to be indispensable to development'; and that the market is a 'space for struggle against economic forces that, in the name of free enterprise, seek monopoly to the detriment of society'. It also advocates protection for Brazilian companies with national capital 'until international competitiveness is actually achieved'.

These counterpoints are striking, but illusory. In nominal ballots, the PMDB's members voted overwhelmingly in favour of the PECs to the chapter on the economic order. In the PECs on the telecommunications and oil monopolies, there were more dissidents, but no more than a quarter of members. The PMDB programme approved in 1996 thus clashes with the party's conduct during the political process of the PECs. The hypothesis that the document was self-critical of positions taken a year earlier cannot be sustained in view of the continuing discrepancies between programme and action. Accordingly, two hypotheses remain: the more benign sees contradiction between the party's leaders or members of Congress and the rank-and-file represented at the convention; the other holds that, on this point, the programme is no more than rhetoric.

Other recurrent items on the amendment agenda during the FHC governments were tax reform and the creation of constitutional instruments to support fiscal policy. Until 2001, the only changes to the constitutional structure of the tax system consisted in: the financial transactions tax (IPMF) introduced by EC03/93 and restored by EC12/96 earmarking the proceeds to funding health care; a confined adaptation of details of the tax system to the social security reform (EC20/98); and another stemming from EC29/00 that set a constitutional floor on funding for health care. The PSDB made a priority of introducing tools to support economic and financial policy; hence its support for swift approval of localised constitutional changes with a view to achieving fiscal balance. The PT's telling criticism of that policy, totalling 21 proposals in 1996, was steadily elaborated further between 1996 and 1999. The PT's tax reform proposal took the form of a 'global amendment' centred on fiscal justice, income distribution through taxation and reduction of taxes on production and employment. This led the party, by 2001, systematically and almost unanimously, to adopt positions counter to all PECs on tax and fiscal matters submitted by the executive or the government's congressional base, whether designed to create instruments to support fiscal policy, to adapt the tax system to the social security reform or to introduce new contributions to fund health care.

The PFL's proposals on tax and fiscal matters appear at the heart of the 1994 document – seen as the most comprehensive – on the subject of reform of the state. This ranking of subject matters expressed a view that conflicted with the PT's, but did not coincide with the PSDB's. It supported the adjustment proposed by the government, without explicitly backing the strategy of localised constitutional amendments. It focused on guidelines for a new tax system, mostly targeting the federative aspect of the tax reform. Unlike what had occurred with proposed amendments to the chapter on the economic order, no direct correspondence can be seen here between the PFL's proposals and the content of the PECs enacted. Nonetheless, its members' support for the PECs almost always bordered on the unanimous, with very few defections.

The PMDB did not add any issues of significance. Its new programme vaguely mentions a tax system able to 'sustain the State's ability to manage currency' and rejects the idea of seeking to balance the budget at the expense of the state performing its role of 'encouraging development and promoting social justice, but also of maintaining public order and providing security against outside threats to our territorial integrity'.

Once again, its opposition discourse contrasted with the strong voting support its members gave to the PECs in Congress.

In the discussion of the constitutionally defined federative design that occurred during the Cardoso administrations, the PFL once again limited itself to specific proposals while the other three parties made general recommendations. Its document on the reform of the state, arguing firmly for decentralisation, resolved the tension present in the proposals submitted to the Review Congress a year earlier. Finding no echo in the executive, the idea did not prosper and, for its change of direction, the PFL had to content itself in practice with the lesser evil: the federative status quo in the Constitution. That about-turn also reflected the new polarisation between the PSDB and PT in the presidential dispute from 1994 on, which further imprisoned both the PFL and PMDB in state-level political subsystems.

The PMDB came to the same point of view as the PFL, but from the opposite direction. It replaced the municipalist proposals of the *Letter from Brasília* with declarations of principle in favour of decentralisation. These are analogous in meaning and generality to the declarations of the PT. The PSDB held silent in its role as the party of the president, whose administration was using ECs to contrive tax stratagems to circumvent the logic of the 1988 Constitution while leaving the overall federative design untouched. While the boost from the PFL's change of direction did not ensure the viability of the PMDB's decentralisation proposals, it did make it difficult for the opposing design to emerge. This may be why, at the time, there were no ECs defining a new federative design. The outcome of mutual vetoes – by the executive on the one hand and by the opposition and federatively inclined parties on the other – was to maintain the constitutional status quo.

The social security reform progressed through Congress between March 1995 and December 1998. It was debated for months in the lower house and for just over a year in the Senate, then returning to the lower house for enactment in the form of EC20/98. The result was an amendment significantly different in content from the original PEC, making for more superficial reform.[3] In the lower house, rapporteurs were appointed from among members of parties allied with the government and greater restrictions were placed on the original proposal. In the upper house, the PSDB rapporteur accepted other changes, but during the second reading in the lower house, both rapporteurs, also members of the PSDB, enforced the executive's instructions more firmly.

In the closing stages, the president's party took over. It declared the present model unworkable and proposed a new one, eliminating early retirements, benefits without equivalent contributions and the disparity between retirement requirements in the public and private sectors. There were defeats on important points, such as contributions by retired persons and a minimum retirement age of 60 for men and 55 for women, which was supported by 307 congressmen, one less than necessary. However, during the second vote, transitional rules were proposed for a minimum retirement age of 53 (men) and 48 (women) for private sector workers. The proposal met with fairly united opposition and strong rejection from left-leaning movements, but PT documents did not examine its merit. The PMDB declared that the public social security system should be social in nature and complemented only by mutual, private entrepreneurial systems. Once again, the PFL tabled specific proposals, which were partly included in the EC: joining the chorus that decried the system's financial impracticability, it proposed measures that went further than the original PEC and further still than the final draft of the EC and even the position of the party's members in Congress (Salles, 1996).

Other constitutional issues either were not targeted in the parties' proposals and in congressional debate or were inadequately processed politically. For instance, the generality and lack of substance of the parties' analyses of the political system were reflected in an absence of amendments on the subject, except one admitting re-election for the president, governors and mayors and another regulating the issuing and subsequent congressional appraisal of provisional decrees. With the exception of the PFL's support for re-election in 1993, those issues were nowhere to be found in the party documents examined.

On the administrative reform, the PSDB supported PEC173/95, which gave rise to EC19/98, including its provisions ending tenure in public employment, setting wage ceilings and introducing mandatory performance assessment in the public administration. However, it was the executive that formulated the proposal, which was not submitted to the parties for consensus-building. Beyond the PSDB's formal support, no party (not even the PSDB) made any documented declarations. Passage of this PEC was turbulent, with the PT involved in civil servants' protests to halt it. The PMDB and PFL were less cohesive, especially the latter, whose members deviated from their standard behaviour of practically unanimous support for the government agenda. The amendment approved at first reading in the lower house stipulates that civil service tenure is conditional on five years' probation and may be forfeit for poor performance. In addition, governments at all three levels of the federation could dismiss civil servants to comply with payroll spending limits. However, the government failed to secure approval for eliminating civil service examinations as the sole condition for access to public employment and was also defeated in its attempt to extend the age of compulsory retirement from 70 to 75 years. The government's defeats were partly reversed in later ballots, but the reform made little progress towards making the civil service more professional.

Among the social policy-related amendments, the landmark of the period was EC14/96, which created the Fundamental Education Development Fund (Fundo de Desenvolvimento do Ensino Fundamental; Fundef). It appears in party documents not as a proposal originating there, but as one meriting support. The PSDB tried to capitalise on it as a government achievement, while the PFL, through Vice-President Marco Maciel, acknowledged it as an advance. The PMDB was also supportive, but the PT did not slacken its opposition, despite the fact that this proposed amendment addressed a social policy and, in Congress, the PT voted unanimously against it. When the PT argued for 'effective' allocation of funds to health care in the fiscal budget, it did not mention EC29, already discussed here. Another two ECs addressing social policies were enacted during that period, but escaped mention by any of the party documents consulted here.

In summary, during the FHC administrations, the four parties' standard conduct on the various constitutional issues was as follows: the PSDB spoke for the executive and thus borrowed the prestige of the president's position, his intellectual endorsement, as well as political and administrative support from the ministries for the programmatic solutions formulated by the PFL. The latter, in addition to operating as a 'think tank', also led the operation of processing the resulting proposals politically through Congress (together with the PMDB), a process in which the PSDB played a supporting role, almost always involving direct confrontation with the opposition. The PMDB had enough leeway and flexibility to contribute to formulations that clashed with the official government line, but not to assist their political processing, a mission that fell by definition to the PT, which was in opposition. The PT, grappling with the pragmatic pressures of a conjuncture that absorbed its interest, was somewhat inconstant in its mission as a think tank, and very active – together with smaller parties such as the PDT, PCdoB, PSB and sometimes the PPS – in its resistance to the political processing of the proposals by the government caucus.

Instead of the PSDB and PT replacing the PFL and PMDB as more active formulators of amendments, what happened while the PSDB was in government was that the former two parties (especially the PFL) continued to be the main sources of proposals. The PT's lesser output is understandable in view of its position as an opposition – and, accordingly, also anti-revisionist – party. However, the PSDB's position may seem surprising for its omission or generality on several issues. It is to be supposed that being the president's party restricted its scope for autonomous formulation, making it difficult to separate party and government agendas. Neither can it be ignored that, like the PT, the PSDB was a novice in its relationship with the Brazilian state, and its intellectuals were more closely associated with universities – unlike the PMDB and PFL, whose political members had extensive administrative experience and were able to make better use of their connections in the state techno-bureaucracy when drafting proposals.

In this way, the PFL, seconded by the PMDB, continued to lead the constitutional debate in both intensity and depth during the FHC administrations. Contrary to the common-sense notion that the PFL and PMDB are more 'immediatist' (as opposed to the more 'doctrinal' PT and PSDB), what was actually seen in the debate on constitutional change during the PSDB governments was the opposite.

Slower pace and new agenda from 2003 onward

The PT's attaining of the federal executive in 2003 was expected, for political and programmatic reasons, to slow the pace of constitutional change. The trend had already been noted during the second FHC administration, not because the revisionist agenda had become saturated (as already mentioned, the social security and administrative reforms remained incomplete and the tax reform had only been provisionally drafted, while the political reform had not even got that far), but rather due to problems of political coordination in the closing stages of the PSDB administration. The incoming government was expected to be a minority in Congress – a simple majority was soon achieved by negotiating positions in government, but the three fifths majority needed to enact PECs had to be negotiated once these were in discussion – and it was programmatically not committed to the reform agenda of the previous decade, all of which led to the belief that the successive extensions of constitutional reform activity would come to an end. It would be time for social policies.

The start of the Lula administration partly frustrated those expectations. Soon after being elected, the president let it be known by the document *Commitment to change* (*Compromisso com a Mudança*) that he would be submitting five reform proposals to Congress on social security, tax, labour and trade unions, land ownership, and the political system. Indeed, the immediate resumption of the social security reform from where PEC20/98 had left it dominated the attention of the political agenda throughout most of 2003, to the point of sending tremors through the left of the government alliance and even the PT itself. Macroeconomic logic and the inertia of the previous institutional agenda held the government to an agenda that was prior to the 'spectacle' of economic growth and the restitution of social debt pledged in the election manifesto. However, together with the social security reform, the government forwarded another PEC proposing a tax reform that, contrary to its predecessor's measures, met important expectations on the part of the state governments.[4]

The political processing of the Social Security PEC shifted the locus of alliance-building and political negotiation from the executive to the legislature, even though – as shown by Melo and Anastasia (2005) – Congress was the main arena of a game whose players competed in at least another three: the ministries, with their power of patronage; the judiciary, with its power of veto; and the 'aware publics' in civil society, especially those whose interests were strongly affected by the reform (civil servants). The ability of coalitional presidentialism to produce governability beyond the informal rule of overwhelming parliamentary majorities was put to the test. The outcome of this process – approval of an amendment maintaining the essence of the design proposed by the executive and at the same time incorporating significant influence from the opposition – indicated that the system had passed the test. Would fulfilment of the government agenda begin with political renewal?

Life gave the lie to this surmise. Once the social security and tax reforms were past, the government arranged a stable, prior majority so as not to be forced to negotiate its agenda item by item. While the political system and governability could dispense with this kind of majority, the government party's strategy could not. The enormous breadth of the alliance assembled from late 2003 might suggest that the effort was expended for the sake of the special quorum needed to resume the agenda of constitutional change. Once again, expectations were disappointed; this time, the earlier prognosis – that the process would finally die down – was confirmed. This was evidenced not only by the dwindling number of amendments proposed, but also in declining party involvement in drafting and processing them. Both trends were connected with the political realignment of 2003–04, the crisis in the governing coalition of 2005–06 and the thematic profile of amendments during PT governments. The proclaimed political, land, trade union and labour reforms, and other pending administrative reforms met other fates: the first never went beyond parliamentary and party rhetoric; the second was handicapped by the managerial pace of a ministry under the influence of the Landless Workers' Movement (Movimento dos Trabalhadores Sem Terra; MST); and the others went nowhere. The government was thus able to turn its full attention to conjunctural concerns. Pragmatic management of political trading would ensure strategic support for macroeconomic and social policy management.

During the two Lula administrations, 28 constitutional amendments were enacted (only seven short of the FHC governments) and three more have been passed under the Dilma government. However, when the subject matter of the amendments, then and now, are compared in the terms of the present analysis, it will be remembered that 23 amendments were considered in the previous section because they involved the political system, 'systemic' areas managed by the executive or social policy designs. That represents approximately two thirds of the total of 35 enacted during the FHC administrations. Applying the same criterion, the 17 later amendments that qualify are only 55% of a total of 31. The two sets differ in subject matter. While amendments on social issues totalled 22% (five out of 23) beforehand, they now represent 35% (six out of 17). Of the 11 other amendments, eight made more permanent – albeit mostly localised – changes in systemic areas (four in the tax system, two in the economic order, one in the social security system and one in the political system). As compared with the 17 systemic amendments under the previous government, now less than half are amendments where parties are expected to contribute in a major way to their formulation and political processing.

After the first year of the Lula government, no constitutional issues stand out as focuses of the political agenda in Congress or in the parties. The documented repertoire of proposals from parties, with the exception of the PT, has shrunk abruptly as compared to previous periods.[5] This evidences the executive's power to induce party agendas. Operating more as political processing plants for government proposals than as autonomous think tanks, the parties exempt themselves from constitutional issues when these are not placed on the agenda by the government. While in previous periods the PFL was a case apart, it forfeited that position when it saw itself waning electorally in opposition. While in opposition, the PT had been more of a political processor of resistance endeavours than a wellspring of proposals; in government, it morphed the activity of formulation into the operation of politically processing the ideas generated within the government. The PFL's leading role as a source of proposals in the 1990s was relatively exogenous, deriving from its experience in government, but it was prior to the FHC administration and served as a credential for accessing the centres of power that would be occupied by the PSDB. The PT's is endogenous and derives first from its access to power and the agenda inherited by the executive, and then from interactions between its party programme and the experience of government.

It is as well to note that the PT combines its pragmatic management of the structure of government with persistently high levels of counter-hegemonic ideology in its programmatic documents. The 2007 programme speaks of a 'crisis in institutional representation', a diagnosis linked to its advocacy of 'participatory democracy'. The counter-hegemonic tone is raised further and regionalised in the 2011 document: flirting with Chavism and its allies, it sets out the thesis that the left's centre of gravity worldwide is shifting from Europe to Latin America, suggesting an ideal identity between democracy on the continent and the electoral advance of this 'new left'.

This conception of politics and democracy inspires a design for reform. At its third congress, the party argued for reform with its historical proposals and issues, such as: advocating party fidelity; prohibiting alliances and closed, pre-ordered party lists in proportional elections; the end of the re-election rule; a limitation on the number of mandates allowed to parliamentary representatives; and affirmative action by means of gender, race and ethnic quotas in political representation. It proposed that the reform be conducted by an 'Exclusive Constituent Assembly' on the following argument: members of Congress, who owe everything to the rules, will not change them.

The Exclusive Constituent Assembly is not mentioned in the documents of 2011; the plebiscite view is upheld and previous proposals are pragmatically condensed. They argue in favour of voting on party lists and exclusively public campaign-funding; they also support the diagnosis of 'decision-making paralysis' in coalitional presidentialism. Descriptively, their criticisms of distortions and failings in the system suggest a preference for wide-ranging political reform; prescriptively, they are prevailingly minimalist.

Of the other three parties, only the PSDB declared its position on political reform in a document at the time. Converging with the PT, it argues even more inflexibly for voting on party lists, declares its dissatisfaction with the proportionality criteria in representation and criticises the excessive proliferation of (non-elective) 'positions of trust'. The latter would be more appropriately addressed by an administrative reform, which none of the parties includes in its agenda. Unlike the PT, it supports district voting and is silent on exclusively public funding for parties and campaigns, which is a priority issue for the PT.

There are no other issues of constitutional change in that period on which to bring party proposals into dialogue. PT documents address the issues of tax reform, social policy designs and social security reform (the latter only in articles in the magazine *Teoria & Debate*). The PSDB document holds silent on these issues and the PMDB and PFL produced no new documents. Of all the other 10 ECs enacted on 'systemic' subjects in the period, in only four cases was their passage through Congress conflictive. Seven amendments enacted in the period deal with fiscal and tax issues: four making changes to the structure of the tax system and three supporting fiscal policy. Of these, only Lula's tax reform and two extensions to time frames for government revenue decoupling (*Desvinculação de Receitas da União*; DRU) sparked any level of political conflict. The four remaining amendments were approved by consensus.

Even greater convergence resulted in six constitutional amendments on social policies in the period. In 12 nominal Senate ballots, only one vote was cast against them. In the lower house, in a total of 12 nominal votes, there were 25 votes against, which is negligible since every ballot involved at least 320 representatives and, in most cases, 380 to 420. Those six PECs were drafted by members of several parties; the rapporteurs too were drawn from different parties.

Limited space precludes any more detailed analysis here. Suffice it to contrast that period with the confrontation that marked constitutional change prior to 2002. By way of illustration, a word about the PEC drafted by the then Senator José Serra (PSDB), which became EC40/2003, one of two amendments approved during that period addressing the chapter on the economic order. This proposal originated under the previous administration, its object revealing that it belonged to the series of market-oriented reforms. It dealt with regulations on credit cooperatives and advocated opening up financial institutions to foreign capital, a proposal that spent six years before the Senate and lower house until being definitively approved in 2003 after the leaders of all four parties studied here recommended voting in favour, and were followed almost unanimously by their fellow party members in both houses. The fact that the final wording of the amendment left regulation to supplementary law certainly helped dissipate conflict, but the nearly unanimous agreement with the change shows that ideological polarisation was already a thing of the past.

Two observations

The material analysed here shows that the PSDB and PT, the leading contenders for the presidency, were not leading policymakers on constitutional matters. The PFL particularly stands out for its more substantial and successful attempts to formulate market-oriented constitutional reforms and make them politically viable.

On the other hand, the other preliminary assumption is confirmed: that parties have performed less as sources of original ideas than as political processing plants for externally generated proposals. The PFL's performance as a formulator in the mid-1990s qualifies that interpretation, without contesting it.

Acknowledgement

I am grateful to Mariana de Carvalho Pinto, who collected and partly organised the data, for her collaboration

Notes

[1] Documents from 1988 to 1994 examined were: PT – Resolution of the first Congress (1991), posted on the party's website (www.fpabramo.org.br/node/5880) and articles in *Teoria & Debate* magazine; PSDB – the 1988 document *Diretrizes básicas* (*Basic guidelines*) by the Teotônio Vilela Institute and a 1990 booklet drafted by Senator Fernando Henrique Cardoso's staff, both posted on the party's website (in www.psdb.org.br); PFL – proposals for the constitutional review, drafted in 1993 and published in 1996 in the *Livro do PFL* (*Book of the PFL*), organised by Mauro Salles; and PMDB – the 1992 *Carta de Brasília* (*Letter from Brasília*), posted on the party's website (in www.psdb.org.br).

[2] Documents consulted: PT – resolution of its second Congress (1999) and articles from *Teoria & Debate* magazine; PSDB – the 1997 document *Balanço do primeiro governo e programa de ação* (*The first year of government on balance and programme for action*), posted on the party's website (www.fug-rs.org.br/site/memoria_man_92); PFL – *Programa de Reforma do Estado* (*Programme for reform of the state*), *Nota da Comissão Executiva* (*Note from the Executive Commission*) and speeches by Vice-President Marco Maciel and Congressman César Maia at the National Convention, and the Party Programme approved at that same Convention, all published in PFL (Salles, 1996); and the PMDB's 19946 *Novo Programa Doutrinário* (*New doctrinal programme*), posted on its website (http://pmdb-rs.org.br/scripts/programa) and which replaced the 1982 document *Esperança e Mudança* (*Hope and change*).

[3] This process was examined by Melo and Anastasia (2005), who compare it with the new social security reform carried out in 2003 on the initiative of the PT government.

[4] Melo and Anastasia (2005) show that state governors played an important role in raising parliamentary support for the social security reform, especially among opposition party members.

[5] Documents for this topic: PT – *Compromisso com a Mudança* (*Commitment to change*), Lula's manifesto after the victory of 2002; documents from *Teoria & Debate*, especially discussing the tax and social security reforms (2003) and the *Balanço do 3o Congresso* (*3rd Congress on Balance*) (2007); Political Resolutions of the third (2007) and fourth (2011) party congresses; and the 2011 *Resolução sobre reforma política* (*Resolution on political reform*). PSDB – *Programa Partidário* (*Party programme*), published by the Teotônio Vilela Institute. PFL and PMDB – no programme documents addressing constitutional issues in the period were found.

References

Arantes, R. and Couto, C. (2008) 'A Constituição sem fim', in S. Diniz and S. Praça (eds) *Vinte anos de Constituição*, São Paulo: Paulus, pp 31–60.

Cantanhede, E. (2001) *O PFL*, São Paulo: Publifolha.

Abranches, S.H. (1988) 'Presidencialismo de Coalizão. O Dilema Institucional Brasileiro', *Dados*, vol 31, no 1, pp 5–34.

Duverger, M. (1980) *Os partidos políticos* (2nd edn), Brasília: UnB.

Fleischer, D. (1981) *Os partidos políticos no Brasil* (2 vols), Brasília: Ed. UNB.

Kinzo, M.D.G. (2005) 'Os partidos no eleitorado: percepções públicas e laços partidários no Brasil', *Revista Brasileira de Ciências Sociais*, vol 20, no 57, pp 65–81.

Mainwaring, S. (2001) *Sistemas partidários em novas democracias: o caso do Brasil*, Porto Alegre/Rio: Mercado Aberto/FGV.

Mainwaring, S. and Scully, T. (1995) *Building democratic institutions: party systems in Latin America*, Stanford, CA: Stanford University Press.

Mainwaring, S. and Shugart, M. (2002) 'Presidencialismo y democracia en América Latina: Revisión de los términos del debate', in S. Mainwaring and M. Shugart (eds) *Presidencialismo y democracia en América Latina*, Buenos Aires: Paidós, pp 19–64.

Mainwaring, S. and Torcal, M. (2005) 'Teoria e institucionalização dos sistemas partidários após a terceira onda de democratização', *Opinião Pública*, vol 11, no 2, pp 249–86.

Mair, P. (2003) 'Os partidos políticos e a democracia', *Análise Social*, vol 38, no 167, pp 277–93.

Melo, C.R.F. (2010) 'Eleições presidenciais, jogos aninhados e sistema partidário no Brasil', *Revista Brasileira de Ciência Política*, no 4, pp 13–41.

Melo, C.R.F. and Anastasia, F. (2005) 'A reforma da Previdência em dois tempos', *DADOS*, vol 48, no 2, pp 301-32.

Melo, M.A. (2002) *Reformas constitucionais no Brasil: instituições políticas e processo decisório*, Rio de Janeiro: Revan.

Melo, M.A. (2005) 'O sucesso inesperado das reformas de segunda geração: federalismo, reformas constitucionais e política social', *Dados*, vol 48, no 4, pp 845–88.

Meneguello, R. (1989) *PT: a formação de um partido, 1979–1982*, Rio: Paz e Terra.

Panebianco, A. (1988) *Political parties: organization and power*, Cambridge: Cambridge University Press.

Salles, M. (ed) (1996) *O livro do PFL: educação e emprego*, São Paulo: Massao Ohno Editor.

Souza, C. (2008) 'Regras e contexto: as reformas da Constituição de 1988', *Dados*, vol 5, no 4, pp 791-823.

FIFTEEN

Business associations and public policy analysis

Renato Raul Boschi

Introduction

The analysis in this chapter will focus on Brazil's main industrial business organisations, aiming to evaluate their ability to produce information, track implementation and monitor policies and disputes in their interest. Our analysis is framed by the period following the neoliberal reforms, because of the impact they had on the organisation of industrial business interests and on the overall productive regime in Brazil. Previous papers by the author with Eli Diniz (Diniz and Boschi, 2004, 2007) have emphasised that one of the main changes in the scenario after the economic reforms was that interest mediation activities shifted from the executive to the legislature, stimulated in part by the re-democratisation process taking place at the same time (throughout the 1990s) in Brazil. That shift was accompanied by a trend for organisations to professionalise, particularly as a result of the lobbying activities that came to predominate in the industrial business community's political activities, which previously had targeted the executive.

More recently, it can be assumed that, as of the Lula administration, the restoration of state capabilities and the emerging prospect of greater (developmentalist) government intervention confronted the sector with a more strategic need to monitor the economic conjuncture, while simultaneously identifying multiple executive initiatives in various different policy fields, and thus reinforced the trends of the 1990s signalled earlier.

The study presented here will focus on certain bodies that represent the interests of the industrial business community in terms of their ability to produce, analyse and monitor public policies relating directly to this segment. The structure for representing the business community's interests, and those of other prominent social actors, was set up in the 1930s with a view to structuring the capital and labour segments to meet the growing challenges posed by an industrial and urban order in Brazil. The original structure underwent significant changes over time, in particular, for the segments of capital that were able to bypass the principles of monopoly of representation that inspired the creation of the corporatist official structure under Vargas. This flexibility led to the emergence and expansion of parallel business interest organisations, defined as a function of sectors of industrial production, which, in some cases, became more important than their official counterparts (Diniz and Boschi, 1979, 1991, 1993, 1999, 2000).

Some entities of the official structure retained their centrality (although not their monopoly over representation of industrial interests), either because they were able to draw together the interests of their constituency as whole nationwide or because of the importance of the region they represented in overall industrial production. In some other cases involving so-called parallel associations, certain bodies gained significance because they represented different schools of thought or outlooks on development projects for Brazil. It is along these lines that the following organisations have been chosen for analysis: the National Confederation of Industries (Confederação Nacional da Indústria; CNI); the São Paulo State Federation of Industries (Federação das Indústrias do Estado de São Paulo; FIESP); the Rio de Janeiro State Federation of Industries (Federação das Indústrias do Rio de Janeiro; FIRJAN); and the Industrial Development Studies Institute (Instituto de Estudos para o Desenvolvimento Industrial; IEDI). The first three belong to the official corporative structure set up in the 1930s to represent business interests, and they continue to be the industrial sector's main mouthpieces, despite a series of changes in the characteristics of the political system and the production regime. The latter is an independent association set up in the 1980s as a think tank by a group of developmentalist business leaders, primarily for the purpose of evaluating industrial performance in recent years and drafting alternative proposals.

Our analysis involves examining these organisations to identify the new trends towards policymaking and analysis. In the first part, our concern is to identify centres within organisations' structures directed to producing information (an analytical capability), to monitoring and to producing documents to bolster companies' activities in matters in their interest. We will also specify activities distinguishable as policy orientations, complementary to public policies undertaken within the official sphere. As is well known, the state in Brazil has played a central role to make up for deficiencies in dimensions not covered by private firms. In contrast with developed countries, where complementarities between patterns of labour training, innovation and financing are established at the level of firms and are identified as key characteristics of their specific varieties of capitalism, in developing countries in Latin America, such complementarities tend to be effected by the government, particularly in view of the structural social inequalities and the heterogeneity of production regimes. However, important initiatives in labour training and capacity-building policies have been implemented by industry through the 'S-System', which can be seen as complementary or parallel to policies carried out by the state. Those usually entail a considerable level of specialisation and the development of bureaucratic capabilities. Some such initiatives of a public–private nature carried out by 'S-System' organisations connected with industry will be examined.

In the present context of financial globalisation, business organisations and other civil society organisations have been required to provide responses that depend on understanding a conjuncture of opportunities and limitations. In that context, it is necessary to identify strategic areas of their activity that rest on the production of specific, well-grounded knowledge. The emphasis of the analysis in this chapter is on identifying such areas.

Some recent trends can be identified within the context of corporative associations. These new aspects include thematic areas for action by industry, which entail strategies and endeavours towards public policy analysis. This is the case with the CNI, with a focus on de-bureaucratisation, education, infrastructure, foreign relations, micro-businesses, technological innovation, work, social responsibility and so on. In addition, another novelty consists in the development of a series of indexes designed to guide companies' investment strategies, these include: the Industrial Businessman's

Confidence Index (Índice de Confiança do Empresário Industrial; ICEI); the National Consumer Expectations Index (Índice Nacional de Expectativa do Consumidor; INEC); the Fear of Unemployment Index (Índice de Medo do Desemprego; IMD); and the CNI-IBOPE Survey (National Confederation of Industry- Brazilian Public Opinion and Statistics Institute). The experience of the CNI's Council of Legislative Affairs (Conselho de Assuntos Legislativos; COAL) emerges as one of the most significant since the reforms (Diniz and Boschi, 2004). Set up especially as a centre for monitoring industry claims submitted to Congress, this CNI unit was the subject of a detailed study (Mancuso, 2007b). Here, we will present some recent data on COAL activities in this endeavour to characterise public policies of interest to the industrial business community.

In the cases of FIESP and FIRJAN, it is also possible to identify new activities and internal organs that can be expected to increase the analytical capabilities of business organisations. On one hand, what can be seen in FIRJAN, for instance, is the creation of Business Councils to formulate policies in various areas relating to issues that are important to industry; on the other hand, FIESP, for example, has set up departments and strategic areas specialising in quite contemporary issues, such as energy, infrastructure, environment, social responsibility, technological innovation, water resources, international relations, economic and industrial policy, as well as more permanent topics in the sphere of labour relations, social policy, legislative issues, strategic management for competitiveness and so on. This means that the most important industrial sector federations have increased the complexity of their structures, as well as setting up bureaucratic capabilities to address these issues through policy analysis and development.

National Confederation of Industries

The CNI is the largest institution of Brazilian industry. It comprises 27 industrial federations in states and the Federal District, plus over 1,000 member employers' associations, in addition to 196,000 industrial businesses. Its role is to manage, coordinate and protect the sector's interests. Its activities include knowledge production, especially with respect to operationalising government industrial policy. In order to serve industry interests, the CNI ensures industrial community participation in a number of thematic areas, such as: 1) de-bureaucratisation (restructuring Brazilian business policy and surmounting legal obstacles that, in the CNI's view, are obstacles to Brazil's economic development); 2) education (capacitating workers by technical qualification and vocational training to meet industrial sector demands through the so-called 'S-System', which includes the Industry Social Service [Serviço Social da Indústria; SESI], the National Industrial Training Service [Serviço Nacional de Aprendizagem Industrial; SENAI], the Euvaldo Lodi Institute [Instituto Euvaldo Lodi; IEL] and others); 3) international affairs (foreign affairs and signing undertakings to further the interests of Brazilian industry); 4) infrastructure (improving Brazil's infrastructure for developing production of goods and services); 5) micro and small businesses (offering programmes and support for small-scale entrepreneurship in Brazil); 5) labour (increasing flexibility of payroll tax requirements in Brazil); 6) technology and innovation (technological and scientific development in industry, through public policies favouring scientific progress); and, lastly, 7) social responsibility (social programmes).

According to data provided by the CNI itself, what could be defined as the organisation's developing analytical abilities to monitor public policies is carried out through dialogue with their members. This ongoing process of consultation involves the different hierarchical levels within the organisation, such as federations and unions, in addition to the national industrial associations. The process includes the National Industry Conference (Encontro Nacional da Indústria) and the National Industry Forum (Fórum Nacional da Indústria), which express and convey industry demands to the executive, legislature and judiciary. In this way, through debate with the widest possible range of areas of industry, the CNI builds its position and the actions to be taken to represent Brazilian industry, directly targeting public policy outcomes. Research, studies, seminars and so on are produced in this process in order to help improve action to support Brazilian industry. One of the CNI's main tools to this end is its Legislative Report (*Informe Legislativo*), which lists new legislative proposals submitted to the National Congress, arranged by topic of interest to the industrial sector.

CNI has a technical staff to conduct its research, which regularly includes:

- Industrial Indicators – Produced monthly since 1992 showing trends in operating revenue, labour hours, level of employment, total wages and use of installed capacity in 19 sectors in Brazil's processing industry.
- Industrial Survey – A qualitative opinion survey conducted quarterly at 1,513 companies in 23 states. Of these, 891 are small, 415 are medium and 207 are large companies. Business perceptions of how output, employment, stock, use of installed capacity and the company's status are progressing allow researchers to evaluate current industrial and economic conditions.
- Industrial Business Confidence Index (ICEI) – This quarterly survey conducted in 24 states reveals industrialists' perception of current conditions and their expectations for how Brazil's economy and their companies will perform. The indicator shows changes in industrial production trends.
- National Consumer Expectations Index (INEC) – This quarterly quantitative survey reveals the Brazilian population's outlook with respect to inflation, personal income, financial situation, indebtedness and plans to purchase higher-value goods. This indicator helps predict family consumption trends.
- Fear of Unemployment Index – This quarterly quantitative survey shows the Brazilian population's concern with employment. It complements the INEC information and also helps predict family consumption.
- CNI-IBOPE Survey – This quarterly survey of 2,002 voters in 145 municipalities investigates people's opinions about government performance, policy priorities and topics of interest to industry. From the CNI-IBOPE survey, CNI develops the INEC.

To illustrate some specific actions in response to ongoing public policies, some CNI activities in 2011 include, first, the launch of the Industrial Legislative Agenda (Agenda Legislativa Industrial) itself, which is intended to expedite or slow bills before the legislature. Another important activity that year involved coordination in the joint public–private endeavour to implement a wide-ranging government industrial policy project. Here, the federal government appointed CNI to coordinate the dialogue to be established with Brazilian industry in order to formulate the new stage of the

Production Development Policy (Política de Desenvolvimento Produtivo; PDP), as well as devising a new foreign trade strategy.

Another policy-related initiative, in a field that is both extremely contemporary, but at the same time in line with its interests, was to conduct a study to reduce carbon footprints. According to CNI, Brazil is wealthy in terms of the diversity of its energy matrix, but hydropower is nonetheless its largest source. The centrality of hydroelectric power is coming to be a problem for Brazilian industry in that electric power costs have been rising above inflation, placing Brazil's electricity among the most expensive in the world. For this reason, CNI conducted a study designed to encourage debate about the future of energy in Brazil, with a view to increasing the competitiveness of Brazil's national product.

There are a number of thematic councils responsible for examining developments in structures of the state; COAL being the most important of these. COAL's findings are published in a newsletter or articles published on the federations' websites with a view to publicising legislative positions that are in the interests of industry. This monitoring of legislative activities is replicated at the state level, where the federations work closely with state legislatures. COAL is designed to monitor, examine, understand and anticipate the activities and decisions of the legislature in order to guide the federations' policy action precisely and forge closer links between the federations of industry and state and municipal legislatures. In summary, COAL's goal is to make CNI positions known to the National Congress, to select and rank issues before the National Congress that are of interest to the industrial sector, and to circulate important information to industry councils, commissions, federations, associations and organisations.

Among COAL's achievements in 2011 was having several presidential provisional decrees scheduled for debate, with important consequences for the CNI. These included Provisional Decree No 517 of 2010, extending taxes levied on electricity bills for another 25 years (until 2035). The change proposed by CNI through its congressional representatives would reduce the cost of electricity by 2–3%, providing relief to both Brazilian society and industry.

São Paulo State Federation of Industries

The FIESP is perhaps the most complex and differentiated of all the industrial corporative organisations, because of the importance of the sectors it represents, and the number and size of its member employers' associations. Among the many agencies and departments in its structure that perform some type of policymaking or policy-monitoring role, FIESP has nine Higher Thematic Councils, coordinated by the Roberto Simonsen Institute (IRS), a study centre supported by industry concerned with examining broader national matters. These councils set out guidelines for the work of the various different departments, such as Economic Research and Studies, International Relations and Foreign Trade, Agribusiness, Social Responsibility, Infrastructure, Advanced Studies, Environment, Legal and Legislative Studies, Competitiveness and Technology, and Micro, Small and Medium-Sized Industries.

The Higher Thematic Councils are technical bodies set up to foster discussion and analysis of issues important to industry in São Paulo and Brazil, so as to guide FIESP's position in formulating action and policies to be carried out by its departments, and maximise results. The most important councils are: the Higher Thematic Council on Legal and Legislative Affairs (Conselho Superior Temático de Assuntos Jurídicos e Legislativos; Conjur); the Higher Thematic Council on the Economy (Conselho Superior Temático de Economia; Cosec), which discusses, studies and proposes policies in the economic field; and the Legal Department (Departamento Jurídico; Dejur), which provides the business community with information on all the implications of legislative changes and jurisprudence.

In order to guarantee proper growth in the various different production chains, committees were also set up for the following sectors: Food and Agribusiness, Civil Construction, Mining, Leather and Footwear, Textile and Garments, and the Defence Industry. There are also committees for Young Entrepreneurs, Cultural Action and Social Responsibility.

The mission of the Social Responsibility Committee (Comitê de Responsabilidade Social; Cores) is to offer strategies and tools that will assist industrialists in formulating and implementing Corporate Social Responsibility (CSR) policies that take account of the legal requirements and concerns with promoting citizenship and sustainable development, in addition to the transparency of their activities.

The most important body producing indicators and information in the FIESP structure is the Economic Research and Studies Department (Departamento de Pesquisas e Estudos Econômicos; Depecon). This agency conducts economic research, studies and analyses of industry's performance, its problems and the proposed solutions. Its products include:

- *Macro Vision (Macro Visão)* – a daily publication that provides information to members on the main aspects of the economic situation.
- *Level of Activity Indicator (Indicador de Nível de Atividade*; INA) – summarises all indicators of the Conjuncture Survey, which has been conducted monthly since 1975, of 850 São Paulo companies and forecasts industry trends.
- *FIESP Sensor (Sensor FIESP)* – monthly qualitative survey conducted since June 2006 to gather information about the progress of processing industry activities during the current data collection month, thus eliminating the time lags of traditional conjunctural surveys.
- *Cost of Credit (Custo do Crédito)* – weekly publication that provides business owners with information on credit operations, presenting a comparative study of interest rates applied by major retail banks in Brazil.
- *Monthly Industrial Survey (Sondagem Industrial Mensal)/ Business Owners' Confidence Index (Índice de Confiança do Empresário)* – monthly publication based on company responses to questionnaires on volume of production, utilisation of installed capacity, stock of end products, demand forecasts for the next six months, materials purchases and exports. On the same questionnaire, company CEOs answer questions on overall conditions in Brazil's economy, in São Paulo State and in the company, both current and forecast for the coming six months (in order to compile the ICEI).
- *Industrial Sector Index (Índice do Setor Industrial*; INDX) – monthly index developed to measure the performance of the most representative industrial shares selected from among those most traded on the São Paulo stock exchange (BOVESPA) in terms of liquidity and weighted by the market value of shares available for negotiation.

- *Industry Directions (Rumos da Indústria)* – quantitative survey through 700 interviews monthly emailed to participants to assess companies' point expectations for their business and the economy.
- *Brazil Pulse Survey (Pesquisa Pulso Brasil)* – covering a wide range of topics and conducted nationwide by Ipsos Public Affairs at the request of FIESP and the São Paulo State Industries Centre (Centro das Indústrias do Estado de São Paulo; CIESP), involving a national sample of 1,000 interviewees.

Another important agency producing data and information in the FIESP structure is the International Relations and Foreign Trade Department (Departamento de Relações Internacionais e Comércio Exterior; DEREX), which works in strategic areas. These include International Negotiations, in which it conducts studies and technical analyses to inform decision-making and it also contributes to promoting private sector interests to the Brazilian government. The issues it addresses include negotiations on trade, investments, services, taxation and the environment.

The FIESP has a series of other agencies and departments, all directed to producing analyses and information and focusing on legal activities, the environment, small- and medium-size businesses, agribusiness, innovation and competitiveness, defence and security, regional action, human capital, and so on. Additionally, CIESP, a non-profit civil association that works alongside the FIESP, publishes *In Focus (Em Foco)* a membership newsletter.

Rio de Janeiro State Federation of Industries

FIRJAN undertakes projects, research and studies to inform the business community about actions and investments in Rio de Janeiro State. Like their regional counterparts, FIRJAN acts as a business partner to 9,170 affiliated member companies, basically devoting attention to boosting the state of Rio de Janeiro's position as the second most important industrial region in the country. Fear of losing that position and a possible scenario of de-industrialisation has led FIRJAN to develop campaigns to attract and stimulate investments locally. Other important initiatives involve an active campaign in favour of the state of Rio as the country's largest oil producer, as was the case in the recent debate over the oil royalties in which FIRJAN placed itself against the redistribution of such assets among the states of the federation. Another recent example concerns FIRJAN's very prominent participation in matters related to the ecological debate, as evidenced by its numerous actions in the RIO+20 Forum held in June 2012.

FIRJAN has also operated favourably on a number of issues that traditionally compose the public agenda of industrial associations in Brazil, such as the reduction of the fiscal burden, decreasing interest rates, de-bureaucratisation and simplification of procedures for setting up new enterprises, in addition to providing inputs regarding the production of updated reports on the situation of industry in the state of Rio, as specified later in this chapter.

Actions in the technical and policy fields are guided by business councils and forums. The business councils address topics that are strategic to development in the state and the business forums' purpose is to encourage growth in specific sectors and work towards reducing tax and legislative and bureaucratic obstacles.

The business councils are subdivided into 14 areas that address the following issues of importance to industry: Legislative Affairs, Strategic Management for Competitiveness, Social and Labour Policy, International Relations, Economic and Industrial Policy, Energy, Infrastructure, Environment, Social Responsibility, Technology, Regional Representations, Water Resources, Young Entrepreneurs, and the Construction Industry.

The Business Council on Legislative Affairs (Conselho Empresarial de Assuntos Legislativos) keeps track of bills of interest to industry, so as later to inform the responsible bodies (councils and associations) so that they receive technical information. It also determines whether bills are constitutional and whether they interfere adversely with the state's economy or with industrial competitiveness. On that basis, legal counsel drafts a legal opinion on the bills. Finally, the (technical and legal) opinions are forwarded to members of the legislature as suggestions. The council also works with CNI to draft the Legislative Agenda, as already mentioned.

The Business Council on Economic and Industrial Policy discusses current economic issues, providing supporting information so that the FIRJAN system and board can take positions on such matters. Structural, tax and labour reforms, as well as the economic and political conjuncture, are among the central issues.

The business forums are divided into nine specific areas: Defence and Security, Metal-Mechanical Industry and Related Segments, Ornamental Stone, Tourism, Cosmetics and Perfumery, Sand and Gravel Industry, Climate Change, Footwear, Bags and Accessories, and Agroindustry.

The FIRJAN also has publications such as the *Industry Letter* (*Carta da Indústria*), which comes out weekly and publishes the federation's institutional news and promotes projects in the state economy. *Economic Rio* (*Rio Econômico*), a monthly e-zine, provides an overview of the Rio de Janeiro State economy, addressing legal, infrastructure and investment issues. The monthly *Legal Report* (*Informe Jurídico*) clarifies current legislation, legal decisions and other legal issues of interest to the business community. The annual *FIRJAN Municipal Development Index* (*Índice FIRJAN de Desenvolvimento Municipal*; IFDM) enables human, economic and social development to be monitored in terms of employment and income, education, and health, and is elaborated on the basis of official statistics produced on these policy areas. Another publication concerns the monthly Rio Exports bulletin, which analyses the influx of foreign capital and the volume of foreign trade in the state. In addition, monthly research is carried out with the major industrial firms in the state of Rio in order to provide a picture about recent trends, sales, production levels, occupied personnel, salaries, utilisation of installed capacity and other relevant data. And, lastly, the *Rio de Janeiro State Industrial Legislative Agenda* (*Agenda Legislativa da Indústria do Estado do Rio*) is published annually to inform the state legislature and general public of industry positions on bills being discussed in the state.

Worthy of attention in the case of FIRJAN is the association's concern with environmental issues, for example, its participation in the Rio +20 Forum, as already mentioned. Action in this area involves not only the production of specialised information, but also technical assistance in order to promote sustainable development and stimulate investments in environmental protection. The Carbon Office, for instance, is a virtual information centre addressing the enterprises' doubts on issues of climatic changes and carbon credits. The *Environmental Report*, a monthly publication issued by FIRJAN's department of Innovation and Environment, and the Research of Environmental Management constitute two other important initiatives in this area. The latter constitutes a basis for planning environmental actions in Rio de Janeiro, in addition to representing a sound thermometer for environmental diagnosis in a state that prides itself for the quality and beauty of its natural environment.

Industrial Development Studies Institute

IEDI consists of 44 business leaders representing Brazil's major corporations. It was set up in 1989 to conduct studies of industry and national development, working autonomously as a developmentalist think tank. Its studies address a variety of areas including liberalisation and integration of trade with the rest of the world, competitiveness, education, tax structure, economic development funding, regional development policies, and policies to support micro and small businesses, technology policy and others.

IEDI works with organisations that have an interest in industry, in partnership with the state, primarily to formulate and implement an industrial development policy whose main goals are to support Brazilian industry's participation in world industrial production and to increase output of goods with greater added value and technological content. In December 2010, IEDI, a developmentalist organisation, launched their 'Contributions to a Brazilian development agenda' ('Contribuições para uma Agenda de Desenvolvimento do Brasil'), with policy suggestions on reforms to be implemented in subject areas such as: education; infrastructure and macro-economy, industry and development; innovation; and sustainability and long-term funding.

Tables 15.1 and 15.2 summarise the contents of all IEDI Analyses (which are not issued regularly) and Letters produced between January 2003 and September 2011. The results are extremely uniform in terms of the knowledge production or analytical capabilities of the kind being considered in this chapter. All key issues for industry on what could be termed a developmentalist perspective are included in both the Analyses and the Letters.

Table 15.1: **Industrial Development Studies Institute Analyses**

Subject	Period	No Analyses	Content
Foreign Trade	11/03/2003–30/03/2009	22	Exports, Technological Innovation, Brazilian Foreign Trade, Exchange and Reciprocal Trade
Innovation and Sustainability	20/01/2003–28/03/2011	13	Green Economy, Sustainable Energy, Indicators for Science, Technology and Innovation
Industry and Industrial Policy	17/02/2003–18/08/2011	72	Industrial Productivity, Industrial Policies in Selected Countries, Indebtedness and Profitability
Industrial Employment	17/01/2005–09/09/2011	69	Stagnation, Retraction, Deceleration

Between January 2003 and September 2011, the IEDI published 449 Letters on its website, focusing on industry and industrial policy, foreign trade, innovation and sustainability, and labour issues (see Table 15.2).

Table 15.2: **Industrial Development Studies Institute Letters**

Economy and Industry	
January 2003–September 2011	
Total 449 Letters	
Subject	%
Industry and Industrial Policy	46
Foreign Trade	28
Innovation and Sustainability	12
Industrial Employment	14

'S-System' in industry

The 'S–System' comprises several institutions corresponding to different segments of the production sector and working to improve and promote employee well-being in areas such as health, leisure and vocational training. This group of institutions thus formulates and implements social policies complementary to those applied by the state. The various organisations in the system were set up in the period since the 1940s, first in the trade sector and later expanding to agriculture, transport, industry and others, until forming a complex array of sectoral and regional organisations and policies. The organisations currently part of the S–System, in addition to SENAI and SESI in the industry sector, are IEL, CNT, CNC, CNA, SENAR, SENAC, SESC, SESCOOP, SEST-SENAT and SEBRAE, all of which are referenced in the Glossary at the end of this chapter.

Industry Social Service

Established during the administration of Getúlio Vargas, SESI came into being at the same time as other important quality-of-life gains for working people, the foremost being the Consolidated Labour Laws (Consolidação das Leis do Trabalho; CLT). SESI is organised into two basic blocs: normative agencies, comprising the National Council and Regional Councils; and management and production agencies, comprising the National Department (DN) and 27 Regional Departments (DRs).

SESI is able to undertake policy initiatives through the dynamics of relations between the DRs and the DN. While the DN formulates guidelines and sets strategic directions to strengthen unity, the DRs are directly engaged in carrying out the programmes. The main programmes are in areas such as health, culture and education. It is important to emphasise the scope of activities in the health care field. In 2006, for instance, SESI investment in health care resulted in nearly 500,000 medical appointments and vocational interviews and over 1 million instances of nursing care. SESI offers programmes such as Health and Safety Promotion, Workplace Safety, as well as Drug Prevention and Disease Prevention.

SESI's educational endeavour includes programmes such as Worker Education and the Knowledge Industry (an industry initiative launched in 2006 to promote access to information and culture by populations of municipalities with low Human Development Indices) and projects such as Little SESI (*Sesinho*), launched in 1947 to be the main channel for the organisation's actions involving children from four to 14 years old and, today, a prominent and extensive educational resource. To give an idea of the scope of SESI's supplementary activities, suffice it to say that they take place in 324 Activity Centres, 891 Operational Units and 748 Mobile Units, totalling 1,963 units with:

- 35,293 students enrolled in pre-school education;
- 167,801 students enrolled in elementary education;
- 179,062 students enrolled in high school education (youth and adult education and teaching integrated between SESI and SENAI);
- 265,339 students enrolled in worker education (youth and adult elementary and high school education); and
- 892,745 students enrolled in on-site and distance continued professional development programmes.

National Industrial Training Service

Set up in 1942 as part of the system of the CNI and state federations of industry, SENAI supports 28 areas of industry by training human resources and providing services such as assistance to the production sector, laboratory services, applied research and technological information. Its 27 RDs, linked directly to an ND, take its programmes, projects and activities nationwide.

SENAI invests in social responsibility through incentive programmes for education. The SENAI education network comprises 738 operating units (454 fixed and 384 mobile) around Brazil and spans 28 fields of activity. From 1942 to 2008, it trained 47,883,006 students. It offers 1,263 industrial training programmes, 825 high school-level technical courses, 68 undergraduate courses and 74 postgraduate programmes, in addition to professional initiation, qualification and refresher programmes in all 28 areas of activity.

Final remarks

The analysis undertaken in this chapter reveals a very complex scenario in terms of the production, tracking and even implementation of public policies by interest organisations connected with the industrial business community in Brazil.

On one hand, most of what could be defined as the development of analytical skills by such organisations over time is strongly determined by the specific conjuncture and relates to the conditions under which organised interests have access to the apparatus of the state. Variations in regime, greater or lesser centralisation of the decision-making process, and permeability of government agencies to processes of private sector consultation or participation in policymaking have affected how organisations equip themselves with information relevant to furthering their interests. Greater transparency in the publication of information regarding policymaking, implementation and outcomes has an impact on these associations' analytical capability. Increasing use of computer systems in public agencies' activities and the posting of data online also change the scenario of what could be termed business organisations' policy analysis capability.

On the other hand, the business community's organisations have undeniably changed considerably and modernised over time in a process of differentiation of their internal structures, as a result, they are able to monitor their interests more effectively. Although official corporatism may be described as one of the most stable institutions in Brazil's republican history since the 1930s, when a national industrialisation project was established, it has also proven to be a quite agile nexus of public–private communication; it has undergone changes while preserving its central role in industrial business community activities. The parallel associations that formed around it also express the growing process of specialisation, differentiation and complexity that the production regime has experienced throughout the whole import-substitution-based industrialisation period and under the aegis of an open economy that has been integrated with globalised circuits since the 1990s.

The economic transition driven by market-oriented reforms, and its interrelationship with the political transition towards a democracy with increasing degrees of institutionalisation, which occurred almost simultaneously in Brazil, posed enormous challenges for the activities of interest groups, which consequently sought information in the public policy field. Democratisation gave greater centrality to the legislature, towards which lobbies and organised interest groups gravitated. On the other hand, the scenario of globalisation and of performance in the context of an open economy reinforced the traditionally dominant role of the executive, with greater degrees of interventionism and regulatory activity generating the need for extensive communication between interest groups and agencies of the bureaucracy.

This dual process is reflected in the pattern of activities of industry organisations, in some cases reproducing classic thematic areas such as tax policy, foreign exchange policy, wage policy and industrial policy. In other cases, new challenges certainly emerged in areas such as technological innovation policies, environment policies, energy or energy source diversification policies and social responsibility.

In terms of their internal structures and their development of analytical skills, the organisations considered here express the intense process of adaptation to this critical dual scenario. Not only have they set up internal centres to address a diversified agenda of demands, they also come to produce knowledge on a wide range of topics and contents. Even organisations representing regional interests, such as the federations examined here or those based on a programmatic proposal, such as IEDI, and even the entity that gathers together the broadest aggregate interests of industry, the CNI, had to equip themselves in that respect. On the other hand, the endeavour to develop more comprehensive outlooks or approaches better able to contend with different but interrelating thematic public policy fields has forced these organisations to foster strategies to coordinate their joint work and their approaches to different levels of the apparatus of the state.

Finally, it should also be stressed that over time, the official associations of industry, such as the CNI and the federations, have always played a central role in implementing supplementary social policies and labour capacitation through the S-System institutions. These effectively constitute policies that entail a policymaking, implementation and monitoring strategy, so as to complement or coordinate with initiatives by the federal, state and municipal levels of government.

Acknowledgements

I am grateful to Camila Borges and Michelle Salabert Chaves, intern researchers at INCT/ PPED (National Institute for Science and Technology- Public Policies, Strategies and Development), for gathering data for this chapter.

References

Diniz, E. and Boschi, R. (1979) 'Autonomia e dependência na representação de interesses industriais', *Dados*, no 22, pp 25–48.

Diniz, E. and Boschi, R. (1991) 'O Corporativismo na construção do espaço público', in R. Boschi (ed) *Corporativismo e desigualdade: A construção do espaço público no Brasil*, Rio de Janeiro: IUPERJ/Rio Fundo Editora.

Diniz, E. and Boschi, R. (1993) 'Brasil: Um novo empresariado? Balanço de tendências recentes', in E. Diniz (ed) *Empresários e modernização econômica: Brasil Anos 90*, Florianópolis: Ed. da UFSC/IDACON.

Diniz, E. and Boschi, R. (1999) 'O Legislativo como arena de interesses organizados: A atuação dos *lobbies* empresariais', *LOCUS, Revista de História*, vol 5, no 1, pp 7–32.

Diniz, E. and Boschi, R. (2000) 'Associativismo e trajetória política do empresariado brasileiro na expansão e declínio do estado desenvolvimentista', *Teoria e Sociedade*, no 5, pp 48–81.

Diniz, E. and Boschi, R. (2004) *Empresários, interesses e mercado: Dilemas do desenvolvimento no Brasil*, Belo Horizonte: Ed. UFMG.

Diniz, E. and Boschi, R. (2007) *A difícil rota do desenvolvimento: empresários e a agenda pos-neoliberal*, Belo Horizonte/Rio de Janeiro: Editora UFMG/IUPERJ.

Mancuso, W.P. (2007b) *O lobby da indústria no Congresso Nacional: Empresariado e política no Brasil contemporâneo*, São Paulo: EDUSP.

Appendix: Glossary

BOVESPA – Bolsa de Valores, Mercadorias e Futuros de São Paulo (São Paulo Securities, Commodities and Futures Exchange)

CIESP – Centro das Indústrias do Estado de São Paulo (São Paulo State Industries Centre)

CNA – Conselho Nacional de Agricultura (National Council of Agriculture)

CNC – Confederação Nacional do Comércio de Bens, Serviços e Turismo (National Goods, Services and Tourism Trade Confederation)

CNI – Confederação Nacional da Indústria (National Confederation of Industry)

CNT – Confederação Nacional do Transporte (National Transport Confederation)

COAL – Conselho de Assuntos Legislativos (Legislative Affairs Council)

Conjur – Conselho Superior Temático de Assuntos Jurídicos e Legislativos (Higher Thematic Council on Legal and Legislative Affairs)

Cores – Comitê de Responsabilidade Social (Social Responsibility Committee)

Cosec – Conselho Superior Temático de Economia (Higher Thematic Council on the Economy)

Dejur – Departamento Jurídico (Legal Department)

Depecon – Departamento de Pesquisas e Estudos Econômicos (Department for Economic Research and Studies)

DEREX – Departamento de Relações Internacionais e Comércio Exterior (Department of International Relations and Foreign Trade)

FIESP – Federação das Indústrias do Estado de São Paulo (São Paulo State Federation of Industries)

FIRJAN – Federação das Indústrias do Rio de Janeiro (Rio de Janeiro State Federation of Industries)

IBOPE – Instituto Brasileiro de Opinião Pública e Estatística (Brazilian Public Opinion and Statistics Institute)

ICEI – Índice de Confiança do Empresário Industrial (Industrial Business Owners' Confidence Index)

IEDI – Instituto de Estudos para o Desenvolvimento Industrial (Industrial Development Studies Institute)

IEL – Instituto Euvaldo Lodi (Euvaldo Lodi Institute)

IFDM – Índice FIRJAN de Desenvolvimento Municipal (FIRJAN Municipal Development Index)

IMD – Índice de Medo do Desemprego (Fear of Unemployment Index)

INA – Indicador de Nível de Atividade (Level of Activity Indicator)

INDX – Índice do Setor Industrial (Industrial Sector Index)

INEC – Índice Nacional de Expectativa do Consumidor (National Consumer Expectations Index)

IRS – Instituto Roberto Simonsen (Roberto Simonsen Institute)

CSR – Responsabilidade Social Empresarial (Corporate Social Responsibility)

SEBRAE – Serviço Brasileiro de Apoio às Micro e Pequenas Empresas (Brazilian Micro and Small Business Support Service)

SENAC – Serviço Nacional de Aprendizagem Comercial (National Commercial Training Service)

SENAI – Serviço Nacional de Aprendizagem Industrial (National Industrial Training Service)

SENAR – Serviço Nacional de Aprendizagem Rural (National Rural Training Service)

SENAT – Serviço Nacional de Aprendizagem do Transporte (National Transport Training Service)

SESC – Serviço Social do Comércio (Commerce Social Service)

SESI – Serviço Social da Indústria (Industry Social Service)

SESCOOP – Serviço Nacional de Aprendizagem do Cooperativismo (National Cooperativism Training Service)

SEST – Serviço Social do Transporte (Transport Social Service)

SIXTEEN

Policy analysis in non-governmental organisations and the implementation of pro-diversity policies

João Bôsco Hora Góis

Introduction

Unlike what happened in countries such as Canada and the US, Brazil did not experience the institutionalisation and the academic or professional maturation of traditional policy analysis. At the same time, today, it has to address contemporary dilemmas and discussions in this field. That is perhaps the very reason why the mix of policy analysis styles and methodological approaches is so particularly intense in this country.

The purpose of this chapter in studying this mix is to contribute to a broader understanding of how policy analysis is being assimilated in Brazil. It does so – taking as its example non-governmental organisations (NGOs) that advocate for diversity – by showing how the encounter between the production and use of statistical evidence, arguments and advocacy contributed to the process of constituting actors who were an influence in deconstructing negative discourses about certain social segments, each characterised by a different identity attribute. These actors clamoured for different types of recognition and the institutionalisation of policies designed to reduce the inequalities anchored in these adverse discourses. The chapter also attempts to show how the practice of policy analysis can be linked to specific features of the contextual changes that simultaneously allow it to occur and are modelled by it. It also traces different pathways by which policy analysis is learnt even in the absence of the traditional formal structures generally involved in teaching it.

The chapter draws on a diverse set of sources, both print (congress annals, open letters, personal correspondence, policy council minutes, research reports, and so on) and oral (interviews of members of various different groups and government representatives on rights councils).

Struggles to secure respect for diversity in Brazil

The feminist movement, the black movement, the gay rights movement and others have been crucial in spreading the diversity debate throughout Brazil. Especially since the 1970s, in the context of Brazil's re-democratisation, such movements led the struggle to defend and assert cultural differences and went on to demand greater recognition for the rights of segments with a history of social exclusion.

Despite their numerous differences, these movements' activities have been animated by at least one common element: the endeavour to dismantle adverse discourse on women and black and gay individuals. In that regard, these movements can be seen as participants in a 'discourse coalition' understood as 'a group of actors who share a social construct' (Hajer, 1993, p 45). That is why they have been operating on an approach designed to dismantle these discourses and whatever develops from them in various spheres of social life.

Organisationally, in the 1970s and through most of the 1980s, this type of endeavour was pursued on the 'grassroots social movements' model. For that purpose, groups in the movements depended on volunteer action, relied on a small and varying number of participants, and were short-lived and operated with very incipient, informal structures. Gradually, however, such groups started taking the NGO format, with advantages and disadvantages now thoroughly examined in the literature. That and the expanding numbers of activists in Brazil's states have contributed to groups' proliferating across the country.

An exhaustive survey of the universe of groups that form the movements in defence of human diversity is beyond the scope of this chapter. For the purposes of our argument, suffice it to say that it is an ensemble that varies widely in institutional goals and target publics, the body of demands presented, the human and financial resources available, and so on.

Such groups also differ in terms of when they entered the public arena in Brazil: while the black and feminist movements have their origins in the early decades of the 20th century, gay rights groups are a political product rooted in the 1970s. At the same time, however limited a definition of NGO or social movement we use, we will always be talking about very large numbers of entities scattered widely over Brazil's regions. They are highly diversified enough to preclude anything approaching an overall diagnosis as to the presence of policy analysis in the broad field of NGOs taking as subject the defence of human diversity. Notwithstanding, in many respects, although the timings differ, the black, feminist and gay rights movements can be seen to share various aspects of the policy analysis learning and use curve. As a result, statements made in this chapter reflect specific features of the group of organisations studied, while suggesting the existence of broader patterns of applicability.

Pro-diversity movements and the learning of policy analysis

The early groups in these movements functioned in precarious conditions, but, nonetheless, it was in them that a body of militants started to take shape, and was able to put organisational processes in place, define guidelines for action, forge alliances, galvanise coalitions with political parties and so on. This in turn meant learning different forms of conjunctural and scenario analysis.

The experiences, analytical skills and cadres forged in the late 1970s and part of the 1980s in the organisational frameworks then predominant in those movements were transferred to the new – NGO – model on which such movements began structuring, particularly from the mid-1980s onward. That model framed the formation of a whole generation of activists whose struggle for rights drew on the more sophisticated models they had learned for understanding social realities and voicing demands.

Their learning gained density as the channels for dialogue between the state and society on policymaking expanded. As a result, these organisations and their militants began to assimilate specialised knowledge of new topics and trends – budget interpretation, filing legal claims, how to gain access to managers and policymakers, and so on – which were important for policy analysis, but were little known until then. This learning process expanded throughout the 2000s, especially as a result of the systematic endeavour by all three movements to form new leaders and activists.

Some preliminary conclusions can be drawn by examining this learning process. The first is that analytical activities have gained in density thanks largely to state investments in this field. It is the public administration, mainly the federal government, that is funding a significant portion of actions directed to training new activists and groups in the movements and has strong technical influence over such actions. This phenomenon is particularly salient in the gay rights movement due to the strength of the partnerships established between them in the fight against the HIV/AIDS epidemic, the epidemic's incidence in the Lesbian, Gay, Bisexual, Transsexual and Transgender (LGBTT) population and the central place occupied by this issue on this movement's agenda.

The World Bank had a major role in the process of fighting the HIV/AIDS epidemic through loans to the Brazilian government. The loans highlighted the importance of the NGOs in halting the spread of the disease. Likewise, they stipulated that NGOs should be trained and directly involved in the implementation of specific policies and programmes (World Bank, 1998). It is thus no coincidence that federal agencies invested in implementing capacity-building projects, such as SOMOS.

SOMOS was the first systematic effort to train homosexual activists on a large scale in Brazil. Conceived in response to the need to address the spreading AIDS epidemic, it was the outcome of negotiation between the Associação Brasileira de Gays, Lésbicas e Transgêneros (ABGLT) and the federal government, and was modelled on other Latin American experiences led by Salud Integral y la Ciudadanía de América Latina y el Caribe (ASICAL) (Ministério da Saúde, 2005). Formally launched in 1999 to train 24 groups in 11 states, by 2007, it involved 270 organisations. The project was designed to increase the technical capacity of the organisationally most fragile LGBTT groups and thus enhance their ability to dispute public funding for HIV/AIDS-related endeavours (ABGLT, 2012).[1] The federal administration's interest in funding training for leaders of the LGBTT movement has continued, as explicitly stated in the national plan to promote LGBTT citizenship and human rights (Brasil, 2009).

Federal government funding of training projects raises important issues about how LGBTT activism has been shaped in Brazil. This very same funding has influenced the emergence of different groups or has assured initial support for those in formation that was decisive to their continuing; it limited the degree of pressure and tension among actors who, although working in cooperation, belonged to different political camps, and it also influenced the movement's agenda and analyses.

Another conclusion relates to the groups' 'capacity' to pursue their actions. The term 'capacity' refers to a broad set of components, including material factors, such as financial, technological and symbolic resources, for example, trust and the ability to interact with others. This chapter addresses only human resources in movements involved in learning and producing policy analysis. These are few and their skills and stock of academic capital differ significantly, there being no record of people hired specifically for this kind of activity. One major contributor to this is the predominantly voluntary nature of participation in the groups, as well as certain people rising to positions that bring them to take part in analysis without any corresponding professional training. Another adverse influence on this situation is the difficulty of retaining the most qualified staff, because of instability in funding, whether from government agencies or foreign charities. The lack of human resources, combined with growing demand for more skilled analysis, is one of the factors that explains the groups' ever-closer relations with external experts. In the case of the gay rights movement, this can be credited to the solid relationship that, from the early days, it built with academic sectors. However, it was under pressure from the urgent needs imposed by the HIV/AIDS epidemic that dialogue between academics and gay activists working to combat the epidemic gain density, whether from the political support offered by the former or from partnerships formed between them around behavioural and epidemiological investigations. Today, relations with the scientific community continue and are becoming better structured, particularly around research and educational intervention projects.

Another element to be highlighted is their gradual learning about the role of discourse in the struggle for respect for human diversity. This learning often bears no academic seal of approval on how it is used either in creating truths or as a tool for action to counteract negative images of minority groups. Considering the increasing strength of the analyses and interventions that may result, this is not a secondary datum when thinking about the learning and practice of policy analysis. Deeper knowledge of the meanings of discourses implies greater command of the terms used in various debates about race, gender and sexual orientation, better understanding of opponents' and allies' positions (and shifts in position), more clearly demarcated focuses for action, and, above all, distinguishing whom to address for desired political and economic compensations. A clear understanding of contexts implies a grasp of how identifying different feasible courses of action is a fundamental task of the policy analyst (Geva-May and Pal, 1999). Understanding the content, use and historicity of discourse thus implies analysing a series of questions that go beyond the particular features of the discriminations suffered by women and black and gay people.

Not coincidentally, the contradiction between specific and general problems and agendas, which followed in the wake of this learning, has clearly been overcome, although it was the source of enormous disagreement in pro-diversity movements as the 1970s became the 1980s. In the 1970s, most of the groups were practically segregated, denying the importance of traditional politics and seeking to rid themselves of any ties to political parties (which led to much infighting); in the early 2000s, there was a move, at least conceptually, towards accepting the need to work more inter-sectorally, as expressed in the support from significant portions of the black and feminist movements participating in the World Conference against Racism, Racial Discrimination, Xenophobia and Related Intolerance for the 'Background paper for the expert meeting on gender-related aspects of race and discrimination' (Creenshaw, 2002). That seminal paper marked the birth of a tradition in analysis of relations among the multiple forms of discrimination and vulnerabilities. It was also important in stimulating a kind of collective action in which different identity groups pooled capacities. The LGBTT movement also surmounted its initial, almost separatist posture, and, today, its orientation is internationalist and its discourse presents the problems affecting homosexuals as being related to a slew of other social and economic issues (ABGLT, 2005, 2006, 2009), as manifest in the national LGBTT citizenship and human rights plan (Brasil, 2009).

Also, as regards learning about the use of discourse, the movements – in the midst of their differences, which were neither few nor minor – had to formulate coherent narratives about the issues they perceived and their proposed solutions. Those narratives can be understood as amalgams of viewpoints that, although different, are not incompatible for purposes of group formation and political action. All the same, this is not a cumulative process in which all viewpoints are incorporated to create a 'truth' broad enough to meet the expectations of all actors involved in constituting it. Studies of the formation of different types of field of discourse show that the inclusion of certain arguments usually involves the elimination of others. It was no different among the pro-diversity movements. In the gay rights movement, human rights have been held up as a preferred discursive strategy, functioning as a domain within which the movement's different goals have been presented. Note, however, that this choice was made gradually over many years of internal debate in the gay rights movement, during which other alternatives were rejected or relegated to secondary importance.

Another component of this learning history was their progress in using research that furnishes quantitative evidence about dimensions of the lives of marginalised groups. The 'NGO' format, which became predominant among Brazilian social movements, contributed greatly to this. It required that their organisations fulfil certain, then unfamiliar, institutional formalities and posed a need to learn how to work with projects structured around topics, objectives, methodologies, deadlines and goals clearly specified in contracts and with less intuitive analytical and interventional approaches than had predominated until then. Over the years, their Brazilian and international funders – federal, state and local administrations, as well as the Inter-American Development Bank, Petrobrás, Women's Learning Partnership, the Ford Foundation, the Schorer Foundation, and agencies of the UN system, such as UN Women and UNESCO (United Nations Educational, Scientific and Cultural Organization) – ceased to accept generic claims to 'defend rights' and came to prefer projects with a clearly delimited object of intervention connected with problems whose materiality could be expressed explicitly through 'evidence'. In response, the groups and their activists have undergone training in some kind of social research method to enable them to produce and use (particularly statistical) data.

At the same time, the use of qualitative research has certainly also grown in the fields of gender and race relations and social orientation. University research groups – which also engage in pro-diversity activism – have busied themselves with analysing the ideological substrates underlying multiple forms of discrimination. The most influential are: the Programa de Estudos e Debates dos Povos Africanos e Afroamericanos (PROAFRO) at Rio de Janeiro State University; the Centro de Estudos Afro-Brasileiros (CEAO) at Bahia Federal University; the Núcleo de Estudos de Gênero PAGU at Campinas University; the Núcleo de Estudos Interdisciplinares Sobre a Mulher at Bahia Federal University; the Instituto de Estudos de Gênero (IEG) at Santa Catarina Federal University; and the Centro Latino-Americano em Sexualidade e Direitos Humanos at Rio de Janeiro State University. Although it is possible to identify specific theoretical and methodological orientations at the origin of these groups, they all work on interdisciplinary and multi-thematic approaches that correlate among issues of gender and race, race and sexual orientation, and so on.

However, the groups in the movement are more interested in quantitative research. Arguments about social justice, inequity and inequality and many others that are qualitative in nature are certainly useful when presenting analyses and demands. Accordingly, this is not to deny the power of argumentative strategies in the policy process (Majone, 1989); rather, it is to say that such strategies – when deployed in relation to the public administration and society as a whole, in a world where scientific knowledge is commonly expressed and consumed in 'data' – find a powerful ally in quantitative research. This type of research gives greater credibility to arguments and demands, and that is extremely important because 'credibility is a crucial asset in both policy analysis and evaluation' (Geva-May and Pal, 1999, p 262).

One last item to be highlighted in the movements' learning curve is suggested by their adherence to what has been termed the 'participatory style' (Mayer et al, 2004) in policy analysis. This is advocacy, the component concerned with choosing the most appropriate strategies to be used in the contexts where the movements operate and where power is unevenly distributed. 'Advocacy' is a term traditionally used to describe the endeavour by NGOs to defend the interests of groups with a history of exclusion. This is done through negotiations, direct political pressure, public campaigns, media relations and so on. The list also includes the ability to suit how demands are presented to each specific situation encountered, as well as the resources available. The groups studied here present their demands in very different manners, with variations also in frequency and sophistication. The highest impact is achieved through parliamentary public hearings, while reports circulated electronically through their grassroots constituencies offer maximum reach. Seminars are also useful to stimulate thinking about any research conducted, to discuss the agenda and action strategies to be adopted, and to overcome 'language barriers' among participating actors. Written documents are much less used and are restricted to motions, public letters, short informative material and occasionally longer reports. The fact that long reports are rarely used should not be perceived as a handicap; although, at first sight, they may seem to be more influential, the policy analysis literature does not bear this out. On the contrary, it seems to make more sense to say that the more varied the manners (including oral ones) of presenting analyses, the more chance they have of being heard and used.

The advocacy component, in addition to defining the manner of presentation, must also be able to grasp the most appropriate moments for the presentation. The social movements have progressed in their ability to read and interpret contexts, which is particularly important in identifying windows of opportunity for intervention, which appear irregularly and unpredictably. The right moment to present demands leads on to another important discussion about advocacy: its (desirable) capacity to generate collective mobilisation. This potential is consistent with the post-positivist turn in policy analysis and its criticism of the encapsulation of numerous agents in the decision-making process. In that respect, as part of the participatory style characteristic of the movements' policy analysis, advocacy produces 'argumentative inclusion', that is, it enables narratives under construction to be appropriated, assumed or contested by increasing numbers of people besides those who traditionally take part in policymaking. In Brazil, the clash between pro-diversity movements and religious narratives on abortion, same-sex civil unions and violence against Afro-Brazilian worship has had this mobilising effect, engaging enormous numbers of people in massive public, discursive rallies. Vicious attacks against the premises and believers of African-based creeds in Brazil have been perpetrated by Catholics, traditional Protestants and neo-Pentecostal organisations, as well as agents of the state. This has led to demonstrations across the country, the creation of inter-faith coalitions, the lobbying of Congress and the federal government, the creation of state and national committees to address the topic, and the passing and enforcement of stricter legislation with both an educational and punitive eye to faith-related crimes (Estado do Rio de Janeiro, 1991; Brasil, 2007; CCIR, 2009; Da Silva, 2009).

Still, as regards advocacy, networking has boosted the movements' analytical and interventional capabilities. Actors working together tend to reach agreements on core issues, but not necessarily on secondary ones. This, however, does not preclude coalitions of actors in the same or different segments from networking (Sabatier and Jenkins-Smith, 1999), as seen, for instance, in parliamentary fronts comprising agents at different points on the national party-political spectrum together with pro-diversity groups.

It is through the set of analytical and advocacy skills learned in this process that the movements have been intensifying their demands. Sectors such as the business community have certainly been targeted by their actions due to recurrent and multiple forms of discrimination in the labour market (UNIFEM, 2006; Instituto Ethos, 2007; Brasil, 2011). Cooperation among governments and non-governmental groups to act on gender- and race-based inequalities produced conferences and policy proposals, as seen in the proceedings of the second National Conference on Policies for Women (Brasil, 2008) and the first National Conference for the Promotion of Racial Equality (Brasil, 2005), to press companies at least to comply with anti-discrimination legislation and to act towards more inclusive forms of recruitment and internal promotion. By the same token, the LGBTT movement has pressed to remove the barriers facing transgender people in accessing the labour market. In Rio de Janeiro, partnering between the Associação das Travestis e Transexuais do Estado do Rio de Janeiro and the Rio de Janeiro City government resulted in the Projeto Damas, which offered vocational training in a range of income-generation activities as an alternative to their predominant role in the market as sex workers (ASTRA, 2004). The federal government has also made efforts to improve education, labour situations and social protections among transvestites. In 2009, in connection with the workshop 'Políticas Públicas de Trabalho, Oportunidade e Previdência para Travestis e Transexuais – Astral Top', representatives from the sector met with technical staffs of various ministries to discuss alternative manners of placing their members in the formal labour market. This move was led by the ABGLT, the Articulação Nacional de Travestis e Transexuais (ANTRA) and the Frente Parlamentar pela Cidadania LGBT (SEDH, 2009).

The movement's activities, however, have focused incisively on the three powers of the state. Dialogue is most intense and, despite numerous problems, most successful in the executive and judiciary. In the legislature, conversely, analyses and demands are subject to a more highly charged context. Features of our legislative system and its relationship with the executive have brought the debate over recognition for minority rights into an arena where those rights are being used as bargaining chips. Even when such rights are seen to be defended by sectors of the executive and members of Congress, this is done feebly enough to be abandoned relatively easily, either by inaction from supporters or systematic opposition from the detractors. Freedom of sexual orientation, for instance, is being supported strongly enough to attract legislators from different parliamentary fronts. On the other hand, there is systematic opposition from (especially religious) groups to any expansion of legal guarantees for gays, which end up facing opposition: first, to their content; and, second, when exploited as part of a moral panic strategy that manages to 'succeed' among the constituencies of not only conservative members of parliament, but also many others more to the left of the political spectrum.

Over the years, the movements discussed here have expanded their dialogue with institutions and organisations of the state and have been successful, if only partly, in having their demands met. It is correct to say that this success has not only resulted from the increasing quantitative and qualitative refinement of their learning about intervention and analysis. International studies of the utilisation of policy analysis products are discouraging: they find that, even in countries where this occurs systematically and professionally, the results have limited impact or are not necessarily 'heard'. This brings us to the issue of the contexts where policy analysis takes place. In the case of the movements studied here, the development, style and frequency of policy analysis, and the advances it has led to, have in fact been shaped by a number of contextual variables, two of which will be examined in the following.

The social context where analysis and advocacy take place

The first contextual variable to be highlighted is the post-positivist and post-Marxist turn in social and cultural discourses in Brazil in the closing decades of the 20th century. That turn meant reviewing analytical categories that recur in discussion of social problems, helped the claims for recognition gain access to the political arena and contributed to making the state more receptive to dialogue with the demands of 'minorities'.

This kind of review, supported by a new conceptual apparatus, emphasised the plurality and complexity of social life. It also stressed that poverty cannot be understood solely as lack of material resources and that many problems traditionally classified into the 'cultural' field are not derived merely from the relations of production and class structure of capitalist societies. Inspired by such reviews, it has become increasingly evident, for instance, that violence has gender, that inequality has race and that exclusion can also be constructed out of sexual orientation. The process of review has also contributed to an understanding, within those same governmental agencies, that various social problems arise out of complex interactions of factors. This in turn has helped, particularly in the street-level bureaucracy, to dismantle traditional discourses that associate poverty and extreme poverty with 'deviant' behaviour by individuals and groups (Góis et al, 2008). All of this has enabled agencies of the state to arrive at a fuller understanding of notions such as the 'social question' and the like, making it easier for the public agenda to embrace issues (the generational issue, for instance) that until recently were very little explored.

Another very important variable to this context are the growing opportunities for service users, professional bodies, NGOs and so on to participate. This has resulted from Brazil's re-democratisation and from the constitutional provisions and ordinary law that, especially after 1988, created a wide range of opportunities for public participation in public affairs, such as referendums, plebiscites and 'citizens' initiatives'. In addition to these opportunities, there are councils on rights, which are one of the prime destinations, in addition to the three powers, where the movements direct their analyses and demands. The number of councils has grown significantly in recent decades: by 2009, there were over 10,000 of them across Brazil. For all three movements discussed here – and particularly for the gay rights and black movements – this growth has been significant, either because specific rights councils were set up or because their representatives sat on social oversight bodies in several areas. Note also that racial equality and the right to free sexual expression have been gaining a status equivalent to other areas under social oversight, as expressed in the convening of municipal, state and national conferences in the two fields. The calling of regular conferences for these areas has constituted a relevant and 'official' space for producing analyses. However, it should not be forgotten that there were significant shortcomings in the performance of social control bodies in these and other areas in terms of political co-optation, non-compliance with the parity principle, government representatives' resistance to power-sharing, various forms of prejudice and so on.

While these opportunities for movements to participate in social oversight mechanisms have in fact expanded, there is less certainty as to how their analyses and demands are received by their partners in dialogue in these bodies. This problem derives both from the dilemmas experienced within the councils and from the limitations in their human resources that the movements experienced when represented on social oversight bodies. This problem may grow as issues of gender, race and sexual orientation gain legitimacy in the Brazilian state: once they are seen as cross-cutting concerns, they will be discussed by an increasing number of authorities, and thus the movements will require increasing numbers of representatives.

Final remarks

From the 1970s onward, one central pillar of the agenda of the pro-human diversity movements has been 'recognition', which has at its core the notion that social justice and the quality of social relationships cannot be measured simply by how the material resources available in a society are distributed and redistributed, because the recurring injustices in our society are much more often moral in nature than economic. Despite its strong theoretical and political appeal, the debate over 'recognition' is being severely scrutinised. Various thinkers argue that demands for recognition lead, for instance, to the marginalisation of redistributive needs and the consequent decline in demands for redistribution.

In the case of the movements studied here, especially the gay rights and black movements, their initial emphasis on recognition stemmed from the belief in three elements: the own importance of recognition, its urgency and the lack of resources for advocacy. We should add to this list the historical moment, which favored neither more dialogical relations between the state and civil society nor the request of redistributive policies. The contextual changes signalled earlier contributed to changing this scenario. As a result, the endeavours to redefine negative discourses about women and gay and black people managed to attain a new threshold at which they became worthy of inclusion on the agenda of the state.

By constructing knowledge and using argumentative strategies and advocacy, the pro-diversity movements steadily identified various phenomena that were perceived as belonging to the sphere of private life (where it was widely believed that they should remain, as they were not legitimate objects of government intervention) and introduced them into the field of rights. In other words, these movements managed to transform race, gender and sexual orientation into subjects whose importance and scope made them worthy of inclusion on the list of problems to be addressed by government.

This process has had quite different effects on the various different minority groups, indicating the presence of a 'hierarchisation of human rights in Brazil', that is, the government gives more attention to some groups than to others (Góis and Teixeira,

2011). Overall, however, they may be considered favourable given, for instance, the significant institutionalisation of government attention to the dilemmas facing women and black and gay people in Brazil. National councils now exist on women's rights, on the promotion of racial equality and against discrimination of the LGBTT community, there are ministry-level special secretariats for these segments and, in the 2000s, national action plans were introduced to curb violence against gay men, lesbians and transgender people (Brasil Sem Homofobia), to reduce the incidence of certain diseases among the black population (Política Nacional de Saúde Integral da População Negra), and to empower female rural workers (Programa Organização Produtiva de Mulheres Rurais). At the same time, inter-sectoral programmes in which redistributive issues are a marginal or central component have been set up, without neglecting issues of recognition. Pro-diversity activists often contribute to structuring such programmes.

This warrants the conclusion that the growing presence of NGOs has brought much more to the policy process than just pressure. The experiences studied here show that they have transferred essential knowledge to the state that has been crucial to sectoral policymaking. This they have done through a learning process that, at times, involves a more scientific approach and, at others, uses controversial, multivariate data sources; at times, availing itself of discourse structured out of academic reasoning and, at others, taking on a style typical of working practice in this field, one which – almost like investigative journalism – puts together small pieces. This mix of approaches to analysis and action gives grounds for saying that the various policy analysis styles (rational, client advisory, argumentative, and so on) are present in differing degrees. Given the diverse nature, magnitude and complexity of the problems affecting women and black and gay people (and other social groups) in Brazil, the manners in which they can be addressed call for a wide variety of knowledge production and intervention strategies. In that regard, 'informality' and the use of diverse policy analysis styles should not be considered a problem. Rather, it should be seen as a component of the different possible solutions.

Note
[1] Government-funded capacity-building for leaders of the LGBTT (Lesbians, Gays, Bisexuals, Transvestites and Transexuals) movement also included the TULIPA project, directed to the transgender groups (ASTRA, 2004; Ministério da Saúde, 2012).

References
ABGLT (Associação Brasileira de Gays, Lésbicas e Transgêneros) (2005) Resoluções do I Congresso da ABGLT. Avanços e Perspectivas. Curitiba.
ABGLT (2006) Anais do II Congresso da ABGLT. Maceió.
ABGLT (2009) Carta de Belém. Belém.
ABGLT (2012) Projeto SOMOS. Breve histórico, www.abglt.org.br/port/somos. php (accessed 20 February 2012).
ASTRA (Associação de Travestis e Transexuais) (2004) Construindo nossa história, construindo nossa cidadania. Salvador. Datilo.

Brasil (2005) Secretaria Especial de Políticas de Promoção da Igualdade Racial (SEPPIR). I Conferência Nacional de Promoção da Igualdade Racial. Brasília: SEPPIR.

Brasil (2007) Lei no 11.635 de 27 de dezembro de 2007. Institui o dia nacional de combate à intolerância religiosa.

Brasil (2008) Secretaria Especial de Direitos para Mulheres (SPM). II Plano Nacional de Políticas para Mulheres. Brasília: SPM.

Brasil (2009) *Plano Nacional de Promoção da Cidadania e Direitos Humanos LGBT*, Brasília: Secretaria Especial de Direitos Humanos.

Brasil (2011) Secretaria Especial de Políticas Para Mulheres (SPM). Relatório anual do Observatório Brasil da Igualdade de Gênero 2010/2011. Brasília: SPM.

CCIR (Comissão de Combate à Intolerância Religiosa – Fórum de Diálogo Inter-Religioso) (2009) Relatório de casos assistidos e monitorados pela comissão de combate à intolerância religiosa no estado do Rio de Janeiro e no Brasil. Rio de Janeiro: CCIR.

Creenshaw, K. (2002) 'Documento para o encontro de especialistas em aspectos da discriminação racial relativos ao gênero', *Revista Estudos Feministas*, vol 10, no 1, pp 171-88.

Da Silva, J. (2009) *Guia de luta conta a intolerância religiosa e o racism*, Rio de Janeiro: CEAP.

Estado do Rio de Janeiro (1991) Lei n. 1814, de 24 de abril de 1991. Estabelece sanções de natureza administrativa aplicáveis a qualquer tipo de discriminação em razão de etnia, raça, cor, crença religiosa ou de ser portador de deficiência.

Geva-May, I. and Pal, L.A. (1999) 'Good fences make good neighbours. Policy evaluation and policy analysis – exploring the differences', *Evaluation*, vol 5, no 3, pp 259-77.

Góis, J.B.H. and Teixeira, K.C. (2011) 'Diversity in corporate social responsibility: the (almost invisible) place of homosexuality', IASSCS Conference 2011, Naming and framing: the making of sexual (in)equality, Abstract Book.

Gois, J.B.H., Lobato, L.V.C., Senna, M.C.M. and Moraes, J.R. (2008) 'Avaliação do Benefício de Prestação Continuada: características sociais, proteção social e seus efeitos', *Serviço Social e Sociedade*, no 96, pp 65-92.

Hajer, M. (1993) 'Discourse coalitions and the institutionalization of practice: the case of acid rain in Britain', in F. Fischer and J. Forester (eds) *The argumentative turn in policy analysis and planning*, Durham, NC: Duke University Press.

Instituto Ethos (2007) *Perfil Social, Racial e de Gênero das 500 Maiores Empresas Brasileiras e Suas Ações Afirmativas*, São Paulo: Instituto Ethos.

Majone, G. (1989) *Evidence, argument and persuasion in the policy process*, New Haven, CT, and London: Yale University Press.

Mayer, S.I., Van Daalen, C.E. and Bots, P.W.G. (2004) 'Perspectives on policy analysis: a framework for understanding and design', *International Journal of Technology and Management*, vol 4, no 2, pp 169-91.

Ministério da Saúde (2005) Projeto Somos. Desenvolvimento organizacional, advocacy e intervenção para ONGs que trabalham com Gays e outros HSH. Série Manuais, no 65, Brasília.

Ministério da Saúde (2012) 'Projeto Tulipa Capacita Travestis e Transgêneros', www.aids.gov.br/noticia/projeto-tulipa-capacita-travestis-e-transgeneros (accessed 15 June 2012).

Sabatier, A. P. and Jenkins–Smith, H.C. (1999) 'The advocacy coalition framework. An assessment', in P. Sabatier (ed) *Theories of policy process*, Boulder, CO: Westview Press.

SEDH (Secretaria Especial de Direitos Humanos) (2009) *Seminário discute políticas públicas de trabalho, oportunidade e previdência para travestis e transexuais*, Brasília: SEDH, www.direitoshumanos.gov.br/noticias/ultimas_noticias/2009/06/MySQLNoticia.2009-06-02.3351 (accessed 20 September 2011).

UNIFEM ((United Nations Development Fund for Women) (2006) *O progresso das mulheres no Brasil*, Brasília: UNIFEM.

World Bank (1998) Documento de avaliação de projeto sobre empréstimo mundial proposto no montante equivalente a US$ 165 milhões ao Brasil para um segundo projeto de controle de AIDS e DST. Relatório 18338-BR. Washington.

PART FOUR

ACADEMIC AND RESEARCH INSTITUTE-BASED POLICY ANALYSIS

SEVENTEEN

Expert community and sectoral policy: the Brazilian Sanitary Reform

Nilson do Rosário Costa

Introduction

This chapter addresses the policy analysis that underpinned the Brazilian Sanitary Reform (SR), responsible for defining the Unified Health System (Sistema Único Saúde; SUS) and for the proposal to make universal health care a right under the Federal Constitution of 1988 (FC1988). The expert community that produced the policy analysis of the health sector reform has been referred to as the *sanitaristas* (Weyland, 1995; Arretche, 2010). In the social sciences, the 'policy community' of experts is defined as the set of individuals spread across government agencies, research departments and institutes, political parties, non-governmental organisations, and interest groups that act within a specific public policy area (Majone, 1989). The *sanitaristas* exhibited the features of a policy community as described in the literature, in light of their specific role in the national debate on reorganisation of the health system.

From the perspective of social status, the more relevant *sanitarista* trait was their position as teachers and researchers at public agencies and universities. In the 1980s, the *sanitaristas* held a very special place in the state structure: they enjoyed the conditions of a Weberian organisational bureaucracy (particularly job stability), combined with the decision-making autonomy typical of professional and academic bureaucracies. Their professional isolation was reinforced by the expressive participation of medical doctors from the academic sphere who were at the helm of the SR. The influence wielded by the *sanitaristas'* social and professional status was crucial to the scope of the SR.

As analysts of the Brazilian health system, the *sanitaristas* displayed singular attributes: they worked in a specialised area and shared the worldview and independence of a professional public bureaucracy. Their policy analysis, which led to the adoption of a project of a universalist right to health within the 1980s' atmosphere of democratic transition, was undertaken inside the state apparatus and not based on any mobilisation of civil society or social movements. The international literature has not ignored the role of policy analysis by the specialised public bureaucracy (Dobuzinskis et al, 2007).

It should also be emphasised that the *sanitaristas* carried influence primarily because their policy analysis was opportune, timely and propositional. Nevertheless, their successful formation and implementation of a political agenda was not grounded in the mass dissemination of long-standing, consolidated 'scientific evidence' that lent legitimacy to the proposed health system reform. Explorations of the role of expert communities highlight the use of scientific authority to overcome doubts about the adequacy or plausibility of public policy implementation. Reliance on scientific evidence is usually necessary when decision-makers cannot fully distinguish true from false (Haas, 1992). Majone points out, however, that scientific evidence alone is not enough to legitimise the options offered by policy analysis. Specialists have to convince social actors within the diverse realms where they propose to act, and, in this case, arguments are more efficacious than scientific evidence (Majone, 1989).

According to Hall (1989), one must account for the circumstances that afford the dissemination of innovative ideas. With this perspective in mind, the present chapter shows that the SR was the product of the organisation of new political subjects who took advantage of Brazil's pro-democratisation environment in the 1980s and defined the SUS as an institutional objective by means of arguments.

Why did these arguments win out? The national political elites accepted the SUS project in a conjuncture where an authoritarian regime (1964–84) was in crisis and democratic transition was the order of the day (1985–90). There were three essential features to the Brazilian institutional process that enabled the *sanitaristas* to act so efficaciously. First, there was no veto power against a sectoral policy agenda by relevant social actors, like the corporatist trade union sector that had controlled social security and access to individual medical care down through the history of the republic. In the course of the authoritarian regime, unions had suffered specific, concentrated losses that cast worker representatives out of the decision-making process within the sphere of social security and, consequently, out of the decision-making process concerning the organisation of medical care. Malloy (1979) shows that Brazil's post-1964 authoritarian military regime worked diligently to control the labour movement.

Second, the bankruptcy of the authoritarian regime's centralised decision-making automatically brought into the political arena the voices of: leaders of the legislative and judicial branches; states and municipalities, that is, federative levels that were then secondary; and coalitions of sectoral experts. From the perspective of the federation, authoritarian centralisation robbed states and municipalities of the possibility of social intervention in three ways: by concentrating financial resources in the hands of the federal executive; by defining general norms applicable to social policies; and by subjecting applications for federal funds to federal government approval, thus avoiding any automatic transfer of such funds (Draibe, 1999).

Third, in their arguments about the FC1988, the *sanitaristas* received the support of the democratising political elite that defended redemption of the Brazilian 'social debt'. At the time, Jaguaribe and other intellectual leaders, for example, argued that a stable democracy would not be viable in Brazil until the 'yawning chasm between the great masses and the upper strata of the population was substantially reduced' (Jaguaribe et al, 1986, p 15).

In the context of democratic transition, the scope of institutional choices was greatly broadened, temporarily suspending structural constraints on changes in public policies. Interest groups found themselves able to wield influence in the management of new policies. Collective action gained pluralist form, as described by Granados and Knoke (2005), given the heavy competition between emerging interest groups and the fragmentation of power. The transfer of political coordination to the constitutional process (1987–88) reduced the authoritarian government's role in interest mediation.

In the paradigm theory approach to public agenda-setting, the policy window is the moment when advocates of unique proposals 'push' their solutions to problems. Within this window, entrepreneurs act decisively to link solutions to problems, overcoming constraints by adapting proposals to circumstances (Kingdon, 2003). In this regard, the period of democratic transition in Brazil offered a window for new institutional choices in public health policy given the fragmentation of the sectoral arena and the weak veto power held by relevant interest groups, especially trade unions, as mentioned earlier, or even health care companies or organisations that benefitted from the military regime. In light of this picture, the health sector could be taken over by 'public policy entrepreneurs'.

Authoritarianism, national developmentalism and health policy

Over the course of its existence, Brazilian authoritarianism was not completely omissive when it came to the social question. It engaged in redistributive efforts especially during the second half of the 1970s. This intervention was a response to criticisms that the regime's social policy was bankrupt, especially in health. Two sure signs of how its social policy was indeed bankrupt were the increased infant mortality rate noted in the city of São Paulo in the late 1960s – at the height of a cycle of steady economic growth in Gross Domestic Product (GDP) touted by the regime as the 'Brazilian economic miracle' – and the devastating effects of the 1974 meningitis epidemic (Malloy, 1979).

The Geisel government (1974–79) engineered a specific response to the collective perception of social crisis in Brazil. The social activism of the military regime during his autocratic administration led to the establishment of the Ministry of Social Security and Assistance (Ministério da Previdência e Assistência Social; MPAS) in 1974. Dos Santos (1979) has identified a substantial strengthening of social protection following the creation of the MPAS. Noronha and Levcovitz see the Prompt Action Plan (Plano de Pronta Ação; PPA) as an inclusive initiative in health assistance that yielded 'an unprecedented rise in the production of services' after 1974 (Noronha and Levcovitz, 1994, p 78).

In 1977, the increased complexity of the social security system led to the establishment of the National Social Security and Assistance System (Sistema Nacional de Previdência e Assistência Social; SINPAS), which comprised the Financial Administration Institute (Instituto de Administração Financeira; IAPS), the National Social Security Institute (Instituto Nacional de Previdência Social; INPS) and the National Social Security Healthcare Institute (Instituto Nacional de Assistência Médica; INAMPS). INAMPS was charged with providing individual health care to urban workers, government employees and rural workers (Braga and Paula, 1981).

The universalisation of social security made it imperative to ensure that health services like hospitals and clinics were accessible to an unexpectedly large contingent of the population. Malloy (1979) shows that Brazilian social security encompassed 80% of Brazil's urban population. The self-employed, housemaids and the rural population were no longer denied access to social security health services. This attempt at mass provision of social citizenship required investments in the supply of new medical services. The authoritarian regime opted to rely on combinations of the public and private spheres to expand social security services (Braga and Paula, 1981).

Nevertheless, the military regime had such a tenuous hold on legitimacy that the executive was capable neither of garnering recognition nor of providing intellectual leadership in sectoral initiatives. It should, however, be pointed out that the social policy debate in the latter half of the 1970s was no longer restricted to the issue of social inclusion (Dos Santos, 1979). Social policy reflection had turned to new questions: excess spending and the inefficient allocation of public resources. Weyland is perspicacious in his understanding of the complexity of this new scenario:

> Health professionals and experts from academia and research institutes criticized this unequal and wasteful model of health care ever more vocally. In the mid 1970s, they formed a 'sanitary movement' demanding profound reform. This social movement attributed the problems of the established system to its heavy reliance on the private sector. It therefore called for strengthening the public sector in order to guarantee all citizens equal rights and effective access to health care and to shift the emphasis from curative treatments to preventive measures, such as vaccination and sanitation.... It would also limit the explosion of health spending by diminishing the need for the expensive treatment of people falling ill with diseases that are easy to prevent. (Weyland, 1995, p 15)

The author highlights criticisms of the initial scholarship produced by the *sanitaristas* regarding the Brazilian military's national developmentalist decision to favour private companies in the expansion of hospitals and specialised clinics by authorising social security to purchase goods and services from them. Policy analysis in health thus dialogued with decisions that broadened Brazil's social protection structure in the 1970s while not, however, recognising these decisions as legitimate or even necessary.

The legitimacy crisis faced by the health sector expansion model jeopardised the late social protection system shaped by the authoritarian regime, modelled on a partnership between the state and private companies that provided health services to the social security system. Noronha and Levcovitz (1994) note that there was disagreement about the model even within the social security bureaucracy itself.

Policy analysis by the *sanitaristas*

The intellectual foundations of the SR were informed primarily by the results of research contracted by Research and Projects Financing (Financiadora de Estudos e Projetos; FINEP), a body of the federal executive branch headquartered in the city of Rio de Janeiro that was responsible for executing a portion of the programme to modernise scientific and technological research under the Geisel administration (Costa, 1992).

Although the *sanitaristas* had bureaucratic ties to the state apparatus of an authoritarian regime, their scientific production was paradoxically focused on deconstruction of the government's medical assistance policy. For the *sanitaristas*, more than serving as an instrument for broadening social protection, the expansion of health assistance as fostered by the regime subordinated the health sector to the logic of capitalist development in unacceptable terms. Oliveira and Teixeira provide examples of the functional-structural perspective that underpinned the veto of arrangements combining the state sphere and the health market in that context. For the authors, the expansion of social security within the sphere of health was part of the accumulation process, facilitated by the special blending of state and monopoly capital in Brazil.

Oliveira and Teixeira (1985) identified three unique features of this arrangement between social policy and accumulation. The first was the extension of social security coverage to encompass almost all of Brazil's urban population as well as part of its rural; the second was the favouring of curative, individual, welfare-based and specialised medicine in detriment to preventive public health measures of collective interest; and the third was the formation of a medical–industrial complex, responsible for the high rates of capital accumulation by large international monopolies in the area of medications and medical equipment manufacture.

Within the same institutional context, Cordeiro's early 1980s' policy analysis emphasised the process of capitalisation of medical practice, which was to forge links between the institutions that provided health care and trained human resources and the emerging medical–industrial complex that produced drugs and equipment (Cordeiro, 1980).

The author states:

> The material foundations for the privatisation of medicine, a process that stepped up pace as of 1976, lay in both the for-profit and not-for-profit private hospital sectors.... This policy option took as its rational justification the existence of a private hospital sector ... together with growing demand generated by the incorporation of large contingents of urban wage earners into the social security system. (Cordeiro, 1980, p 162)

Those in scientific research enjoyed paradoxical intellectual autonomy that allowed them to reaffirm the functional-structural theoretical perspective that tied growing state provision of health services to accumulation. Scientific research by the *sanitaristas* reaffirmed structuralist representations of the relation between the economy and politics then dominating the Brazilian social sciences. In 1973, for example, Donnangelo, a pre-eminent intellectual in social science research in health that decade, stated:

> The following can be identified as the prime means through which state interference has preserved the private sector: by sustaining quantitatively and qualitatively greater demand through concentrated manipulation of resources; by guaranteeing the continuity and expansion, under private control, of a network of services that progressively incorporates modern technology; and by keeping private producers in direct control of production processes. (Donnangelo, 1975, p 37)

The author did warn, however, that the preferential treatment accorded to the private producer was constrained by the need to reconcile it with guarantees that wage-earners would be able to access and consume services. Still, this same advantage rendered policy decisions less permeable to rationalisation and concentrated pressure on the state to expand the sphere of private action (Donnangelo, 1975).

What is particularly intriguing about the experience of the *sanitaristas* is that the constitutional process demanded institutional arguments that would justify the sectoral reform project. Such arguments were in fact produced, but the imperative of the institutional agenda distanced *sanitarista* policy analysis from the anti-capitalist representations found in their initial intellectual production.

Within the constitutional process, the *sanitaristas'* policy analysis became diffused at a national level through two bodies that, in the 1970s, brought together professors and researchers at the departments of social or preventive medicine within state or federal medical schools and at Fiocruz's National Public Health School (ENSP): the Brazilian Centre for Health Studies (Centro Brasileiro de Estudos de Saúde; CEBES) and the Brazilian Post-Graduate Association in Collective Health (Associação Brasileira de Pós-Graduação em Saúde Coletiva; ABRASCO). Even though the *sanitaristas* were intellectually independent, their social status as part of the public bureaucracy demanded that they create these two civil bodies in order to disseminate their reform agenda. In the 1970s, the authoritarian regime still had the power to limit direct political activism by public organisations.

CEBES was founded in 1976 as an outgrowth of *Revista Saúde em Debate*. As Cohn has pointed out, its members were academics or health professionals from the public sector whose chosen focus of policy analysis was reform of the health system from the perspective of universalisation and equity under the aegis of the state. Two CEBES leaders who were especially important during the constitutional process were physicians Antônio Sérgio Arouca and Eleutério Rodriguez Neto. The same role was played by ABRASCO, created in 1979, another vital actor in the shaping of health reform policy in the context of resistance to the military regime and of democratic transition (Cohn, 1989).

Cohn rightfully calls attention to the influence of the Italian sanitary reform experience, mainly through Giovanni Berlinguer's (1979) *Medicina e Politica*, translated into Portuguese by CEBES in the late 1970s. In this now classic work, published in Italy in 1973 and in Brazil in 1979, Berlinguer defended the *institutional* construction of a national sanitary service with integrated health protection functions, assuaging the anti-capitalist resistance then endemic to the Italian left (Berlinguer, 1979).

The important presence of this physician and senator for the Italian Communist Party reflected CEBES's great affinity for the strategy of occupying institutional spaces, which were expanded by democratic transition, as Cohn (1989) reminds us. Combining its outlook of institutional cooperation with the institutional lessons of the Italian experience, CEBES was able to present a tremendously original proposal for the Brazilian SR. The document 'A questão democrática na área da saúde' ('The democratic question in the area of health'), presented at the First Symposium on National Health Policy, held in the Federal Chamber in October 1979 (Escorel et al, 2005), was the main instrument of this innovative policy analysis.

CEBES proposed that the democratisation of health should present the following components: 1) recognition of the universal right to health; 2) recognition of the social nature of health conditions (employment, wages, nutrition, sanitation, housing and environmental protection); 3) state responsibility for the right to health; 4) creation of the SUS; 5) the establishment of funding mechanisms, with the defined participation of health within federal, state and municipal budgets; 6) decentralised management, with links between the federal, state and municipal levels; and 7) entrusting direction of the SUS to the Health Ministry, along with the task of planning and implementing the National Health Policy in cooperation with states and municipalities (Fleury et al, 2007).

The *sanitaristas* eliminated or minimised the anti-capitalist components of their original intellectual production, instead positing as a crucial strategic choice in SR the development of the state sector of the health economy. In the section entitled 'Política de assistência médica' ('Medical assistance policy'), the document 'A questão democrática na área da saúde' called for:

the immediate suspension of agreements or payment contracts by service units involving the purchase of physician services from the private entrepreneurial sector, replacing them with general subsidies; ... the immediate creation ... of a regionalised network of [government] clinics and health posts focused on the provision of preventive measures, in coordination with primary health care, emergency care and work accident care. SUS physicians should be used to staff these posts; ... definition of a policy for the production and distribution of medications and medical equipment ... aimed at reducing dependence on foreign capital, through greater state participation in research, researcher training and the development of national technology aimed at the production of raw materials vital to the industrialisation of essential medications. (Fleury et al, 2007, pp 14–15)

CEBES's sectoral reform proposal was further fortified by the successful experimentalism in health management practised by municipal governments. In the frail and restricted federative context that outlived the military regime, the *sanitaristas* enthusiastically disseminated experiences in the organisation of health care by progressive municipal governments. Municipal governments adopted the proposals to expand primary care that were disseminated through channels of interaction within the public health policy community. At this stage, the development of municipal policy depended above all on the idiosyncratic characteristics of local governments and progressive municipal leaders (Costa et al, 2011). Municipalism soon became a fundamental value on the democratising agenda of the *sanitaristas*: the Integrated Health Actions (Ações Integradas de Saúde; AIS) policy, in place during the brief period of democratic transition, reinforced the policy community's localist outlook. In 1986, 2,500 municipalities threw their support behind the AIS proposal (Noronha and Levcovitz, 1994).

The document *Pelo direito universal à saúde* (*For the universal right to health*; ABRASCO, 1985) was the *sanitaristas'* second show of force in policy analysis during the democratic transition. The document ratifies their advocacy of 'including health in the Constitution of Brazil as one of the basic elements in affirming the citizenship of the Brazilian people, defining it as a right to be safeguarded by the state' (ABRASCO, 1985, p 7). According to ABRASCO, the reorganisation of the Brazilian health system would be grounded in the universalisation and equalisation of health care, managerial decentralisation of service management, institutional integration among bodies and agencies and among the various levels of care, new relations between public and private services, the definition of a human resource policy and a science and technology policy, and the development of forms of participation for health professionals and users of services (ABRASCO, 1985).

Falleti (2010) is correct when she says that the *sanitaristas* arrived at both the Eighth National Health Conference (8th CNS), held in 1986, and at the constitutional process with their own agenda. Cohn and Elias (2003, p 45) also highlight the fact that: 'When the National Congress elaborated the country's new constitution in 1988, it was the health sector that presented the most complete proposal both in terms of governing principles and in the organisation of the system.'

The same impression was had by physician Carlos Mosconi, an influential member of the constitutional assembly from the Partido da Mobilização Democrática do Brasil (PMDB), Minas Gerais, who said:

> I have received a number of proposals from all areas. Of the proposals I received, in the health area, perhaps the most wide-ranging of all is [that] of the National Commission for Sanitary Reform, a proposal already in constitutional terms. I ask Your Honour's permission to read the proposal, which goes as follows: Art. 1 – Health is a right guaranteed by the state to all inhabitants of the national territory without distinction. (Mosconi, 1987, p 6)

The recommendations of the 8th CNS ratified CEBES's and ABRASCO's theses that the health of each individual is a collective interest, that the state's duty in health should be given priority treatment in social policies and that the right to health and equal access should be extended to actions and services to promote, protect and recover health at all levels of complexity (Comissão Nacional da Reforma Sanitária, 1987). The 8th CNS reiterated the need to change the historical standard of government action in health through the decentralisation of health services at sub-national levels.

To fund the new SUS, the 8th CNS proposed that the sector be allocated 'a minimum percentage over public revenue' or 'a minimum percentage equal to 15% of public revenue' (Comissão Nacional da Reforma Sanitária, 1987, p 24). The 8th CNS held that direct subsidies to private health plans be vetoed by revising the personal income tax deduction and by eliminating deductions allowed to companies for health care costs (Comissão Nacional da Reforma Sanitária, 1987, p 24).

Ratified by democratising political leaders, the 8th CNS document called for: the reorganisation of the Ministry of Health as a coordinating body for the sector; the shifting of the centre of financial decisions to states and municipalities; democratised decision-making through the establishment of state and municipal Deliberative Councils, comprising workers, employers, health professionals and the government; and a steady increase in tax-based funding of health until reaching 8% of GDP in 1990 (Brasil, 2007).

Some of the more distributive items on the agenda drawn up by the 8th CNS had inarguably garnered broad support from the political leaders who had risen to victory in 1985 under the New Republic (1985–90). It should be remembered that one of the most representative intellectuals and physicians in the sanitary field during the New Republic, Hésio Cordeiro, became president of INAMPS in 1985. It was in this environment that the Unified and Decentralised Health System (Sistema Unificado e Descentralizado de Saúde; SUDS) was created by decree law, as a continuation of the AIS programme, especially to reinforce the role of state governments within the federative public system then taking shape (Ministério da Saúde, 1985).

The mobilising strength of the 8th CNS influenced the establishment of the National Commission on Sanitary Reform (Comissão Nacional da Reforma Sanitária; CNRS), a consultative board entrusted with drawing up suggestions on the institutional and legal reshaping of the health system. Existing from August 1986 to May 1987 (Comissão Nacional da Reforma Sanitária, 1987), the CNRS devoted itself to further developing the Final Report produced by the 8th CNS, to systematising proposals and to the national integration of the sanitary movement, with special attention to legislative power and the constitutional process (Brasil, 1988).

The chapter on health in the FC1988 and its subsequent laws and administrative rulings would essentially ratify the organisational engineering that followed from the *sanitarista* policy community's proposition (see the Appendix). The FC1988 continues to hold the idea of health as a universal, equal right delivered through promotion, protection and recovery actions (Brasil, 1988, article 196). From the angle of systemic organisation, the FC1988 adopted the proposal for a unified, decentralised, integrated system with social participation (FC1988, article 199).

Institutional incentives for expanded, participative decision-making found expression in the decision to provide for Health Conferences (Conferências de Saúde) and Health Councils (Conselhos de Saúde) within the SUS at all levels of government (Ministério da Saúde, 1993). The Health Councils were to be ongoing, deliberative bodies comprising the government, service providers, professionals and users. They were to help oversee the implementation of health policy at their corresponding level, and decisions would be 'homologated by the legal head of the executive branch in each sphere of government' (Ministério da Saúde, 1993). The legislation that instituted the National Health Council (Conselho Nacional de Saúde; CNS – Decree no. 99.438/1990) gave it the power to 'act in the formulation of strategy and in the control of the execution of National Health Policy' at the federal level.

Final remarks

Assessments of the development of the SUS in the 1990s were overridingly pessimistic. It is widely, and surprisingly, maintained that the reform unfolded under precarious conditions and was incomplete, distorting its formulators' original conception. It is generally argued that there is a dissociation between the formulation and implementation of the SR. In this regard, the literature has stressed the complex relation between the public and private spheres. Paim (2008) and Ocké-Reis and Marmor (2010) have said that the SUS imagined by the community of *sanitaristas* became 'a broken promise'. Ocké-Reis and Marmor (2010, p 327) state: 'The state is incapable of responding to the coverage-related problems caused by budget constraints and this both prevents the SUS from becoming stronger and leaves ample room for the growth of an oligopolistic private health insurance market.' Paim, Travassos, Almeida, Bahia and Macinko are in surprising agreement in their diagnosis that 'implementation of the SUS has been complicated by state support for the private sector, the concentration of health services in more developed regions and chronic underfunding' (Paim et al, 2011, p 1778).

Now, more than 20 years after the enactment of the FC1988, the Brazilian health system has solidified into a hybrid system. The prevalence of funding for private insurance and out-of-pocket pay for medical care by families is pushing the sector towards organisational fragmentation. At the level of collective action, the institutionality of the FC1988 has served merely as a civic reference for individuals who can use it to ensure enforcement of the right to universal access to health care and to expensive medications.

Some authors have endeavoured to attribute the dissociation between the formulation and implementation of the SUS to Brazil's historical legacy of individual medical care. The origin of health care, grounded on differentiation in the realm of Brazil's retirement and pension institutes, has not favoured the Brazilian working class's universalist values of solidarity (Manicucci, 2006).

Others underline the constraints of developing an agenda based on the expansion of the state's role and of public spending in the early 1990s' environment of monetary stability and fiscal adjustment (Pereira, 1996). From this viewpoint, even the theme of federative decentralisation is seen as an expression of the minimal state agenda that was part of the executive branch's neoliberal project in the 1990s (Ugá, 1997). Pereira (1996) and Gerschman (1997), proponents of this perspective, hold that the SR coincided with a new era of Brazilian liberalism, where social policies were subordinated to macroeconomic policy.

From another prism, Diniz (1997) underscores how the new Brazilian democracy broke with a rigid state institutionality that showed little potential for political incorporation. The new democracy brought a multifaceted system of interest representation, rendering anachronistic the model of the omnipotent, concentrating state. Furthermore, the new political party system was to support segmentation in the composition of interests (Vianna, 1998).

Vianna (1998) and Manicucci (2006) call special attention to the role of the trade union movement, which did not support the SR, immersed as it was in the contradictions between an egalitarian ideological posture and the defence of corporatist interests. Concomitant with implementation of the SR, the demand for private medical care became an item on the collective bargaining agenda of various trade unions, constituting an 'implicit veto' of the reform's public, universal model.

Faveret and Oliveira (1990), on the other hand, raise the hypothesis of excluding universalisation, that is, when the SUS was set up, the preferential option for providing care to the poor distanced the middle class and unions from state-based care. Public underfunding and the massification of access prompted social actors with stronger voices to exit the public sphere. The authors see the entrenchment of the private health care insurance market as a consequence of the strategy of focusing the SUS on the poor and of limiting services.

A less sceptical reading of the performance of the SUS ties into the decentralisation experience. Arretche (2002, 2003) defends the thesis that the SR was especially successful in establishing federative decentralisation. She notes that He local autonomy in programme management, incentivised by the Ministry of Health, created institutional opportunities for government leaders to implement decisions in tune with their own preferences within the realm of the SUS. The preferences of municipal executives have not produced any collective ill will; the main advances in health indicators in Brazil are seen as attributable to the decentralisation process (Hunter and Sugiyama, 2009; Falleti, 2010).

The social sciences recognise the public bureaucracy's ability to put in place distributive developmentalist policies (Evans, 1999). The features of distributive policy are very attractive to national elites: social costs are spread out and benefits concentrated in certain social sectors and strata. Distributive developmentalist decisions have a marked presence in Brazilian economic history because they generate no opposition or veto from any social group.

This chapter has shown that the SR proposal included an agenda of a redistributive nature, which clashed openly with the distributive decisions of Brazil's authoritarian regime, in the grip of a legitimacy crisis. There is no doubt that implementation of a redistributive agenda under the SR in the context of the new democracy would mean specific, concentrated losses for entrepreneurial sectors and health professionals. The literature on redistributive institutional models is, however, sceptical about the public bureaucracy's ability to enforce a redistributive agenda on its own, without the acquiescence of social groups that wield obstructionist power (Esping-Andersen, 1996). The analysis of the institutional limits of redistributive public policies in Brazil presents a challenge to the SR's epistemic community today.

Acknowledgements

The author would like to thank Jeni Vaitsman, Deborah Uhr, Domingos Sávio Nascimento Alves and Elize Massard da Fonseca for their valuable comments on this chapter.

References

Abrasco (Associação Brasileira Pós-Graduação em Saúde Coletiva) (1985) *Pelo Direito Universal à Saúde*, Rio de Janeiro: Comissão de Políticas de Saúde.

Arretche, M. (2002) 'Federalismo e relações intergovernamentais no Brasil: A reforma dos programas sociais', *Dados*, vol 45, no 3, pp 431–57.

Arretche, M. (2003) 'Financiamento federal e gestão local de políticas sociais: O difícil equilíbrio entre regulação, responsabilidade e autonomia', *Ciência & Saúde Coletiva*, vol 8, no 2, pp 331–45.

Arretche, M. (2010) 'Toward a unified and more equitable system: health reform in Brazil', in R. Kaufman and J. Nelson (eds) *Crucial needs, weak incentives*, Washington, DC: Woodrow Wilson Center Press.

Berlinguer, G. (1979) *Medicina e Política*, São Paulo: Cebes/Hucitec.

Braga, J.C. and Paula, S.G. (1981) *Saúde e previdência: Estudos de política social*, São Paulo: Cebes/Hucitec.

Brasil (1988) *Constituição da Republica Federativa do Brasil (Constitution of the Federative Republic of Brazil)*. Brasília. Imprensa Nacional

Brasil (2007) *Anais da 8a Conferência Nacional de Saúde: 17 a 21 de março de 1986*, Brasília: Ministério da Saúde, Centro de Documentação.

Brasil Ministério da Saúde (1985) *Primeiro Plano de Desenvolvimento do Setor Saúde*, Brasilia: Imprensa Nacional.

Brasil Ministério da Saúde (1993) *Descentralização das Ações e Serviços de Saúde. A ousadia de fazer cumprir a lei*, Brasília: Imprensa Nacional.

Brasil Ministério da Saúde and Secretaria de Gestão Estratégica e Participativa (2006) *A construção do SUS: Histórias da Reforma Sanitária e do Processo Participativo*, Brasilia: Imprensa Nacional.

Cohn, A. (1989) 'Caminhos da reforma sanitaria', *Lua Nova*, no 19, pp 123–40.

Comissão Nacional da Reforma Sanitária (1987) *Documentos II*, Rio de Janeiro: Secretaria Técnica da Comissão Nacional da Reforma Sanitária.

Cordeiro, H. (1980) *A indústria da saúde no Brasil*, Rio de Janeiro: Graal.

Costa, N.R. (1992) 'Política e projeto acadêmico: notas sobre a gênese do campo da saúde coletiva', *Cadernos de História e Saúde, Casa de Oswaldo Cruz*, no 2.

Costa, N.R., Siqueira, S., Uhr, D. and Da Silva, P.F. (2011) 'Reforma psiquiátrica, federalismo e descentralização da saúde pública no Brasil', *Ciência e Saúde Coletiva*, vol 16, no 12, pp 4603–14.

Diniz, E. (1997) 'Crise, governabilidade e reforma do estado: em busca de um novo paradigma', in S. Gerschman and M.L.T.W.Vianna (eds) *A miragem da modernidade: democracia e políticas sociais no contexto da globalização*, Rio de Janeiro: Editora Fiocruz.

Dobuzinskis, L., Howlett, M. and Laycock, D. (2007) *Policy analysis in Canada – the state of the art*, Toronto: University of Toronto Press.

Donnangelo, M.C.F. (1975) *Medicina e Sociedade*, São Paulo: Pioneira.

Dos Santos, W.G. (1979) *Cidadania e justiça. A política social na ordem brasileira*, Rio de Janeiro: Editora Campos.

Draibe, S.M. (1999) 'Há tendências e tendências: com que estado de bem estar social haveremos de conviver?', *Cadernos de Pesquisa*, NEPP/UNICAMP, no 10.

Elias, P.M. and Cohn, A. (2003) 'Health reform in Brazil: lessons to consider', *American Journal of Public Health*, vol 93, no 1, pp 44–8.

Escorel, S., Nascimento, D.R. and Edler, F.C. (2005) 'As origens da reforma sanitária e o SUS', in N.T. Lima, S. Gerschman, F.C. Edler and J.L. Suzez (eds) *Saúde e democracia: história e perspectiva do SUS*, Rio de Janeiro: Editora Fiocruz.

Esping-Andersen, G. (1996) 'After the golden age? Welfare state in a global economy', in G. Esping-Andersen (ed) *Welfare state transition – national adaptations in global economics*, London: Sage Publications, pp 1–31.

Evans, P.B. and Rauch, J. (1999) 'Bureaucracy and growth: a cross-national analysis of the effects of "Weberian" state structures on economic growth', *American Sociological Review*, no 64, pp 748–65.

Falleti, T.G. (2010) 'Infiltrating the state. The evolution of health care reforms in Brazil, 1964–1988', in J. Mahoney and K. Thelen (eds) *Explaining institutional change: ambiguity, agency, and power*, Cambridge: Cambridge University Press.

Faveret, P. and Oliveira, P.J. (1990) 'A universalização excludente: reflexões sobre as tendências do sistema de saúde', *Planejamento e Políticas Públicas*, no 3, pp 139–62.

Fleury, S., Bahia, L. and Amarante, P. (2007) *Saúde em Debate: Fundamentos da reforma sanitaria*, Rio de Janeiro: Cebes.

Gerschman, S. (1997) 'Democracia, políticas sociais e globalização: relações em revisão', in S. Gerschman and M.L.T.W. Vianna (eds) *A miragem da modernidade: democracia e políticas sociais no contexto da globalização*, Rio de Janeiro: Editora Fiocruz.

Granados, F.J. and Knoke, D. (2005) 'Organized interest groups and political networks', in T. Janoski, R. Alford, A. Hicks and M. Schwartz (eds) *The handbook of political sociology – states, civil societies and globalization*, Cambridge: Cambridge University Press.

Haas, P.M. (1992) 'Introduction: epistemic communities and international policy coordination', *International Organization*, vol 46, no 1, pp 1–35.

Hall, P. (1989) *The political power of economic ideas – Keynesianism across nations*, Princeton, NJ: Princeton University Press.

Hunter, W. and Sugiyama, N.B. (2009) 'Democracy and social policy in Brazil – advancing basic needs, preserving privileged interests', *Latin American Politics and Society*, vol 51, no 2, pp 29–58.

Jaguaribe, H., Santos, W.G., De Abreu, M.P., Fritsch, W. and Ávila, F.G. (1986) *Brasil, 2000 – Para um novo pacto social*, Rio de Janeiro: Paz e Terra.

Kingdon, J.W. (2003) *Agenda, alternatives, and public policies*, New York, NY: Longman.

Majone, G. (1989) *Evidence, arguments, and persuasion in the policy process*, New Haven, CT: Yale University Press.

Malloy, J. (1979) *Política de previdência social no Brasil*, Rio de Janeiro: Editora Graal (English: Malloy, J. [1979] *The politics of social security in Brazil*, Pittsburgh, PA: University of Pittsburgh Press).

Manicucci, T.M.G. (2006) 'Implementação da reforma sanitária: a formação de uma política', *Saúde e Sociedade*, vol 15, no 2, pp 72–87.

Mosconi, C. (1987) *Atas da Constituinte*, Brasília: Senado Federal.

Noronha, J. and Levcovitz, E. (1994) 'Os caminhos do direito à saúde', in R. Guimarães and R. Tavares (eds) *Saúde e Sociedade no Brasil nos anos 80*, Rio de Janeiro: Relume Dumará.

Ocké-Reis, C.O. and Marmor, T.R. (2010) 'The Brazilian National Health System: an unfulfilled promise?', *International Journal of Health Planning and Management*, no 25, pp 318–29.

Oliveira, J.A. and Teixeira, S.M.F. (1985) *(Im)Previdência social: 60 anos de história da previdência no Brasil*, Petrópolis: Vozes/Abrasco.

Paim, J.S. (2008) 'A reforma sanitária brasileira e o Sistema Único de Saúde: dialogando com hipóteses concorrentes', *Physis: Revista de Saúde Coletiva*, vol 18, no 4, pp 625–44.

Paim, J.S., Travassos, C., Almeida, C., Bahia, L. and Macinko, J. (2011) 'The Brazilian health system: history, advances, and challenges', *Lancet*, no 377, pp 1778–97.

Pereira, C. (1996) 'A política pública como caixa de Pandora: organização de interesses, processo decisório e efeitos perversos na reforma sanitária brasileira (1985–1989)', *Revista Dados*, vol 39, no 3, pp 423–77.

Ugá, M.A. (1997) 'Ajuste estrutural, governabilidade e democracia', in S. Gerschman and M.L.T.W. Vianna (eds) *A miragem da modernidade: democracia e políticas sociais no contexto da globalização*, Rio de Janeiro: Editora Fiocruz.

Vianna, M.L.T.W. (1998) *A americanização perversa da seguridade social no Brasil*, Rio de Janeiro: REVAN/IUPERJ/UCAM.

Weyland, K. (1995) 'Social movements and the state: the politics of health reform in Brazil', *World Development*, vol 23, no 10, pp 1699–712.

Appendix

Table 17.A1: Historical evolution of the SUS: first years

Document / Topic	The Democratic Question in Health	Eighth National Health Conference	Federal Constitution of 1988	Law 8080 of 1990	Law 8142 of 1990
Concept of health/universalisation	Universal right to health. Recognition of the social determinants of health.	Health as a product of the social organisation of production.	Health as a right of all, guaranteed through social and economic policies that seek to reduce the risk of illness and achieve universal access.	A human right. Advocacy of universal and equal access to actions and services to promote, protect and restore health.	–
Health as a duty of the state	Health as a responsibility of the state	Health as a duty of the state	Duty of the state	Duty of the state	–
SUS	Creation of the SUS	Creation of the SUS	Creation of the SUS	Enactment of the SUS	–
Decentralisation/municipalisation/equity	Decentralisation of the SUS, aimed at local needs.	Decentralisation and equal access. Strengthening of the role of municipalities.	–	Emphasis on decentralisation down to the municipal level.	–
Democratic participation/Health Councils	Democratic participation of the population at different levels of the SUS.	People's participation in policy formulation and in planning, management, execution and evaluation of health actions. Creation of Health Councils.	Community participation.	Veto of joint bodies (Health Conferences and Health Councils).	Within each sphere of government, the SUS will have Health Conferences and Health Councils.
Leadership of the SUS	Health Ministry will direct the SUS. INAMPS becomes part of this system.	The SUS should have a single leadership.	The SUS has a single leadership in each sphere of government.	Political and administrative decentralisation, with a single leadership in each sphere of government.	–
Regionalisation/integrality	Creation of own regionalised network.	The SUS should be regionalised and hierarchised and should provide integrated care. Progressive nationalisation of sector.	Regionalised, hierarchical network. Integrated care, with priority on preventive action.	Emphasis on regionalisation and hierarchisation of the health service network. Integrated execution of health care and preventive action.	–
SUS funding	Expansion of the proportional participation of the health sector in federal, state and municipal budgets.	Creation of the social policy budget. Creation of Unified Health Funds (Fundos Únicos de Saúde) at federal, state and municipal levels. Setting of a minimum percentage of public revenue.	The SUS is funded with resources from social security and from federal, state (including the Federal District) and municipal budgets, in addition to other sources.	In accordance with estimated revenue, the social security budget will allocate to the SUS the funds needed to achieve its purposes.	Speaks to the allocation of funds from the National Health Fund (Fundo Nacional de Saúde) and the transfer of funds to municipalities, states and the Federal District.

EIGHTEEN

Brazilian think tanks: between the past and the future

Tatiana Teixeira[1]

Introduction

In-depth study of think tanks (TTs[2]) has only recently begun in Brazil, and the number of academic papers and press articles is increasing (Cançado, 2004; Barcellos, 2006; Sá, 2011), reflecting growing interest in these public policy analysis research institutes. In Brazil, such studies are still restricted to a niche, with papers addressing analysis of specific fields, such as international relations and administration. Examples of this segmentation are: business organisations, such as liberal institutes[3] (Gros, 2004); institutes of applied economics (Durand, 1997); foreign policy institutes (Soares, 2011); or those representing TTs clusters (Lima, 2010).

How do Brazilian TTs differ from their North American counterparts?[4] If the term does not figure in Portuguese or in Brazilian law, how are they framed legally? What challenges do they encounter in establishing and maintaining themselves? These are some of the questions that this chapter aims to answer. Although reference is made to the US, it should be noted that this is not a comparative study.

This exploratory, descriptive research was based on a literature review, analysis of institutional websites and a semi-open-ended questionnaire used as a script for semi-structured interviews. Institutions were selected according to the literature – above all, McGann's (2012) global ranking and its 81 Brazilian TTs, and Rosa-Soares's (2009) dissertation, which listed 20 of them – and to answers given by interviewees, who spontaneously mentioned approximately 100 purported TTs. Between August 2011 and March 2012, 99 experts, including Brazilian scholars, diplomats, former ministers and members of TTs, were interviewed; roles quite often overlapped.

Origins and boundary porosity

Just as policy analysis studies had their origin in the central nations, such as the US, then becoming paradigmatic for academic discussions in other countries, so the same can be said of TTs. Accordingly, it is imperative to refer back to the North American model in order to understand this type of institutional arrangement in Brazil. After all, 'think tanks are an American invention, and their development is largely an American phenomenon' (McGann, 2011, p 35).

For most (78.79%) of the interviewees, TTs are a type of institution now present in Brazil: answers ranged from "certainly" to "embryonic" and "yes, some – only a few considering the magnitude of the agenda and its complexity and the size of the country, the size of its academia". Many said that it was impossible to speak of TTs in the strict sense in Brazil, but only of "adapted models" or "experiences that point in that direction".[5] The answer to this question seems to be directly related to what definition is used to describe a TT.

Such institutions first emerged in the Anglo–Saxon political environment and, today, are spread worldwide. Their increasingly transnational nature and their adaptation to different socio–political contexts heighten the challenges to those intending to study them. The US remains the country with the greatest number of simultaneous ideal conditions for TTs to spread and survive, such as: the multiplicity of centres of power with a system of checks and balances highly receptive to external agents; strong civic voluntarism with financial contributions from individuals and legal entities to these institutions; a fiscal regime favourable to private fund donations; independence and continuous exchange of information between academic and politic circles; and strong government interest in research (McGann, 2005; Teixeira, 2007).

North American TTs consolidated and became significant particularly because of the need to understand the US role in the world, and the world itself, after 1945, with the focus on high politics. In Brazil, TTs are still more focused on thinking about the country domestically and are still looking for a model of their own to administer a number of challenges.

In the US, for instance, philanthropy is at the source of these institutions, which receive contributions to maintain them and fund long-term projects. In Brazil, 'the word "foundation" is often used in Latin America to mean a non-profit operating organisation rather than a donating one' (Truitt, 2005, p 541). There is no culture of private philanthropy, and large fortunes are seldom donated to research organisations, which narrows the funding bottleneck. As a result, research is mostly publicly funded, institutions have limited staff and facilities and more modest budgets, and institutions are more often subject-specific than generalist.

In addition, Brazilian TTs do not have the holding tank role they do in the US. When senior members of government step down, they often migrate to private consultancies, resume their positions at universities (usually public ones) or run for office.

In the classic literature,[6] independence from governments and parties is considered an essential condition for these institutions to operate and for them to be recognised as such. Recent studies, such as Acuña (2009), have begun to put this view into perspective. Even in the US, however, to speak of a 'pure think tank'[7] greatly simplifies the realities. As described by McGann:

> In other parts of the world, sponsorship by a government ministry is a legal necessity for a think tank to exist.... *A middle course in defining think tanks therefore makes the most sense.* Think tanks are policy research organizations that have significant autonomy from government and, by inference, from the corporate world as well. But autonomy is a relative rather than an absolute term.... These ideal think tanks have served as models for new organizations being established or points of departure for existing institutions that wanted to reinvent themselves. But most think tanks do not fit neatly into any one category. (McGann, 2011, pp 17, 22, emphasis in original)

Medvetz (2008, p 2) also takes issue with the rigidity of the original concept and argues that it favours the North American and British models, and that even in the case of the US, 'the first organisations to exist under this banner were not independent at all'. Suffice it to mention the origins of the Rand Corporation, the Democratic connections of the Center for American Progress and the Progressive Policy Institute, or the Republican ties of the Heritage Foundation and of the American Enterprise Institute. Connections and political positions cannot be neglected or minimised.

North American TTs are politically and ideologically charged, and the same happens in Brazil, where several take a political stance, directly or indirectly, with their 'theoretical stamps':[8] by their institutional connections, such as the Fundação Perseu Abramo and the now extinct Instituto Cidadania, both linked to the Workers' Party (Partido dos Trabalhadores; PT); by their agenda profile (Instituto Millenium); or by their activity profile, such as Instituto Pólis and Centro Brasileiro de Estudos de Saúde, both directed to social movements.

Think tanks, non-governmental organisations, universities and lobbies

It is still difficult to establish institutional boundaries between TTs and other advocacy, party-political or academic research organisations (see Goodman, 2005; Abelson, 2006; Teixeira, 2007; Rosa-Soares, 2009; Pinto, 2010). In Brazil, this distinction between TTs and foundations, non-governmental organisations (NGOs), universities and consultancies is very tenuous, leading to the existence of hybrid institutions. That is the case with the Brazilian Social and Economic Analyses Institute (*Instituto Brasileiro de Análises Sociais e Econômicas*; Ibase), Institute for the Study of Labour and Society (Instituto de Estudos do Trabalho e Sociedade; Iets) and Religious Studies Institute (Instituto de Estudos da Religião; Iser), all of which are NGO-TTs and strongly involved with social issues; Centre for Integration and Development Studies (Centro de Estudos de Integração e Desenvolvimento; Cindes), Brazilian International Relations Centre (Centro Brasileiro de Relações Internacionais; Cebri), Study Center of International Negotiations (Centro de Estudos das Negociações Internacionais; Caeni) and Institute for International Trade Negotiations (Instituto de Estudos do Comércio e Negociações Internacionais; Icone), which are consultancy-TTs and provide the private sector and government with support on international affairs and negotiations; Applied Economic Research Institute (Instituto de Pesquisa Econômica Aplicada; Ipea), which is a government agency-TT that operates as a 'research and State advisory institution' (Pochmann, 2011); or Getúlio Vargas Foundation (Fundação Getulio Vargas; FGV), which is a teaching institution-consultancy-TT.

Interviewees found it particularly controversial to classify certain institutions such as Ipea, FGV and the now-extinct Higher Institute of Brazilian Studies (Instituto Superior de Estudos Brasileiros; Iseb). Ipea was the most controversial: while acknowledging the quality of its research and its historical importance, some interviewees nonetheless criticised its alleged party-ideological capture in recent years and the fact that it is a government agency – two features regarded as compromising its policymaking independence and autonomy. FGV was questioned mostly for being more a teaching institution than a TT. Many considered it chronologically inappropriate to identify Iseb (founded in 1955 and closed in 1964) as a TT.

Another source of confusion is that 'third sector' has become a catch-all covering diverse terms and types of activity (Montaño, 2002). 'The presence of civil society on the political stage has brought new subjects into the public space, and this has led to series of inaccuracies as to their nature' (Pinto, 2010, p 185). In order to minimise distortions, a good alternative might be a less flexible description, as suggested by one interviewee.

In the endeavour to differentiate TTs from NGOs, it might help to observe the vocabulary used by the organisation and apply a negative concept, since TTs are neither a platform to empower civil society nor a space for activism and militancy by social movements. Furthermore, NGOs are usually of a more beneficent, educational nature and focus on different subjects, such as social assistance or the environment, (often) involving voluntary work. TTs seek no such 'representation'. The same distinction serves for the national policy councils, which have become popular throughout Brazil and cannot be regarded as TTs, because they actually seek to represent groups in society. Another point is that NGOs are not concerned with research, one of TTs' core activities. Thus, investigating modus operandi also helps in this differentiation (see Table 18.1).

Table 18.1: **How do TTs operate?**

How do TTs operate?	Number of mentions[*]
Does not know/did not answer	14
They conduct research/studies/reflection/intellectual production	49
Influencing policy and political debate/direct intervention	31
Events (debates, workshops, seminars, etc)	30
Publishing (reports, policy briefs, position papers, etc)	23
Publicising analyses/projects/proposals	14
Media (publishing articles, interviews)	10
They train people	5
They create courses	5
They provide data and information	5
Researchers' individual visibility and influence	4

Notes: *Number of individual mentions made among 99 interviewees. Each interviewee could mention more than one item. Another 22 topics were mentioned one to three times.

Source: Table prepared by the author based on interviews.

Although lobbying occurs in Brazil, it is not regulated. The lack of explicit standards adds to the confusion regarding the activity performed by TTs, particularly in terms of supporting partners' expectations as to the results such institutions should achieve. In that respect, there is some tension to be managed between TT sponsors and partners. While the former may try to intervene in the research agenda, looking for the immediate influence and more palpable results afforded by lobbying, the latter are interested in a long-term venture. As Abelson (2007, pp 565, 571) explains:

> What think tanks can offer is the time to reflect and to think critically about important policy matters... Policy influence ... is not simply about

achieving desirable outcomes. It is a process that allows various individuals and organizations to exchange ideas with journalists, academics, members of the attentive public, and policy-makers throughout government.

Teaching is not the main activity in TTs; the concern is more with strategic ideas and applied research and they have greater facility for bridging, in terms of knowledge production and dissemination, among society, academia, governments and companies. One of the reasons for this greater institutional flexibility is that their bureaucratic structure is smaller than in university departments. According to Goodman (2005):

> Think tanks tend to be goal-oriented. Their scholars research specific topics and encourage solutions to well-defined problems…. Think tanks are graded based upon their success in solving real world problems. Universities are graded based according to the academic prestige of their faculty members.

Brazilian think tanks: dilemmas and changes

Less than 10 years ago, Chacel (2005, p 567) remarked that 'the think tank concept is alien to Brazilians'. Nowadays, even though few researchers delve into the subject,[9] the concept is no longer so obscure:"The institutions are not new. The change grew out of theoretical discussions about their action. This raised the need to discuss the knowledge and the ideas they produce".[10] After McGann's (2012) report was published, listing the latest annual ranking, at least six Brazilian institutions – Brics Policy Center (BPC), Brazilian Analysis and Planning Centre (Centro Brasileiro de Análise e Planejamento; Cebrap), Cebri, Cindes, FGV and Fernando Henrique Cardoso Institute (Instituto Fernando Henrique Cardoso; iFHC) – publicised and celebrated their positions.

Considering that the concept is under constant analysis (Medvetz, 2008; Acuña, 2009; McGann, 2011), the idea of TTs in Brazil is believed to relate more to their agency, to the 'strategic choice' made by the institution and the 'identity it seeks to build',[11] than to any specific label. In legal terms, there is no single possible or expected framing for Brazilian TTs or *organizações de pesquisa e aconselhamento em políticas públicas* (policy research and advisory organisations)[12] (Rosa-Soares, 2009).

Nonetheless, we have developed some basic criteria to identify them. They must: not be an ad hoc group; be a formally institutionalised collective actor; be mentioned in the literature, in the media or by interviewees; conduct research; organise debates and events, such as seminars or workshops; have current publications and diverse sources of funding; and aim to contribute to or intervene in public agendas by producing and transmitting knowledge (Acuña, 2009; McGann, 2011; see also Table 18.2).

There are also differences as to the institute's chosen policy area and the history of NGO participation in each of them. As one interviewee stated, health care and foreign policy, for instance, have very different backgrounds and profiles in terms of their openness to participation by civil society, with foreign policy being 'in that respect, barely rooted socially'.[13] As regards foreign policy (Lima, 2013), the bureaucratic insulation and professionalism of Itamaraty (Ministry of Foreign Affairs) seem to have had a limiting effect on the expansion of TTs in this field, where there are many institutions whose profile is more consultancy-oriented.

With the changing nature of Brazil's foreign standing and the new responsibilities and demands it entails, and considering the depth of current issues and the need for more technical knowledge in international bodies, such as the World Trade Organization (WTO), TTs will increasingly be called upon – as is the case with Icone, which was set up 'to assist the Brazilian government and private sector in developing positions in international trade negotiations and litigation' (Schaffer et al, 2010, p 67).

This endeavour to narrow concepts down also calls on the classification by McGann (2011, p 23):

1. *Independent and autonomous* – a public policy organisation that has significant independence from any one interest group or donor, and autonomous in its operation and funding from government.
2. *Quasi-independent* – autonomous from government, but controlled by an interest group, donor or contracting agency that provides most of the funding and has significant influence over the TT.
3. *University-affiliated* – research centre at a university.
4. *Political party-affiliated* – formally affiliated with a party.
5. *Government-affiliated (federal, state or municipal)* – organisation that is part of the structure of government.
6. *Quasi-governmental* – funded exclusively with government funds and contracts, but not part of formal government structure.
7. *For profit* – operates as a for-profit business.

The idea of cluster is also used for institutions that house TTs, such as universities – Universidade de São Paulo (USP), FGV, Pontifícia Universidade Católica (PUC) or Universidade Estadual de Campinas (Unicamp) – with their study centres. Note, in this case, that this attribute is neither static nor permanent, and that not all research centres inside universities are actually prominent and visible.

Table 18.2: **Definition of TTs**

Features most often mentioned[*]	Number of mentions
A centre for thinking, research and knowledge production	55
Influencing political decisions	33
Specialisation/specific subject field	17
Politicised institution/ideological bias	17
Independent research	14
Discussion forum	13
High-level research/expertise	13
Autonomy from government	10
Communities of researchers/policy experts	10
Applied/instrumental research	9
Not-for-profit organisations	8
Permanent researchers and staff	8
Public–private funding	8
A bridge among society, academia, governments and business	7
Organisations that started in the US	7
Linked to parties/governments/interest groups/corporations	6
Public–private institutions	5
Consultancy	5
Training/providing people for parties and governments	5
Clear orientation to a specific clientele	5
Drafting political projects for institutions, parties, states	5
Idea factories/idea banks	5
Virtual communities/networks	5
Production, systematisation, publication and communication of specific knowledge	5

Note: [*]Another 53 features were mentioned one to four times by interviewees.

Source: Table prepared by the author based on interviews.

As regards Brazil, another category to be considered, although still only incipient, is vanity/legacy TTs (Abelson, 2006). In the US, former presidents commonly offer their collected material to seed university libraries, which in time become important foreign policy research centres. Some presidents were successful during their term in the White House; others, because of political constraints while they were in office or unfavourable circumstances, are remembered for what they were unable to do. These TTs serve to fill this void, their import deriving from the former president's visibility and symbolic and social capital. The desire not to be forgotten and to shape how they want to go down in history prompt this endeavour to leave other accomplishments that may overshadow past failures.

The recently established Instituto Lula (formerly Instituto Cidadania) and the iFHC can be thought of in this category, even if the institutes do not see themselves as TTs. Instituto Lula is considered to be building that identity. As described by one member, its Latin America Initiative, Africa Initiative and Democracy Memorial may have features usually considered characteristic of a TT, but not yet the institute as a whole. At the iFHC, whose dual role is to give public access to documents from its founder's history and to be a source of, and a centre for, debate, there is 'a concern with the public importance of what we are doing, but we do not mean to "take a position" and influence policymaking directly, as think tanks tend to do'.[14] An alert should be sounded to the risks of ideology in excess and the need for redoubled attention so that such institutions do not become electoral platforms and representatives of party agendas.

Challenges

The most important problem to be overcome is funding (see Table 18.3), which relates to another challenge: having funds to hire high-profile researchers for long-term projects and ensure the institution's survival and the quality of its work. Lack of interest from politicians and society, and the lack of a tradition of philanthropy, also have direct impacts on funding: 'The private sector sees little use in think tanks (it prefers lobbying, pure and simple). These days, foreign foundations only fund projects and do not cover fixed costs.'[15]

The funding sources mentioned most often in interviews and by Montaño (2002) and Lardone and Roggero (2011) were: government agencies; Brazilian and international funding agencies, for example, National Scientific and Technological Development Council (Conselho Nacional de Desenvolvimento Científico e Tecnológico; CNPq) and Coordination for Postgraduate Personnel Improvement (Coordenação de Aperfeiçoamento de Pessoal de Nível Superior; CAPES); public and private sector subsidies and donations; international funding, for example, Inter-American Development Bank (IDB), United Nations Development Program (UNDP) and others, such as Heinrich Böll Foundation; budget items; cooperation agreements; educational and consultancy service provision; management contract ('social organisation'; OS); partnership agreement ('public interest social organisation'; Oscip); and tax exemption ('public utility entity').[16]

Many of the institutions examined by the author,[17] without actually being TTs, already see themselves as such: they have yet to embody a larger number of the components listed in this chapter. Some lack importance and visibility and their analyses lack robustness; others lack continuous activities and output, and involvement with public agendas. Curiously, others that do not consider themselves TTs, or in fact are not, because they do not meet the criteria of this study, were classified as such by interviewees.

Overall, Brazilian TTs still speak mostly to themselves and their peers. Except for government agencies such as Ipea, interaction with the government is neither constant, systematic nor comprehensive and these institutions function more as places for debate and sources of data and analyses, or are called on to create programmes or evaluate ongoing projects. There is 'little tradition of "osmosis" between institutions of state and these independent research institutions'.[18]

Interviewees occasionally recalled more tangible examples of influence, showing that TTs 'intervene timidly in public debate and in the media – generally through members' individual opinions rather than institutional diagnosis' (Sá, 2011). That observation holds for Brazilian TTs overall, including those in Rio de Janeiro, such as BPC, Casa das Garças, Cebri or Cindes. Most work with a small structure and staff of researchers and, according to

Table 18.3: **The biggest challenges?**

Challenges[*]	Number of mentions
Does not know/did not answer	6
Lack of disinterested funding/resources	49
Lack of interest from politicians	13
Lack of tradition in philanthropy/political entrepreneur/sponsor with broad vision	13
Lack of support/interest from civil society	10
Being/staying independent	9
Being/staying autonomous	8
Strong government presence in funding	8
Conceptual challenge (spread the term TT and differentiate it from NGO, lobby, advisory body and academic body)	7
Patrimonialism	7
Lack of tradition of civil society organisation	6
Lack of critical mass	6
Immaturity of institutions and democratic debate	5
Government short-term focus	5
Technical bureaucracy a strong presence in research	5
Brazilians' level of education	5

Note: [*]Another 72 topics were mentioned one to four times by interviewees.

Source: Table prepared by the author based on interviews.

directors of several of these institutions,19 their major concern is to be an alternative space for debate, more than to influence the political process. Wiarda (2010) explains that smaller TTs with lesser power resources generally aim to influence those who influence politicians.

Examples of influence mentioned in literature and in interviews include: the book *É possível: gestão da segurança pública e redução da violência* (Veloso and Ferreira, 2008), which resulted from a seminar in 2007 at Casa das Garças and is claimed to be one source for the public security plan of the present Rio de Janeiro State government; Icone's technical support for Itamaraty on the agriculture chapter in the Doha Round of WTO negotiations; projects drafted by Instituto Cidadania and adapted by the Lula administration, such as Fome Zero (Zero Hunger); the impact of partnering between the Inter-Union Statistics and Socioeconomic Studies Department (Departamento Intersindical de Estatística e Estudos Socioeconômicos; Dieese) and the Ministry of Labour (Gamarra, 2009); the impact on the federal government of studies conducted by Marcelo Neri (FGV) on the new Brazilian middle class (Neri, 2011); and research conducted by Cebrap for São Paulo municipal government and for the Ministry of Health in the social, demographic and health and reproduction fields.

Brazilian national political debate is still shallow and poorly informed. Added to which are: re-democratisation and the influx of new actors; mounting social demands and increasing 'complexity of public policies and foreign policy' and the need to effectively 'constitutionalise citizenship';[20] and economic expansion and Brazil's growing political stature (Melo Neto and Froes, 2001; Farah, 2011). In other words, even though TTs are not routinely consulted and do not influence the various stages of the policy cycle directly, broadly or frequently, most interviewees (71.72%) believe there is scope for TTs to intervene more in politics. Their influence could be direct – by 'members of TTs achieving positions of command, or their thinking influencing those who work in the apparatus of state', or 'on members of congress connected with TTs' causes' – or indirect, 'within the sphere of public opinion and academic analysis'.[21]

At the same time, there is disbelief as to whether Brazilian politicians will begin using this space more often since, as one interviewee pointed out, 'it is always difficult to persuade politicians to think in the long term.'

Final remarks

It may not yet be possible to think of Brazilian TTs in terms of an ideal type, since the concept still seems to be undergoing adaptation. Indeed, discussion of TTs in Brazil is beginning in a world that is very different from when they first appeared: their (deliberate and conscious) inspiration in the American model was a recent phenomenon dating from 1990–2000. This suggests that they are strongly hybrid. In the interviews, there was considerable agreement as to what a TT is. However, that agreement disappears when considering their Brazilian counterparts and the nature of such institutions.

Reactions to TTs in the interviews span a wide range of opinion: they start in pessimism with respect to their growth and survival and their importance to Brazil, together with mistrust of their ideological, party and political profile, and end in the certainty that they are essential in any democratic system and in enthusiasm over their possible action, practical results and beneficial, innovative contributions to politics and society.

This means that orthodox definitions are still insufficient to understand the phenomenon in Brazil and that, for now, the legal framework is not the most significant aspect. Understanding their institutional role is more useful than any simple categorisation. This change is being picked up by more recent Latin American studies, which show that each researcher adopts specific criteria for what a TT is understood to be in different countries. The concept's flexibility will depend on who is thinking about those organisations (how they see them and from what standpoint) and the purpose to be achieved by using a given classification, because 'the label is charged with social consequence' (Medvetz, 2008, p 2).

In Brazil, the lack of conceptual clarity encourages indiscriminate, random use of the term, whether deliberate or not, and makes them difficult to identify. To date, the concept is apparently being absorbed as something necessarily favourable, as certifying quality and especially useful to institutes wishing to internationalise more intensively.

It can often lead institutions, even when not actually TTs, to refer to themselves as TTs for advertising and marketing purposes.

What can be seen in Brazil is 'state patronage', because the state (together with foreign foundations, such as the Ford Foundation) has been foremost in inducing what Brazilian TTs would eventually become and because research in Brazil is still primarily funded by government investment. Furthermore, in Brazil, TTs include not only parastatal agencies (such as OSs, OSCIPs or public interest entities), spanning a few agencies and public foundations. The scenario also comprises TT clusters, such as Brazil's leading universities and their research centres, and hybrid TTs, such as foundations (whether party-political or otherwise) and NGOs of acknowledge competence that operate with the expectation of spreading or influencing a particular political agenda.

As mentioned earlier, the lack of an institutionalised field for ideas to be discussed more fully, shallow political debate and the persistence of certain historical elements of Brazilian political culture, relating to the political grammars described by Nunes (2003), are all mentioned as obstacles to the progress of such institutions. However, more conscious efforts to reproduce the North American TT model and methods are already visible. The work of the newest generation of Brazilian TTs is now clearly based on a 'TT format', focusing more on policy briefs than on dense academic research, with some of their publications available in English. This means that Brazilian TTs may also try to increase their presence and influence in political debate in Brazil in years to come.

The topics studied by those TTs, it is believed, will become increasingly cross-cutting and more flexibly bounded. In order to meet growing demand resulting from Brazil's repositioning on the world stage, they are expected to concentrate more on fields such as foreign trade and international relations (the rise of China, Africa, sustainable development and the environment, oil and energy resources, BRICs,[22] South–South relations, security and defence, and so on).

The profile is expected to be more internationalist with increasing researcher exchange and partnerships with foreign institutions to obtain funding, as means to surviving and improving research quality and capacity. Funding issues will also keep institutions small in size and staff numbers, and more personal and specialised. That kind of institutional choice can also be risky: specialise too narrowly and you may be tied to an issue that no longer matters, and become irrelevant in the medium or long term. Although a permanent research staff is expected, TTs should not be bound to a physical location, because networking is one way to minimise the impact of scarce funding.

Finally, and in conclusion, to study the evolution of a new type of institution in Brazil also means observing a country that has been extensively pondering and discussing itself and its place in the world.

Acknowledgements

This chapter was funded by Faperj. I would like to thank: the interviewees, the key elements of this research; André Machado for tabulating data and transcribing interviews; Professors Cesar Guimarães, Erica Resende and Williams Gonçalves, the diplomat Paulo Roberto de Almeida and Christiane Sauerbronn, for the large network of contacts; and the editors of this book and again Cesar Guimarães, Paulo Roberto de Almeida and Williams Gonçalves for their careful reading and comments, which have enriched and improved the final version. The author would also like to thank Professor James McGann, head of the Think Tanks and Civil Societies Program and supervisor of the doctoral internship in the University of Pennsylvania in 2012.

Notes

[1] Email: tteixeira.iuperj@gmail.com

[2] See the Appendix for a list of abbreviations and acronyms.

[3] Liberal institutes are 'organisations set up by businessmen in the early 1980s to spread the principles of neoliberalism among members of Brazil's elites … and turned into a national network' (Gros, 2004, pp 143, 145).

[4] This chapter addresses Brazilian institutions and excludes branches of foreign institutes, such as the Konrad Adenauer Foundation and the Friedrich Naumann Foundation for Freedom, mentioned in interviews, and the Heinrich Böll Foundation (Rosa-Soares, 2009), or those established abroad, such as the Brazil Institute at the Woodrow Wilson International Center for Scholars (Rosa-Soares, 2009).

[5] Interviewed by the author.

[6] See the literature review in Teixeira (2007).

[7] As mentioned by one interviewee.

[8] Interviewed by the author.

[9] Authors who do address the issue include Almeida (1989), Miceli (1989), Paulics and Bava (2002), Chacel (2005), Truitt (2005), Ducoté (2007) and Gamarra (2009).

[10] Interviewed by the author.

[11] Interviewed by the author.

[12] Rosa-Soares (2009) argues the need to have and use a concept translated into Portuguese.

[13] Interviewed by the author.

[14] Interviewed by the author.

[15] Interviewed by the author.

[16] Act 9.637/98 (OS), 9.790/99 (Oscip), 2.730/98 (Titles of Public Municipal Interest – Rio de Janeiro) and 3.377/00 (Public State Interest/RJ). The recent Research Support

Act, 11.487/07, allows companies to use tax incentives in innovative projects conducted by universities and research institutes.

[17.] The TTs most mentioned in interviews (and the number of mentions): BPC (8); Cebrap (26); Cebri (50); Cedec (11); Cindes (12); Dieese (5); ESG (5); Funcex (5); FGV (28); FPA (16); Ibase (6); Instituto Cidadania (5); Icone (12); Iedi (7); Iets (7); iFHC (25); Casa das Garças (12); Instituto Liberal (8); Instituto Lula (5); Instituto Millenium (12); Ipea (32); Instituto Pólis (7); Iseb (8); Instituto Teotônio Vilela (7); and (the former) Instituto Universitário de Pesquisas do Rio de Janeiro (Iuperj) (8).

[18.] Interviewed by the author.

[19.] Interviewed by the author.

[20.] Interviewed by the author.

[21.] Interviewed by the author.

[22.] Brazil, Russia, India, China, and South Africa.

References

Abelson, D.E. (2006) *A capitol idea: think tanks & US foreign policy*, Montreal: McGill-Queen's University Press.

Abelson, D.E. (2007) 'Any ideas? Think tanks and policy analysis in Canada', in L. Dobuzinskis, M. Howlett and D. Laycock (eds) *Policy analysis in Canada: the state of the art*, Toronto: University of Toronto Press, pp 551–73.

Acuña, C.H. (2009) 'Análisis comparativo de cuatro estudios de caso sobre institutos de investigación de políticas (o *think tanks*) en México, Brasil, Ecuador y Uruguai', in V. Weyrauch (ed) *Acercando la investigación a las políticas públicas en América Latina: repensando los roles y desafíos para los institutos de investigación de políticas*, Buenos Aires: Fundación CIPPEC.

Almeida, M.H.T. (1989) 'Dilemas da institucionalização das Ciências Sociais no Rio de Janeiro', in S. Miceli (ed) *História das Ciências Sociais no Brasil* (vol 1), São Paulo: Vértice/Ed. Revista dos Tribunais/Idesp, pp 188–216.

Barcellos M. (2006) 'Ideias para dar e vender', *Valor Econômico*, Eu&Fim de Semana p 12.

Cançado, P. (2004) 'Discreto clube da elite', *Revista Época*, no 320, Available at: http://revistaepoca.globo.com/Revista/Epoca/0,,EDG65186-6012,00.html

Chacel, J. (2005) 'Think tanks in Brazil: the case of Instituto Brasileiro de Economia as an Illustration', in J. McGann and R. Weaver (eds) *Think tanks & civil societies: catalysts for ideas and action*, New Brunswick: Transaction Publishers, pp 567–83.

Ducoté, N. (2007) 'El desarrollo de algunas capacidades internas críticas para la incidencia efectiva de los *think tanks* en políticas públicas', in A. Garcé and G. Uña (eds) *Think tanks y políticas públicas en Latinoamérica: dinámicas globales y realidades regionales*, Buenos Aires: Prometeo Libros, pp 221–44.

Durand, M.R.G.L. (1997) 'Formação das elites político-administrativas no Brasil: as instituições de pesquisa econômica aplicada', *Revista do Serviço Público*, vol 48, no 2, pp 100–22.

Farah, M.FS. (2011) 'Administração pública e políticas públicas', *Revista de Administração Pública*, vol 45, no 3, pp 813–36.

Gamarra, M.R. (2009) 'El impacto de la producción científica del DIEESE en la implementación de políticas públicas específicas para la protección de la calidad del empleo por el Ministerio de Trabajo del Brasil', in Weyrauch, V. (ed) *Proyecto 'Espacios para el Compromiso: usando el conocimiento para mejorar las políticas públicas a favor de los pobres*, La Paz: GDN-CIPPEC, pp 137-73.

Goodman, J.C. (2005) 'What is a think tank?' National Center for Policy Analysis (NCPA), Special Publications, www.ncpa.org/pub/what-is-a-think-tank.

Gros, D.B. (2004) 'Institutos Liberais, neoliberalismo e políticas públicas na Nova República', *Revista Brasileira de Ciências Sociais (RBCS)*, vol 19, no 54, pp 143–60.

Lardone, M. and Roggero, M. (2011) 'El rol del Estado en el financiamiento de la investigación sobre políticas públicas en América Latina', in N. Aste and E. Mendizabal (eds) *Vínculos entre conocimiento y política: el rol de la investigación en el debate público en América Latina*, Lima: CIES, pp 115–63.

Lima, M.C. (2010) 'O futuro das ideias: análise estrutural & incertezas-críticas prospectivas para think tanks', MBA thesis, Ebape/FGV, Rio de Janeiro.

Lima, M.R.S. (2013) 'Relações Internacionais e Políticas Públicas: a contribuição da análise de política externa', in E. Marques and C. Faria (eds) *Política pública como campo disciplinar*, São Paulo: Ed. Unesp.

McGann, J. (2005) *Comparative think tanks, politics and public policy*, Northampton: Edward Elgar.

McGann, J. (2011) *Global think tanks: policy networks and governance*, New York, NY: Routledge.

McGann, J. (2012) *2011 global go to think tanks report*, Philadelphia, PA: University of Pennsylvania.

Medvetz T. (2008) *Think tanks as an emergent field*, New York, NY: Social Science Research Council.

Melo Neto, F.P. and Froes, C. (2001) *Responsabilidade social & cidadania empresarial* (2nd edn), Rio de Janeiro: Qualitymark.

Miceli, S. (1989) 'Condicionantes do desenvolvimento das Ciências Sociais', S. Miceli (ed) *História das Ciências Sociais no Brasil* (vol 1), São Paulo: Vértice/Ed. Revista dos Tribunais/Idesp, pp 72–110.

Montaño, C. (2002) *Terceiro setor e a questão social: crítica ao padrão emergente de intervenção social*, São Paulo: Cortez.

Neri, M. (2011) *A nova classe média: o lado brilhante da base da pirâmide*, Rio de Janeiro: FGV-CPS/Saraiva.

Nunes, E. (2003) *A gramática política do Brasil: clientelismo e insulamento burocrático* (3rd edn), Rio de Janeiro: Jorge Zahar Editora.

Paulics, V. and Bava, S.C. (2002) 'Em busca do conhecimento e da afirmação da cidadania', *São Paulo em Perspectiva*, vol 16, no 3, pp 48-53.

Pinto, C.R.J. (2010) 'As ONGs e a política no Brasil: presença de novos atores', in C.W. Andrews and E. Bariani (eds) *Administração pública no Brasil: breve história política*, São Paulo: Editora Unifesp.

Pochmann, M. (2011) 'O Ipea é o grande centro para se pensar o Brasil', *Revista Desafios do Desenvolvimento*, vol 8, no 69, Interview. pp 74-75, www.ipea.gov.br/desafios/images/stories/PDFs/desafios069_completa.pdf.

Rosa-Soares, J. (2009) 'Think tanks: um esforço para a estruturação de conhecimentos sobre o fenômeno e sua influência sobre políticas públicas no Brasil', MBA thesis, Universidade do Estado de Santa Catarina, Florianópolis.

SÁ, Nelson de (2011) 'A descoberta do mundo', Folha de S. Paulo. Ilustríssima, www1. folha.uol.com.br/ilustrissima/951970-a-descoberta-do-mundo.shtml

Schaffer, G., Sanchez, M.R. and Rosenberg, B. (2010) 'Winning at the WTO: the development of a trade policy community within Brazil', in G. Schaffer and R. Meléndez-Ortiz (eds) *Dispute settlement at the WTO: the developing country experience*, Cambridge: Cambridge University Press, pp 21–104.

Soares, N.O. (2011) 'Os think tanks e a política externa brasileira: estudo de caso do Cebri e do Icone', final course project, Pontifícia Universidade Católica de Minas Gerais, Belo Horizonte.

Teixeira, T. (2007) *Os think tanks e sua influência na política externa dos EUA*, Rio de Janeiro: Revan/PPGRI.

Truitt, N.S. (2005) 'Think tanks in Latin America', in J.G. McGann and R.K. Weaver (eds) *Think tanks & civil societies: catalysts for ideas and action*. New Brunswick: Transaction Publishers, pp 529– 49.

Veloso, F. and Ferreira, S.G. (eds) (2008) *É possível: gestão da segurança pública e redução da violência*, Rio de Janeiro: Contracapa Editora.

Wiarda, H.J. (2010) *Think tanks and foreign policy: the foreign policy research institute and presidential politics*, New York, NY: Lexington Books.

Appendix: Acronyms and abbreviations

BPC – Brics Policy Centre

CAPES – Coordenação de Aperfeiçoamento de Pessoal de Nível Superior (Coordination for Postgraduate Personnel Improvement)

CEBRAP – Centro Brasileiro de Análise e Planejamento (Brazilian Analysis and Planning Centre)

CEBRI – Centro Brasileiro de Relações Internacionais (Brazilian International Relations Centre)

CEDEC – Centro de Estudos de Cultura Contemporânea (Contemporary Culture Studies Centre)

CINDES – Centro de Estudos de Integração e Desenvolvimento (Centre for Integration and Development Studies)

CNPq – Conselho Nacional de Desenvolvimento Científico e Tecnológico (National Scientific and Technological Development Council)

DIEESE – Departamento Intersindical de Estatística e Estudos Socioeconômicos (Inter-Union Statistics and Socioeconomic Studies Department)

ESG – Escola Superior de Guerra (Brazilian War College)

FGV – Fundação Getúlio Vargas (Getúlio Vargas Foundation)

FUNCEX – Fundação Centro de Estudos do Comércio Exterior (International Trade Studies Foundation Centre)

FIOCRUZ – Fundação Oswaldo Cruz (Oswaldo Cruz Foundation)

FPA – Fundação Perseu Abramo (Perseu Abramo Foundation)

IBASE – Instituto Brasileiro de Análises Sociais e Econômicas (Brazilian Social and Economic Analyses Institute)

ICONE – Instituto de Estudos do Comércio e Negociações Internacionais (International Trade and Negotiation Studies Institute)

IEDI – Instituto de Estudos para o Desenvolvimento Industrial (Industrial Development Studies Institute)

IETS – Instituto de Estudos do Trabalho e Sociedade (Institute for the Study of Labour and Society)

iFHC – Instituto Fernando Henrique Cardoso (Fernando Henrique Cardoso Institute)

IPEA – Instituto de Pesquisa Econômica Aplicada (Applied Economic Research Institute)

ISEB – Instituto Superior de Estudos Brasileiros (Higher Brazilian Studies Institute)

PUC-Rio – Pontifícia Universidade Católica-Rio (Rio de Janeiro Catholic University)

UNICAMP – Universidade Estadual de Campinas (Campinas State University)

USP – Universidade de São Paulo (São Paulo University)

NINETEEN

Policy analysis by academic institutions in Rio de Janeiro State

Cristiane Batista[1]

Introduction

The political, social, economic and administrative changes that Brazil underwent in the late 1980s and early 1990s led to expansion of the policy analysis field. The advent of federalism and social policy decentralisation contributed to public policy receiving greater attention not only from sectors of government and social movements, but also from academic institutions. In that period, technical and scientific papers addressing public policies proliferated in universities and social research institutes, heightening the influence of this scientific production on government policy actions. In other words, the changes that have taken place in Brazil in the past two decades have contributed to shaping expertise proper to public policy and have broadened the spectrum of actors involved in producing it.

The pattern of policy analysis in Brazil has been strongly influenced by literature on decision-making processes, especially the neo-institutionalist literature, which focuses on how government structures and political behaviour shape public policy models. In the Brazilian case, analysis tends to be approached largely in terms of government institutional structures, including here the corresponding constitutional arrangements, to consider the type of regime, federalism, separation of powers, the role of the judiciary, the composition of Congress vis-a-vis the executive and so on, all in the context of the re-democratisation process and reorganisation of the electoral system at the time. Such studies usually attribute considerable weight to institutions, but make little room for the political and social actors involved in the policy process, such as state managers, private organisations, non-governmental organisations, social movements, stakeholders and academia, although the international policy analysis literature acknowledges the importance of these actors, in addition to the macro institutions, in public policy production.

This chapter analyses the contribution of one specific actor that has proved paramount in shaping Brazilian public policy: the academic community, represented here by certain university centres and applied social research institutes. The main purpose is to ascertain what kind of policy-oriented production is performed in academic institutions and to what extent its products influence government decisions. Can academia be said to figure as one more actor in Brazilian policy networks? Can academia be said to be an important actor in policy networks? Put succinctly, analysis of policy networks seeks to understand the processes surrounding policymaking and to identify actors outside the circles responsible for offering such policies, even if they are interconnected in numerous ways in a vast communication network. In other words, it aims to understand policies arising from the relationship among the state, individuals, groups and organisations.[2]

In order to understand the nature of academic production on public policy, as well as the destination of this production in practice, the authors conducted a survey of studies produced and published on official websites, and interviewed a state government manager and coordinators at four teaching and research institutions in Rio de Janeiro State, recognised for their work on housing, urban planning, poverty, employment and income, violence, and human rights, all of which are crucial areas not only in Rio de Janeiro City and State, but also throughout Brazil. These institutions were: 1) the Núcleo de Estudos e Projetos Habitacionais e Urbanos (NEPHU/UFF), a centre for housing and urban studies and projects, at Fluminense Federal University; 2) the Laboratório de Análise da Violência (LAV/UERJ), a laboratory for the analysis of violence, at Rio de Janeiro State University; 3) the Laboratório de Responsabilidade Social, Desenvolvimento Local e Políticas Públicas, a laboratory for social responsibility, local development and public policies, at Rio de Janeiro Federal University's Institute for Urban and Regional Research and Planning (IPPUR/UFRJ); and 4) the Centro de Políticas Sociais (CPS/IBRE/FGV), a social policy centre connected with the Brazilian Institute of Economics at the Getulio Vargas Foundation.

The key characteristic of these academic centres is that they conduct studies and analyses intended to influence government policy decisions and people's lives. Accordingly, they can be described as bodies focusing more on producing policy analysis and policy evaluation[3] than on policy research and academic research.[4] Proportionally, however, is policy analysis or policy evaluation preponderant in these academic institutions' overall applied policy-related production? In order to answer this question, a theoretical distinction must be made between different lines of investigation.

Policy analysis and policy evaluation

No clear, definitive boundary between policy analysis and policy evaluation has been drawn in the public policy literature. It is common for the two concepts to be confused. However, various papers show substantial conceptual, methodological and functional distinctions between policy analysis and policy evaluation.[5]

Policy analysis can be defined as 'a discipline of the applied social sciences that uses multiple research methods in a context of argument, public debate and political endeavour to create, critically evaluate and generate substantial political knowledge' (Dunn, 1994, cited by Geva-May, 2002, p 248). It assists political decision-making by proposing goals, the means to achieve them and analyses of costs and target publics. Policy analysts' main concern is to recommend to government not only the best policy options, but also the best strategy for taking and implementing those options. In practice, their task is to identify the political, economic, social and cultural context[6] and identify intervening variables of social problems such as health, education, unemployment, criminality, urban sanitation, poverty and income, and to propose means to solve or mitigate them (Behn, 1981).

Policy evaluation, on the other hand, relates to existing or ongoing policies or programmes. It involves critical analysis of the programme (or policy) designed to discover how far the goals proposed in the original model are being achieved and at what cost, and to point to new and more effective courses of action. In other words, evaluation means systematic analysis of a programme's or policy's results as a way to improve them; that is, looking beyond the official goals set in the model to learn whether the results being achieved are positive or negative, whether the policy or programme is good or not. This is to say that while policy analysis is prospective, policy evaluation is retrospective (Lima et al, 1978; Weiss, 1998).

In methodological terms, while policy evaluation studies are based on original data and directed to investigating a specific problem, policy analysis usually draws on secondary data gathered from the literature. Put differently, the evaluator's role is to suggest alternative policies based on primary research conducted in the field in order better to understand the object of analysis. The analyst's role, on the other hand, is to make policy recommendations based on formal conceptual and mathematical models; it is to collect, interpret, criticise and synthesise ideas and data already presented by others (Geva-May, 1999).

Policy analysts regard the survey conducted for evaluation purposes as one more tool, but not the only one. Analyses are universally acknowledged to be based on political institutions, on values and on organisational dynamics. They are not specific or focused, but rather are comprehensive and universal, although contextualised (Behn, 1981; Geva-May, 1999).

In both policy analysis and policy evaluation, the literature acknowledges the participation of multiple actors involved in the process of policy evaluation, formation and making. As Weiss (1998, p 44) attests: 'in our system, particularly in public agencies, decisions usually involve a range of people at different stages of the process. In many cases the Legislative and Judiciary are also involved. Multiple actors have something to say.' That is, both take the view that public policies involve not only one main actor, in this case the government, but rather a group of actors and organisations that work on the same problem and participate in various phases of the process through to the final stage (Hjern and Porter, 1981). This means viewing public policies as the outcome of interaction between state agents and non-state organisations.

In the 1930s, Laswell (1958 [1936]) defined policy analysis as a way to reconcile scientific and academic knowledge with governments' empirical production, and encourage dialogue between actors involved in the process, such as governments, interest groups and social scientists. Along the same lines, but more recently, Lindquist (1990, cited by Dobuzinski et al, 2007) identifies and acknowledges the importance of the actors involved in public policy analysis and intervention, separating them into three groups: 'proximate decision-makers', 'knowledge brokers' and 'knowledge generators'. The first group comprises decision-making agents with the authority to decide policy directions, and includes ministry cabinets, the executive and legislators, in addition to administrators and government officials with the authority to make policy decisions. The second group consists of 'knowledge agents', meaning research teams and permanent government experts, who serve as intermediaries between decision-makers and 'knowledge generators'. The third group includes academia and research institutes responsible for providing the economic and social data on which analyses are performed.

In Brazil, although the policy field has broadened in recent years, systematic analyses of the policy studies produced by this third group, the 'knowledge generators', are still scarce. That is the analysis undertaken in this chapter.

Academic production on public policies in Brazil

The NEPHU/UFF was set up in 1982 as an extension project. The intention was to extend technical and scientific resources generated and accumulated by the university to socially disadvantaged population groups by proposing urbanism and social solutions for vulnerable areas. These would include socio-economic registration, urbanism and land title regularisation, land use and occupation, and treatment of hillsides in risk areas, all in response to demands from the communities' representative bodies, such as community associations.[7]

The LAV/UERJ was set up in 2002 at the UERJ Social Sciences Department to:

> to produce knowledge applied to the fields of security, violence and criminality, justice and human rights and to contribute, through diagnoses and proposals, to monitoring and evaluating the impacts of public policies in these fields, particularly in Rio de Janeiro State.[8]

Accordingly, in addition to its strictly academic activities, which include organising courses and seminars and supervising undergraduate and graduate students, the LAV offers consultancy and technical support to government agencies, Brazilian and international non-governmental organisations, and the press.

The IPPUR/UFRJ was founded in 1987 as a product of the Postgraduate Programme in Urban and Regional Planning (PUR), which the UFRJ has offered since 1971. It was set up initially to offer undergraduate degrees in urban and regional planning – then unprecedented in Brazil – on a multidisciplinary approach combining knowledge from sociology, economics, geography, urbanism, political science and law. In addition to guaranteeing interdisciplinary degrees, the institute is concerned to promote interaction between intervention-oriented and more analytical studies.[9] Although the IPPUR comprises several laboratories, for the purpose of this analysis, the Laboratory for Social Responsibility, Local Development and Public Policies has been selected. Set up in 1993, its main purpose is to contribute to public policymaking directed to human, community and social development and to the formation of civic communities.

The CPS/IBRE/FGV was set up in 2000 to engage in activities directed to monitoring social goals, perception studies and evaluation, design and operationalisation of public policies implemented both by the state and civil society. Its focus is on issues such as poverty, inequality, employment and income, human development, education, health, savings, and social security.[10]

Since the 1980s, when these institutions originated, production of public policy research by academic institutions has increased in terms of the number of researchers involved at each, as well as in demand from government agencies. As the websites of the institutions surveyed do not provide full quantitative information on research they have conducted to date, no numerical data can be provided on this growth. However, the magnitude of growth is reflected in the interviewees' declarations.

The LAV, for instance, has stood out as a leading actor in public security and human rights studies since the 1990s and, consequently, is increasingly in demand. The NEPHU, which stresses the importance of connecting basic sanitation conditions and housing improvements with citizenship from the outset, recently saw its discourse incorporated by the Ministry of Cities. The latter was set up in 2003 with an agenda based on involving social movements, including trade union and social leaders and university researchers and professors in its policies to foster urban development, improve housing conditions and reduce social inequalities. Creation of the Ministry of Cities had an impact on policy research production levels at NEPHU, which was also noticed at the Laboratory for Social Responsibility (IPPUR).

Another reason why academic production on public policies increased was that these studies came to be more widely publicised in the media. This contributed not only to increased demand, but also to recognition for the institution as an important political actor in the analysis and evaluation of government policies. In this respect, the role of the media is crucial: the more exposure academic papers receive, the greater the demand for policy studies.

Characterising the institutions' work

Most of the academic institutions – units, laboratories or centres – considered in this chapter work on three different fronts: teaching, research and extension, the three pillars that sustain the university. Their teaching activities focus on organising courses and seminars and supervising undergraduate and graduate students; in research, they run projects and studies involving students and researchers of their own or from partner institutions; and their extension activities include research for intervention focused on socially disadvantaged groups. On all three fronts, the focus is on producing knowledge about applied public policies.

Thus, the main feature of these academic institutions is that they produce policy analysis and policy evaluation, either commissioned by public (or private) agencies or conducted on the institution's own initiative. They conduct original and evaluative research, as well as using theoretical models and secondary data in their analyses. The LAV/UERJ and IBRE/FGV, for example, make more frequent use of quantitative methodologies, which involve secondary data surveys, but also primary data collection, even though they do apply qualitative research methods through focal groups, interviews and fieldwork, just like the other academic centres investigated here, which rely more heavily on the latter type of methodology.

The academic studies can thus be said to focus on policy analysis and policy evaluation. What cannot be concluded from the available data, however, is which of these areas of policy studies is the strong point in research. This difference can be gauged when commissioned research is compared with studies conducted on the institution's own initiative: commissioned studies represent half of all public policy research conducted by these academic institutions, while the other half corresponds to research conducted on their own initiative. Nevertheless, the interviewees themselves draw attention to the difficulty of distinguishing accurately between studies conducted on the institution's own initiative and those commissioned by government agencies. This is because it is common for academic research to be funded by public bodies, such as scientific and technical research funding agencies,[11] and the outcomes also influence public action in some way.

This is the case with academic studies not undertaken directly on commission from public agencies, but funded by them, which also influence the actions of decision-makers and are reflected in public policies. That is to say that the influence on policy results often occurs indirectly: the government uses the results of policy studies conducted on academic initiative, but which it has funded.[12] However, academic studies are commissioned not only by government public agencies, but also by non-governmental and private organisations.[13] This analysis will focus only on partnerships entered into with Brazilian public agencies.

NEPHU/UFF has working agreements with the Ministry of Cities, Petrobras, Rio de Janeiro state government, through its Secretariat for Land Affairs and Human Settlements, Rio de Janeiro municipal government, through its Municipal Secretariat for Housing, as well as with the São Gonçalo, Itaboraí, Nova Friburgo and Duque de Caixas municipal governments, the latter through its Education Secretariat.[14] In the specific case of the NEPHU/UFF, all studies and interventions begin in response to demands from social movements, that is, via neighbourhood associations. This academic body thus treats public mobilisation as a factor crucial to public policy implementation. Based on that demand, they partner with public institutions at the federal, state or municipal level.

The LAV/UERJ partners more, domestically and internationally, with federal governments, even though public security, one of the laboratory's chosen issues, is the responsibility of the state government. Its domestic partner agencies include the federal government, through its Special Secretariat for Human Rights, Rio de Janeiro state government, through its Institute for Public Security, and Minas Gerais state government, through its Secretariat for Social Defence, the latter directed to assessing public policy performance in Minas Gerais State.[15] The CPS/IBRE/FGV, on the other hand, works in partnership with Rio de Janeiro state government through its Sub-Secretariat for Social Programme Integration, with the Pereira Passos Municipal Institute of Urbanism (an agency of Rio de Janeiro municipal government's Special Secretariat for Development), with Banco do Nordeste do Brasil S/A (a federally owned development bank for Northeast Brazil), and with the Fundação Banco do Brasil (a not-for-profit, public interest foundation), in addition to partnering with social movements, such as Ação da Cidadania (Citizens' Action).[16]

Most projects at the IPPUR Laboratory for Social Responsibility are undertaken on the institution's own initiative even though, as with other academic institutions, it receives funding from Brazilian scientific research funding agencies, such as the National Council for Scientific and Technological Development (Conselho Nacional de Desenvolvimento Científico e Tecnológico; CNPq) and the Carlos Chagas Filho Research Support Foundation of Rio de Janeiro State (Fundação Carlos Chagas Filho de Amparo à Pesquisa do Estado do Rio de Janeiro; FAPERJ). In terms strictly of teaching, which has direct impact on public policies, the Laboratory offers an undergraduate course in Public Management for Economic and Social Development, set up in partnership with other departments at the UFRJ.

But on what basis does a public agency opt for a given academic teaching and research institution? The nature of the research, the issues investigated, the approaches, the methodologies applied, the track record of results from analyses and evaluations, and technical competence all influence the public sector's choosing of one institution over another. However, changes in the public administration, including its ideological alignment and government 'affinity' with certain institutions, may also influence the decision. On the other hand, it is reasonable to suppose that academic institutions are not neutral, especially those with institutionally cohesive agendas of their own. Accordingly, the academic institution's 'ideological profile' also influences public agencies' preferences. The IPPUR Laboratory for Social Responsibility, for instance, has a more or less systematic relationship with Rio de Janeiro's municipal governments, which can be explained by occurrences of municipal governments associated with right–wing ideologies.[17] Other institutions, such as NEPHU, experience an association between changeover in the party in office and terminations of contracts and agreements.

This 'ideological affinity' between contracting and contracted parties also contributes to reducing conflict. The relationship between those actors becomes especially delicate when academic research or analysis detects what are regarded as unacceptable or illegal practices in government. Some governments are highly resistant to criticism and have difficulty recognising their weaknesses. This is often the reason why research is 'shelved', that is, results from academic analyses are filed away because they do not meet the contracting agencies' expectations. Conflict worsens when the agreement contains a confidentiality clause, because researchers are then prevented from publishing their results.

In summary, public managers' choice of academic institution to carry out policy analysis and policy evaluation can be seen to be neither entirely neutral and/or random nor based solely on technical criteria, but also on political and ideological criteria. Appropriate choice of academic institution bears directly on the transfer of knowledge to the government agency: the happier the choice, the more likely results will be used and the smaller the chance of their being shelved.

Knowledge transfer

Researchers always immediately expect the findings from their analyses and evaluations to influence decision-makers' actions and government policies. They expect political decisions to be based on the technical criteria furnished by the studies conducted at their institutions. Now, does this happen in Brazil?

Research by academic institutions in Rio de Janeiro reveals that academic studies – whether commissioned by government agencies or conducted on an institution's own initiative – do have some influence on policies that, although limited, can be identified in practice. The CPS/IBRE/FGV, for instance, at the request of Rio de Janeiro state government's Secretariat for Social Security and Human Rights, has developed an indicator of presumed income for families in the municipality of Rio de Janeiro, which informed implementation of the Better Income Programme (Programa Renda Melhor). That programme is an integral part of the Plan to Extinguish Extreme Poverty in Rio de Janeiro, designed to grant benefits ranging from R$30 to R$300 (equivalents €10 to €100) to assist families on the federal government's family allowance programme (Programa Bolsa Família).[18] The LAV/UFRJ, at the request of Rio de Janeiro state government, has analysed the impact of vigilante activities on societies in Rio de Janeiro. It is also negotiating to evaluate the policy of implementing Police Pacification Units (Unidades Polícia Pacificadora; UPPs), a public security and policing policy introduced by the state government. The IPPUR Laboratório Responsabilidade Social has conducted urban and regional planning projects in Cidade de Deus, a borough that forms the 34th Administrative Region of the municipality of Rio de Janeiro.[19] The IPPUR also offers specialisation courses designed to prepare graduates for dialoguing with the city, and which train municipal managers.

As regards whether commissioned studies or those conducted on an institution's own initiative have greater influence on policy decision-making, it can be seen that commissioned studies tend generally to be more used by government agencies.

However, decision-makers usually monitor the output of their partner institutions and also make use of research conducted on those institutions' own initiative and posted on their websites and published in specialised journals. In some cases, they prefer to draw inspiration from research conducted on academic initiative rather than commissioning specific studies. This is because academics work at their own pace, often taking longer than public agents' time frames (the term of their administration or budget endowment) (Weiss, 1998). In other words, when there is no time to wait for the results of commissioned academic research, managers avail themselves of research conducted on an institution's own initiative.

Although researchers are concerned that it is important for government decision-making to employ technical criteria, the use made of academic research results usually goes beyond the strictly technical in order to meet political criteria. Academic studies are unlikely to provide the whole basis for political decisions. In addition to technical reports, a number of other factors intervene in the policymaking process, such as the economic and political costs of change, support or opposition from significant political actors, the interests of the team involved in formulating or changing the policy or programme, the political context, stakeholder pressure, and so on. Therefore, academic research results constitute an important source of information: they contribute to discussion and debate and thus influence action taken by decision-makers, thus impacting public policies, even if indirectly or partly (Weiss, 1998).

Academic influence on policymaking becomes more efficient the greater and more efficient the channel for communication between academia and sectors of the media. Public demand for policies has an even more significant effect when academic research results are reported outside the scientific journals and gain attention in the mass media, prompting public debate and pressuring the government to take action. That is, the more exposure academic papers achieve, the more likely they are to impact on public policies. In other words, access to the media – or, rather, being able easily to publicise academic research results in the media, supplanting the scientific journals – will leverage academic influence on policy outcomes and thus recognition for academia as an important political actor in the policy network.

Final remarks

Since the 1990s, the production of academic research into applied public policy has increased, both in terms of studies conducted at the institutions' own initiative and as commissioned by government agencies. That increase is due both to the redistribution of social responsibilities among levels of government after the 1988 Brazilian Constitution, and the recognition that academic actors are key to discussion and knowledge production on public policies. In that connection, the media played a crucial role. Wider media coverage of academic research results has contributed to increasing their visibility and consequently to expanding demand for research.

One of the questions this chapter proposed to answer goes further: what impact has that increase in academic production had on public policies? What practical use has been made of the findings of studies, whether conducted by institutions on their own initiative or commissioned by government? Rephrasing that question, is academic knowledge transferred to government agencies, that is, do academic research results influence decision-makers? Going beyond that, what is the nature of academic research into public policies?

Analyses of key informant reports and interviews warrant the assertion that academic research results do influence public policy design in Brazil, although that influence is limited. Political and economic factors make it unlikely that technical findings from academic research will account entirely for public managers' decisions, but they are one of the many information sources that go into those decisions. Moreover, as the academic institutions investigated here are recognised for their studies of applied public policies, their research (as shown earlier) is concentrated in policy analysis and policy evaluation, even though it cannot be gauged how important these two areas are relative to overall research production.

However, there is still room to expand academic influence on public policies. That expansion would be made possible by greater flexibility in universities' internal management of funding and by administrative support. Administrative limitations, inflexibility in management of research funding and university budgets, excessive bureaucratic controls, and unresponsive institutional management all represent constraints on academic production, because they limit knowledge production and restrict researchers' creative activities. On the other hand, the government needs to become more receptive to research results and more sensitive to the importance of academic findings. That, however, is a discussion for another research agenda.

What can in fact be concluded from this study is that academics do play a crucial role in policy evaluation, development and implementation in Brazil, given that they propose new concepts, new viewpoints and new alternatives. They are not the sole or most important source of information, but undoubtedly figure as one of them. At the limit, academics wield influence over people's beliefs and opinions, including those of opinion leaders, pressure groups and public decision-makers, and in that way have an impact on public policies. That is to say that, along with government managers, private organisations, non-governmental organisations, social movements and stakeholders, academia can also be acknowledged to be an active and important political participant in Brazil's policy network.

Notes

[1] Collaborating author: Iris Jordão Lessa de Morais, MSc (Health Science, ENSP/FIOCRUZ).

[2] For a literature review on policy networks, see Klijn (1998), Marques (2000, 2006), Schneider (2005) and Santos (2005).

[3] For a literature review on policy analysis and policy evaluation, see Lima et al (1978), Behn (1981), Figueiredo and Figueiredo (1986), Greene (1994), Weiss (1998), Geva-May (1999, 2002) and Weimer (2002); for an analysis of networks, see Klijn (1998) and Marques (2000, 2006).

[4] For the difference between policy research and academic research, see Weimer and Vining (1999).

[5] For details on those differences, see Geva-May (1999).

[6.] Geva–May (2002) states that culturally contextualised policy analyses provide more appropriate solutions to social problems.

[7.] See: www.proex.uff.br/NEPHU.php

[8.] See: www.lav.uerj.br/

[9.] See: www.ippur.ufrj.br/

[10.] See: http://cps.fgv.br/

[11.] For example: Conselho Nacional de Desenvolvimento Científico e Tecnológico (CNPq), an agency of the Ministry of Science and Technology; Coordenação de Aperfeiçoamento de Pessoal de Nível Superior (CAPES), a federal government agency responsible for drafting the National Plan for Degree Graduate Programmes; and Fundação Carlos Chagas Filho de Amparo à Pesquisa do Estado do Rio de Janeiro (FAPERJ), an agency linked to the Rio de Janeiro State Secretariat for Science and Technology.

[12.] Curiously, one interviewee's perception was that research institutions often see government agencies as funding agencies; their aim is to conduct research on a particular topic and they look for funding. In such cases, the demand comes from the outside, from academia to government agencies.

[13.] NEPHU, on principle, does not conduct research for private institutions, because it supports the concept that public universities should provide public services.

[14.] NEPHU also works in partnership with the Fundação Legião Brasileira de Assistência (LBA), with two German institutions that fund social projects, MISEREOR and Deutshe Gesellschaft für Technische Zusammenarbeit (GTZ), as well as Associação Fundação (FEMI-BRASIL), legal representative of the Foundation for Earth, Mankind and Initiative. Also interesting is that although the institution's headquarters are in Niterói, there is no partnership between this centre and the local municipal government.

[15.] Partner international agencies include UNICEF (United Nations Children's Fund), police academies in the Caribbean, the Inter-American Development Bank and the Red Cross. Social organisations include the Favela Observatory (Observatório de Favelas) and the Brazilian Forum on Public Security (Fórum Brasileiro de Segurança Pública), an organisation with members from universities, civil society and police forces and supported by international foundations, such as the Ford Foundation, Open Society Institute and Tinker Foundation.

[16.] International organisations involved include the United States Agency for International Development (USAID), a US agency responsible for economic and humanitarian assistance programmes, and the Committee for Democratisation of Information Technology (Comitê para a Democratização da Informática; CDI). CPS/IBRE/FGV also operates projects commissioned by private foundations and organisations, such as Sun Microsystems (computing company), Instituto Votorantim, Fundação Educar Dpaschoal, Instituto Unibanco, Sebrae (public-interest private organisation), Escola Nacional de Seguros

(Funenseg), SESC Pernambuco (an organisation supported by goods, service and tourism trade owners), Todos Pela Educação (a movement funded by private enterprise, but which includes civil society organisations, educators and public managers), and the Instituto Trata Brasil (a public-interest civil society organisation [OSCIP]).

[17.] For example, Cesar Maia was elected mayor representing the following parties: from 1993 to 1996, the PMDB; from 2001 to 2004, the PTB; and from 2005 to 2008, the PFL/DEM. Also, Luiz Paulo Conde was elected mayor from 1997 to 2000, for the PFL.

[18.] See: www.rj.gov.br/web/seasdh/exibeconteudo?article-id=459324

[19.] See: http://mpprio.com.br/downloads/Pfeiffer_Cl%C3%A1udia_Beneficio_colabora%C3%A7%C3%A3o_p-p.pdf

References

Behn, R.D. (1981) 'Policy analysis and policy politics', *Policy Analysis*, vol 7, no 2, pp 199–226.

Dobuzinski, C., Howlett, M. and Laycock, P. (2007) *Policy analysis in Canada*, Toronto and London: University of Toronto Press.

Dunn, W. N. (1994) *Public policy analysis: An introduction*, Englewood Cliffs, NJ: Prentice-Hall.

Figueiredo, M.F. and Figueiredo, A.M.C. (1986) 'Avaliação política e avaliação de políticas: um quadro de referência teórica', *Análise de Conjuntura*, vol 1, no 3, pp 107–27.

Geva-May, I. (1999) 'Reinventing government: the Israeli exception. The case of political cultures and public policy making', *International Management Journal*, vol 2, no 3, pp 112–26.

Geva-May, I. (2002) 'Cultural theory: the neglected variable in the craft of policy analysis', *Journal of Comparative Policy Analysis: Research and Practice*, vol 4, pp 243–65.

Greene, J.C. (1994) 'Qualitative program evaluation: practice and promise', in N.K. Denzin and Y.S. Lincoln (eds) *Handbook of qualitative research*, Thousand Oaks, CA: Sage Publications, pp 531–44.

Hjern, B. and Porter, D. (1981) 'Implementation structures: a new unit of administrative analysis', *Organizational Studies*, vol 2, pp 211–27.

Klijn, E. (1998) 'Redes de políticas públicas: una visión general', http://revista-redes.rediris.es/webredes/textos/Complex.pdf

Laswell, H.D. (1958 [1936]) *Politics: who gets what, when, how*, Cleveland: Meridian Books.

Lima, O.B., Jr., Silva, A.A. and Leite, M.C. (1978) *Intervenção planejada na realidade social: escopo e limites da pesquisa de avaliação*, Rio de Janeiro: IUPERJ.

Lindquist, E. A. (1990) 'The third community, policy inquiry and social scientists', in S. Brooks and A. C. Gagnon (eds) *Social scientists: Policy and the state*, pp 21-52. New York: Praeger.

Marques, E. (2000) *Estado e Redes Sociais: permeabilidade e coesão nas políticas urbanas no Rio de Janeiro*, Rio de Janeiro: Revan/Fapesp.

Marques, E. (2006) 'Redes sociais e poder no estado brasileiro: aprendizado a partir das políticas urbanas', *Revista Brasileira de Ciências Sociais*, vol 21, no 60, pp 15–41.

Santos, H. (2005) 'Perspectivas contemporâneas para a constituição de redes de políticas públicas', *Civitas*, vol 5, no 1, pp 59–68.

Schneider, H. (2005) 'Redes de políticas públicas e a condução de sociedades complexas', *Civitas*, vol 5, no 1, pp 29–58.

Weimer, D.L. (2002) 'Enriching public discourse: policy analysis in representative democracies', *The Good Society*, vol 11, no 1, pp 61–5.

Weimer, D.L. and Vining, A.R. (1999) *Policy analysis: concepts and practice*, Englewood Cliffs, NJ: Prentice-Hall.

Weiss, C.H. (1998) *Evaluation: methods for studying programs & policies*, Englewood Cliffs, NJ: Prentice-Hall.

TWENTY

Postgraduate instruction and policy analysis training in Brazil

Eliane Hollanda and Sandra Aparecida Venâncio de Siqueira

Introduction

Policy analysis has been developing worldwide as a branch of political science since the Second World War. At its origins, in both Europe and the US, lie the war effort of the 1940s and the need to rationalise public decisions and action. With time, policy analysis became increasingly independent of its field of origin and consolidated into a distinct object of study. Political science is concerned with subjects directly connected with the field of *politics*: political theory, institutions and how they operate, political behaviour and ideologies, interest groups, political parties and elections, and so on. Policy studies, meanwhile, are concerned with analysing the policy process and evaluating policies; their field is thus *policies*. Their distinctive feature is that they are a theoretical and applied field, which assumes some capacity for intervention. Although discussion persists at the theoretical level as to what the public policy studies field is, it always relates to the idea of the identification and solution of social problems by governments.

In Brazil, there is no specific training in policy analysis, although the activities of public managers, consultants, private entities and sectoral specialists have increasingly been furnishing knowledge about how policy options are taken, implemented and evaluated. What we call 'policy analysis' is being conducted by professionals in technical and bureaucratic careers in ministries and other government agencies, and is produced in private education, research or advisory institutions.

Although there is empirical production in the public policy field, there is no discussion in Brazil of what policy analysis is or the work of a policy analyst as they appear in the international literature – or, at best, that discussion is only incipient. Policy analysis is defined by the importance given to systematically analysing the development of policy options, and may be performed by both government and non-governmental agents (Weimer and Vinning, 1995; Geva-May and Maslove, 2007; Bardach, 2009).

The activity of policy analysis as understood in Brazil relates first to subjects dear to Brazilian intelligentsia in the 20th century. At that time, intellectuals and academics in several fields devoted their efforts essentially to studying the state and the patterns of its development (Villas Boas, 1991; Loureiro, 1992, 1997; Forjaz, 1997; Melo, 1999; Liedke Filho, 2005; Carvalho, 2007; Jackson, 2007; Souza 2007; Lessa, 2010). Already in the 1940s, the course to be set for economic planning in Brazil, as regards the level of government intervention in the economy, was a point of debate.

Several factors can be regarded as responsible for this gradual shift in research objects. The international crisis of 1980 prompted interest in finding new objects and methodologies for more empirically referenced analysis relating more closely to the concrete problems that Brazil was undergoing. That interest was grounded in an increasingly diverse and robust scientific community in Brazil. The context given by Brazil's democratic transition in a late capitalist formation (Reis, 1989) is also taken to explain why academic analysis specialised during this period.

There was possibly some level of specialisation among academics in the field of policy studies, policy research and government planning and, from the 2000s onward, in policy and programme evaluation. Of these academics, policy analysis specialists had backgrounds in the various disciplines that address policy issues and, unlike the North American tradition, did not receive any specific training.

In this text, we draw a distinction between 'instruction' and 'development'. To begin with, we stress the idea that instruction is part of the policy analyst's development, but that development is not limited to academic instruction and also incorporates professional practice. This chapter examines the contribution of postgraduate programmes to policy analysts' development.

Technical elites and policy analysis

It is impossible to understand the processes involved in forming the academics who were to staff the public policy and policy analysis fields without considering major historical processes that culminated in the production of a technical and intellectual elite in Brazil.

As regards instruction, Brazil's quest for modernisation lasted two centuries. The first vocational schools were founded in the 19th century, extending government regulation to the training of those who would later replace the *práticos*, that is, practitioners with experience, but no formal accreditation, in treating the sick, for instance, or fulfilling the needs of the building trade. However, it was not until public universities were set up in the 1950s, bringing together isolated schools of higher education, that various areas of knowledge began progressively to institutionalise and professionalise. The model for university activities hinged on the person of the university professor, often brought in from abroad. These professors established a tutorial relationship with small groups of students, who also took on the roles of assistant professors and researchers, mainly for the purpose of supervising theses. This process was very limited and did not favour the quantitative development of a postgraduate system (Balbachevsky, 2005).

At first, undergraduate and postgraduate faculty were poorly trained, lacked technical quality and often resorted to assistance from professors from other countries. The exception was a small contingent of Brazilian professors, generally from the social upper classes and/or educated abroad, who combined their teaching activities with technical positions in government and private enterprise. Professors were often recruited from other disciplines. The legacy from the early years of the Republic (1889–1930) was a higher education system whose structure did not include a research function and was staffed by 'bachelors', military engineers and other personnel left over from Imperial times (Carvalho, 2007). Academic disciplines such as economics, administration and political science would not become autonomous in their theory and as professions until decades later, with the founding of postgraduate programmes, university research units and public and private research centres.

Politically, academic training proved to be closely bound up with the national development projects implemented under a variety of democratic and authoritarian governments, which called for a techno-bureaucracy to be formed to produce analyses and to plan policies. The strategy of modernisation began in the 1930s during one of Brazil's periods of national-developmentalist, authoritarian rule: the regime pursued an industrialisation agenda for which it needed the expertise of technical elites. It was not until the 1960s, especially under military rule, that postgraduate instruction began to be given consistently in Brazil.

The willingness of the military government (1964–85) to develop a new generation of technicians – through which Brazil would gain access to the leading-edge technology crucial to development without depending on the 'central' countries – interacted with the development of universities and postgraduate programmes, a process already ongoing in Brazil. In 1965, the Ministry of Education recognised and regulated postgraduate programmes separately from undergraduate studies, designating them as subsystems of Brazil's university system (Santos, 2003; Souza, 2004; Balbachevsky, 2005).

In the 1970s, the development of postgraduate programmes came to be regulated by National Postgraduate Education Plans (Planos Nacionais de Pós-Graduação; PNPGs), whose duration varied. The plans show that postgraduate instruction had reached the stage of strategic planning in view of an analysis of Brazil's needs. PNPGs have diagnosed asymmetries in policy implementation and shown a need to expand and diversify the range of professions represented by existing human resources, as well as encouraging strategic programmes that integrate with medium- and long-term public policies.

Development of instruction in public policy and policy analysis

As already mentioned, policy studies did not institutionalise in Brazil as an academic field with undergraduate degrees, specific disciplines, journals and professional associations, but rather as an area of knowledge that cut across a number of other academic fields. Neither did any specific type of instruction take shape, of the kind that exists in the US and other countries, involving a policy analysis methodology as defined in Chapter One of this book. However, given that today those who perform policy analysis in its various forms and in different sectors do so strongly influenced by their initial academic training, this chapter seeks to identify recent characteristics of instruction in the policy studies field. Accordingly, it asks whether policy studies are taught in Brazil's postgraduate programmes by examining the study of public policy in different areas of knowledge.

However, it is no easy task to identify what is taught in the way of policy analysis and by whom, since instruction in policy analysis is often scattered across disciplines that address subjects such as the state, democracy, federative relations and so on. Here, this teaching has been identified by mapping institutions in the fields of administration, political science, international relations, economics and social work whose MA or PhD programmes included policy studies as areas of concentration and/or of research in 2000 and 2009, and comparing them. Also examined are disciplines whose syllabus listed public policy as a central topic for discussion.

As in the North American and European models of training in policy analysis, in Brazil, the first technicians to fulfil the function came from traditional academic disciplines (Geva-May and Maslove, 2007). For this reason, these courses became the starting point for this study. The field of international relations was included because Brazil's postgraduate studies coordination office (Coordenação do Aperfeiçoamento do Pessoal do Ensino Superior; CAPES) classifies it in the same assessment area as political science. The social work field was added because it traditionally organises its programmes in coordination with federal government proposals (Silva and Carvalho, 2007).[1]

In Brazil, postgraduate courses in public policy date from the 1960s and form part of the endeavour to expand and develop the state. This expansion continued until the 1980s, centring on the major fields that drive Brazil's development. The first doctoral programmes appeared in the 1970s; Masters programmes had started a decade earlier and were expanding strongly.

One feature in common among the initiatives in different fields of knowledge in that period was that programmes were concentrated in Brazil's Southeast administrative region, particularly in the Rio de Janeiro–São Paulo area. These states were favoured by the model of development implemented in Brazil, which concentrated industrialisation processes in that region, making it more attractive for setting up, among the various other activities, vocationally oriented educational and capacity-building processes (Brasil, 2004, 2010; Steiner, 2005).

Another important aspect was the strong public sector presence in supply of policy-related disciplines. Public universities and institutes were the main providers of education in the various different areas examined here. After this period of expansion, the supply of public policy-related programmes and disciplines changed little in the 1980s. The severe economic crisis that Brazil experienced in that period may partly explain this behaviour. In terms of development, this was considered the 'lost decade', given the adverse impact of the crisis on various indicators of national development.

The period after 1988 marks a new phase in terms of relations between the problems that entered the political agenda and the teaching of policy studies and policy analysis. The re-democratisation of Brazilian society and enactment of the 1988 Federal Constitution redefined the rules for the transfer of federal government funds and responsibilities to state and municipal governments. This paved the way for these issues to be incorporated as important elements in policy analysis.

In the 1990s, the reform proposed by the Fernando Henrique Cardoso government to ensure a more modern and efficient state introduced new parameters for policy analysis and instruction in policy studies. Among other things, this reform made it mandatory for teaching institutions to offer postgraduate programmes in order to be recognised as universities. This expanded the number of Masters programmes in private institutions interested in changing status.

Moreover, CAPES adopted new assessment parameters for its ratings of postgraduate programmes. These replaced the idea of the 'course' with the 'programme', integrating instruction and research and focusing on academic production as the criterion for evaluating faculty. These changes left postgraduate programmes in a privileged position in terms of knowledge production and researcher training, rather than just facing the challenge of producing faculty. In that context, it is the lines of research and no longer individual faculty preferences that shape the syllabus and what is to be taught in the disciplines (Balbachevscky, 2005; Kuenzer and Moraes, 2005).

In the 2000s, the government of Luiz Inácio Lula da Silva (2002–10) expanded tax incentives introduced during the Fernando Henrique administration to a larger set of private education institutions in order to reduce regional inequalities and speed up access to university education, especially for lower-income groups. As a result of this effort, the supply of programmes practically doubled (see Table 20.1). This expansion featured institutions migrating to other areas of Brazil, especially the Northeast and Mid-West regions.

Table 20.1: **Supply of courses with public policy studies as areas of concentration and disciplines on postgraduate programmes in selected areas, 2000 and 2009**

2000				
Postgraduate programmes	No institutions with Masters and/or Doctoral programmes	No programmes with policy studies areas of concentration	No programmes with policy studies research areas	No policy studies disciplines in programmes
Political science	8	4	4	19
International relations	2	0	1	1
Economics	30	5	5	20
Social work	13	6	7	29
Administration	27	3	7	17
TOTAL	80	18	24	86
2009				
Postgraduate programmes	No institutions with Masters and/or Doctoral programmes	No programmes with policy studies areas of concentration	No programmes with policy studies research areas	No policy studies disciplines in programmes
Political science	15	7	11	47
International relations	11	3	5	19
Economics	41	9	16	51
Social work	27	27	27	83
Administration	54	3	9	36
TOTAL	148	49	68	236

Source: Brasil Ministério da Educação (2000, 2009)

This spread, together with other factors, including increased social investment and measures to modernise the state, led to strong growth in the number of programmes with areas of concentration and courses in policy studies offered in the past decade. That growth shows the effort being made by institutions not only to expand the supply on offer, but also to improve their expertise in policy analysis. Greater dialogue between social work and the government's agenda and the importance social assistance gained as public policy in the 2000s explain why such programmes incorporated more disciplines concerned with policy analysis.

Despite the growth, on the whole, few courses addressing policy analysis are offered by these postgraduate programmes. Most courses concentrate on discussing the concepts and theories of their own professional field. Even those that do incorporate public policy as an object of analysis usually do so on a theoretical perspective rather than using applied methodologies specific to policy analysis.

Broadly speaking, the content of courses on policy analysis was divided into three areas: public policies, social policies and the policy cycle.[2] Group I – public policy – includes disciplines that focus on conceptual aspects of public policy and on public policy and its relationship with the state (Table 20.2). Group II – social/sectoral policies – includes literature on the welfare state, and social and sectoral policies (Table 20.3). Finally, Group III – the policy cycle – relates to disciplines that discuss the decision-making process, agenda formation, policy implementation and evaluation, as well as theories and models of the policy process (Table 20.4).

Table 20.2: **Group I: public policy — number of courses, 2000 and 2009**

| Area | Public policy | | | | | | | | | |
| | Economics | | Administration | | Social work | | Political science | | International relations | |
Subject matter/year	2000	2009	2000	2009	2000	2009	2000	2009	2000	2009
Conceptual aspects	3	8	3	9	2	9	5	11	–	9
Public policies and government	10	16	3	4	5	6	5	22	–	6

Source: Brasil Ministério da Educação (2000, 2009)

The first group comprises the disciplines where discussion focuses on conceptual aspects of public policy and its relationship with the state. Much effort in these disciplines goes into discussing the various different theoretical approaches, the principles and the nature of policy, and the analytical assumptions and dilemmas that underlie a government's decision whether or not to implement a given public policy.

With the changes in the design of the Brazilian state stipulated in the 1988 Constitution, certain topics gained prominence as objects of analysis, whether in research or instruction. One of these is the discussion about decentralisation and intergovernmental relations in public policy in a democratic environment, which has become more important as an object of analysis since the 1988 Federal Constitution established that power should be devolved to sub-national levels. Another is the discussion of the state reform agenda, which in policy studies course prospectuses appears in connection with the topics of globalisation, fiscal adjustment, reform of the state, public sector efficiency and the third sector regarded as an alternative to state intervention.

The programmes examined also began to discuss new concerns that had already been addressed by the government agenda. This was the case, for instance, with discussions of poverty, inequality, distributive justice and economic and social sustainability. In some programmes – political science, for instance – this discussion is approached in more theoretical terms; others, such as social work, include more applied aspects of social policies.

Table 20.3: **Group II: social/sectoral policies — number of courses, 2000 and 2009**

Area	Social/sectoral policies									
	Economics		Administration		Social work		Political science		International relations	
Subject matter/year	2000	2009	2000	2009	2000	2009	2000	2009	2000	2009
Social security policies	1	4	2	1	9	30	1	4	–	–
Environmental policies	3	2	1	2	1	3	–	1	–	–
Urban/energy policies	2	–	–	–	1	1	1	–	–	–
Agriculture policy	6	2	–	2	1	–	–	–	–	–
Industrial policy	1	1	–	–	–	–	–	–	–	–
Labour market policies	–	3	1	–	2	2	–	–	–	–
Regional policies	1	–	–	–	–	1	–	1	–	–
Policies targeting specific population groups	–	–	–	–	3	8	–	2	–	1
Human rights, national defence policy, policy to counter violence	–	–	–	–	–	–	–	3	–	1

Source: Brasil Ministério da Educação (2000, 2009)

Table 20.4: **Group III: policy cycle — number of courses, 2000 and 2009**

Area	Policy cycle									
	Economics		Administration		Social work		Political science		International relations	
Subject/year	2000	2009	2000	2009	2000	2009	2000	2009	2000	2009
Policy cycle	–	–	3	7	2	3	2	1	–	–
Development/implementation		3		2		1	5	10		2
Monitoring	1	–	–	–	–	–	–	–	–	–
Evaluation	7	4	2	9	–	19	1		–	–

Source: Brasil Ministério da Educação (2000, 2009)

The advance of the social agenda in the 2000s manifested itself in 2009 in the proliferation of disciplines that offered content relating to social and/or sectoral policies. In this period, a more favourable economic environment – resulting from the international situation and positive effects of changes made to the macroeconomic policy framework in order to halt the economic crisis of the 1990s – enabled social policy expansion in the 2000s. The emergence of sectors of the population with access to new levels of consumption and income transfer programmes are some of the outcomes of increased social investments (Bacha and Schwartzman, 2011).

The increase in the number of subject areas addressed represented an endeavour to improve the quality of discussions of the social programmes introduced by the federal government in recent decades to provide citizens with social protection, reduce inequities and promote development. The subjects addressed comprise various different issues: social security; environment and sustainability; national defence; agrarian policy; local development; gender and family; child labour; hunger and minimum income; and labour.

The expansion of state actions in the policy field leads academic courses to concern themselves more with the empirical nature of policy analysis, particularly with social programme efficiency. This concern finds expression in academic programmes taking an evaluative approach or directing their attention to mechanisms for managing and/ or monitoring social policy programmes.

Instruction and training in policy analysis

The activity of policy analysts is at the same time social and political (Bardach, 2009). Academic instruction is only one aspect of their training. However, the manner in which theoretical and social debates are reflected in postgraduate programmes shows the discipline's historical importance to the training of policy analysts. Differences in policy analysts' training have an impact on the types of policy analysis. The way postgraduate programmes are organised is shaping approaches to how to conduct policy analysis.

For decades in Brazil, economists have occupied a privileged position high up in the federal bureaucracy and their influence on public policymaking has not resulted solely from the expanding technical needs of the state (Loureiro, 1992). On the contrary, it reveals that, already in the 1930s–1950s, this group was turning 'technical information into political resource' (Loureiro, 1992, p 51). With backgrounds in other areas of knowledge and often self-taught in the field of economics, they acquired expertise connected with the production of technical information and very specific work methodologies – constructing price indices, measures of inflation and so on. That situation turned their knowledge into technical and political competences, that is, into the capacity to influence government decisions. Meanwhile, as early as the 1940s, the subject of economic planning divided economists into two opposing camps.

Those who supported greater state intervention in the economy and protectionist measures to assist industrial growth faced off against those who proposed restricting the state's activities and its protectionist corollaries and assuring greater freedom to market forces. This shifted academic debate into the field of politics. This complex context led universities, in the 1960s, to reformulate their economics courses so that curricula placed the emphasis on studies of mathematics and economic theory. The purpose was to endow these programmes with distinctive features of their own and differentiate them from management studies (Loureiro, 1997).

The founding of the Economic Sciences Faculty at Minas Gerais Federal University in 1941 is a good illustration of the dynamics of institutional evolution in the field of economics in Brazil. The course in administration and finance, the first to be implemented, was replaced in 1945 by the course in economics given by a group of university professors. At first, the main challenge was to train qualified professors, which was accomplished by 'arduous' self-teaching. Between 1940 and 1960, major methodological changes took place in instruction: Keynesian ideas prevailed, the phenomenon of underdevelopment was discovered and theorists proposed that it should be surpassed. Human resource policies encouraging the admission of new professors to faculty by way of titles and examinations put an end to the customary clientelist practices in university professors appointing their assistants. Constant updating of theory, methodologies and curricula led to publications and the founding in 1967 of the Regional Development and Planning Centre (Centro de Desenvolvimento e Planejamento Regional; CEDEPLAR), directed to postgraduate instruction and the study of regional problems, thus making it what might be called a policy analysis agency (Paula, 2006).

The social sciences were a very different case, especially sociology and political science. The development of the field of sociology at São Paulo University shows that between 1930 and 1950, this discipline organised with a view to forming a generation of academics intellectually. Claiming their work to be an expression of modernity in opposition to the oligarchic order, sociologists insulated themselves from social and political events in order to maintain their intended activity of analysing the capitalist social order in Brazil and the changes arising from the process of industrialisation and urbanisation. In order to maintain their status as public intellectuals, they had, contradictorily, to refrain from public debate and intensify academic debate over what characterised Brazil and the directions it was taking (Carvalho, 2007; Jackson, 2007).

Political science gained firm outlines between 1960 and 1970 as a field of knowledge and professional practice. Forjaz (1997) argues that an institutional structure was set up thanks not only to the introduction of a postgraduate system associated with a scientific and technological development project, but also to the support of US international agencies, especially the Ford Foundation.

In the 1980s, new patterns of research would emerge, as new methodologies and new themes were incorporated, under strong US influence, decisively changing the course of the social sciences (Melo, 1999). It is perhaps in the field of political science that the teaching of policy studies has acquired greatest theoretical substance.

A different trajectory is to be observed in the social work field. As it is an area typically concerned with the action of vulnerable social groups and influenced by various currents of left-wing thought, from the 1960s onwards, social workers engaged in opposition to the military government. At that time, they sought a theoretical framework in Marxism to underpin their activities. Their knowledge production in that persuasion expanded during that period, which saw a surge in postgraduate academic production, more specifically, social policy analyses.

The field consolidated in the 1970s, as research was conducted and postgraduate programmes in the strict sense set up. With the 1988 Constitution, social assistance policy gained the status of a policy of state, and together with health policy and social insurance policy, formed the bases of Brazil's social security system (Silva and Carvalho, 2007).

Final remarks

The original trajectory of policy analysis in Brazil, diverging quite significantly from what happened in North America and Europe, is related to different factors, especially: the tardy expansion of higher education in Brazil; the tradition of producing analyses in essay form, a legacy from the 19th century and a significant presence until the 1960s, when policy-oriented types of analysis became established; plus the presence of authoritarian governments (1937–45 and 1964–85), which were crucial to the organisation of the modern Brazilian state. Despite of their exclusionary and repressive features, those regimes had a modernising side that drove the development of economic and social policies and posed the need to build up technical elites able to analyse them.

With these socio-historical bases as its backdrop, the chapter examined the characteristics of postgraduate academic instruction in policy analysis, highlighting the importance of political and social changes in Brazil over recent decades in relation to universities and teaching institutes setting up areas of concentration and research that take public policy as their object of analysis. In addition to expanding instruction in this field, this movement has led at the same time to greater professionalisation and expertise at the education centres themselves.

Notes

[1] Postgraduate education in Brazil is organised in programmes where a set of Masters and doctoral courses in the same higher education institution share one academic structure and faculty. Programmes are structured on the basis of specific major fields of knowledge, termed 'areas of concentration'. These areas must be interrelated with the areas of research conducted in the institutions. Areas of research are the themes that group the scientific studies conducted according to the methodology of scientific investigation. Programmes are evaluated by CAPES, which groups them by broad field of knowledge.

[2] The empirical material was drawn from information posted on the website of CAPES, a Ministry of Education agency that regulates higher education in Brazil.

Acknowledgement
We are grateful to Letícia Strozenberg, who collected and partly organised the data, for her collaboration.

References

Bacha, E.L. and Schwartzman, S. (eds) (2011) *Brasil: a nova agenda social*, Rio de Janeiro: LCT.

Balbachevsky, E. (2005) 'A pós-graduação no Brasil: novos desafios para uma política bem sucedida', in C. Brock and S. Schwartzman (eds) *Os desafios da educação no Brasil* (1st edn, vol 1), Rio de Janeiro: Editora Nova Fronteira, pp 285–314.

Bardach, E. (2009) *A practical guide for policy analysis: The eightfold path to more effective problem solving* (3rd edn), Washington, DC: CD Press.

Brasil Ministério da Educação (2000) *Coordenação de Aperfeiçoamento de Pessoal de Nível Superior. Caderno de Indicadores 2000. Coordenação de Nível Superior*, Brasil, DF. CAPES. www.capes.gov.br/caderno avaliação.

Brasil Ministério da Educação (2004) *Coordenação de Aperfeiçoamento de Pessoal de Nível Superior. Plano Nacional de Pós-graduação. PNPG 2005–2010, Coordenação de Nível Superior*, Brasil, DF: Capes.

Brasil Ministério da Educação (2009) *Coordenação de Aperfeiçoamento de Pessoal de Nível Superior. Caderno de Indicadores 2009. Coordenação de Nível Superior*, Brasil, DF. CAPES. www.capes.gov.br/caderno avaliação. www.capes.gov.br/caderno avaliação

Brasil Ministério da Educação (2010) *Coordenação de Aperfeiçoamento de Pessoal de Nível Superior. Plano Nacional de Pós-graduação. PNPG 2011–2020 – Coordenação de Nível Superior*, Brasil, DF: Capes.

Carvalho, M.A.R. (2007) 'Temas sobre a organização dos intelectuais no Brasil', *Revista Brasileira de Ciências Sociais*, vol 22, no 65, pp 17-31.

Forjaz, M.C.S. (1997) 'A emergência da Ciência Política no Brasil: aspectos institucionais', *Revista Brasileira de Ciências Sociais*, vol 12, no 35, pp 101-20.

Geva May, I. and Maslove, A. (2007) 'In between trends: developments of public policy analysis and policy analysis instruction in Canada, the United States, and European Union', in C. Dobuzinsky, M. Howlett and P. Laycock (eds) *Policy analysis in Canada*, Toronto and London: University of Toronto Press.

Jackson, L.C. (2007) 'Tensões e disputas na sociologia paulista (1940–1970)', *Revista Brasileira de Ciências Sociais*, vol 22, no 65, pp 30-49.

Kuenzer, A.Z.R. and Moraes, M.C.M. (2005) 'Temas e tramas na pós-graduação em Educação', *Educação & Sociedade*, vol 26, no 93, pp 1341–62.

Lessa, R. (2010) 'O campo da Ciência Política no Brasil: uma aproximação construtivista', in C.B. Martins and R. Lessa (eds) *Horizontes das Ciências sociais no Brasil: ciência política*, São Paulo: ANPOCS.

Liedke Filho, E.D. (2005) 'A Sociologia no Brasil: história, teorias e desafios', *Sociologias*, no 14, pp 376–437.

Loureiro, M.R. (1992) 'Economistas e elites dirigentes no Brasil', *Revista Brasileira de Ciências Sociais*, vol 20, no 7, pp 47–69.

Loureiro, M.R. (1997) 'Formação de elites dirigentes no Brasil: o papel das instituições Relatório de Pesquisa no 18, Núcleo de Pesquisas e Publicações, Escola de Administração de Empresas de São Paulo, Fundação Getúlio Vargas, p 43.

Melo, M. A. (1999) 'Estado, governo e políticas públicas', in S. Miceli (ed) *O que ler na Ciência Social Brasileira (1970–1995), Ciência Política* (2nd edn, vol 3), São Paulo/Brasília, DF: Editora Sumaré, ANPOCS/CAPES.

Paula, J.A. (2006) 'O ensino e a pesquisa em Economia na Universidade Federal de Minas Gerais', *Análise*, vol 17, no 2, pp 329–44.

Reis, E.P. (1989) 'Política e políticas públicas na transição democrática', *RBCS*, no 9, vol 3.

Santos, C.M. (2003) 'Tradições e contradições da pós-graduação no Brasil', *Educação e Sociedade*, vol 24, no 83, pp 627–41.

Silva, M.O.S. and Carvalho, D.B.B. (2007) 'A pós graduação e a produção de conhecimento no Serviço Social brasileiro', *Revista Brasileira de Pós-Graduação*, vol 4, no 8, pp 192–216.

Souza, A.R. (2004) 'As trajetórias do planejamento governamental no Brasil: meio século de experiências na administração pública', *Revista do Serviço Público*, no 4.

Souza, C. (2007) 'Estado da arte da pesquisa em políticas públicas', in G. Hochman, M. Arretche and E. Marques (eds) *Políticas públicas no Brasil*, Rio de Janeiro: Editora Fiocruz, pp 65–86.

Steiner, J.E. (2005) 'Qualidade e diversidade institucional na pós-graduação brasileira', *Estudos Avançados*, vol 54, no 19, pp 341-65.

Villas Boas, G. (1991) 'A tradição renovada', in H. Bomeny and P. Birman (eds) *As assim chamadas Ciências Sociais: formação do cientista social no Brasil*, Rio de Janeiro: UERJ, Relume-Dumará.

Weimer, D.L. and Vinning, A.R. (1995) *Policy analysis: concepts and practice*, New Jersey, NJ: Pearson and Prentice Hall.

Index

Note: The following abbreviations have been used – *n* = note; *t* = table